AGAINST THEIR WILL

D1599274

AGAINST THEIR WILL

The History and Geography of Forced Migrations in the USSR

by
Pavel Polian

CEU PRESS

Central European University Press
Budapest   New York

© 2004 by Pavel Polian

First published in Russian as *Ne po svoyey vole...*
Istoriya i geografiya prinuditel'nykh migratsii v SSSR
by OGI–Memorial in 2001

Published in 2004 by
Central European University Press

An imprint of the

Central European University Share Company
Nádor utca 11, H-1051 Budapest, Hungary
Tel: +36-1-327-3138 or 327-3000
Fax: +36-1-327-3183
E-mail: *ceupress@ceu.hu*
Website: *www.ceupress.com*

400 West 59th Street, New York NY 10019, USA
Tel: +1-212-547-6932
Fax: +1-212-548-4607
E-mail: *mgreenwald@sorosny.org*

Translated by Anna Yastrzhembska

ISBN 963 9241 68 7 Cloth
ISBN 963 9241 73 3 Paperback

Library of Congress Cataloging-in-Publication Data

Polian, P. M.
    [Ne po svoyey vole. English]
    Against their will : the history and geography of forced migrations in the
USSR / by Pavel Polian.
        p. cm.
    "First published in Russian as Ne po svoyey vole—istoriya i geografiya
prinuditelnykh migratsii v SSSR by OGI Memorial, in 2001."
    Translated by Anna Yastrzhembska.
    Includes bibliographical references and index.
    ISBN 963 9241 68 7 (cloth)—ISBN 963 9241 73 3 (pbk.)
    1. Migration, Internal—Soviet Union—History. 2. Forced
migration—Soviet Union—History. 3. Political persecution—Soviet
Union—History. 4. Deportation—Soviet Union—History. 5. World War,
1939–1945—Forced repatriation. I. Title: History and geography of forced
migrations in the USSR. II. Title.
    HB2067.P6513 2003
    325—dc22

                        2003019544

Printed in Hungary by
Akaprint Nyomda

The builders of Egypt treat the human mass as
building material in abundant supply, easily obtainable
in any quantity.

OSIP MANDELSHTAM [1923]
[tr. Jane Gary Harris, 1991].

There is no way communism can be founded on
permanent domicile: neither is there any joy for it, nor
an enemy.

ANDREY PLATONOV [193?]

The peasants keep disappearing from the countryside,
and those employed in manufacturing are not genuine
"muzhiks" any longer.
Where are those millions? It seems right to say:
the peasants, the real ones, are now on trains.

MIKHAIL PRISHVIN [1935?]

To Comrade Beria: We must crush them into oblivion.

JOSEF STALIN [1940?]

Dedicated to Robert Conquest and Alexander Nekrich,
the first researchers of Soviet deportations.

Table of Contents

List of Tables

List of Figures

Foreword
to the English Edition

Dear Reader!

A relatively brief time has passed since the Russian edition of this book was published; and, it seems, all that a new edition of the book or its translation to a foreign language may require is mere correction of minor inaccuracies rather than any serious update.

However, this is not the case with regard to the studies of deportations. Nearly every month brings about fresh publications that contain new data and often shed more light upon familiar facts and events. Even every new visit to the archives often involves surprises and additional findings.

There is no lack of current political events either: in the North Caucasus, Crimea, Baltic republics, Moldavia and Western Ukraine. These events are typically largely predetermined by the surviving legacy of the deportations that once took place.

All the factors in question condition constant reconsideration of the content of *Against Their Will*, which is likely to lead to the appearance of an entirely new book.

Nevertheless, certain chapters of general significance, namely the introduction, first chapter and the conclusion, including a comprehensive list of 53 deportation operations conducted by the USSR, were improved specifically for the present edition.

Supplements 1 and 2 underwent considerable changes, involving certain amplifications and the introduction of additional data.

The rest of the chapters do not contain changes apart from corrections of minor mistakes and typos.

The author regards it as his pleasant duty to thank Nikita Okhotin who came up with the idea of the translation of *Against Their Will* into English, the Central European University Press that responded to the idea, Anna Yastrzhembska who took the trouble of translating the ever resisting text, and three friends of mine: Evgeniy Permyakov, the publisher of the Russian edition, John Crowfoot for his valuable comments on the translation and Nikolay Pobol for his support in providing prompt responses to numerous inquiries on the translator's part.

PAVEL POLIAN
Moscow–Cologne, March 2003

Introduction

There is no established terminology in the selected area. This is the reason why corresponding basic and key notions should be defined in the first place (original Russian terms follow in italics).

Forced migrations denote resettlement [*pereseleniye*] by the state of large numbers of people, either its own citizens or foreigners, using *coercive methods*. The coercion itself may be *direct* or *indirect*.

In the former case we are dealing with *repressive migrations*, or *deportations*.[1] The latter term denotes *"voluntary–compulsory" migrations* [*dobrovolno-prinuditelnyye*],[2] i.e., those instances when the state imposes circumstances and factors that influence individual decision taking regarding resettlement in such a way that it leads them to take the decisions preferred by the state. Putting it another way, in the former case we mean the overtly repressive (coercive) impact the state exerts on its citizens (or foreign subjects); the latter refers to the purposeful administrative pressure to determine individual choice.

There is a subtle though important nuance here. Pressure is exerted by all states on their citizens and is a universal feature characteristic of their relations; in some sense it is both common and normal. However, the citizen is left to take his or her own decision and, with whatever qualifications, the decision is voluntary. That is why non-repressive or "voluntary–compulsory" migrations are not covered by this study, and are instead referred to when making comparisons with migrations of the repressive type. Such migrations can be interpreted as impelled by force in certain exceptional cases, when the state "goes too far." As an example one could cite the resettlement of demobilized Red Army servicemen and women on warrants issued by military registration and enlistment offices; and most instances of "planned resettlements to the plain," which were an economically conditioned measure in the highland areas of the Caucasus and Central Asia, also come into this category.

Deportations (repressive migrations) are one of the specific forms or types of *political repression*.[3] They also represent a procedure designed by the state to persecute its political opponents and keep track of them—it does not matter whether the latter are real or imagined. Cases where virtually an entire group (social, ethnic, or confessional), rather than only part of it, is subjected to deportation are referred to as *total deportations*.

We have intentionally tried to avoid the term "ethnic cleansing." This came into common usage in the 1990s in the course of familiar events in Yugoslavia. In our view, the term is too vague and inclusive. In addition, certain types of deportation, which are commonly referred to below as *sweep operations* [*zachistki*],[4] of territories or border zones, were not determined by ethnic factors.

Two features qualify *deportations* as a distinctive type of *repressive measure*: their *administrative* (i.e., non-judicial) *nature* and their *collective application*, i.e., they focus on an entire group, which meets criteria imposed from above and is sometimes rather numerous, rather than on particular individuals. As a rule, decisions concerning deportation operations were issued by the ruling Communist Party and Soviet government following initiatives taken by the security service (OGPU-NKVD-KGB) and by other agencies. This locates deportation operations outside the judicial field of the Soviet system of justice,[5] and outside international and Allied legislation concerning POWs. It also draws a sharp distinction between the system of special settlements [*spetsposeleniya*], on the one hand, and the systems of prison labor camps and POW and internee camps, the GULAG and GUPVI "archipelagos," on the other.

Throughout its existence the USSR was a country of intensive population mobility. However, this mobility was not due to citizens' free choice of their place of residence, based on their individual preferences, market situations or variations in living standards. Rather, it was a different type of mobility characterized by its planned, large-scale and coercive—or, in short, forced—nature. "Mobility" of this type culminated in population deportations that are justifiably recognized as one of the essential components of the Stalinist repressive system.

The clear intention of *uprooting large numbers* of people from their habitual living environment and, therefore, *resettling* them sometimes many thousands of kilometers away, is another component linking the subject of forced migrations to that of "classical migration" research, and qualifies this area as requiring a *geographical perspective*.

During or immediately after the end of the Civil War (1918–1921), localized operations for the forced resettlement of certain population groups were first launched in the USSR. In the 1930s and 1940s forced deportation was practiced with such intensity and enthusiasm in the Soviet Union that the impressive achievements of the world's "first workers' and peasants' state" in this respect are hardly surprising. Nevertheless, it would be incorrect, in our view, to consider forced migration a phenomenon exclusively specific to the USSR or socialist systems in general. The Soviet Union was neither the trailblazer nor the only practitioner as far as deportations were concerned. It was, rather, the regime that most consistently and insistently *implemented* such a policy.

One cannot resist mentioning the unprecedented *rational justification* and *cruel simplicity* of the deportations carried out in the USSR, which predetermined their extraordinary expansion and smooth *technologized methods*, and—as a consequence—their unthinkably *large scale*. This careless toying with millions of souls, manipulating the fates of entire peoples (Germans and Chechens, in particular) cannot but astound one in a most chilling way!

Even the semantic meaning of some terms was distorted. For example, what happened to millions of former Ostarbeiter [East European forced labor workers] and Soviet POWs in the post-war period led to the loss of the neutral meaning of such concepts as *repatriation* and *repatriate*, which acquired the semantic "shade" of the adjective that justifiably complemented them; in other words, the terms "repatriation" and "forced repatriation" became synonyms in a sense.

One can maintain, however, that the practice of deportations as a repressive method used to restrain citizens is a specific feature typical of *totalitarianism* in general: after all, the German Nazis would never shrink from either driving millions of Ostarbeiter and evacuees into the Third Reich, nor deporting and methodically exterminating Jews and Gypsies!

T. F. Pavlova appears to be right in saying: "...It was only a totalitarian society that was capable of producing such a phenomenon as forced expulsion of peoples."[6] It is also appropriate here to refer to

P. Sorokin and his valuable and shrewd remark that totalitarian regimes feel comfortable only under the conditions of crises and cataclysms: the more profound the cataclysm, the more thorough the totalitarian inversion of being.[7]

This work represents *historico-geographical research of forced migrations in the USSR*, those that were carried out by the Soviet organs endowed with respective powers both on USSR territory (*internal forced migrations*) and beyond the borders; and those that were practiced by corresponding bodies of the Third Reich on USSR territory (*international forced migrations*).

In their entirety, *internal forced migrations*—from the deportation of Cossacks in 1919 up to the deportation of "spongers" in the mid-1950s—represented a large-scale historical phenomenon that involved around 6 million people. These deportations constituted a part of the USSR state totalitarian migration system, which was conditioned by a number of political and economic factors. It was the so-called "kulak exile" along with the total deportations of the "punished peoples" [*nakazannyye narody*] during the Great Patriotic War that became the key and determining components, or milestones, of the deportations.

International forced migrations affected an even greater number of people. For example, the number of Soviet citizens that were deported by German occupying forces to the Third Reich as forced labor force exceeded 3.2 million persons. The majority of these people were repatriated to the USSR in the first post-war months with, as a rule, overt elements of violence and coercion threaded into the process. The total number of the repatriates was considerably larger than the number of the civilian workers that had been driven into the Third Reich, for the repatriates also included some other categories of Soviet citizens (POWs, refugees, etc.) that were returned home. The deportation of ethnic Germans from the countries of Southeast Europe (which was not the most significant in terms of numbers of deportees, especially as compared to other groups) can be characterized as extremely important typologically, as Stalin's attempt to spread the Soviet rules of the game to the occupied European countries, and simultaneously acquire an additional source of labor.

All these—large in their scope, and seemingly chaotic—removals of millions of people produced a most serious demographic and economic impact in the regions of their departure and destination, and in the entire country.

Since the moment of their launch and nearly until the late 1980s, the forced migrations were one of the taboo topics in the USSR. Neither any information concerning the deportations and deportees, nor even as much as mentioning the exiled peoples were allowed in public (and—to a considerable extent—even in official) discourse up until the mid-1950s, when first disclosures were made by Khrushchev.

The only way for a common person to learn about the existence of Ingushetians or Kalmyks, for example, was by comparing corresponding reference sources (encyclopedias, administrative maps) issued before and after the deportations. The ban on publishing "unnecessary" information was not completely lifted even after the partial rehabilitation was decreed, and the non-disclosure strategy thus remained prevalent. Apart from the official interpretations, some exceptional toned-down factual allusions to the matter were allowed (and as a rule, in some upbeat context containing analysis of the party and Soviet bodies' activities in particular regions in certain periods of time).

It was in the West that the forced migrations in the USSR were first publicly discussed. It was from there that information filtered out, and conclusive and systematic research appeared for the first time, and early into the process at that. For example, as early as in 1960, i.e., only three years after the beginning of the rehabilitation process with regard to the "punished" ethnic groups, the book *Soviet Deportations of Nationalities* by Robert Conquest came out.

Robert Conquest saw the war-time ethnic deportations in the USSR as a logical extension of tsarist Russia's colonial policy, which was facilitated by the Russian Empire's compact configuration and its being a land power. He based his research on extremely scarce sources, namely those produced by Soviet officialdom (for example, administrative maps and encyclopedias, compared as was mentioned above; the population censuses of 1926, 1939 and 1959; materials concerning the campaign for the exposure of Shamil as an agent of British imperialism; and even the lists of the Soviet subscription press periodicals!), along with the testimonies given by Austrian POWs that had been repatriated from Kazakhstan (where they had encountered Chechens), and even the reports of English mountaineers about their expedition to the Elbrus mountain region (when the Balkars were returning).[8] Much was gathered from the confessions of Soviet defector Lieutenant Colonel Burlitsky, a participant of all deportation operations (except the Balkar one),[9] and from Khrushchev's "secret" speech at the 20th CPSU Congress (which omitted mention of the Soviet Germans and the Crimean Tatars).[10]

Notwithstanding the scarcity of the sources, Conquest succeeded in drafting the very first—and rather realistic at that—chronology and statistics of the deportations of the "punished peoples," and even made a fragmentary and somewhat more tentative estimation of the statistics concerning the death rate of the deportees during the resettlement. He also drew a logical conclusion that it was Georgians in the Caucasus and Ukrainians in the Crimea that "gained" most privilege and advantage from the deportations.

In addition, Conquest drew the first (rather provisional and not quite accurate) map of deportations of the "punished peoples" in the USSR.[11] In 1972, the first edition of the *Atlas of Russian History* by Martin Gilbert appeared, which included a map of general directions of the ethnic deportations in the USSR (it was more accurate than Conquest's, but still rather sketchy).

In a general context of Stalin's repression, dekulakization and ethnic deportations were depicted by Aleksandr Solzhenitsyn in *The Gulag Archipelago*. In essence, the deportation of any particular group always "delegated" the group's most prominent and "dangerous" leaders to the GULAG (on an individual basis, one might say). In "History of our sewage system" (second chapter of the *Archipelago* first volume), Solzhenitsyn described the majority of the deportation "flows," which perfectly matched the time span of 1918–1956. While, perhaps, overestimating the extent of the GULAG's "power" as an NKVD structural component to a degree, he did not exaggerate its collective semantic meaning or its widely spread perception as a common term. The impact of this epic, creative and truly experienced research work, published all over the world, cannot be exaggerated: taking into account the numerous translations of *The Gulag Archipelago* into every significant literary language, the theme of Stalin's deportations was exposed on a truly global scale.

A special consideration should be given to the book *The Punished Peoples* by Aleksandr Nekrich, which was written in the early 1970s during the author's stay in the USSR and appeared in 1978–79 (first in Russian and later in English). It was in this book that ethnic deportations in the USSR were looked at as an integral, poorly researched and—importantly—*academic* matter. Some chapters are devoted to the deportations from the Crimea, Kalmykia and the North Caucasus, to the period when the "punished peoples" held the status of "special resettlers" [*spetspereselentsy*], and to the process of their returning (or non-returning) to their homelands. Nekrich used scarce Soviet and foreign publications on Second World War history as factual sources (NB: the Soviet archives were strictly inaccessible even to the majority of historians holding party membership[12]). He also made use of sources dealing with party development in the remotest areas of the USSR during the war and post-war period: these sources sometimes contained "grains" of information valuable for the study of the "punished peoples"; and of oral testimonies by repressed peoples' representatives themselves. Nekrich refers to his predecessors as "pioneers in the field" naming A. Kh. Dzukayev (who wrote about the Chechens), Kh. I. Khutuyev (the Balkars), Ch. S. Kulayev (the Karachais), D-Ts. D. Nodinakhanov and M. L. Kichinov (the Kalmyks), V. I. Filkin and S. N. Dzhuguryants (the Chechens and Ingushetians) and R. I. Muzafarov (the Crimean Tatars). While paying due esteem to these academics that were focused, as a rule, on the history of one particular people or region, we would like to put additional stress on the achievement of A. Nekrich himself, who produced a study on the "punished peoples" as an independent academic problem, and who undertook the first, and thus especially arduous, steps in investigating and analyzing the issue.

It was not until the late 1980s, i.e., the Perestroika time, that Soviet academic papers and publications dealing with the topic first appeared. Gradual opening of the relevant reserves of central and regional archives in Russia and other CIS countries resulted in an explosion of interest in the problem, and stimulated the appearance of numerous publications and deportees' memoirs, starting from the early 1990s. Among these publications, the most prominent works were produced by the following authors: S. U. Aliyeva, V. A. Auman, V. G. Chebotareva, N. F. Bugay, M. A. Vyltsan, A. Ye. Guryanov, V. P. Danilov, A. N. Dugin, I. Ye. Zelenin, V. N. Zemskov, Kh. M. Ibragimbeili, N. A. Ivnitsky, V. A. Isupov, G. N. Kim, A. I. Kokurin, S. A. Krasilnikov, V. N. Maksheyev, O. L. Milova, T. F. Pavlova, V. S. Parsadanova, V. I. Passat, D. B. Shabayev, and others (predominantly historians, archivists, and ethnographers). Publications (collections of materials prepared using archaeographic methodology) by N. F. Bugay, V. N. Zemskov, O. L. Milova, and V. I. Passat, which gave publicity to hundreds of the most consequential documents, deserve a special merit. Thematic collections of papers about repression of Poles and Germans prepared by historians from the Memorial Society are significant. Among the works dealing with the outcomes of the deportations, in particular with the process of rehabilitation of the repressed peoples and with ethnic conflicts, books by A.G. Zdravomyslov and, especially, by A. A. Tsutsiyev about the Ossetian–Ingushetian conflict, and by A. G. Osipov on the ethnic discrimination of Meskhetian Turks in the Krasnodar region are of considerable note. The research by V. A. Kozlov concerning outbreaks of mass unrest in post-war USSR, including the protests involving repressed peoples in the locations of their exile, also adds greatly to our understanding.

Russian publications of the 1990s contain plentiful empirical data that reflect many aspects of the forced migrations, in particular related to the legal system, ethnic matters, statistics, organizational issues and national economy. However, most of these publications badly need further archaeographic and semantic commentaries along with historical interpretation. Attempts to systematize the accumulated empirical data are far more uncommon. Among the most significant of such attempts are monographs by N. F. Bugay *L. Beria to I. Stalin: "Following Your Order…"* (1995) on the deported peoples, and by N. A. Ivnitsky *Collectivization and Dekulakization (The Early 1930s)* (1996) on "kulak exile," and a series of papers about "kulak exile" by V. N. Zemskov.

In the West, the theme of Stalin's repression in general, and that of the labor camps in particular, has forced the problem of forced migrations away from the limelight to a certain extent. I can only refer to a few historians who wrote monographs, or at least a series of papers, dealing with the topic. Combining empirical data analysis with their traditional adherence to literary sources (predominantly memoirs), Western historians sometimes produced more accurate colligating evaluation and conclusions than their Russian and Ukrainian colleagues.

The topic is still being elaborated on in Germany and the USA. German historians studied the deportations of Germans from the Volga region (A. Eisfeld, V. Herdt, D. Dahlman), and the history of the "kulak exile" (S. Merl). Papers by American academics are characterized by highly efficient critical study of highly diverse and heterogeneous sources. Among these are works by M. Gelb (about the deportations of Koreans, Finns, and other national minorities) and P. Holquist (about the deportation policy practiced in tsarist Russia during the First World War, and in Bolshevik Russia during the first years of the Soviet rule; this author should be merited for showing the continuity that clearly can be traced throughout pre- and post-revolutionary Russia). The deportations, or rather the deportees, are paid significant attention to in the monograph by J. Pohl about the USSR prison system. An interesting new perspective is offered by N. Naimark and T. Martin in their analyses of the deportations of Chechens, Ingushetians, and Crimean Tatars in the broader context of ethnic cleansing in Europe in the 20th century (remarkably, they incorporated substantial empirical data from the Russian archives on academic "circulation").

The problem of the *Westarbeiter*, i.e., civilian German "internees" deported to the USSR during the first post-war months and used as a labor force, remains scarcely researched. Some studies, directly or indirectly dealing with this theme, were published in the West (monographs by G. Weber et al., S. Karner, and other authors). It was in 1994 that the first publications on the topic came out in Russia (papers by V. B. Konasov & A. V. Tereshchuk, P. N. Knyshevsky, M. I. Semiryaga).

As yet no works that cover the full scope of forced migrations have been produced either in Russia or in the West. Similarly, no analytical publications specifically dealing with the geographical aspect of the deportations have appeared so far. And yet, there is a pressing academic demand for systematizing all available empirical data, discerning particular logic behind the related facts and events, and searching for common—in particular geographical—patterns of the deportations.

It is to the above-mentioned demand that this book hopefully has become a response. The research covers repressive forced deportations that involved the Soviet population and were launched in the very first years of the Soviet rule, gained a powerful momentum during the years of dekulakization, and underwent further intensive development in the second half of the 1930s, the period of Second World War and the post-war years. In fact, forced migrations continued in the USSR until the mid-1950s. This study deals with both forced migrations inside the Soviet Union and international ones that involved the Soviet population, as well as those which were initiated by the USSR and destined for the Soviet territory, but targeted foreign citizens (in particular Romanian, Hungarian, Yugoslavian, Czechoslovakian, German and Polish nationals). It should be noted that those international forced migrations that were carried out by Germany, and not by the USSR, remain outside the scope of this book (for example, driving civilian population from the occupied regions into the Third Reich).

An especially careful consideration is given to the *territorial aspect* and *historico-geographical features* and regularities of the forced migrations in the USSR, their evolution and resulting space pattern, along with their impact on the economy of the regions of departure and destination at the moment of deportation up until today.

Remarkably, the space scope appears to comprise several levels: predominantly the USSR itself within its pre- and post-war boundaries. However, while dealing with the war-time deportations to the USSR territory, one cannot avoid touching upon a broader European context. The chronological span of the main research covers as much as one-third of the century starting from 1919–1920, up until the mid-1950s (yet the historical preamble has no temporal limits; and the discussion of the problems surrounding the "punished peoples" rehabilitation and the consequences of the deportations in chapter 4 takes into account events that happened in the most recent period until 1999 inclusive).

While working on the book, we aimed at addressing the following mutually linked and specific tasks:

- Retrospective consideration in a broad historico-political context of the forced migrations as a historical phenomenon; eliciting from the historic roots of the Soviet deportation policy and practice;
- Elaboration of related terminology, and development of a comprehensive classification of forced migrations;
- Generating a comprehensive list of available literary and archival data related to particular operations and stages of the forced migrations (including the witnesses' testimonies introduced into academic circulation), and critical analysis and systematization of these materials;

– Creating a data bank on forced migrations in the USSR (following the model: "period"—"legal basis"—"target group, its size and administrative status"—"regions of departure"—"regions of destination"), which would be organized chronologically and tied to the spatial context as strictly as possible;
– Determining the scale of forced migrations in the USSR, as far as both particular operations and stages, and their totality, are concerned;
– Analysis of the USSR deportation policy, its evolution, the magnitude of its social and spatial outreach and its associations with various forms and types of migrations;
– Historico-geographical evaluation of the outcomes that the forced migrations in the USSR brought about, and of the spatial patterns of these outcomes.

In terms of methodology, the research is based on the following three principles:

a) addressing trustworthy, reliable facts;

b) putting them into a system;

c) search for regularities, analysis and interpretation.

Based on the proposed classification and space-time systematization, the research suggests a structural geographical description of the forced migrations in the USSR, and attempts to discern their hallmarks and common geographical patterns as linked to the political, social and economic development of the USSR and to the contemporary situation in the CIS countries and Baltic states.

The book is an attempt to provide an analysis of the Soviet repressive migration policy and practices, and an evaluation of the impact they produced on the political and economic situation in the entire country and its particular regions both at the time of their implementation and at present (the origins of some of today's hot spots, for example the Ossetian–Ingushetian conflict, can be traced back to the deportation policy of the Soviet state).

While revealing the historic excesses of the Soviet Union, one of the most powerful totalitarian countries of the 20th century, and disclosing the state's repressive system and its mechanisms, the book also represents a rather topical study. First of all, it concerns the regions where the rehabilitation process has not been completed and thus caused countless problems. There is no doubt that the book's topicality is also enhanced by the apparent "popularity," in the late-

20th century, of tackling ethnic conflicts by means of deportations and other methods of territorial "cleansing" (e.g., recent events in Africa, in the Balkans, and—regrettably—once again on the territory of the former USSR).

The *information basis* of research comprises primarily *archival data* and *academic publications*. International migrations were approached with predominant reference to primary archival sources (namely, those from the GUPVI and RGVA collections), while internal migrations are documented by materials published by Russian academics in recent years (the monographs by N. F. Bugay and N. A. Ivnitsky were used as principal sources). In addition, oral history documents and memoir testimonies were referred to in the work, but their role is rather limited.

Dealing with "voluntary–compulsory" migrations, which made a setting for the forced migrations, we relied on the materials provided by the Russian State Archive of the Economy (RGAE), particularly on the vast holdings of the Agricultural Ministry Chief Resettlement Agency, which maintains a compiled collection of materials produced by all predecessors of the organization starting from 1924, naturally with certain blanks and gaps, not least due to endless structural reorganizations and changes of the official affiliation of the country's resettlement headquarters (RGAE, h. 5675). In this context, it is also worth mentioning the reserve of the Resettlement Department of the RSFSR (GARF, h. A-317), a similar organization distinguished for its employment of "alleviated compulsion" and typically engaged in performing tasks in the sphere of compensatory migrations.

In the early 1990s, regional archives started to be explored too. These archives sometimes contain records providing a level of detail that can rarely be found in central archives. With regard to this, it would be appropriate to pay due tribute to works by S. A. Krasilnikov and his colleagues, and V. A. Isupov and V. N. Maksheyev, who used the reserves of the Novosibirsk and Tomsk regional state archives. Regrettably, archives possessed by some official bodies are still hardly accessible, although there is an urgent need for this material; and this makes any exhaustive research unrealistic.

As a rule, the text omits references to various decrees, resolutions, rulings, orders and other legal documents authorizing various official practices and operations in the area of forced migrations in the USSR. A compiled annotated list of these documents, which was compiled as a result of the examination of academic sources, is offered as an attachment.

The bibliography contains two separate lists: of monographs and article collections, and of papers and articles. The bibliography comprises only titles of fundamental sources from the field and those papers that are referred to in the text on more than two occasions. Other sources are cited in the footnotes to the chapters.

The author has been studying forced migrations since the early 1980s. He has approached the area from different perspectives during this period: first by exploring the migration processes in the Caucasus related to the so-called planned resettlement of highlanders from mountain regions to the plain. Later the author was engaged in elaborating a classification of forced migrations in the USSR, chiefly of ethnic deportations and compensatory migrations. Intense efforts were made in 1991–1996 while inquiring into the subject of forced migrations in the course of writing the book *Victims of Two Dictatorships: The Ostarbeiter and POWs in the Third Reich and their Repatriation* (1996), which dealt with the forced resettling of Soviet POWs and civilians from the USSR territory to the Third Reich by the German authorities, and the consequent—essentially imposed—repatriation in accordance with the Yalta agreement. Simultaneously, materials were gathered and analyzed with regard to the deportation of ethnic Germans that were "interned and mobilized" by the USSR in a number of European countries.

The research area is located at the intersection of geography, history and demography, and the monograph is designed for experts in corresponding fields. However, it is also aimed at numerous victims of deportations in the USSR and their family members, who are interested in understanding and comprehending their individual fates in a broad context of Soviet history.

The book was based on the doctoral dissertation "Geography of Forced Migrations in the USSR," defended by the author in April 1998. Compared to the dissertation, the text of the monograph was thoroughly updated. At the same time, some chapters devoted to international forced migrations, elaborately analyzed in the book *Victims of Two Dictatorships* (1996), were omitted in this monograph.

Work on the book was carried out in closest the contact with Russian historians, ethnographers, demographers, and archivists, for example N. Bugay, A. Vishnevsky, A. Guryanov, V. Danilov, S. Zakharov, Zh. Zayonchkovskaya, V. Zemskov, N. Ivnitsky, R. Kuliyev, Sh. Muduyev, D. Nokhotovich, N. Okhotin, N. Petrov, T. Plokhotnik, N. Pobol, A. Roginsky, and others. Besides, substantial valuable advice, comments and information came from foreign colleagues: S. Debski (Kraków), G. Klein (Freiburg), G. Superfin (Bremen), F. Ther (Berlin), P. Holquist (Ithaca, USA), P. Gatrell and N. Baron (Manchester), and others. Memorial Society members and experts of the State Archives of the Russian Federation A. Eisfeld (Göttingen) and A. Nikolsky (Moscow) provided significant help in selecting illustrations.

Most sincere gratitude and appreciation are addressed to all these people.

NOTES

1 From the Latin *deportatio*: exile, banishment.
   The Russian calque *deportatsiya* has the English meaning of forcible expulsion of one or many individuals from a city or territory. Specialized terms (see below) distinguish the various forms of punitive banishment and internal exile (*ssylka*, *vysylka* etc.) and those to whom such measures are applied: *ssylny*, *vyslany* and so on.
2 This paradoxical formulation is common in the old Soviet bloc, applying to relatively innocent activities like *subbotniki* ("voluntary" work days by the free population), and to the most brutal forms of repressive measure.
3 From the Latin *repressio*: punitive measure of retribution, aimed at suppression or putting an end to particular events. Cf. the formulation in the Russian Federation Law "On rehabilitation of victims of political repression," 18 October 1991, Art. 1: "By political repression is meant various measures of coercion imposed by the state for political considerations and taking the forms of: deprivation of life or freedom; forced placement in psychiatric institutions; expulsion from the country and deprivation of citizenship; removal of population groups from their homelands; sending [individuals and groups] into [internal] exile; special resettlement or deportation; forced labor under conditions of restricted freedom; along with other types of deprivation or infringement of the rights and liberties of persons recognized as socially dangerous to the state or political system on the basis of social, national, religious, or other criteria. These measures are executed in accordance with decrees issued by courts or other bodies endowed with judicial authority, or through administrative measures implemented by executive power organs, officials, non-government organizations or their branches endowed with administrative power."

4 We make rather wide use of the term "sweep operation," which is expressive and precise, although it was hardly ever employed in documents produced during the epoch under consideration.

5 Neither the Criminal nor Civil Codes were taken into account and even such Soviet surrogates of justice as the "troika" or Special Council [Osoboye Soveshchaniye] were not involved. (Often the latter issued juridical decisions providing for "banishment to remote areas of the USSR" after a term in the GULAG or supervision by the special settlement bodies that were responsible for "ordinary" [internal] exiles but this is a different matter.)

6 Pavlova, *Spetspereselentsy v Zapadnoy Sibiri*, 28.

7 Cited in *Yusupov*, 181.

8 See R. Jones "Climbing with Russians," *Geographical Magazine* (June 1959).

9 Published in journal *Life* on (5 July 1954).

10 In addition, some information originated from Soviet "non-returnees" who managed to avoid the post-war repatriation. In particular, according to Conquest, the Kalmyk Diaspora headed by Naminov was especially active and well organized, and it constantly addressed international organizations appealing to public opinion in both Western countries and in the East.

11 Conquest, *Soviet Deportations of Nationalities*, 94.

12 This mere fact renders any criticism regarding Nekrich's unawareness of archive materials rather inappropriate (see Bugay, Gonov, 25, 26).

Forced Migrations: Prehistory and Classification

FORCED MIGRATIONS BEFORE HITLER AND STALIN: HISTORICAL EXCURSUS

World history has seen many examples of "deportations" and "forced migrations." It will suffice to recall a succession of events described in the Old Testament, largely involving accounts of particular episodes from the life of Jews "resettled" in Egypt, Babylon, and other countries of the Old-Testament Diaspora.

At the other end of the Eurasia mainland, back in the 3rd century BC, Chinese emperor Qin Shi Huangdi ordered the execution of 500 scholars and the resettlement of hundreds of thousands of families from northern to southern China. The Incas practiced forced resettlement too.

There is much in common between the intercontinental "resettlement" of black slaves from Africa to America and the driving of the Ostarbeiter into the Third Reich, and between the dekulakization and Mao's Village Campaign in China. The driving forces behind forced migration practice have not changed significantly during the centuries: they are motivated by a particular combination of *political and pragmatic factors*.

Political motives—preventing rebellions, dispersing discontent, weakening and suppressing protests, homogenizing regions of either departure or destination, and so on—often dominate. However, the role of *economic* factors is colossal, and it tends to gradually overshadow the initial political momentum: deportees are a cheap (and even preferably free, or almost free) labor force that is moved to a particular location at a particular time at the discretion of the authorities administering the deportation.

There is also an evident connection between outbursts of forced migrations and historical cataclysms.

One conspicuous example is the African *slave trade*. Approximately 11 million black slaves were brought to America in the period from the 16th through the mid-19th century. Taking into account those who perished while hunted or during the journey, the figure for the number of people "affected" by the slave trade should be increased to 15 million.[1] Table 1 shows approximate "bottom line" estimations of the numbers of black slaves deported from Africa, by century and colonial empire.

Europeans operated primarily on the West African coast, while the East coast was exploited by Arabs for the same purpose, and from much earlier than the beginning of the European trade (i.e., starting from approximately the 13th century): in particular, slave labor was used at sugar cane plantations near Basra. Gradually, the "reservoir" of black slaves on the African coast became exhausted: the "depleted zone" which could not maintain an active slave trade, which initially appeared in the area of contemporary Senegal, shifted in the direction of the Ivory Coast, then to Nigeria, and then, by the late 19th century, to Congo and further south up to Angola, which by this time had already been "drained" by the Portuguese and Brazilians. The Arab slave trade continued even after Europe abandoned the practice and dissociated itself from slavery, following the European colonization of Africa: in Oman and Zanzibar slave markets were still functioning at the end of last century.

The history of *the Jewish people* is another rich in examples of

Table 1. Deportations of black slaves from Africa by some European countries in the 16th–19th centuries (thousands persons)

Country	Century				
	16th	17th	18th	19th	TOTAL
Portugal	50	600	2,000	1,200	3,850
Spain	75	300	600	600	1,575
England	—	300	1,800	—	2,100
France	—	160	1,400	50	1,650
Holland	—	Unknown	Unknown	Unknown	1,000
TOTAL	125	over 1,360	over 5,800	over 1,850	10,175

Source: Meyer J. Sklaverei und Sklavenhandel Mitteilungen. AvH-Magazine, Nr. 57, July 1991, 6.

deportations and forced resettlement. Just recall the "special resettlement" to Egypt, and the Exodus, along with the First (Assyrian and
Babylonian) and Second (Rome) Diasporas, etc. In both ancient and
contemporary times, the intensity of Jewish migrations has been
extraordinary. And very rarely were these migrations voluntary.

In essence, the entire contemporary history of the Jewish people
has been a succession of ceaseless migrations, a sequence of mass
wandering and suffering. This is a history of "The Galut," or expulsion.

In 1290, all Jews were expelled from England, and then from
France in 1292. The expellees settled predominantly in Spain. However, in 1492—under the pressure of the Inquisition—all Jews (except
those baptized, or *Marranos*) were driven out of Spain, and in 1497
from Portugal too: they moved to Italy, North Africa, and Turkey.
Approximately at the same time, a mass resettlement of Jews from
Germany to East Europe, particularly to Poland and Lithuania, was
taking place.

After most of these territories were integrated into Russia, it was
this country that was destined to become—and for a long time—the
Jewish Diaspora's demographic leader. And yet, simultaneously, Russia turned to the implementation of a tough anti-Semitic state policy
that comprised the introduction of the Pale of settlement and episod-
ic banishment of Jews who managed to evade the anti-Semitic Russian legislation by fair means or foul.

At this point, it is worth underlining that such Soviet deportation practices have a substantial pre-Revolutionary precedent. Fur-
thermore, it was not exclusively Jews that were the victims.

Until 1861, in the Russian Empire it was only the serf peasants
whose great number and degree of personal subjection exceeded
those of the Jewish population. And yet after 1861, it was the Jews
themselves who were "inferior" to every other equivalent group.
Expulsion and other types of repression of Jews only increased in the
late 19th century, thus placing increased pressure on them to leave
and triggering a new wave of mass Jewish emigration from Russia,
predominantly to the USA, and to Palestine, when possible.

It was large-scale deportation of Jews from Moscow and Rostov-
on-Don in 1891–1892 that played the decisive role in this process. The
Jewish population in Moscow comprised categories holding different
status. Merchants, qualified physicians, engineers and lawyers enjoyed

the right to *unconditional* residence, along with retired (so-called *Nicholas'*) soldiers. Craftsmen, chemists, pharmacists and apprentices enjoyed a *conditional* residence right, i.e., valid only when they were actually employed in the trade indicated in their "craft" identity cards. A number of categories—such as personal secretaries or clerks—were permitted to stay only provided they possessed the local administration's authorization.[2]

On 29 March 1891, Alexander III issued a decree that banned Jewish craftsmen from settling in Moscow and the Moscow Oblast, and envisaged the expulsion of those that were already living there. In actual practice, the decree was extended to many other categories of Jewish population. On 14 July, a secret order was issued allowing for the expulsions to commence but also stipulating the right for deferment for various time periods, with the maximum of one year. Few permissions to stay were issued: virtually the only one was given to Isaac Levitan. And yet, a part of the Jewish community did stay, although—to use Vermel's expression—at the cost of "moral migration," i.e., converting to Christianity (typically to Lutheranism).

From 14 August to 14 July 1892[3] (depending on deferment terms), Moscow railway stations were overcrowded with great numbers of Jews. Many of them departed to places beyond the "Pale of settlement," predominantly to the territory of the former Kingdom of Poland (first of all, to Warsaw and Łódź), and to the south, namely to Odessa. According to an indirect estimation made by S. Vermel, approximately 38 thousand people were deported from Moscow during the period of 1891–1892.[4]

Most of them headed directly abroad, primarily to German seaports. This event, though it seemingly affected only Moscow and was hardly statistically significant, nevertheless had a colossal aftermath, namely, it produced the decisive momentum for mass Jewish emigration from across the entirety of Russia to North America. S. Vermel maintains that 42,145 Jews emigrated from Russia in 1891; and as many as 76,417 in 1892. And this was happening despite the closure of American ports at the beginning of 1892 due to the threat of epidemics.[5]

In 1895, a new ruling on the expulsion of Jews from Russia followed. This time it concerned Persian Jews (several hundreds of natives of Herat and Meshkhed had settled primarily in the Merv region). Soon, however, the expulsion was replaced by permission to stay in the Transcaspian Obl. though with the status of "temporary residents." However, in 1910 virtually all Herat Jews were expelled from the Russian Empire as foreign Jews.[6]

As it has already been mentioned, Jews were not the only group subjected to forced migrations in tsarist Russia. For example, at the very beginning of the 19th century, during the Russian–Turkish wars in the Black Sea region, the entire Muslim population (Tatars, Turko-mans, and the Nogays) was deported from the Prut–Dniester inter-fluve area (or the Budzhak Steppe) to the Crimea.[7]

Deportations and resettlement in general came to be a well-established method of fighting the Caucasian war and consolidating hard-fought territorial gains. Even in the course of, or in conjunction with, some military actions, many highland *auls* were moved to the plain or enlarged. For example, the whole population of the Larger Kabarda was grouped into as few as 33 big *auls*. Thousands and sometimes even tens of thousands of Chechens were moved from the "piedmont" areas to the plains, namely the places allotted to them by the Russians.[8]

The Russian authorities also made attempts to impose their order on the internal arrangement of highlanders' settlements. For example, the merging of smaller Chechen *auls* into larger ones under-mined the internal clan [*teip*] unity.[9] Shamil realized the danger the stable domicile and enlarged settlements represented for his cause, and made the principle of establishing small auls and even forest camps a constituent of his settlement policy, which naturally placed additional pressure on the ordinary population.

After Shamil was captured and the Caucasian war came to a vic-torious end in the eastern Caucasus, the Russian government intend-ed a total resettlement of the highland Chechens from the Caucasus. The plan was even partly implemented, but merely with regard to small—most uncompromising—sections of the population.

After the Russians achieved victory in western Caucasus too, and—to an extent—under the influence of Turkish propaganda, mass moving of so-called Mukhadjirs, highlanders from the conquered western Caucasus, to Turkey took place. During the period of 1863–64, the total of some 418 thousand Adyghians, Abazians, and Nogays left their homelands for Turkey, and around 90 thousand were moved to the plain, namely to the left-bank Kuban region (obvi-ously, internal deportation was the only alternative to emigration, which, as a matter of fact, stimulated the latter process). Some 20 thousand highland Muslims that resided in the Tsebeld, Abkhazia, were subjected to administrative expulsion to Turkey in 1866, after they organized a revolt and tried to storm Sukhum. Another 100 families were resettled to Turkey from the Trans-Katal Okrug.[10] Those emigrants' descendants still live in Turkey as well as in other Middle East countries, in Western Europe, and in the USA.[11]

Turkey, however, was not the only destination of the tsarist repressive deportations. For example, participants of the 1871 revolt in the western Daghestani district of Unkratl were resettled to Siberia, inner Russian *gubernias* and other parts of Daghestan.[12] Participants of the uprising led by imam Ali-Bek in 1877 in the Vedeno Okrug were partly resettled to the plain and partly left as labor force for making cuttings through the forests. Administrative expulsions (on a scale of up to several hundred persons) were still occasionally practiced in the Caucasus later: for example, the fact of the expulsion of 300 Ossetians for anti-government insurgent actions in 1905–1906 has been established.[13] The actions of Chechen gangster leader Zelimkhan Gushmazukaev and his gang in 1905–1911 (attacks on trains, treasuries, shops, etc.) once again made the government contemplate deporting "evidently vicious persons with their families"[14] or at least "the male lineage of any gangster along with their family"[15] from the Caucasus to East Siberia. Roughly 3 thousand of Zelimkhan's relatives were indeed exiled or resettled, and they were not allowed to return until the beginning of the First World War.[16]

The First World War brought about an unprecedented scale to the forced migrations in Russia (affecting both Jews and non-Jews). It was tsarist Russia (although it was not only Russia) that initiated and implemented the policy of "preventive ethnic cleansing" and deportations.

There was nothing unusual about this, since it was the Russian Empire that possessed the notoriety of having gained long-term practice and ideological justification of such dubious activities. "Military statistics"—traditional and typically one of the principal subjects taught at the General Staff Academy—was a discipline responsible for developing and perfecting the techniques. Due to its dependence on the acquisition of conscripts, the army was extremely interested in reliable data on, and studies of, the geography of the Russian population.

At the end of the 19th century, leading Russian military statisticians A. Maksheyev, N. N. Obruchev, and especially V. A. Zolotarev, developed a specific doctrine that could be appropriately summed up as the "geography of unreliability." [17] It was based on the actual geography of "reliable" and "unreliable" populations, and on their ratio within particular territories: the former group included the population of Slavic origin, and the latter predominantly comprised Jews, Germans, Poles, and the peoples of the Caucasus and Central Asia. Only those regions where the Russian population exceeded 50% were evaluated as favorable in terms of the population's reliability. The degree of reliability, according to Zolotarev, decreased the further you looked for support from the center to the outskirts of the empire. The Military Academy students—future officers and commanders of the Tsarist, White and Red Armies—listened to this, studied it, and definitely took note.

Military statistics were not limited to mere assessment and speculation. To be sure, they were used to support an active and evolving policy that dealt with the "reliability" differentiation among Russian territories: regions with a highly concentrated unreliable population were registered and kept under control. In case of war it was recommended to "improve the situation," especially in frontier zones. Taking civilian hostages, confiscation or liquidation of property and cattle, along with *deportations based on national and ethnic group membership* were identified as the most efficient and practical measures. Based on this doctrine, special punitive military units were created honed on the use of systematic cruelty in stamping out any minor manifestations of discontent or rebellion against the Russian colonization of the empire. In particular, such operations were carried out in Central Asia, where it was not deportations but civilian killings that were used as the extreme measures of choice.[18]

In fact, the Jewish deportation from Moscow in 1891 was a mere actualization of a concept of Jewish population redundancy in the city, which was scientifically grounded by military statisticians. All the more, this was so with regard to the deportations carried out in the western frontier zones of Russia in the course of the First World War. As P. Holquist remarks, such measures cannot be explained solely by military necessity: "Their logic becomes clear only if one accepts the idea of the possibility to transform the population structure by means of either the introduction of particular elements into the structure or their removal."[19] According to some evaluations, the deportations in the west of the country affected around 1 million people, with Jews constituting half of this number and Germans one-third.[20]

The haste and simultaneous efficiency that distinguished the deportation operations conducted by the Russian authorities might seem surprising. However, everything becomes clear in the context of the concepts taught at the Military Academy of the General Staff of the Russian Empire.

As early as the night of 18 July 1914 (Old Style), i.e., even before the official declaration of war, Russia launched arrests and deportations of German and Austro-Hungarian nationals.[21] The number of the latter that were subjected to the measures was high (the total amounted to at least 330 thousand people). They had lived for decades in Saint Petersburg, Moscow, Odessa and Novorossia, in Volyn, Poland and the Baltics. Deportees were sent to remote inland regions (in particular, to the Vyatka, Vologda, and Orenburg Gubs.; residents of the Siberia and Primorsky Kray were exiled to the Yakutsk Oblast). In the second half of 1915, they were removed to considerably harsher environments: deportation destination shifted to the Trans-Ural part of the Perm Gub., Turgaysk Obl., and Yeniseysk Gub. Not only "espionage suspects" were subject to deportations, but also all men of conscription age (as a preventive measure against their joining the enemy armies). Along with Germans, Austrians and Hungarians, Poles, Jews and others were deported too (the only exception was allowed for Czechs, Serbs and Rusyns who signed a pledge "not to undertake any harmful actions against Russia"). Germans from Volyn were subject to exceptionally cruel treatment: virtually all of them were sent to Siberia in summer 1915.[22] Incidentally, the exile was carried out at the expense of the deportees themselves. If they did not have sufficient means for relocating, they were conveyed to the destination as prisoners.

In fact, people were often interned indiscriminately; they were termed "civilian POWs." This arbitrary policy reached its climax at the point when General N. N. Yanushkevich,[23] the chief of staff of the Supreme Commander-in-Chief, issued an order on 5 January 1915 to cleanse a 100-*verst*-wide[24] zone along the Russian Baltic coastline of all German and Austro-Hungarian nationals aged from 17 to 60. Those who refused to leave were labeled German spies. It was only some time later that these measures were weakened to an extent—

mainly for sections of the Slavic peoples—under public pressure and due to a number of negative results, which they had brought about.[25]

Besides, Turkish nationals were exiled (at least 10 thousand people, with many Crimean Tatars among them). According to S. Nelipovich, they were deported to the Olonets, Voronezh, Kaluga, Yaroslavl, and Kazan Gubs. In his turn, E. Lohr believes the destinations were the Ryazan, Kaluga, Voronezh, and Tambov Gubs., and—especially—the region of Baku, where a 5,000-capacity camp with horrific conditions was created for the deportees.

Naturally, Jews were not forgotten either. In 1914–1915, 250–350 thousand Jews were deported from the territories of Poland, Lithuania, and Belorussia into inland Russian gubernias; and they were allowed only 24 hours to get prepared. It took even shorter time for the local population thoroughly to plunder the houses and shops left by Jews. (Ironically, despite the Jewish deportation, the military still managed to claim that the Jews were responsible for the subsequent Russian military failures.)

The Jewish population of the town of Janowiec, Radom Gub., was the first to be deported. A little later, Jewish residents of Ryki (most likely located in the same gubernia), Myszyniec in the Lomzyn Gub., and New Aleksandria in the Lublin Gub. were deported (in two stages: 23 August and at the beginning of September). In October, all Jewish residents were ousted from the towns of Piaseczna, Grodzisk and Skierniewicy in the Warsaw Gub., in particular 4 thousand people (including a 110-year-old woman) from Grodzisk. Later they were allowed to return, but were deported again in January 1915, along with Jewish settlers of another 40 towns and villages (remarkably, as in the case of Sochaczew, a number of Jews were taken hostage, and some of them were later hanged). In March 1915, on the eve of Jewish Easter, 500 families were expelled from Radoszczicy, Radom Gub., and from Mniew in Kieleck uyezd. The majority of expelled Jews headed for Warsaw, where their number climbed to 80 thousand, but subsequently they were banned from entering large cities.

However, as noted by S. Vermel, the author of a series of general papers on the topic, all these individual expulsions and adversities "...pale beside the monstrous mass expulsion from Kovno and Kurland Gub." Due to the rapid advance of the German army, the Russian military authorities issued orders for the immediate deportation of all local Jews from Kurland Gub. and then from Kovno, and partially from Suwalki and Grodno Gubs., on 30 April 1915 and on 3 May 1915 respectively. The total number of Jews expelled then from Kurland Gub. was around 40 thousand[26]; and 150–160 thousand were deported from Kovno Gub. A number of uyezds of Poltava, Yekaterinoslavl and Taurida Gubs. were assigned as destinations of new settlements of the deportees.[27]

Baltic general governor P. G. Kurlov opposed the deportation of Jews from Kurland. It was for this reason that he visited the commander-in-chief and convinced him that the latter's order should be cancelled. During the course of the German advance, the authority over deportation-related matters was transferred to military commanders, who had neither time nor willingness to deal with such issues. As a result, the actual implementation of deportations was often at the discretion of middle-ranking police officers or even counter-intelligence services.[28]

Nevertheless, the process of expulsion of Jews—which expanded this time to cover the southwestern region, namely Podolsk and Volyn Gubs.—was resumed in June 1915. All this was happening in spite of the fact that at least one member of nearly every Jewish family was fighting at the front, and Jewish young men, including those expelled, were still drafted into the army!

(At this point, it would be appropriate to divert from the subject and make a somewhat premature comment: while at the initial stage of the Soviet rule Jews were freed from discrimination, the deportations of Jews were recommenced later, yet only barely on a lesser scale. So, in the 1920s some residents of Daghestani and Azerbaijani highland villages, populated by Tats and highland Jews, were "moved down" to Derbent and Kuba. Iranian Jews were deported from the border zone of Turkmenistan's Mary Obl. in its northern deserted part, within the 1937–1938 policy envisaging the deportation of foreign nationals. In 1940, Jewish refugees who escaped from the German-occupied western part of the former Polish state were deported from the Polish territory annexed by the USSR.[29] One has to note that this saved them from the Nazi genocide.[30] Due to the absence of respective direct documentary evidence, we will not touch upon the deportation of Jews to Siberia allegedly planned by Stalin in 1953.)

So how many Russian "displaced persons" did the First World

War produce in all? The estimation made by Ye. Volkov based on the data of state authorities and the Tatyaninsky Committee appears to be the most reliable: 7.4 million as of 1 July 1917, with 6.4 million of them refugees and the rest deportees.[31]

However, it is not mere numbers that matter. As P. Gatrell accurately observes refugee status came to be a type of "civil status" in Russia, i.e., refugees turned into a *new* informal *social class*, cast to the very marginal position in society, to say the least, by the force of circumstances. This was a group of people that had lost (temporarily, or at least so they hoped) everything they possessed: dwelling, property, occupation, and particular social status. In no time, respectable and independent citizens were rendered a gathering of "vagrant elements," hordes of homeless beggars, fully and totally dependent on the state and private and charitable initiatives arranged by non-refugees. And to a greater extent, even, the above refers to deportees.

On the whole, we have to state that *the tsarist government's treatment of interned "adversary nationals" was a remarkable precursor of the horrifying deportation policy implemented by the Soviet state.*

However, Russia was not the first country in the 20th century to produce deportees. This phenomenon was first noted in the Balkans, as a result of two Balkan wars (some sort of prelude to the First World War) between Bulgaria and Turkey in 1912 and 1913. At least 500 thousand persons were displaced from their homelands and became refugees. In 1913, after the Second Balkan War had ended, Bulgaria and Turkey signed an agreement that provided for the resettlement of national minorities (an actual total of around 50 thousand people was deported by either side).[32] Turkey and Greece made a similar agreement in 1914, and Greece and Bulgaria in 1919.[33] One of the most gruesome episodes of "ethnic cleansing" in world history occurred in Turkey in 1915, when a massive massacre of Armenians took place accompanied by the flight of escapees abroad, in particular to Soviet Armenia.

The Greek–Turkish Treaty on population exchange of 30 January 1923 and the Lausanne Treaty of 23 July 1923 stipulated an exchange of citizens unprecedented in its scale. It was not an exchange of national minorities that Turkey and Greece agreed on, but mutual peaceful "ethnic cleansing" of larger parts of the countries' territories[34]: around 400 thousand Turks were expelled from Greece to Asia Minor, from where around 1.2 million Greeks were deported in their turn. This instance set a "promising" precedent for international dispute and conflict resolution through ethnic cleansing.

After the defeat of Germany in the First World War and the consequent reduction of its territory, around 1 million Germans resettled from the Baltic states to the remainder of German territory. Simultaneously, a current of refugees rushed from eastern Ukraine and Belorussia to Poland.

According to different estimates, numbers of emigrants from the Bolshevik Russia ranged from 1.5 to 3 million persons. However, these were refugees rather than deportees (with perhaps one exception of the *Philosophers' ship* with some 150 people aboard). In 1921 a Refugee Settlement Commission headed by Fridtjof Nansen was founded under the aegis of the League of Nations. A so-called Nansen-Amt was organized in 1931, and a Refugee Convention was concluded in 1933. The subsequently issued International (or *Nansen's*) passports, and the activities of the Nansen Foundation and other organizations helped millions of people, in particular Jewish refugees from Germany, to survive and assimilate.

FORCED MIGRATIONS AND THE SECOND WORLD WAR

It was the Second World War and events related to it that caused an unsurpassed boom of forced migrations. The war introduced all too many new and tragic twists to the concept of forced migrations. As a result of military operations, some 30 million people were forced out from their places of residence in Europe alone. After the war, some 13.5 million displaced persons were registered. Such huge numbers in such a short space of time had been unheard of in the history of mankind!

The first powerful momentum came from Spain seized by the Civil War. Some 2 million people fled the territory controlled by General Franco's forces and crossed over to the Republicans; and around 0.7 million left Spain altogether (mainly heading for France and its North African colonies, but also for Latin America and the USSR). After the end of the war, some 180 thousand Spanish nationals stayed in France.[35]

The total number of refugees in France itself amounted to 5 million persons, including 70 thousand Alsace residents that fled in 1940, after the German annexation, being unwilling to seek glory in battles wearing the *Wehrmacht* uniform.

If one looks upon the war as a global fight between two coalitions, one has to recognize the fact that both sides contributed to the ensuing historical and human catastrophe. However, first of all blame can be attached to the individual totalitarian leaders of the coalitions, namely the Stalin Communist regime and Nazism under Hitler.

Merely in the USSR some 15 million people fell into the category of "forced migrants," including those deported by Germany to its territory. However, since the USSR will be essentially dealt with in what follows, now it would be interesting to describe the deportation policies implemented by the enemies of the Soviet Union (first of all, Germany and Japan) and even by its allies (e.g., the USA).

Undoubtedly it was primarily Germany that was able to rival the USSR when it came to forced migrations. And in the case of Nazi Germany it was the *ethnic* criteria that played the foremost role in corresponding practices. The two peoples that received singular and most careful attention on the part of the Nazis were Germans and Jews.

As far as the German population residing outside the Third Reich (so-called Volksdeutsche) was concerned, the Hitler state developed—and consistently implemented—resettlement projects, that were far-reaching and impressive in scope.

On 6 September 1939 (i.e., right after the German conquest of western Poland), Hitler delivered an inflamed speech in the Reichstag: there should be clear and precise boundaries dividing the European nations, which requires resettling hundreds of thousands of the Volksdeutsche. As soon as the next day, a special Reich commission on strengthening the German nation was founded under the leadership of Himmler, which was assigned to implement the following tasks: a) repatriation of all Volksdeutsche residing abroad into the Reich in the shortest possible time-frame; b) prevention and suppression of all possible harmful influences dangerous for the "German nation"; c) formation of new settlement areas for ethnic Germans through repatriating Germans—primarily from East and Southeast Europe—to these new locations.

This was the beginning of the *Heim ins Reich!* (Back home, to the Empire!) campaign. Only two matters remained to be settled for successful completion of the project: a scientific way to distinguish a

German from a non-German had to be formulated, and the concept of *Reich* had to be specified, preferably through some enlargement of its territory.

The latter problem having already been addressed to some extent, the former was not neglected either. On 11–13 October 1939, a special Immigration Center (EWZ)[36] was founded. Its competency covered primarily matters relating to the immigration and naturalization of the Volksdeutsche.[37]

Primary attention was paid to the Germans that resided in the Soviet-controlled zone, as it was established by the Molotov–Ribbentrop Pact. A secret protocol of 28 September 1939 contained a stipulation of mutual assistance to ethnic Germans residing in the Soviet-controlled zone and wishing to move to the German-controlled zone (a corresponding regulation referred to Ukrainians and Belorussians who intended to move to the USSR).

The opening of the first regional EWZ office in Gotenhafens (contemporary Gdynia), on the Baltic coast, as early as 12 October was not a coincidence. The office was given the title the Northeastern Immigration Bureau (Einwanderungsstelle Nordost).[38] So, it is easy to explain the boldness of the Germans in conducting negotiations with the USSR on evacuation of Germans from the Baltic region and Transdniestria: Berlin had no illusions about the way Stalin would treat the German population in these areas in the event of war or preparation for it.

A joint German-Soviet commission on evacuation was established as early as October 1939; and a corresponding agreement was signed on 16 November. The key representatives of the Soviet and German sides respectively were Ya. N. Sinchin and Hofmeier, both of whom resided in Lutsk. Besides, there were two Soviet representatives in Helm (S. N. Troitsky) and in Jaroslaw (V. S. Zhegarov). Available data show that up to 128 thousand ethnic Germans, including 15 thousand Poles claiming German origin, were evacuated to the West by 8 February 1940. The number of people that were willing to move in the opposite direction constituted some 40 thousand, in particular many Jews, but the Soviet side agreed to accept only 20 thousand persons.[39]

The Soviet–German agreements on repatriation into Germany envisaged the right of ethnic Germans residing on the territories annexed by the USSR to "repatriate" from the USSR. This repatriation was based on ethnic criteria exclusively. Neither Slavs, nor Jews—even if they were family members of the "Aryans"—qualified for the resettlement. Aryans were strictly recommended to divorce with such "undesirable" spouses.[40]

The resettlement was proclaimed absolutely voluntary, however it was not such in practice: it was obvious that the Soviet side would regard those that stayed as German agents and an untrustworthy element. This was realized perfectly well by the Volksdeutsche themselves, and German propaganda did not need to be too insistent in representing these "voluntary-forced" migrations as utterly free. Nevertheless, one has to point to the coincidence—so rare in history—of the interests of all the interested parties, namely the USSR, Germany and Germans themselves.

In accordance with the first Soviet–German agreement of 16 November 1939, initial evacuations of ethnic Germans from the Polish lands annexed by the USSR (i.e., Western Ukraine and Western Belorussia) were carried out.[41]

Germans found the process manageable and hurried to expand it to incorporate Bessarabia and North Bukovina, places of residence of at least 110 thousand Germans.[42] Ambassador Schulenberg met with Molotov on 25 June 1940, and on 9 July he addressed the NKID of the USSR in a memo, which suggested that negotiations on the matter be started immediately in order to complete the resettlement before the winter set in. Eventually, a treaty on the evacuation was signed on 5 September 1940.[43]

A joint Soviet–German commission was charged with the responsibility for the operation. Remarkably, it was usually the Soviet side that made concessions when it came to debatable points. By the end of October 1940, the operation for the resettlement of Germans from Bessarabia and North Bukovina had already been largely completed. By this time, 106,872 out of the registered 126,242 persons had departed by cars, trucks, ships, or horse-drawn carts. Some 17 thousand persons (primarily in North Bukovina) still remained to be resettled. Taking into account 260 persons evacuated in 1941, the total number of the Volksdeutsche resettled from the regions in question constituted 124 thousand persons.[44]

A similar agreement concerning the Baltic states was signed by the USSR and Germany on 10 January 1941 (see below). The total of the Volksdeutsche evacuated from western regions of the USSR came to 392 thousand[45] (according to other sources, it equaled 350 thousand[46]).

All these evacuations were termed "treaty resettlements," since Germany undertook to conclude international agreements concerning each particular group of *Volksdeutschen*. The first treaty of this kind was signed with Estonia (15 October 1939), then with Italy (21 October 1939, with regard to Germans from Adige in South Tyrol), after that with Latvia (30 October 1939) and twice with the USSR (16—according to other sources 11—November 1939: concerning Germans from Western Ukraine and Western Belorussia; and 5 September 1940: regarding Germans from Bessarabia and North Bukovina). There followed an agreement with Romania (22 November 1940), and subsequently two more treaties with the USSR (both signed on 10 January 1941, the first concerning Germans from Estonia and Latvia, and the other on the resettlement of Lithuanians, Russians and Belorussians from the Memel and Suwalki regions). Then it was Italy's turn again (31 August, on the resettlement of Volksdeutsche from the province of Leibach), and eventually came an accord with Croatia (30 November 1942). The total number of "treaty resettlers" amounted to 751,460 persons.[47]

By the time that Lodz was liberated by the Red Army,[48] and the EWZ was thus dissolved, its register comprised files for 1,055,400 ethnic Germans, who were divided into 16 categories. The largest of the categories comprised Germans from the Soviet Union (apparently within the borders of 17 October 1939), who numbered 275 thousand persons. Further followed (in descending order by number of persons; the data are rounded): Germans from Bessarabia and Dobrudja and their relatives—118,000; persons in the process of Germanization (*im Deutschstämmigenverfahren*)—113,000; persons in the process of resettling (*im Umsiedlungsverfahren*)—107,000; Germans from Bukovina—96,000; Germans from Volyn and the Narew district—79,400; Germans from Latvia and Estonia—72,200; Germans from Galicia—57,800; Germans from Lithuania—51,100; Volksdeutsche from France—19,800; Germans from Bosnia—18,500; resettlers (*Absiedler*) from Slovenia—15,900; Germans from Gottschee in Slovenia—15,000; persons of German origin (*Deutschstämmige*) from France—5,600; Germans from Serbia, Greece and Slovakia—3,400; Germans from Bulgaria—2,300; "special resettlers" from the New World—550; and "Germanic returnees" (*Germanische Einwanderer*)—

150. In addition, 10–12 thousand persons received German citizenship on Hitler's order of 19 May 1943, according to which those joining the operating army forces or the SS were granted corresponding
privileges.

One should also take into account those persons whose "racial
files" were still at different stages of consideration: their total number
ranged from 120–126 thousand, with some 110 thousand Germans
from the USSR and 10–15 thousand from the Sudeten region.[49]
Therefore, the total number of the Volksdeutsche registered by the
EWZ constituted 1,180 thousand.

It was planned to settle Volksdeutsche, eligible in terms of race,
in new eastern territories: in the newly established Gau Danzig-West-
preußen and Gau Warteland, mainly on former Polish territory. Some
parts of the plan were carried out: the number of Volksdeutsche resettled during the war totalled 650 thousand, including 80 thousand
from South Tyrol.[50]

Hitler's plan envisaged a gradual (within about two years post-
war) establishment of an actual colony of the Reich in the east, which
presupposed expansion of the state borders for at least 500km to the
east from the original ones. "Today—Colonies. Tomorrow—Settlements. The day after tomorrow—The Reich!"—this was the overt and
cynical way that Himmler used to express his view of the issue.[51] To
start with, special "corridors" that divided the mass of German settlements—to the east of Warsaw and in southern Poland, in
Beskidy—were to be cleansed and appropriated.

However, the territories that Hitler set out to appropriate for the
sake of "tomorrow" and "the day after tomorrow" had to be cleansed
from local residents for one thing: partly (when the Slavic population
was implied), or totally (as far as Jewish people were concerned). In
the latter case, it was no longer "ethnic cleansing" that was meant, as
in the former case, but genocide: it was Polish Jews from Wartergau
that became the first to be transported to death camps. At the same
time there were some voices, heard from the very top, that supported
total deportations with regard to the Slavic population too, for example Czechs from Czech and Moravian territory.[52]

Therefore, there is a very transparent sinister link between the
games of theorizing Social Nationalism and the practice of Holocaust.[53] The Resettlement Center, an organizational counterpart of
the EWZ, was specifically dealing with matters relating to vacating

suitable territories.[54] Taking into account the role it played in the fate
of Jews from Poland and other countries, this agency should be
placed among the list of criminal organizations without any reservation.

Simultaneously, the successful activities of German agencies
engaged in the "voluntary–compulsory" hiring of Poles for work in
the Reich, which seemingly was not directly linked to the Reich resettlement projects, largely reduced the population density in Poland—
which was not the most "crowded" country in Europe as it was—
merely due to the sheer scale of numbers of people involved (at least
2.8 million persons were transported to the Reich).

In no way were other peoples and regions "neglected" by Germans either. For example, a plan developed by Commissar-General
K. von Gotberg envisaged that the Cossacks, who had to leave their
native settlements in Kuban and at the Don river following the
retreating Wehrmacht, should be placed in so-called "military settlements" or "stations" in Western Belorussia, where they were to be
used for fighting the regime's enemies, local guerrillas in this particular case. This required that the vast 180,000-hectare territory, which
was to be transferred under their control, had to be cleansed of
"unreliable" local population and replaced by "reliable" migrants
(mainly those evading service in the Red Army). For this purpose
"...separate villages united into defense districts with strong military
garrisons and multi-branch systems of decentralized fortified
bases."[55]

And yet, it was certainly not the Cossacks, or even the Poles but
the Jews that remained the matter of greatest concern on the part of
the Reich. Hitler wrote about the need to "cleanse" Germany of them
as early as 1919; and after taking power in 1933, he went for a practical solution to the problem. Although—due to all the "niceties" of the
Nazi policy—Jews themselves started rushing to leave Germany, the
expectation of their "voluntary–compulsory" emigration from Germany was fulfilled only to an extent. After over 400 thousand Jews
(some 3/4 of Germany's Jewish population) had left the country,
Hitler placed his stake on the "deportation" principle.

Total deportation, along with the establishment of a ghetto system and death camps, was the most important constituent of the
Nazi's planned "Final Solution" of the Jewish question, which was
shaped at the fateful conference in Wannsee on 20 January 1942. The

plan comprised several stages and essentially targeted the entire 10-million strong Jewish population of Europe.[56]

As the territorial expansion of the Reich was underway in 1938–1939, increasing numbers of Jews were becoming subject to German anti-Jewish legislation. It was in Vienna in March 1938, soon after the annexation of Austria, that a special Central Office for Jewish Emigration was founded. Engaged primarily in routine matters relating to Jewish emigration, this agency turned its hand to the "genre" of deportation that same year. It was this office that deported some 70 thousand Jews of Polish citizenship, permanently residing in the Reich, on 28–29 October 1938: 31 October was the deadline established by the Polish government for these immigrants to exchange their passports, and those who arrived after this date were not allowed to enter Poland and remained on neutral territory in the area of Zbaszyn.

After the occupation of Poland in September 1939, the Nazis made up for lost time. They allocated a special 20,000-square-kilometer reservation between the rivers Vistula, Bug and San, with its capital in Lublin.[57] This was to be the destination for all Jews from across Europe, though initially those from Germany, Austria, Poland and Czechoslovakia. As soon as the end of October 1939, the first trains with deportees—some 22 thousand people from Vienna, Moravian Ostrawa and Katowice—were brought to the Nisko camp on the San river, from which many fled to Soviet territory.[58]

After some time, these "wild deportations" (as the Nazis themselves referred to them) were halted and resumed only in early 1941: however, as of March 1941 the deportations had affected some 380 thousand Polish citizens (both Jews and Poles). In October 1940, all the Jews from Alsace and Lorraine (70 thousand persons) and from Baden and Saar-Pfalz (6.5 thousand) were deported to Vichy France. After the war against the USSR had started, some 50 thousand Jews were deported from Germany and other European countries to Łodź and even to occupied Soviet territory; some of these deportees were wiped out in Riga and Kaunas.

When the project of the physical liquidation of the Jews was launched and death camps were founded, the deportations, which this time targeted ghetto populations too, acquired an extremely sinister undertone. These deportations were carried out in waves rather than consistently (e.g., in the period of mid-January to mid-May

1942, in September 1942, in the early months of 1943, and in 1944[59]). It would not be an exaggeration to regard the deportations as an essential and largely crucial constituent of the Nazi technology of mass extermination of Jews.

It should be noted that before and during the Second World War, forced deportation and labor policy, rather similar to that exercised by the Nazis and Soviet authorities, was implemented by other countries too, chiefly by Germany's anti-Comintern coalition allies (especially Romania). For example, Bulgaria (as back in 1913) launched ethnic deportations and exchanges: in 1940, after Bulgaria incorporated Dobrudja, eastern Macedonia and West Frakia (that had belonged to Romania and Greece), it deported around 100 thousand Romanians, 300 thousand Serbs and 100 thousand Greeks, subsequently placing 125 thousand Bulgarians in the vacated territories. Thousands of Serbs were also deported by Croatia in 1940.[60] Three new treaties on population exchange were concluded in 1943–1944 by three East European allies of Germany: Romania, Hungary and Bulgaria. The total number of persons resettled in accordance with these treaties made up some 500 thousand.[61]

The case of Japan, however, deserves special attention. This country's treatment of civilian deportees (as well as POWs) was exceptional in its brutality, even compared to equivalent practices in Germany and the USSR. Koreans[62] constituted the key ethnic target (although not the only one) of this policy. During the war, approximately 4.6 million Koreans were subjected by Japan to forced labor, primarily on Korean territory: starting from 1944, all children from the age of the fourth school year and older were obliged to work.

The deportations of Koreans were launched as early as 1939 (even earlier dates are cited by some sources, which in some sense would have been noted by the Soviets), but a corresponding legislative act was issued only late in 1941.[63] First 49.8 thousand Korean workers were driven to Japan in 1939. The number increased in 1940: 59.4 thousand persons (including those transported to Sakhalin). In 1941, another 67.1 thousand persons were subjected to deportation, among them were first 1.8 thousand persons transported to the islands of the southern part of the Pacific Ocean (the war years' total number of the latter reached 5.8 thousand people). In 1942–1943, the number of deported workers amounted to 120 and 128.4 thousand respectively. And finally, 16.4 thousand persons were deported in

1944. The number of Koreans deported in the period of 1939–1944 totaled 444.3 thousand.[64] The key employment sphere of Korean workers in Japan was coal mining.

However, one has to point out that the USA—wary during the Second World War of a possible attack by the Japanese—also resettled some 400 persons (chiefly Eskimos), constituting the entire population of the Aleutian Islands and Pribiloff Islands, to inland territory.[65] After Japan's attack on Pearl Harbor, the USA also interned and deported the American Japanese (incidentally, as in the case of Soviet Germans, with no grounds for accusing them of disloyalty to their new home country): 120 thousand Japanese that had resided in the western parts of the country were transported to the east, with the term of their deportation limited to four years. After the war was finished, official apologies and monetary compensations were offered to the deportees.[66]

German researcher P. Ther appears to have been the first to note the following fact: it was not only "large" legitimate states that enthusiastically practiced ethnic cleansing and deportations of representatives of "hostile" nationalities during the war, but also clandestine and guerilla formations, which had virtual control over large territories in the rear of the German and Allied armies which were getting increasingly embroiled in the east. It was not solely Wehrmacht or the Red Army that such groups were fighting, but also they were struggling with each other demonstrating no lesser degree of cruelty and without the slightest respect for international law. Ther refers to the Serbian and Croatian, and Ukrainian and Polish guerillas as the most merciless enemies. The researcher believes that the numbers of victims on both sides in these confrontations amounted to hundreds of thousands. It should be noted also that the Ukrainian nationalists' vision of the Jewish question was virtually equivalent to that of the Nazis.[67]

At the end of the war and afterwards, the German population was destined to suffer the most large scale forced migrations of their national history. However, these migrations were not related to the Führer's resettlement plans described above, apart from being a direct result of the impending military defeat and the crash of the German policy, which included the resettlement plans as an essential component. Moreover, in a way these migrations were entirely opposite with regard to the Nazis' resettlement plans. Unlike in the case of the "eastward" resettlements inspired by Hitler, the new migrants were moving in the opposite direction: to the west. When the Soviet (in July 1944) and British and US (in September) troops reached the boundaries of the Reich, Germany faced a most acute need to evacuate civilians into inland territories. Trains with refugees from Upper Silesia started for Berlin in January 1945. In a few weeks, the actual population of the towns and villages west of the Oder river increased 1.5 to 3-fold. The German High Command data show that 8.35 million refugees had concentrated in Germany by 19 February, and over 10 million by mid-March. Evacuation from western German regions was halted from 20 February, while the evacuation from eastern territories continued until the end of April, i.e., virtually until the end of the war.[68] Among the evacuees were hundreds of thousands of *Volksdeutsche*, i.e., ethnic Germans, from Romania, Yugoslavia, Hungary, Slovakia, and some 350 thousand from the occupied Soviet regions.[69]

The post-war fate of ethnic Germans was rather unenviable, especially that of the native residents of East Prussia and Upper Silesia. Prior to the war, approximately 11.5 million Germans had lived in these regions, and almost all of them—apprehending vengeful violence on the part of the Slavic population of Poland and Czechoslovakia, but especially out of fear of the advancing Red Army—had to leave their homes in the last months of the war. Some of the German population found it safe to evacuate or merely flee to German territory. As far as the number of people involved in this movement is concerned, estimates range between 5 and 5.7 million.[70]

According to a reasonable classification made by P. Ther, three stages of this semi-flight/semi-exile can be distinguished: first (end of 1944–spring 1945)—*evacuation* measures undertaken by the German authorities; second (March–April–July 1945)—so-called wild exile; and third (after the conclusion of the Potsdam Treaty and a number of consequent accords)—the stage, at which the exile was legitimized and acquired relatively "civilized" forms.[71]

Nevertheless, the methods used to oust Germans from Poland, Czechoslovakia and other countries were not particularly "civilized," especially if one recalls the numbers of people that perished. Until recently a number as high as 2.2 million persons was officially recognized.[72] However, as the most recent research by R. Overmans showed, one can speak with a reliable degree of certainty of some 400 thousand that perished in the process of exile,[73] which—in itself—is a sufficient figure to stun the imagination.

The Allied Control Commission's POW and DP Directorate elaborated a plan concerning the "civilized" stage of the resettlement of Germans. A corresponding treaty was concluded on 22 May 1945 (in Potsdam) stipulating that Germans from Poland be distributed between the Soviet (2 million people) and British (1.5 million) zones, and Germans from Czechoslovakia between the US (1.75 million) and Soviet (0.75) zones. Besides, 500 thousand Germans from Hungary were assigned to the US zone; and Germans of Austrian descent (150 thousand) were to be settled in the French occupation zone. This resettlement was to be carried out between December 1945 and August 1946.[74] For example, the resettlement from Poland to the British zone was launched in February 1946 (by routes Stettin—Lubek, and Korford—Gelmannstadt) and was carried out with rather high intensity: 22 trains per week. Not having capacities for handling such a flow, the British closed their border in the middle of August and limited the weekly number of accepted trains to two. They even addressed the Soviet authorities with a request to halt the flow temporarily, since the Poles continued sending trains with Germans to the west at the same rate.[75]

In general, however, the implementation of the plan faced numerous political and organizational obstacles, which conditioned the fact that eventually the number of those resettled totaled 3.5 million persons. In other words, the outcome exceeded half of the pre-planned figure by a narrow margin (thus the US zone accepted 50% of the envisaged number; the USSR 52%; the UK 63%). By 1 October 1947, 5.4 million persons were resettled, with the Soviet side in the lead this time (92.7%), overtaking the British by 0.3%, and with the US (72.4%) and French (5.9%) zones following behind. Another 4.5 million Germans were distributed over the zones in accordance with their pre-war locations of residence.[76]

The multilateral agreement between the UK, USA, France and the USSR stipulated conducting a special census of German refugees and resettlers in the zones, controlled by the treaty signatories, on 29 November 1946. Nine million displaced Reichsdeutsche were registered in the course of the census, with the majority of them—some 6.15 million persons—having resided in the eastern territories of the Reich that were lost after the war: 3.5 million in Poland and 2.5 million in Czechoslovakia.

These Reichsdeutsche forced out of their pre-war places of residence as a result of war or post-war events, received the status of "exiled" (*Vertriebenen*)[77] in West Germany, unlike those called "displaced/evicted" (*Zugewanderte*) Germans, i.e., persons that had not resided on Reich territory before the war. The latter included, in particular, some 500 thousand Germans from Hungary and 150 thousand from Austria. Around 400 thousand German refugees (mainly from the former Czechoslovakia and Yugoslavia) were concentrated in Austria,[78] another 160 thousand in Denmark, and some 40–50 thousand departed for the New World.

In total, around 2/3 of the German refugees gathered in the western occupation zones (approximately 5.94 million persons), 3 million of whom were located in Lower Saxony. The FRG census of September 1950 showed that 14,447 thousand German refugees resided in the country: 8,078 exiles and 6,369 evictees,[79] including Germans that had arrived from the Soviet-occupied zone. The largest share of the refugees—some 33%—settled in Schleswig-Holstein.

In the period of 1944–1949, some 4.3 million exiled Germans were brought into the Soviet occupation zone in Germany, while around 8 million had been settled in the western occupation zones by 1950. In the former case the share of the "exiled" in the entire population reached almost one-quarter (24.2%), whereas it made up 17% of the population in the latter.[80] Subsequently, the difference between these figures decreased, since approximately 800 thousand of the "exiled," having considered the situation in East Germany, preferred to flee further, to the western part of the country.[81]

The territories vacated as a result of the eviction of the Germans who had inhabited them before, were populated by the titular nationalities of the corresponding countries. Sometimes these resettled people changed their place of residence voluntarily, such as the many people in central Poland that hurried to occupy the lands left by the Germans, while by and large the resettlement was coerced by the authorities, as in the case of Poles and Ukrainians from eastern Polish regions, which had been annexed by the Soviets in 1939 and ultimately integrated in the USSR in the post-war period.

As P. Ther appropriately remarked, there is a certain historical irony behind the fact that these particular people, who were leaving their homes as a result of option (i.e., exchange of population due to territorial exchange), were termed "repatriates" by the Soviet and Polish propaganda, implying they were returning to their homeland.[82]

These optations, however, had nothing in common with voluntary or civilized policy, but were implemented through typically Soviet coercive and humiliating methods.[83]

It should be noted, however, that this action was a joint Soviet–Polish one: the USSR was removing suspicious aliens, and Poland was using them to populate its western border areas recently cleared of Germans, thus reserving its unlimited right to these territories. The joint nature of the operation did not prevent the "elder" partner from degrading the "younger" one on more than one occasion. For example, initially the treaties on repatriation were concluded by the Polish Committee for National Liberation, acting on behalf of Poland (the Polish government in exile was intentionally ignored!), and not with the USSR per se, but with particular Soviet republics: with the Ukrainian SSR on 6 September 1944, with the Lithuanian SSR on 22 September 1944, and so on. It was not until 6 July 1945, when the "formal" status of Poland was established, that a corresponding frame agreement with the Soviet Union itself was signed.[84]

Consequently, as of 31 October 1946, almost 1.1 million persons had been resettled from the USSR to Poland (out of this number, 789,982 were moved from the territory of the Ukrainian SSR; 231,152 from the Belorussian SSR; and 69,724 from Lithuania). Simultaneously some 515 thousand had moved to the USSR from Poland (in particular, 482,109 to the territory of the Ukrainian SSR; 35,961 to Belorussia; and 14 thousand to Lithuania).[85] There were not many "repatriates" that were leaving for the USSR voluntarily: they were being resettled in the best spirit of "Soviet tradition," and the number of those who died in the process of resettlement amounted to a mere 4 thousand. Notwithstanding the pressure on the part of the Polish authorities, some 150 thousand Ukrainians still remained in Poland as of spring 1947. However, virtually all of them were resettled between 20 April and 31 July 1947 to the Polish western border areas instead of being moved to the east, to USSR territory. Essentially, this operation under the code name "Action Vistula" was nothing else but an "ethnic cleansing" campaign in the western border areas of Poland.[86]

As a result, the degree of ethnic homogeneity in the East European countries grew very significantly as early as spring 1945. The policies practiced by states like Poland and Czechoslovakia pursued this aim too: these countries saw the titular ethnic homogenization as a precondition of their security in the future. As early as 1948, the level of such homogeneity (the share of representatives of the titular nationalities) in the countries in question made up 94–95%, while the corresponding figure of 1938 had been only 67%.

The first post-war Hungarian government had a somewhat different political approach, as compared to Poland or Czechoslovakia. However, in practice it had to follow the same practices: the Soviet occupation authorities forced the government to deport 500 thousand of its German population from the country. It was only the Yugoslavian version of homogenization that had been initially complicated by the federal nature of the Yugoslavian state, which still was characterized by an obvious Serbian dominance.

Remarkably, Czechoslovakia was banishing Hungarians along with Germans from its territory. In 1945–1948, 89,660 Hungarians, mainly from Bratislava and other cities, were deported to Hungary, while 73,273 Slovaks were moved from Hungary to Slovak territory.[87] Similar processes took place along the Yugoslavian–Italian (Istria) and Yugoslavian–Hungarian (Vojvodina) borders: in the latter case, the scale of the mutual exchange amounted to "only" 40 thousand people.[88] It is in this context that Poland's policy towards the Jewish survivors residing on its territory can be explained. Poland did virtually nothing to limit the anti-Semitic sentiments and practices (in some cases, for example, in Kielce, taking the form of pogroms) in the country, which resulted in the hasty drift of the remaining Jewish population from the country.

Consequently, the displaced Jewish nationals were leaving East European countries, and—unless they managed to move to Palestine—settled in the western occupation zones of Germany (in the course of the year 1946, the number of Jewish settlers there grew from 50 to 185 thousand), Austria (45 thousand at the end of 1946), and Italy (20 thousand).[89] Sections of these people remained there, and others subsequently moved to the USA, UK and other countries. The majority, however, waited to emigrate to Palestine or repatriate to the state of Israel (after the latter was founded).

By way of summing up the prehistory of forced migrations, a tentative assumption may be made from a global historical perspective that it was the Jews that could be considered the people that were exposed to the gravest hardships brought about by deportation. Sadly, the harrowing fate of those expelled was once again—and in the harshest thinkable way—confirmed in the 20th century. Meanwhile the list grew of peoples that were subjected to deportations in several (not merely one) countries, including Germans, Poles, Greeks, Turks, Koreans, along with Russians, Ukrainians and Belorussians, extending the national make-up of the core body of "kulak exile" and the Ostarbeiter "slave" community.

CLASSIFICATION OF FORCED MIGRATIONS

The cases of forced migration are so plentiful in world history that one can discern essential typological differences between them along with certain common features they possess. Earlier we proposed that a classification of forced migrations[90] be used for their cataloguing and better understanding. The classification has been updated and improved now (see table 2). The proposed classification arises from a fundamental division between "repressive" and "non-repressive" migrations.

Apart from their punitive function, the "repressive migrations" involve as their defining feature a *direct action* engendered by a supreme political decision (more rarely by an international agreement, as in the case of the Yalta agreement with regard to forced repatriation), which is not subject to appeal or even discussion.

The proposed classification certainly represents a simplified model. In reality, more complex combinations of migration types have occurred. For example, to which type—*socially* or *ethnically-determined*—do the pre-war deportations of Estonian, Latvian, and Lithuanian kulaks belong?

In general, forced migration study reveals the stunning and gradually increasing adherence of the Soviet system to *ethnically* rather than *socially determined* repression criteria (the policy in question reached its apogee during Stalin's rule). In other words, the state declares its loyalty to international and class awareness publicly, while in practice gravitates towards essentially nationalistic goals and methods.

The deportation of so-called punished peoples can provide a most prominent example of this approach, the deportation itself serving as the punishment. All such peoples were deported not merely from their historical homeland, but also from other cities and districts, as well as demobilized from the army, which shows that such ethnic deportations embraced the entire country (we term this type of repression "total deportation"). Apart from their homeland, the "punished people" were deprived of their autonomy if they had any before, in other words, of their relative sovereignty.

In essence, ten peoples in the USSR were subjected to total deportation. Seven of them—Germans, Karachais, Kalmyks, Ingushetians, Chechens, Balkars, and Crimean Tatars—lost their national autonomy too (their total number amounted to 2 million, and the land populated by them before the deportation exceeded 150,000 square kilometers). According to the criteria formulated above, another three peoples—namely Finns, Koreans, and Meskhetian Turks—fall under the category of "totally deported peoples."

Table 2. **Classification of forced migrations in the USSR**

A. REPRESSIVE MIGRATIONS (Deportations)

   I ON SOCIAL GROUNDS
     1. *Decossackization (1919–1920)*
     2. *Dekulakization*[91] *(1930–1933)*
     3. *Expulsion of nobility (1935)*

   II ON ETHNIC GROUNDS
     1. *"Political preparation of the theatre of war" and "border sweeps":*
     a) *total,*
     b) *partial.*
     2. *Total deportations of "punished peoples":*
     a) *preventive,*
     b) *"retributive."*
     3. *Compensatory migrations*
     4. *Imposed "Pale of settlement"*

   III ON CONFESSIONAL GROUNDS
     1. *Entire confessions (True Orthodox Christians,*[92] *Jehovists*[93] *and others)*
     2. *Clerics from various confessions*

   IV ON POLITICAL GROUNDS
     1. *Members of banned organizations and parties*
     2. *"People's enemies' " family members*

3. *"Socially unsafe" elements*
4. *The treaty repatriates*
5. *Foreign nationals*

V PRISONERS OF WAR
1. POWs
2. *Civilian internees*

VI PRISONERS
1. Political (prisoners of conscience)
2. Criminals

B. NON-REPRESSIVE ("Voluntary–Compulsory") MIGRATIONS

VII PLANNED RESETTLEMENTS AND RESETTLEMENTS "ON CALL"[94]
1. To remote and non-reclaimed territories
2. *From the mountains to the plain*
3. As an effect of military, industrial, power production-related and other types of construction work
4. *Resettlement of demobilized army service members*

VIII EVACUEES (re-evacuees), REFUGEES, VOLUNTEER REPATRIATES
1. Displaced by war
2. Displaced as a result of genocide, ethnic or confessional conflicts
3. Displaced by natural disasters and environmental catastrophes

Remark: Italics are used in the table to indicate the types of forced migrations that constitute the specific subject of this study.

Based on the suggested classification, we can now elaborate on and specify the object of our research. The research will cover the first four classes of repressive migrations, or deportations, distinguished by *social, ethnic, confessional,* and *political* indicators.

Forced displacement of POWs and prisoners, including both political and criminal offenders,[95] will remain outside our research area. At the same time, the case of the Ostarbeiter falls within the studied area, but should be qualified as a mixed one. The Ostarbeiter deportation appears to be most closely related to resettlement "on call." A relevant legal basis was created, and a stable recruiting mechanism, or even a ritual, was elaborated. This is why, in a fit of temper, even some prominent Nazis[96] compared the industrial Third Reich seated at the heart of Europe to Siberia!

A few more details are worthy of note. In particular, the Ostarbeiter—as a certain unified target group (*kontingent*)—had a well-defined ethnic composition.[97] Only Russians, Ukrainians and Belorussians received such a status. Not merely Roma and Jews, but also the natives of the Caucasus and Central Asia were deprived of this "honor." The national criterion was also decisive when women were selected: Ukrainian girls were considered most appropriate as maids in German homes.

In addition, after the Battle of Stalingrad, and especially the Kursk engagement, the "theatre of war preparation" factor was undoubtedly taken into account, i.e., forced *evacuation* of civilians—or, as it was then generally referred to, the clearing of the territory—took place. In this way, the German authorities tried to render themselves secure against the mobilization of civilians into the troops of the advancing enemy, and simultaneously to turn the civilian labor supply to Germany's advantage.

By the end of the war, elements of yet another type became evident. Hundreds of thousands of refugees and so-called evacuees joined common Ostarbeiter. When the war was over, the POWs, Ostarbeiter, and refugees composed a single complex unity, namely *Soviet citizens subject to repatriation.*

The fact that the post-war "repatriation" of Soviet citizens falls under the category of forced migration does not imply that people were made to return to their homeland, when none of them was willing to do so. The forced nature of the repatriation was predetermined by the Yalta agreements, which essentially ignored any individual say in the matter.

In the case of "non-repressive" forced migrations, a supreme decision or command was not necessarily a determining factor. The mechanism that governed this migration type was absolutely different, namely indirect (that is, incorporating an understated threat), which would prove conclusive in most of the cases. An official would not come with a resettlement order, but people would be put into a situation in which they had willingly to take the decision that suited the authorities. This method was simpler and more advantageous for the state: the burden of cost in such cases was most likely to be borne by the "volunteers" themselves. In reality, the degree of "voluntariness" may well have approached zero.

The inclusion of evacuees in the table arises from the fact that, being unable to overcome bureaucratic obstacles, many of them were precluded from returning to their homes, from which they had been forced. Added to that, this was one of the most massive migrations that had ever occurred in world history: as many as 25 million people were transported to the eastern regions of the USSR in 1941–1942.[98]

In a similar way, our table (but not this study) includes a so-called planned, organized, or agricultural resettlement, which was carried out in order to compensate for the internal dislocation of labor force and land resources on the territory of the USSR (which partly occurred due to historical circumstances and partly due to misaligned national and economic policies implemented by the Soviet authorities). Formally, this type of resettlement was "voluntary." However, in reality—under the conditions imposed by the totalitarian regime—things were different. It was not a mere coincidence that not only interior ministry bodies, but also the system of military registration and enlistment offices, were involved in the process, and all relevant documentation was administered under tight restriction.

The methods of "voluntary" recruitment, especially those used in the 1930s, dismiss any doubt with regard to the forced and inefficient nature of the resettlement. For example, the "Report on the results of resettlement of Red Army households into the North Caucasian region" dated 10 December 1933 reads: "Driven by their aspiration to hit the 'planned figures,' some military units resorted to virtual force while carrying out the recruitment, often taking the form of an order. Party identity cards were taken away from some Communists who refused to resettle to the Kuban region, and other members were expelled from the party. One 'volunteer' on train No.170 was forced to produce a signed undertaking not to leave the Kuban. Some Red Army servicemen were ordered to leave for the region from their active front-line positions."[99]

Simultaneously, a natural question arises concerning the parallels between the typological, organizational and especially geographical features of the three migration approaches—of planned voluntary resettlement, deportations and prison camp (GULAG) resettlement. The deportation policy was closely linked with the general forced labor policy that was pursued in the USSR, and can be understood only in conjunction with the practice of forced convict labor in the GULAG and that of planned voluntary resettlement.

In particular, the failure to implement planned resettlement in the 1920s, combined with the hard currency profits earned from wood exportation, largely predetermined the forms of resettlement and labor exploitation which the state introduced in the 1930s, through the use of both prisoners (GULAG labor camps) and the deported (special resettlers, those exiled by administrative orders, etc.). Forced labor was for the most part considered more productive than free employment. The macro-geographic division of labor between the three types of migrants, i.e., those resettled within the planned-voluntary, prison-camp, and deportation programs, was discernible, though not always clear cut. Thus, the planned migrations targeted areas experiencing labor force deficit, but offering relatively mild climatic and social conditions (for example, the North Caucasus, or some southern areas in the Far East). The "GULAG archipelago," however, specialized in developing areas with extremely harsh climate, or provided the labor force for highly classified establishments (uranium mines, restricted towns, etc.).

The system of special settlements and commandant districts for the deported occupied an intermediate position between the other two systems, and therefore it embraced the European north, the Urals, West Siberia, Kazakhstan, and Central Asia, with the exception of border areas.

NOTES

1 Estimation made by F. Kurten. See J. Mejer, 1991, 6.

2 Vermel, 1924, 20–21. Short reference: Solomon Samoylovich Vermel (1860–1940) was a Jewish physician and political writer. We base our description of Jewish deportations in 1914–1915 on his two unpublished, as far as we know, articles "The Expulsion of Jews" and "The Role of administration in the expulsion of Jews" (manuscripts: RGALI , h. 119).

3 Following S. Vermel, we were stunned by the coincidence of dates: precisely 400 years prior to the day—on 14 July 1492—the expulsion of Jews from Spain was completed.

4 Vermel, 1924, 44–45.

5 Vermel, 1924, 38.

6 Kupovetsky, 1992, 57.

7 Bugay, Gonov, 1998, 25.

8 A review by an unknown author "The Caucasus during the 25-year rule of the Emperor, 1855–1880" (GARF, h. 678, r. 1, f. 682, sh. 1–54; dated 1880 the earliest. The information was provided to us by T. Tsarevskaya).

9 Cf.: "...Bringing the highlanders together as a result of the resettlement of several family clans to larger auls undermined their clan arrangement,

which poses considerable danger to us, since the village elder ceased being a family head, and became an official public figure instead." From a sketch by an unknown author on the history of conquering and administering the Caucasus (GARF, h. 677, r. 1, f. 511, sh. 1–36; written 1878 at the earliest. The information was provided to us by T. Tsarevskaya).

10 Avksentyev, A. V. and V. A. Avksentyev, *The North Caucasus in the Ethnic Picture of the World* (Stavropol, 1998), 96.

11 It was where the group of Adyghians that lived in Kosovo had originated. When the situation in Kosovo grew tense, they immigrated to Russia, to the Republic of Adyghea (as ordinary scholars, not politicians, we would not use the term "repatriation" in this case).

12 From a sketch by an unknown author on the history of conquering and administering the Caucasus (GARF, h. 677, r. 1, f. 511, sh. 1–36; written in 1878 at the earliest. The information was provided to us by T. Tsarevskaya).

13 A report of 1906 by the acting governor-general of the Terek Oblast and Ataman [Commander] of the Terek Cossack army Lieutenant General Kolyubakin (GARF, h. 601, r. 1, f. 926, sh. 1–6; dated 1878 the earliest. The information was provided to us by T. Tsarevskaya). Incidentally, the name of the island, Chechen, near the estuary of the Terek river at the Caspian Sea is connected with the fact that it was one of the traditional places where Chechens would be exiled.

14 A report by Count Vorontsov-Dashkov, governor of the Caucasus, to the chairman of the Council of Ministers, P. A. Stolypin, of 4 May 1910, concerning the robbing of the Kizlyar treasury by Zelimkhan's gang on 27 March 1910 (GARF, h. 109, OODP 1910, f. 111, part 1, sh. 75. The information was provided to us by T. Tsarevskaya). A. Avtorkhanov claims that the transition from individual Chechen exiles to the banishment of families was associated with the change of power in the Vedeno Okrug, when the duties of Colonel Dobrovolsky, killed by Zelimkhan, were taken over by Colonel Galayev, who was also killed by Zelimkhan subsequently.

15 A memorandum of 3 November 1911 submitted by the 4th Record-keeping office of the Police Department to the Special Police Department, concerning Zelimkhan Gushmazukaev's gang (GARF, h. 102, 109 (?), OODP 1910, f. 111, part 2, sh. 42–45t. The information was provided to us by T. Tsarevskaya).

16 For example, according to B. Gatsayev, Zelimkhan's nephew and a bolshevik, his family was exiled to Elets: *V Borbe za Vlast Sovetov* [Struggling for the Soviet Rule]. Memoirs of participants of revolutionary struggle in the Chechen-Ingush republic (1917–1920), Grozny, 1970.

17 See Holquist, 1998. Incidentally, similar ideas were circulated and enjoyed popularity in respective spheres in Germany and the Austro-Hungarian Empire.

18 Holquist provides remarkable examples concerning Central Asia and especially Semirechye [Region of Seven Rivers]. As a result of the practical application of military statisticians' recommendations, the total of the

Semirechye native population dropped from 66% to 20% by January 1917 (Holquist, 1998, 35–37).

19 Holquist, 1998, 39–40.
20 The evaluation is made by Eric Lohr, who defended a dissertation (at Harvard University in 1999) on Russia's policy toward aliens during the First World War (see Holquist, 1998, 38–39).
21 The same operations were conducted against Turkish nationals starting from the end of October 1914.
22 See Auman and Chebotareva, 1994, 500. There is a widely spread yet wrong belief that Nicholas II signed a decree ruling that all German settlers living on Russian territory be deported to Siberia. There was no such decree. The idea itself, however, existed: Society Za Rossiyu [For Russia], founded in 1914, was its most active propagator. (Nelipovich, 1996).
23 After the Great Prince left the position of supreme commander-in-chief, general M. V. Alekseyev took over Yanushkevich. Cf. P.G. Kurlov's character reference for Yanushkevich: "… always kind, very friendly, attentive to all reports delivered to him, he issued orders promptly, and attracted everybody by his lucid mind beaming from his eyes. As far as civilian matters were concerned, Yanushkevich was as inexperienced as his princely chief…" (Kurlov, 1992, 176).
24 One hundred *versts* equals approximately 66.3 miles.
25 Nelipovich, 1996. See also Ther, 1999.
26 The defeat of a Russian military unit near the town of Shavli, that allegedly happened as a result of Jewish espionage, served as a pretext for the repression in Kurland Gub. (Kurlov, 1992, 214–215).
27 Resettlement was permitted exclusively within the Pale of settlement, with the exception of gubernias under martial law (gradually this affected most gubernias).
28 See Kurlov, 1992, 215–216, 181–182.
29 See next footnote.
30 Except Jews (from the German-occupied western Polish territories) that had served in the Polish army and were taken prisoner by the Red Army: following the stipulations of the Soviet–German treaty signed on 30 October 1939, these Jews, along with other POWs, were exchanged for Polish POWs from eastern Poland (the Soviet side ignored individual appeals to the Soviet authorities not to hand them over to the Germans).
31 See Volkov, 1930, 72–73. The validity of the estimate is acknowledged by P. Gatrell too (Gatrell, 1999, 211–215). Interestingly, this cup did not pass from Germany either: after its defeat in the First World War and the subsequent reduction of its territory, some 1 million Germans moved from the Baltic republics to the remaining German territory. At the same time, a current of Polish refugees rushed to Poland from eastern Ukraine and Belorussia.
32 The precise figures were 48,570 Turks and 46,764 Bulgarians (Ladas, S. P., *The Exchange of Minorities: Bulgaria, Greece and Turkey*, New York, 1932, cited by Martin, 1998, 818).

33 See Djodzevic, 1989, 117 and Sundhaussen, 1996, 35, cited by Ther, 1999.

34 Exceptions were allowed with regard to Greeks that had resided in Istanbul before 30 October 1918 and Muslims living in East Frakia.

35 Data taken from the report by R. Tostorf "Spanish refugees after the end of the Civil War in Spain," given at the symposium "Expulsion. Flight. Deportation." (Vertreibung—Flucht—Deportation) that was held in Vienna on 22–23 October 1993.

36 EWZ: Einwanderungszentralstelle. In organizational terms it was a subdivision of the Reich Chief Security Agency (RSChA), and was subordinate to the SD.

37 The procedure was standard for all immigrants: each individual was registered by name, photographed, and tested as to health condition, race and political views. Those that "passed" the race test were granted German citizenship. In addition, the EWZ was engaged in the drafting and practical application of the criteria for distinguishing the "Aryan race," a problem that had been thoroughly studied by German race experts for a long period. The criteria were supposed to be used for clear differentiation between German and non-German population, but also for distinguishing between particular "inside" species among the Germans. For example, the existence of two categories of "blood quality" was officially recognized. These categories corresponded to the "strong" and "weakened" species of the nation: the O-category (Ost-Fall) and A-category (Altreich-Fall). Germans that belonged to the former category qualified for resettlement to the east, where their blood would contribute to the Germanization of corresponding areas, while members of the A-category qualified for residence within the Reich only. See The Holdings..., 1994, 10–18.

38 This body combined regional and central competencies. Remarkably, the office itself was "migrating": it moved from Gotenhaven to Posen (Poznan) in November 1939, to Lodz and Berlin in January–February 1940, and back to Łodź (this time Litzmannstadt), where it stayed until January 1945.

39 I express my sincere gratitude to my Polish colleague S. Debski (Kraków, Poland) for his kind permission to use related data that he discovered in Polish and Soviet archives.

40 Passat, 1994, 21, 99–121.

41 GARF, h. R-5446, r. 3, f. 216, sh. 5; cited by Passat, 1994, 18.

42 According to the data of the late 1930s, 81 thousand Germans resided in Bessarabia (the Right-Bank Moldavia), with 56 thousand of them living in the Akkerman district. The German population of North Bukovina constituted 29 thousand people. Besides, another 11 thousand Germans lived in Left-Bank Moldavia, which had an administrative status when Moldavian ASSR merged in Ukraine, in 1928. (Passat, 1994, 65).

43 Agreement between the government of the USSR and the government of Germany on the evacuation of persons of German nationality from the territories of Bessarabia and North Bukovina to Germany, signed by

Dr. Neldeke and Vasyukov (RGVA, h. 1458k, r. 40, f. 195). The process of evacuation was controlled by German staff comprising 600 persons, 60 of whom, according to the NKVD, were intelligence agents. In its turn, the NKVD also used the resettlement in order to send their operatives into German territory. (Passat, 1994, 20–21).

44 The resettlers took away 22,613 horses and other assets stipulated by the treaty. At the same time, they left behind 59 hectares of land, 22,425 houses, over 5 thousand horses, some 16 thousand cattle, 60 thousand sheep, 2 thousand pigs, and 147 thousand poultry, along with 4 million rubles, and a considerable amount of agricultural products including those not harvested yet. The freed lands were passed over to peasants that had none or little land, or were used to establish kolkhozy and sovkhozy. Some 1,718 poor households were moved from northern parts of the Moldavian ASSR to the Kagul, Bendery, and Kishinev districts within the resettlement project by spring 1941 (Passat, 1994, 21).

45 Mariansky, 1966. It should be noted that German population was simultaneously being evacuated from Romania.

46 According to Polish researcher Ja. Sobczak, at least 350 thousand ethnic Germans left the USSR (in its post-war borders) during the period of 1939–1940, in particular (in thousands of persons): 77.2 from Estonia, 51.1 from Lithuania, 104 from Galicia, 67.5 from Volyn, 43.9 from Belorussia, 43.7 from North Bukovina, and 93.4 from Bessarabia (Sobczak, 1996, 321, cited by Kabuzan, 1996).

47 The Holdings…, 1994, 34, 37. Other data of January 1944 refer to 770,577 people. The number came up to 583 thousand persons even before the war with the USSR started (Ther, 1999, citing Bierschenk, 1954).

48 The EWZ archives were evacuated to Bad Worishofen near Augsburg. The collection of the applications for naturalization, held in the BDC, contains approximately 110 thousand personal files of USSR citizens, 100 thousand of Polish Germans, 82 thousand of Germans from Romania, 73 thousand of Germans from the Baltic states, 23 thousand from Yugoslavia, 14 thousand from France, and 700 from Bulgaria. See The Holdings…, 1994, 17–19.

49 See The Holdings…, 1994, 17–19, 40.

50 For detail see Stuhlpfarrer, 1985.

51 Quoted from the speech Himmler delivered at a military cadet school at Telz (The Holdings…, 40).

52 In particular, the voice of General Friderici, a predecessor of Heidrich at the highest occupational post in the Protectorate. See unpublished paper by A. Schmidt "A garden of experiment: The implementation of the racial theory in Czech lands," which was presented at the conference "Second World War" at Siena College (June, 1999).

53 See Aly, 1995.

54 The Umwanderungszentrale (UWZ), was founded in 1940 as a successor of the Agency for the Resettlement of Poles and Jews (Amt für die

Umsiedlung der Polen und Juden). It was also engaged in the selection of Poles, racially eligible for Germanization.

55 See Remark No.1 by A. Okorokov to the collection of Colonel A. I. Medynsky's memoirs (*Materials on the history of the ROA,* 1999, 473).

56 The "Final Solution" did not necessarily imply the immediate physical liquidation of all European Jews: after a victorious conclusion of the war, Jews from western Europe were to be deported to the occupied east European territories, which were planned to have been "cleansed" (literally) from the local Jewish population. And again, as in the case of ethnic Germans, the key issue was who is and who is not to be regarded as a Jew (see Martin, 1998).

57 Remarkably, at some point the island of Madagascar was discussed as the alternative to Lublin!

58 Browning, 1995, 366. Deportees were allowed to take up to 5kg of luggage that would fit into the shelf over the train seat. Work devices and instruments were to be checked in as baggage. It was allowed to take 2 warm suits, a winter coat, a raincoat, 2 pairs of high boots, 2 pairs of underwear, handkerchiefs, socks, work-wear, a spirit-lamp, a gasoline lamp, a set of cutlery, a knife, scissors, a pocket torch with a spare battery, a candlestick, matches, threads and needles, talcum powder, a backpack, a thermos, and food. It was sanctioned to have no more than 200 Reichsmarks. Only those who had official medical certificates confirming sickness or documents for migration to other countries received exemptions from otherwise compulsory appearance at departure stations. One has to note that the Nazi plans were supported by some Russian immigration circles in Germany, in particular by the National Labor Union. See Zaborovsky, D., *"Opyt razresheniya yevreyskogo voprosa"* [The experience of solving the Jewish question] (*Za Rodinu,* 15 December 1939), No. 95. (see *Sintaksis,* Paris, 1991, no. 31, 179–182).

59 The deportation of 437 thousand Hungarian Jews in May–July 1944 was the largest operation of the year. Ironically, when the Reich started experiencing a shortage of labor force, the Germans had to go as far as deporting some Hungarian Jews, in particular from Budapest, into Germany!

60 See Martin, 1998, 820.

61 See Ther, 1999, citing Magocsi, 1993, 166.

62 See Buruma, J., "Erbschaft der Schulf," *Vergangenheitsbestatigung in Deutschland und Japan* (Munich, 1994), 349–368.

63 Die Geschichte Koreas, vol. 22. *Die Entwicklung der nationale Bewegung.* Seoul, 1978, 435–442 (published in Korean). I am grateful to Ms. Zen Suk Khan for the data she kindly sent to me.

64 "Die Zeit des nationalen Leidens," *Die Zeitgeschichte Koreas,* vol. 4. (Seoul, 1969), 46 (published in Korean). Similar data—422 thousand deported Koreans—are referred to in: Tae-Woon Moon, *Die japanisch-koreanischen Beziehungen nach dem Zweiten Weltkrieg unter besonderer Berucksichtigung der Nationalstereotypen* (Reihe *Geschichtswissenschaft,* vol. 11 (Centaurus-Verlagsgesellschaft, Pfaffenweiler, 1989),16–17 (with reference to: Chen

Ching-Chin *Police and Community Control Systems in the Empire* in Peattle, M., R. Myers (eds.)). *The Japanese Colonial Empire, 1895–1945* (Princeton, 1984), 232; apart from the above-mentioned, another 2,616.9 thousand Koreans served so-called labor duty, ibid., with reference to: Han, Woo-Keun, *The History of Korea* (Honolulu, 1976), 496. An absolutely different figure—661.7 thousand persons—is cited in Wontroba, G. and U. Menzel, "Stagnation und Unterentwicklung in Korea. Von Yi-Dynastie zur Perepherisierung unter japanischer Kolonialherrschaft / Transfines." (eds.) von M. Mols, D. Nohlem and P. Waldmann, vol. 9. (Verlag Anton Hain, Meisenheim am Glan, 1978), 192–193, with reference to: Pak Sung-Jo, *Die Wirtschaftsbeziehungen zwischen Japan und Korea* (Wiesbaden, 1969), 80). The annual distribution of deported Koreans also considerably differs from the above-cited, with the discrepancy especially prominent in the case of 1944 (thousand of persons): 38.7 in 1939; 59.9 in 1940; 53.5 in 1941; 112 in 1942; 122.2 in 1943; and 280.3 in 1944. Interestingly, Japan, in the same way as Germany, drafted particular plans concerning the deportations. The total number of deportees was to reach 937.3 thousand persons in the period 1939–1944 (according to other sources, 907.7 thousand persons), with only 400 thousand persons "scheduled" for 1944. At the same time, in 1942–1943 the "planned tasks" were almost—by 80–90%—fulfilled.

65 Bugay, 1995, 4.
66 Critchlow, 1991, 11.
67 Ther, 1999. See also Snyder T. "'To resolve the Ukrainian Problem Once and for All.' The Ethnic Cleansing of Ukrainians in Poland. 1943–1947," *Journal of Cold War Studies*, 1999, vol. 1, no. 2, 86–120.
68 Yakushevsky, 1995, 56–57.
69 Yakushevsky, 1995, 49, citing: Bullock, A., *Hitler and Stalin: Parallel Lives* (London, 1991), 913–915. However, at least 3 million Reichdeutschen and 0.4 million Volksdeutschen were not evacuated from West and East Prussia, Danzig, Pomerania, Warteland and Silesia.
70 See Ther, 1999, citing: Schieder, T. (ed.), *Dokumentation der Vertreibung der Deutschen aus Ostmitteleuropa Band I/1–3. Die Vertreibung der deutschen Bevölkerung aus den Gebieten östlich der Oder-Neiße* (Bonn, 1953–1961), vol. I/1; Magocsi, P. R., Historical Atlas of East Central Europe (Seattle and London, 1993), 168.
71 See Ther, 1996, 786.
72 According to the official data of the Federal Statistics Service, 1,618,400 persons—out of the 2,239,500 Third Reich civilian casualties related to deportations in one way or other—perished in the process of resettlement. See Ther, 1996, 785 (see also Naimark, 1997, 190).
73 See Overmans, 1994.
74 See GARF, h. 7317, r. 20, f. 1, sh. 56–57.
75 See the record of the talks between Colonel Bryukhanov and Colonel Brei, the chief of the UK Occupation Administration Department for POW and DP Affairs of 10 September 1946 (GARF, h. 7317, r. 20, f. 64, sh. 98–99).

76 See GARF, h. 7317, r. 20, f. 1, sh. 60–80.

77 Later the status was established by the Federal Law on the Exiled (*Bundesvertriebenengesetz*) of 1953.

78 For example, mass forced resettlement of the so-called Gottscheer, i.e., German settlers that had lived on Yugoslavian territory for many generations, from the Slovenian province of Krajina to the Austrian province of Styria (occupied and controlled by the Soviets at that time) was administered in June 1945. Before the occupation of Yugoslavia in 1941, the settlers had Yugoslavian citizenship and tacitly became German citizens under the Reich occupation. The deportation was carried out by the Yugoslavs' unilateral decision, without concluding corresponding agreements with either the central Austrian government or the Soviet occupation authorities. The Austrian side protested against the infringement on its sovereignty by the Yugoslavs, stating that the Gottscheer were not related to Austria or Austrians by either citizenship or nationality. The pre-war total number of the Gottscheer in Slovenia made up several tens of thousands, 1,700 of whom arrived in Styria by 7 June 1945 (900 persons were placed in the Keiserwald camp near Wilden, 500 in Leibnitz, and 300 in Graz at the city railway station). (See the Political report of 13 June 1945 by Major General Tsinev, the chief of the political department of the 57th Army, to Lieutenant General Anoshin, the chief of the political administration of the 3rd Ukrainian front. TsAMO, h. 413, r. 10389, f. 46, sh. 35–37).

79 Certainly, the pre-war linguistic (dialect) and cultural communities were intermingled under these circumstances. See *Die Vertrebenen in Deutschland*, 69–123.

80 Ther, 1996, 779, citing Reichling, G., *Die Heimetvertriebenen im Spigel der Statistik* (Berlin, 1958), 14–15, and also Reichling, G., *Die deutschen Vertriebenen in Zahlen: 40 Jahre Eingliederung in der Bundesrepublik Deutschland* (Bonn, 1989), 30–34.

81 This figure refers to the period between the moment of establishment of both German states in 1949 and the ultimate closure of borders between them in 1961. These 800 thousand constituted around 1/3 of the total number of GDR citizens that fled to the FRG. See Ther, 1996, 800, citing: Heidemeyer, 1993.

82 See Ther, 1996, 782–783.

83 Nevertheless, the resettlers were provided with transportation means and allowed to take up to 2 tons of their belongings and home implements, while the Germans, whose houses the new settlers were to occupy, mainly had to move on foot carrying no more than one item of luggage per person (Ther, 1996, 786).

84 See Ther, 1996, 785–786 and Ther, 1997, 514–515, citing the storage locations of the treaties in Poland: *The Archive of New Documents*, Warsaw (Archivum Akt Novych, or AAN), the foundation of the Government Plenipotentiary for Repatriation Affairs of the Republic of Poland (Generalny Pelnomocnik Rzadu RP do Spraw Repatriacji, sygn. 1, 16–21, 28–37 and others). Ther does not refer to an exact date of the treaty con-

cluded with the Belorussian SSR. However, it is likely to be close to or coincide with the date of agreement with the Ukrainian SSR. The texts of the accords themselves were never published in the press.

85 GARF, h. 9401, r. 2, f. 139, sh. 299–303. See also RGASPI, h. 17, r. 121, f. 545, sh. 47–51.

86 See Ther, 1999, quoting: Chojnowska, A., "Operacja Wysla (przsiedlenie ludnisci ukrainskiej na ziemie zachodnie i polnocne w 1947 r.)," *Zeszyty Historychne*, 1992, no. 102, 3–102.

87 See Ther, 1999, quoting: Sutaj, S., *Madarska Mensina na Slovensku v Rokoch 1945–1948*, (Bratislava, 1993), 138–139.

88 Magocsi, 1993, 168.

89 Lavski, H., "Displaced Persons," *Jewish Encyclopedia of the Holocaust*. Vol. 1 (New York, 1990), 377.

90 See Polian, 1990c, 1990d, 1992, etc.

91 Derived from the Russian *kulak* [fist]: a well-to-do peasant.

92 True Orthodox Christians (The True Orthodox Christian Church): A clandestine church that split from the Russian Orthodox Church in the 1920s as a protest against the latter's collaboration with the Soviet authorities. The True Orthodox Church was subjected to harsh persecution on the part of the state

93 Jehovah's Witnesses, or Jehovists: A Protestant sect, whose members did not recognize army service and most state institutions, and which practiced active missionary policy thus rapidly spreading its doctrine among the population. (The term "Jehovists" was also used to refer to the sect of Jehovisty-Ilyintsy that emerged in the Urals in 1846 and combined elements of Christianity and Judaism. However, judging by their geographical presence today (Ukraine, the North Caucasus and Kazakhstan), the sect is likely to have been caught up in deportations too).

94 A form of "voluntary–compulsory" labor service offered for the greater good of the Party, state and ideology. However, "on call" soon took on a tone of compulsion and threat with talk of prosecution for disloyalty etc.

95 Further, politicals and criminals, more consistent with the Russian *politicheskiye* and *ugolovniki* [transl.]

96 For example, A. Rozenberg.

97 Nazis were rather indifferent to social and confessional membership, but not to the ethnic and national one, essential for them.

98 About 17 million were transported to the east of the country in July–December 1941. The second evacuation wave started in the summer of 1942, when Nazi troops advanced on the southern front (see "Eshelony idut na Vostok: iz istorii perebazirovaniya proizvoditelnyh sil SSSR v 1941–1942 gg" (Moscow, 1966, 13).

99 RGAE, h. 5675, op.1, f.43. sh. 49. The fact that no contact with the local population was permitted en route is no less telling.

PART I

FORCED MIGRATIONS WITHIN THE USSR

Forced Migrations before the Second World War (1919–1939)

THE FIRST SOVIET DEPORTATIONS AND RESETTLEMENTS IN 1919–1929

There is a widely shared view that it was not before the 1930s that the Soviet authorities took up such measures as deportations. In reality, however, the very first years of the Soviet rule, while the Civil War was still in full swing, featured these harrowing and extreme practices.

In the western part of the North Caucasus the events were largely predetermined by the long-lasting confrontation between the "white" Cossacks and Ossetians allied with them on the one hand, and—on the other—poor landless Vainakhs, who cherished naïve hopes of gaining advantage from land redistribution that could be brought about through their union with the Bolsheviks. The first order for population movement was issued by a congress of the Soviets of Terskaya Obl. in April–May 1918. The populations of four *stanitsa* settlements—Tarskaya, Sunzhenskaya, Vorontsovo-Dashkovskaya, and Feldmarshalskaya[1]—were assigned for removal. And on 24 January 1919—and this time at state level—the Russian CP Central Committee issued a directive on decossackization, which envisaged forced resettlement as one of the measures to be taken.[2]

In March 1920, after the Red Army gained full victory, Sovietization took severe forms. The *Terek Cossacks* were bound to be the first to be expelled as a response to their rebellions against the Soviet authorities. Residents of three *stanitsa* settlements located on the plain—Tarskaya, Sunzhenskaya, and Vorontsovo-Dashkovskaya (and apparently those of Tarsky *khutor*)—were resettled on 17 April 1920. Following an order issued by G. K. Ordzhonikidze (a member of the Revolutionary Military Council of the Caucasus Front) in October

1920, residents of the *stanitsa* settlements of Yermolayevskaya, Romanovskaya, Samashkinskaya, Mikhaylovskaya, and Kalinovskaya,[3] aged
between 18 and 50, faced the same fate (others were resettled too, but
to nearby villages and settlements, but beyond a 50km radius of their
previous places of residence). A total of 9 thousand families (or some
45 thousand persons) were removed to the Donbass region, and to
the European north (in particular to Arkhangelsk Gub.). Any return
of the Cossacks to their homelands was prosecuted.[4]

The vacated lands (some 98 thousand *dessiatina* of arable fields)
were handed over to the Red Cossacks and to poor Chechen and
Ingushetian highlanders, which stimulated the latter to move from the
mountains to the plain and provide the most reliable backing to the
regime in the Caucasus. It turned out, however, that the support for
the regime did not imply any regard for its order: gangsterism became
an ever-present phenomenon after the deportation of Cossacks.[5] The
traditional settlement in the mass of the Russian-speaking population
in the Caucasus was thus disrupted. Later, the Cossack okrugs as
administrative units (Sunzhensky, Kazachy, Zelenchuk, and Ardon
Okrugs) were themselves disbanded.

Remarkably, it was at that time, during the very first Soviet
deportations, that toponymic[6] repression was already in place too. If
a *stanitsa*'s population was expelled, but the settlement itself was not
destroyed, then it would be renamed and ascribed the status of *aul*.
For example, in the Nazran Okrug *stanitsa* of Sunzhenskaya was renamed *aul* Akki-Yurt, Vorontsovo-Dashkovskaya *stanitsa* was renamed
Tauzen-Yurt, Tarskaya *stanitsa* became Angusht, Tarsky *khutor* was
turned into *aul* Sholkhi, Feldmarshalskaya *stanitsa* became Alkhaste.
In Chechen Okrug, Mikhaylovskaya *stanitsa* was renamed *aul* Aslan-
bek, Samashkinskaya *stanitsa* Samashki, Romanovskaya *stanitsa* Zakan-
Yurt, and Yermolovskaya *stanitsa* became Alkhan-Yurt.[7]

The resettlement of well-off Russian peasant Cossacks from
Semirechye was carried out in the spring and summer of the famine
of 1921, in the course of a land reform that was implemented under
the slogan of fighting "kulak chauvinism" and liquidating inequality
between non-native European settlers and the natives (the former
group was regarded historically as being an enemy of the latter).
Those subjected to this resettlement had inhabited Semirechye, Syr-
Darya, Fergana, and Samarkand Obls. for a relatively short term,

namely since the Stolypin agrarian reform, when over 438 families moved to Turkestan. These settlers founded some 300 peasant and Cossack villages, and engaged in some arbitrary seizures of the best areas of land.

Resolutions dealing with this matter were issued by the Russian CP Central Committee on 29 June and 5 December 1920 and stipulated a set of deportation measures, and even the transporting of kulaks to concentration camps by way of "punitive sanction," although still based on individual rather than group assumptions.

The entire campaign was initiated by G. I. Safarov, Stalin's co-speaker at the 10th RKP(b) congress, which took place in March 1921. Speaking about the land reform carried out in Turkestan, he proudly mentioned resettling whole kulak communities. The first deportation that was documented was carried out on 16 April 1921 from the village of Vysokoye in Chimkent Uyezd, Syr-Darya Obl.: a corresponding "komissiya po rassloyeniyu" [lit.: commission for stratification] (Sic!—P. P.) exiled more than 20 families. The exiles were sent away from the Turkestan Kray, to the Kaluga Obl. according to the official version, although in practice it was physically impossible to reach the destination at that time.[8]

The next development in deportation took place in fall 1922: two famous "philosophers' ships" transported about 50 outstanding Russian scholars (around 115 persons including their family members) from Petrograd to Germany (Stettin).[9] This was the first case of a relatively large scale international forced migration in Soviet history.

Apparently, this deportation was administered under the All-Union Central Executive Committee decree "On administrative banishment" of 10 August 1922, which stipulated three types of expulsion from particular places of residence as an isolation measure and alternative to arrest: a) banishment from the place of residence and other particular localities in the RSFSR; b) deportation to particular localities in the RSFSR; c) expulsion from the country. The established term of banishment was from two months to three years. Decisions on deportation were taken on an individual basis,[10] and those exiled within the state borders were transferred under the supervision of the local GPU body, which assigned the "exiles" to a particular place of residence (where the latter had to report once every three days). The decree supplement authorized a special NKVD commission to subject certain categories of citizens (especially activists of anti-Soviet political parties) to forced labor in camps for the assigned terms, as an alternative to mere exile.[11]

Available data on other forced migrations in the 1920s, and especially in the early 1920s, are more than fragmentary. As a rule, these resettlements were local, taking place within regions. For example, it is a known fact that a number of highland Jewish *auls* in Daghestan were forced to move down to the plain, namely to Derbent and Kuba. It is also recognized that an intensive process of forcing Armenian population out of Tiflis began, etc.

We do not have any other data at our disposal regarding deportations or forced resettlement in the USSR in the 1920s, up until the beginning of the collectivization campaign. One can mention maybe only the plans—elaborated at the end of 1926, but never carried out—to resettle Koreans from the southern Far East to its northern part, beyond Khabarovsk, at 48.5 degrees latitude north of the equator.[12] Virtually the same plans reared up again in spring 1928, but this time the resettlement plan (to be administered in 1930) concerned only disloyal Koreans, not all of them. In actuality, 1,342 Koreans were resettled in 1930, 431 of them by force (in 1931, when the number of resettled Koreans reached 2.5 thousand, the plan was abandoned).[13]

However, in this period of time, forced migrations represented the exception rather than the rule. Behind the totality of the local operations, one could not yet discern the tough political will, the systematic and methodical approach that would emerge and develop in the 1930s. And yet, such actions as punishment through forced resettlement of some groups of population for their alleged disloyalty during the Civil War or for the unfair—from the Bolshevist perspective—land distribution they imposed, on the one hand, and—on the other hand—encouraging the "loyalty" of more deprived population groups (highland national minorities) by transferring the vacated lands to them constituted clear and menacing indications of what was to come.

Such factors as the land reform implementation in the 1920s or national administrative rearrangement in the RSFSR (and later the USSR) predetermined certain crucial changes in the nature and organizational structure of resettlement. In a number of cases it required the imposition of a non-nomadic lifestyle on the local, or indeed supplemental, population of a newly established administrative unit as the artificially created ethnic grouping assimilated.

American researcher Terry Martin paid due attention to the latter circumstance.[14] Besides, he made a subtle observation with regard to the contradictory link between the domestic and international policies exercised by the young and territorially deprived Soviet state in its border areas. On the one hand, there appears to have been a tendency to found ethnic autonomous administrative units along the borders with states with corresponding dominant population (for example, the Karel Autonomous Republic on the border with Finland, or the Moldavian on the border with Romania). Referring to the struggle between various forces and groups either supporting or opposing the establishment of an analogous Korean Autonomous Republic in the Far East, the researcher came up with a possible model of causal link between this process and subsequent deportations. He named the model itself a "Principle of Piedmont," thus alluding to the process of consolidation of Italian state around the northern province of Piedmont at the end of the 19th century (although, in our opinion, the precedent of the peaceful—through a referendum—splitting off of northwestern Italian territories, namely Savoy and Nice, from Italy, and their inclusion into France, is no less notable). The American researcher says that the "Principle of Piedmont" can be considered an alternative to what he calls "Soviet xenophobia" meaning the traditional Soviet suspicious attitude to foreigners and the tendency to keep the borders strictly closed, etc.[15]

It is this opposition between the "Principle of Piedmont"[16] and "Soviet xenophobia" that T. Martin shows to be the root of the entire Soviet policy in the sphere of ethnic cleansing, and deportation policy in particular. An actual consolidation of Ukrainians and Belorussians did take place in 1939, but it was brought about not by the triumph of either principle. It was a result of a temporary geopolitical conspiracy between the USSR and Germany, which was based on the Curzon Line rather than on the contours of particular ethnic areas. The process required an additional exchange of population for one thing, and an additional cleansing operation on the western border—only this time the Soviet–German one.[17]

These are rather subtle and shrewd constructs, which are based on a new flow of Russian archival materials. In our opinion, they do inevitably lead to adjacent research areas (such as "The Great Terror and ethnicity"), but ultimately cannot be regarded as holding sufficient weight of argument.

For example, if one follows Martin's logic, similar buffer zones designed to spread the Soviet influence abroad were bound to emerge (at least in the 1920s) on the borders with Turkey, Iran and Afghanistan, which never transpired. On the contrary, Kurds were deported from Transcaucasia before the war and Meskhetian Turks from the territories adjacent to the Turkish border during the war, as a preventive measure. Besides, it would be problematic to explain the deportations in question by making an analogy with the deportation of Koreans from the Far East, where the Korean autonomous formation (which eventually took a compromised form of national district and national uyezds) was likely to become a promoter of the Japanese influence in Primorsky Kray rather than Russian influence in Korea occupied by Japan, due to the general weakness of Russia in the Far East at that time.

In our opinion, it was another Bolshevik illusion that became a much more feasible and significant factor that determined resettlement practices. It was their deep material belief in their ability to "repair" all natural and social "defects," in particular by means of planned resettlement, thus overcoming the historic discrepancy between the natural and demographic resources of the giant country that was Russia/USSR.[18]

Such moving of population has been referred to as "planned" or "organized resettlement" in both literature and in everyday life (sometimes the term *agrarian resettlement* was also employed). Officially this type of resettlement was regarded as voluntary, and—although its voluntary nature was highly questionable in many cases—by no means should this practice be confused with the "classical deportations."

At least in the 1920s (especially in the second half of the decade) it was planned resettlements that represented a domestic political issue and received most attention. In order to draft and implement related policies, a special state body—the All-Union Committee for Resettlement [VPK] of the All-Union Central Executive Committee—was founded.[19]

The basis on which the VPK carried out its activities involved both a *planned component* and a combination of measures designed as *economic stimuli* (for example, granting at least token privileges and compensations to the resettlers along with employing certain *elements of administrative pressure*).

The logic of organized resettlement was dictated by, on the one hand, excess of peasant population in the central regions and consequent unemployment there, and—on the other—there was a need to bring huge reserves of unused lands of the Far East and Siberia into agricultural production. There was unused land in the European part of the country too (in particular in the Volga region, after the famine of 1921), and in the North Caucasus (partly as a result of the decossackization measures). Indeed, in four central regions of the Russian Federation 34% of the countryside population was employed in temporary jobs outside their places of residence. Paradoxical as it may sound now, the total of 13.5 million peasants was considered "excessive" in the republics of Russia, Ukraine and Belorussia.[20]

Simultaneously, there was a significant lack of labor force in Karelia and the Murmansk Obl. in the forest and fishing industries. Some 20–25 thousand people from other regions were employed in these areas. Western Siberia had suffered a massive loss of labor force as a result of the Civil War: hundreds of villages were totally destroyed, and a vast region, where agricultural production used to be highly efficient, had simply ceased to exist in economic terms.

The importance and necessity of the resettlement campaign was confirmed by a number of state resolutions. The campaign started in 1924 when resettlement was carried out in the Volga region, and continued in 1925 when resettlement to Siberia and the Far East took place. In 1926, it was the Urals and North Caucasus that became new resettlers' destinations.

The First All-Russian Congress of Resettlement Officials took place in Moscow on 4–8 March 1927. Among other things, the congress substantiated the need to populate the Far East (Sakhalin, in particular), Siberia and Karel-Murmansk Kray, while simultaneously launching the construction of railways and industrial facilities in these areas. Such regions as Karelia were especially keen on populating their underdeveloped territories.

However, the project soon turned out to be deficient. The plan envisaged the resettlement of 5 out of 13.5 million of the "excessive" agricultural labor force in the course of ten years. The implementation of the plan for particular republics would look as follows (see table 3):

Table 3. **Excessive population of the RSFSR, BSSR and UkSSR** (millions)

Republic	Excessive population	Resettlement plan	
		In 5 years	In 10 years
RSFSR	6.9	1.5	2.5
BSSR	1.2	0.3	0.5
UkSSR	5.4	0.7	2.0
TOTAL	13.5	2.5	5.0

The case of the Jewish rural population (it had been prohibited by the tsarist government for Jews to undertake agricultural production) represents an interesting instance with regard to attempts to enforce planned resettlement. In the second half of the 1920s, two alternative projects concerning the issue were put forward. Both of them had the political aim of producing a constructive alternative that would undermine the Zionist concept of Jewish settlement in Palestine. The first plan envisaged the resettlement of half a million impoverished Jews to Ukraine and to the Crimea, and even the creation of a Jewish autonomous administrative unit on the territory of the latter.[21] However, local Russians, Ukrainians and Tatars showed an extremely hostile attitude to the suggestion. The second plan foresaw the resettlement of Jewish rural population to the rich and uninhabited lands of the Far East, in the region of the rivers Bira and Bidzhan on the left bank of the Amur. However, less than 2 thousand Jews moved to the region during the first two years (starting from 1928). Neither the forced demobilization of Jewish Red Army service members, nor propaganda campaigns abroad, nor even the proclamation of a Jewish Autonomous Oblast produced the desired effect. In the course of 1928–1933, some 20 thousand Soviet Jews and around 1.5 thousand Lithuanian Jews moved to the region, but over 11.5 thousand (or 3/5 of) resettlers left "Red Zion" in the Amur region at the same time.[22] Therefore, Bolshevism was unable realistically to produce a competitor to Zionism.

Sometimes, resettlement projects were brought about on the back of plans for hydropower and ameliorative construction work, for example in the Caucasus and Central Asia, which was aimed at rendering the country's economy self-sufficient as far as the production of cotton and other crops was concerned. This type of resettlement was carried out mainly *within regional boundaries*, which usually implied migration from highlands to flatlands in the areas with highland-flatland settlement patterns, or—to use the expression of the period—*resettlement from mountains to the plain.*

Resettlements of this type took place in Tajikistan in 1925–1926: some 500 Dekhan households moved from the highland Garmsky *vilayat* [district] in Pamir to the lands under development in the Kurgan-Tyubin and Djilikul *vilayats*. Some privileges were introduced for such settlers on 5 March 1927 (in particular, they were allowed to retain their highland land plots as "possessions" for three years). On 15 March a Resettlement Committee was founded within the Tajik SSR Central Executive Committee. As a result, the movement became even greater between 1927 and 1928 (over 4.5 thousand households moved), which allowed for dozens of new villages, collectives and soviet farms to be founded, and was subsequently meant to increase cotton production capabilities.[23]

It should be noted that a similar policy was exercised during the resettlement into the Vakhsh valley in the 1930s, especially after the issuance of the state resolution "On the development of the Vakhsh lands in 1933" and the decree "On resettlement to Vakhsh." Both documents established a 16-thousand target group for resettlement in 1933, which was aimed at developing 21.6 thousand hectares of land by spring 1933. Those targeted by the resettlement project were mainly qualified cotton planters from Uzbekistan, the republic's internal labor force, and demobilized Red Army service members.[24] The required number of settlers to move into the region in 1935–1938 was 12,360 households, on the assumption of assigning three hectares per household.[25] The total number of Dekhan households that moved to the Vakhsh valley in the course of the organized resettlement period from 1925–1926 to 1940 is estimed by Sh. I. Kurbanova as 48.7 thousand (apart from the households of re-emigrants and builders). However, some 12.2 thousand of the households (i.e., about 24% of the total) could not bear the hardships of the relocation and left their new places of residence.[26]

At the same time, the financial and informational basis of the resettlement programs was critically deficient. The state sought to shift the burden of resettlement costs onto the resettlers themselves. Consequently, it comes as no surprise that a maximum 5% of the targeted population actually took the risk of moving.

Therefore, one can regard the policy of voluntary planned resettlement as one that failed.

At the same time there were still vast areas to be developed on the territories that were unattractive to free citizens. Forestry was especially profitable: timber export provided the country with significant and stable currency inflow, and its share of the country's export economy was steadily growing. It goes without saying that to bolster this sector the concept of "involuntary resettlement" and "involuntary labor" would come into their element.

It appears that the first person to articulate the idea was N. M. Yanson, deputy people's commissar of the Workers' and Peasants' Inspection of the RSFSR, who proposed that the labor of convicts (convicted for common crimes) should be used more actively in order to develop remote lands, especially as far as forestry was concerned.

In 1930, while analyzing the tendencies of the prison and camp systems' development in the RSFSR during 1929, he (at that time already the people's commissar of justice of the RSFSR) noted in particular: a general increase in the number of convicts (up to 1.2 million persons); a decrease in the percentage of those sentenced to short (less than one year) terms; and a dramatic growth in the number of persons sentenced to forced labor (up to 50.3% as compared to 15.3% in 1928). The policy of the transfer of prison and reformatory inmates to the OGPU labor camps, which were being established based on the principle of self-support (the number of camp prisoners reached 166 thousand by the end of the year, with another 60 thousand prisoners used as labor force in the RSFSR NKVD reformatory colonies) was established. Both Yanson and people's commissar of internal affairs of the RSFSR, V. N. Tolmachev, were convinced that convict [zeka] labor was efficient, and their productivity was often higher than in the case of free employment.[27] An experiment that started out with such promise was bound to have far-reaching results.

The bodies in charge of resettlement were restructured too. A circular "On organizing the arrangement of resettlers into labor collectives" was issued by the Committee for Resettlement at the end of 1929 and sent to the People's Commissariats of Agriculture of the Soviet Union republics.[28] The document regarded planned resettlement as a policy assigned to promote the reorganization of agricultural production on the basis of *collectivization* and likely to prove very advantageous in two spheres: the development of uninhabited lands and relief from overpopulation in a number of agricultural regions.

This perspective provided a meeting point for the ideology of resettlement and the fundamental political campaigns of the Bolsheviks, namely collectivization, dekulakization and "kulak exile." It was almost immediately, in December of the same year, that the Communist Party Central Committee took up the implementation of the resettlement program after Stalin proclaimed the move from the policy of mere restriction of kulak commercial activity to the policy of the liquidation of the kulaks as a social class.[29] It still should be noted that non-systemic dekulakization was already underway in 1929, namely through the impositions of state grain purchases and tax collection.

Interestingly, forced migrations in the form of the cleansing of the border zones were put into practice at approximately the same time.[30] The first resolutions on the resettlement of socially dangerous elements in the western border zones of the USSR, in UkSSR and BSSR were adopted at the end of 1929, quite surprisingly by the republic—and not All-Union—Councils of People's Commissars. For example, the resolution adopted by the Council of People's Commissars of the UkSSR on 13 November 1929 refers to "the soonest possible improvement of the economic conditions in the UkSSR border zone and the facilitation of reconstructive measures in the area," which conditioned "voluntary" inclusion into resettlement groups of citizens recognized as socially dangerous for further residing within the 22 km-wide border zone (and, of note, irrespective of their social status: both peasants of moderate and low income were among those resettled). Siberia, primarily the taiga zone, was the exclusive destination for those banished from the border areas.[31] Statistical reports on persons banished from Ukrainian and Belorussian border zones referred to those resettled as "individuals of special assignment," although they were deported within the joint campaign that included the "kulak exile" (for example, in 1930 18,473 persons were resettled). Subsequently, their family members were given permission to reunite with them.

The decision taken on repopulating the territories vacated as a result proved an interesting enterprise: obviously, it could not be seen to be a matter of chance and natural demographic movement. An appropriate solution was found at the end of the 1920s: so-called Red Army *kolkhozy* were to be established along the frontiers of the USSR, and they would employ demobilized Red Army soldiers and their family members. These were seen by T. Martin (who appears to have been the first one to refer to these establishments) as a symbolic form of the manifestation of "Soviet xenophobia."[32]

DEKULAKIZATION AND "KULAK EXILE" IN 1930–1931

The chronicle of "kulak exile" is an integral component of the history of dekulakization and collectivization, which involved such key concepts as denying kulaks the access to *kolkhozy*, kulaks' property expropriation, along with the isolation and deportation (or liquidation in cases of resistance) of the kulaks as a social class. The main cereal-producing areas of the country became targeted by "blanket" collectivization that involved deportations from the territories.

The OGPU issued rulings concerning resettlement as early as 18 January 1930. However, it was the resolution by the Communist Party Central Committee "On the measures for the liquidation of kulak farms in the areas subject to blanket collectivization," issued on 30 January 1930, that set the unprecedented depth and scale of the anti-peasantry repression.[33] A mass collectivization was launched as early as January 1930. While kulak farms made up around 2.3% of the total of peasant households, according to the official statistics, the number of dekulakized households reached 10–15% (instead of the "planned" 3–5%) in many districts. Naturally, the plans for arrests among the first-category kulaks were over-fulfilled as early as in mid-February. Dekulakization was carried out even in areas where it had not been pre-planned: for example, in the northern region and, in particular, among the sparsely populated areas of the north, which took a special CP Central Committee resolution to be brought to an end.[34] The colonization of underdeveloped or non-reclaimed territories, which initially had been contrived as a parallel plan to be implemented through the use of cheap kulak labor force in forestry, the mining industry and agriculture, was considered a "secondary" task at the beginning, but gradually was brought to the fore. The secretary of the Northern Kray Communist Party Committee, S. A. Bergavinov, wrote to Stalin on 12 March 1930: "...Consequently this [resettlement of hundreds of thousands of dekulakized peasants to the Kray— P.P.] will become a tremendous factor not merely solving the problem of the Kray colonization, and enormously reinforcing the Kray's potential by providing a labor force, but also will hasten the development of the productive potential of new territories, since 250–300 thousand people are a great force."[35]

It was only in February that the mechanism for the exiling of kulaks was fully set in motion. However, the OGPU directives concerning the impending mass deportations had already been sent to the local executives in the areas subject to blanket collectivization in January.[36] The measures were to be carried out by special commissioners appointed by district executive committees (in cooperation with the OGPU and local committees of poor peasants [*kombedy*]) in the period of February–May, i.e., for the most part before the spring crop-sowing season. Those subject to dekulakization were divided into three categories: 1) counter-revolutionary activists—these were sent to concentration camps or even shot without legal trial (their family members were often subject to expulsion to special settlements as a high priority, but in some cases were left at home. Later on, in 1931–1932, those remaining under this category were again transferred to special settlements accompanied by their families if possible); 2) the remaining elements of the active kulaks, well-to-do kulaks, and semi-landowners—these were expelled to remote territories of the USSR or to isolated areas of their native regions; 3) kulaks staying within the district boundaries—these were transferred to small settlements outside the kolkhoz-owned lands. Naturally, most of their property and savings were confiscated from all three categories. The means appropriated in this way were used to pay off the kulak "debts" to the state, or transferred into the indivisible kolkhoz funds.

Directives specifying concrete numbers and destinations of those to be repressed were issued: 60 thousand kulak families were subject to deportation under the first category, and 150 thousand under the second. After these figures were supplemented in late February 1930 with "restricted" contingents from the so-called consuming regions of the USSR (Moscow, Leningrad, West and Ivanovo-Voznesensk regions, the Nizhny Novgorod Kray, and the Crimean ASSR) and from the national districts of Central Asia, Transcaucasia, and North Caucasus, the total number of households subject to deportation reached 245 thousand.[37]

The first deportations were to be carried out in the North Cau-

casus and on the Central and Lower Volga (10 February), then in
Ukraine and in the Central Black-Earth Region (15 February), and
finally in Belorussia (1 March). The completion of the resettlement
was scheduled for the beginning of June, while the first stage was to
be implemented by 15 April.[38]

The initial planned destinations for the kulak populations
expelled from the zones of blanket collectivization were the North
Kray (a warrant for 70 thousand households was issued[39]), Siberia
(50 thousand, local Siberian kulak families being exempted from the
number), the Urals and Kazakhstan[40] (20–25 thousand each). In particular, it was envisaged that underdeveloped and isolated areas would
be targeted, where those deported were to be employed in such
industries as fishing and timber works at first, agriculture taking a
lower priority. The intended deportation "pattern" looked as follows:
Ukrainian kulaks were to be sent to the Northern Kray, kulaks from
the Central and Lower Volga and Belorussia were to be exiled to
Siberia, and those from the Caucasus were to be transported to the
Urals and Kazakhstan (23 and 5 thousand respectively).

The plan of settlement within the North Kray was as follows:
30 thousand families were to be settled in the Arkhangelsk Okrug,
12 thousand in the Komi Autonomous Republic (in these regions,
fishery and fur trade were to be developed), 10 thousand in the Volog-

Table 4. **Number of kulaks of the first and second categories,**
by regions of departure (thousands of families)

Region	Category	
	1st	2nd
Middle Volga	3–4	8–10
Lower Volga	4–6	10–12
North Caucasus and Daghestan	6–8	20
Central Black-Earth Region	3–5	10–15
Siberia	5–6	25
The Urals	4–5	10–15
Kazakhstan	5–6	10–15
Ukraine	15	30–35
Belorussia	4–5	6–7
Consuming regions of the USSR	17	15
National regions of Central Asia, Transcaucasia, and North Caucasus	2.95	

Source: Invintsky, 1996, 69–70

da Okrug (cattle breeding and farming), 9.5 thousand in the Severodvinsk Okrug (flax growing), and 8.5 thousand in the Niandom Okrug.[41] In Siberia, the deported were to be placed in the Priangarsky Okrug (30 thousand families) and along the Tomsk–Yeniseysk railway (20 thousand), while the local kulaks were to be settled in the Vasyugan territory and Narym Kray[42]: "The areas... represent at present a virtually uninhabited space, which is impossible to populate without at least a minimal preparation... The establishment of a special territory is not stipulated. It may be sufficient to merely allocate sites for settlements, all the indicated areas having been explored for the most part."[43] The settlement in the Urals was carried out primarily in the Verkhnekamsk Obl., Komi–Permyak National Okrug, Nizhny Tagil, Irbit, and Tobolsk Obls., with the use of the labor force mainly in forestry and fishery.[44] A part of the Siberia and the Urals deportations was carried out internally on these territories.

Generally speaking, a tendency can be detected in the proposed plans: namely the tendency to ignore the natural and climatic conditions (and therefore traditional skills of the deported kulaks) of the destination areas, and to avoid the placement of kulaks in the areas bordering those from which they had been expelled. This tendency was especially evident in the case of kulaks from the Lower and Central Volga, for whom both Kazakhstan and the Urals were inaccessible (the situation changed in 1931, when the economic factor became significantly more important).

Reality, however, confused matters: to ruin the lives of kulaks (to dekulakize and force them into transfer stations) is entirely different from transporting people to the destination area and providing them with minimal facilities. And inevitably, Siberia and Kazakhstan declared that they were not in a position to receive and settle kulaks. Consequently the entire deportation process was divided into three stages. The first stage, planned to be completed by May 1930, embraced 60 thousand kulak households (i.e., around 300 thousand people), three-quarters of whom were sent to the North Kray (20 thousand Ukrainian families and 8 thousand each from the Central Chernozem zone and Central Volga, 6 thousand from the Lower Volga, and 3 thousand from Belorussia), and one-quarter to the Urals (10 thousand families from the North Caucasus, and 5 thousand from Belorussia, but—let us stress again—not from the Volga territory). However, this plan was soon (16 February) altered by Stalin himself:

70 thousand dekulakized families were now destined for the North Kray, 20 thousand for the Urals, and 15 thousand for Siberia.[45]

On 9 March 1930, the RSFSR Council of People's Commissars created a commission (under the chairmanship of the people's commissar of internal affairs of the RSFSR, V. N. Tolmachev) that was to elaborate particular recommendations concerning the settlement, employment, and use of labor of the "special resettlers." On 1 April 1930, a special Council of People's Commissars commission chaired by deputy chairman of the Council of People's Commissars, V. V. Schmidt, was established for the general supervision of related matters.[46] Similar commissions were organized at the regional level too.

As a result of the inter-regional plan of settlement, 66,445 fam-

Table 5. **Deportations of kulaks of the second category,**
by region of departure (as of 1 January 1930; families and persons)

Region of departure	Planned		Resettled		Remarks
	Families	Persons	Families	Persons	
Ukraine	20,000	100,000	20,761	98,743	
		15,000		14,894	Individuals of "special assignment"*
Belorussia	8,000	40,000	9,231	44,083	
		3,500		3,579	Individuals of "special assignment"*
Central Chernozem Obl.	8,000	40,000	8,237	42,837	Another 700 families expected
Lower Volga	8,000	40,000	7,931	40,001	
Central Volga	6,000	30,000	5,566	29,211	Another 350 families expected
North Caucasus	10,000	50,000	10,595	51,577	Except Daghestan
Crimea	3,000	15,000	3,179	14,029	
Tatarstan	2,000	10,000	650	3,310	4 trains en route
Central Asia	400	2,000	80	281	
Transcaucasia	200	1,000	—**	—**	
TOTAL	65,600	346,500	66,445	342,545	
		18,500		18,473	Individuals "of special assignment"*

Remarks:
 * Deported from the border zones of Ukraine and Belorussia irrespective of social status.
** Due to a harsh political situation, the deportations from Transcaucasia were not carried out.
Source: Invintsky, 1996, 69–70

ilies, or 340,753 persons, were deported by 1 May, and 31,557 families, or 158,745 persons, were resettled within the regions. The total thus constituted 98,002 families, or 499,498 persons.[47]

With the exception of Central Asia and Transcaucasia, the plans regarding the resettlement of kulaks of the second category was virtually fulfilled (see table 6).

The table shows that at this stage neither Siberia nor Kazakhstan played any significant role as regions of destination in the case of interregional kulak deportations. In other words, the recommendation Stalin made on 16 February 1930 was practically ignored, and the major-

Table 6. **Deportations of kulaks of the second category,**
by region of destination (as of 6 January 1930; families and persons)

Region of Destination	Departure	Number Families	Persons
North Kray		**46,562**	**230,065**
	Ukraine	19,658	93,461
	Central Chernozem Obl.	8,237	42,837
	Lower Volga	7,931	40,001
	Central Volga	5,566	29,211
	Belorussia	4,763	22,810
	Crimea	407	1,745
The Urals		**31,343**	**151,249**
	North Caucasus	10,595	51,577
	Belorussia	4,468	21,273
	Crimea	2,722	12,284
	The Urals	13,708	66,115
Siberia		**17,196 +** appr. 14,894 individuals	**100,481**
	Ukraine	1,135 + appr. 14,894 individuals	20,176
	Siberia	16,061	80,305
Kazakhstan		**1,421**	**7,816**
	Central Asia	80	281
	Kazakhstan	1,341	7,535
Far East		**1,280**	**7,352**
	Tatarstan	650	3,310
	Belorussia	183	1,787*
	Far East	447	2,235

Remark:
* Including "individuals of special assignment."
Source: Invintsky, 1996, 141–142, 233–234, 236.

ity of dekulakized peasants were sent to the European North and the Urals, with the ratio of distribution between the two regions around 3:1. All kulaks from the North Caucasus, the majority of those that came from the Crimea, and around a half of the Belorussians became the new "Urals settlers." Kulaks from Ukraine, Central Chernozem Oblast and the Volga region (without taking into account half of the Belorussian kulaks and part of the Crimean ones) were sent to the European North. The table indicates that it was residents of the western border zones ("individuals of special assignment") that were sent the farthest, namely to East Siberia and even to the Far East.

Kulaks were settled in small settlements under the supervision of commandants (so-called labor settlements). The deportees were officially termed as the "special resettlers" (until 1934), then "labor settlers" (in 1934–1944), and starting from 1944 their status was changed to "special settlers." The rights and duties of the special resettlers were stipulated by special resolutions and instructions of the central and local authorities, and subsequently—from 20 May 1931—by the OGPU.[48] Special settlements were under the control of special *komendaturas* [commandant's offices], which in actuality were informal low-level local Soviet authority bodies.

The exact number of special settlements that existed in 1930 and 1931 is unknown, their approximate number being estimated as exceeding 2,000 with 574 located in the Urals region[49] alone. Dekulakized evictees' settlements were supposed to comprise 30–50 households, and only in exceptional cases exceed 100[50] (however, there were some settlements that consisted of 250 and even 500 households).

Obviously, a large percentage of those deported were subjected to resettlement wrongly or represented debatable cases—even from the perspective of the regulations and criteria established by the OGPU itself. This matter was investigated by a special CP Central Committee commission chaired by A. Bergavinov. Notwithstanding the commission's conclusion that the number of deportees resettled without proper grounds generally exceeded 41%, Bergavinov insisted that only 6% of deportees were wrongly dekulakized, and 8% of cases were debatable, and it was these latter figures that were officially recognized by the Communist Party Central Committee Politburo. However, even among these 6% the right to return to the homeland was granted merely to those that had been distinguished while taking part in the revolution or had family members serving in the Red Army. The rest of the non-kulaks were to remain in the North Kray, but were offered the status of free citizens and special privileged conditions.[51] In other words, the resettlement had taken place and so be it, there was no way back, and there was no chance that the Stalinist Politburo would admit the scale of error of its arbitrary actions.

One is left merely to speculate on the percentage of "mistakes" made in the course of the dekulakization of the third category, and during the resettlement of this category's representatives within their regions in March–April 1930. Unlike in the case of inter-regional deportations, no clear criteria ever existed with regard to this category make-up.[52] For example, in Nizhny Novgorod Kray all those subject to resettlement (512 families, or 2,451 persons) were collected from all districts and placed in a single, scarcely populated and rather remote Sinegorsky district of Vyatka Okrug, where three labor settlement were founded for this purpose (specializing in tree felling).[53] In the Urals, the deportees were settled in a number of northern remote locations and employed in peat harvesting, stone-pits, and construction work. In the North Caucasus, a chess-style "castling" move was played out: kulak households were resettled from fertile areas and exchanged their places of residence with impoverished peasants from dry and low-harvest territories. Thus two large arrays of settlements for kulaks employed in agriculture were founded: the first one in the Divensky and Argiz (Prikumsky, according to other sources) districts (some 10 thousand households), and the other one in Donetsk and Shakhtinsk Okrug (around 2,000 families). In the Far East and Central Chernozem Oblast, the "castling" was conducted within the villages of districts (kulaks were moved into poor households, while the owners of the latter took over the kulak houses). No special settlements were founded, those resettled were employed in *kolkhozy* (although the OGPU actively disliked this model, which did not render kulaks "politically harmless"). In other areas subjected to blanket collectivization, kulaks were resettled beyond the boundaries of collectivized lands.

The scale of the "kulak exile" regarding the third category was as follows: by August 1930, according to the OGPU data, 51,889 families, i.e., 250 thousand persons, were settled in 11 districts of the USSR. Later on, the number kept decreasing (for example, it went down to 44,990 by February 1931), which can be explained by the fact that it was easy for kulaks belonging to this category to escape (with time, the proportion of escapees reached 72%). They would make numerous escapes to cities, and to large scale construction sites,[54] which were in abundance all over the country during the first five-year plan period: Donbass, Kuzbass, Magnitka, and even Metrostroy. It was not only kulaks that escaped, but also peasants of moderate and poor income. It was as early as summer 1930 that the number of these "self-dekulakized" peasants reached 250 thousand.[55]

The total of those removed from the areas of blanket collectivization by the end of 1930 made up 77,795 families, i.e., 371,645 persons, including 123,807 men, 113,653 women, and 134,185 children.[56] Most of them (almost 3/5) were banished to the North Kray, without permission to return even for those (as a reminder) that were subsequently recognized as wrongly dekulakized, although they were at least allowed to stay in the resettlement areas with the status of "free citizens." Taking into account the inter-regional migration (as of 1 January 1931), the total of kulaks deported in 1930 reached 109,352 families, i.e., 530,390 persons, or—including the resettled kulaks belonging to the third category—161,241 families, i.e., 780 thousand persons. Strictly speaking, one should subtract from this total the 18,473 "individuals of special assignment," and those deported from the border zones of Ukraine and Belorussia. It is equally true for the dekulakized peasants who were banished but under different regulations, namely due to the "border zones cleansing" and irrespective of social status (let us recall that moderate- and low-income peasants were among those deported too). Therefore, the number of peasants that were dekulakized and banished in 1930 equaled some 750 thousand persons.

At the same time, at least one million former kulaks still remained in their places of residence, but their fate was virtually predetermined: they had to face a winter of hunger and impending exile. Naturally, many did not like the prospect, and a wave of peasant revolts and assassinations of *kolkhoz* activists and propagators gripped the country. However, the majority preferred another form of rebellion, namely resorting to temporary jobs outside their homes.

The OGPU was inclined to think that the third category of kulaks should be merged with the other two and accordingly this group's members would also be banished to labor settlements in remote areas and employed at timber works and peat harvesting, at stone-pits and apatite extraction and railway construction.[57] As a matter of fact, this idea was put into practice the next year, when the categories virtually ceased to have any effective significance, although this "merger" of targets had not been sanctioned officially.

The party plenary meeting of June 1931 declared collectivization completed in the key grain-growing areas of the Soviet Union. However, the imposed collectivization resulted in a dramatic decline of agricultural production.

On 25 January 1931, an operation for the inter-regional deportation of kulaks was carried out in the North Caucasus. Some 9 thousand families (i.e., 45 thousand persons) were resettled from the seaside and forest highland areas of Kuban and the Black Sea to the dry lands of Stavropol region and the Salsk Steppe. Simultaneously, around 8.5 thousand families of members of communes and cooperative associations from Stavropol region and the Salsk Steppe settled on the vacated lands in the Kuban region. As a matter of fact, this was the completion of the resettlement of 1930 rather than the beginning of the "kulak exile" of 1931, since this particular resettlement decision had been taken by the North Caucasian regional Communist Party committee as early as August 1930.[58]

The decree "On authorizing kray [oblast] executive committees and governments of the Union republics to banish kulaks from the areas subject to blanket collectivization" was adopted on 1 February 1931, essentially heralding even larger deportations of peasants, as compared to those of 1930. Inter-regional deportations were cancelled at this time for kulaks belonging to both the second and third categories (Siberia, the Urals and the Far East constituted exceptions).[59]

Krasilnikov wrote: "The rate and scale of dekulakization in the year 1931 were not coordinated with the needs of collectivization any longer, and instead were largely determined by the claims put forward by economic bodies."[60]

A new wave of deportations gained momentum in mid-March 1931. Apart from the areas of kulak departure of the previous year, it spread over the republics of Central Asia (in particular, the following districts were declared territories of blanket collectivization: Kokand, Yangiyul, Deynauss, Saryassiysk, Gizhduvan, Akdarya, the Mirzachul districts of Uzbekistan; and the Charjou, Farab, Sayat, Ashkhabad districts of Turkmenistan[61]), Kazakhstan, (Arys, Lbishche and other districts), Transcaucasia,[62] the Far East, North Kray, Nizhny Novgorod Kray, Bashkir ASSR, Moscow, Leningrad[63] and Ivanovo industrial regions. The deportations were carried out from 20 March through 25 April and from 10 May through 18 September 1931 (i.e., with the traditional crop-sowing break).

There appeared a need to establish a single coordinating body that would supervise and control the work of resettlement, placement and employment of deported kulaks. Such a body was founded on 11 March 1931. This was a so-called Andreyev Commission, a special Communist Party Central Committee commission chaired by Council of People's Commissars deputy chairman, A. A. Andreyev.[64] The commission's proposals were usually represented in the form of decisions by the Politburo.

The resolution of the Communist Party Central Committee "On kulaks," adopted on 20 March 1931, was one of the decisions in question. It provided for the banishment of an additional 150 thousand kulak households to Kazakhstan (to Akmolinsk and Karkalinsky Okrugs, and to the locality of the river Tokrau to the south of Lake Balkhash) during May–July 1931. Apart from agriculture, the deportees were to be employed in mining (for coal, copper and iron ore) and railway construction. Another 40 thousand were to be resettled to northern areas of West Siberia Kray, primarily to Narym,[65] their main assignment being the development of arable land and timber harvesting. Eventually the kulak deportations resulted in the placement of over 80 thousand families, i.e., 363 thousand persons, under the supervision of the Siberia Camp Administration *komendatura*s (i.e., in West Siberia), with 68 thousand families, or 284 thousand persons, of the total settling in Narym Kray. The share of Siberia natives among the deportees amounted to 3/4 and constituted higher percentages further to the north. Consequently, the Kuzbass population rose two-fold, and that of northern areas of West Siberia even tripled, reaching some 300 thousand persons.[66]

There were plans to carry out deportation to Eastern Siberia in 1931, but its scale was not indicated. The party Central Committee assigned the OGPU to prepare the total of more than 200 thousand families for resettlement[67] (it was OGPU local representatives L. Zakovsky and Ye. Yevdokimov who initiated the kulak resettlement). However, this proved impracticable; and 110 thousand families were distributed equally between Kazakhstan and the Urals, without taking into account the resettlers *within* these regions, namely the Urals and West Siberia (12 thousand persons per region). Ukraine and North Caucasus (respectively 30 and 15 thousand families) were the key "exporters" of the kulak mass to the Urals; while a number of regions along the river Volga (this time including those adjacent to the Urals, and similar to it in terms of environmental conditions) and the Central Black-Earth Region and Moscow Obl. supplied resettlers to Kazakhstan.[68] In addition, another 6 thousand *bai* families were moved from Central Asia to the territories in southern Ukraine and the North Caucasus, provisionally usable for growing cotton.[69]

Comparing the geography of kulak departure areas of 1931 with that of the previous year, one can note a dramatic expansion of the affected territories. As far as the geography of destinations is concerned, there was a significant decrease in the percentage of deportees received by the North Kray and, on the contrary, a large increase in Siberia and Kazakhstan (while the Urals' share in this distribution remained notably sizeable[70]).

The initial placement and employment of kulaks in the places of destination was not merely inefficient: it was downright appalling. The number of resettlers at the destinations was actually decreasing (up to 1935). Correspondingly, the labor productivity was slipping too. This led to the transfer of all economic, administrative and organizational functions to a single, although rather authoritative and ambitious body, namely the OGPU.[71] This organization's interest in rationalizing dekulakized resettlers' labor and increasing its productivity was truly direct and immediate: the corresponding monetary payments to the OGPU made up 25% until August 1930, then 15% until February 1932, and 5% further on.[72] Therefore, as G. Adibekov put it, in 1931 the "repressive body turned into a profit-making monster with expansive infrastructure." [73]

A Communist Party Central Committee Politburo resolution "On kulaks," issued on 20 July 1931, stated that the task of mass banishment of kulaks had been essentially completed, and stipulated that in the future any resettlement of kulaks from the areas of blanket collectivization should be carried out on an individual basis.[74] In reality, however, the ban on mass deportations did not work, and although Andreyev Commission authorizations of banishment became more rare, they were far from being curtailed. For example, in July–August 1931, the commission sanctioned the banishment of kulaks from

Kazakhstan (5,000 families, with *intra-regional* resettlement permitted), from Central Asia (6,000 families) and from the Kalmyk region (1,100 families). Intra-regional resettlement was allowed in the Central Volga Kray (2,500 households) and Bashkir ASSR (6 thousand). Another 3,000 of the specially resettled moved from Bashkir and Tatar ASSRs and Nizhny Novgorod Kray to Belsky district, North Kray.[75]

On 12 October 1931, Yagoda reported to Stalin that some 200 thousand families had been dekulakized in 1931, which meant more than a two-fold decrease from the figure in 1930, and that simultaneously there was a two-fold increase in the number of deported kulaks: 162,962 families, i.e., 787,241 persons, including 242,776 men, 223,834 women, and 320,731 children. The total number of families deported in 1930–1931 was 240,757, which made 1,158,986 persons.[76]

Taking into account intra-regional resettlement, according to the data of the OGPU GULAG department on special resettlements, 388,336 families, i.e., 1,803,392 persons, were moved in 1930–1931.[77] Therefore, the number of kulaks of the first and second categories resettled during 1931 made up 1,273,002 persons. According to A. N. Ivnitsky,[78] the total of 381,026 kulak families, i.e., the same 1,803,392 persons, were banished in 1930–1931, including 133,717 families (or about 35%) subjected to intra-regional resettlement and 247,309 families deported to other regions. Then, if one adds to this number some 250 thousand third-category kulaks, resettled in 1930, the total of kulaks deported within two years will amount to around 2.05 million persons! Figure 1 shows the main currents of the "kulak exile."

Yagoda's report to Stalin of 4 January 1932 cites the total figure of kulak special settlers registered in 14 districts of the USSR: it is 1,421,380 persons. In one way or other, the discrepancy between the two figures (0.6 million persons) can be put down to mortality, to successful escapes, or to the change of status of special settlers after arrival at the destinations due to various reasons (after the establishment of a wrongly ruled banishment or due to a marriage with a free citizen, among others). In order to better demonstrate the immense scale of the "kulak exile" as a means of administrative repression, let us compare the provided data with the number of GULAG prison camp inmates: as of 1 January 1932 it equaled only 268,700 persons,[79] i.e., less than 1/5 of the number of kulak "specially resettled people."

Ukraine was the biggest "exporter" of dekulakized peasants in 1930–1931, the number reaching 63.7 thousand families, with more than a half, (32.1 thousand) banished to the Urals and another 20 thousand to the North Kray. West Siberia is rated second on the list (52.1 thousand families). However, in five regions, namely Northern, Western and Eastern Siberia, the Far East and Kazakhstan, the resettlement was administered exclusively within the corresponding kray boundaries. The Urals can be added to the list, since 95% of resettlements carried out there were of an intra-regional nature. In the Bashkir ASSR the figure reached around one-half of total deportations. Therefore, almost the entire Asian and most of the European areas of the USSR became zones of intra-regional "kulak exile." This is hardly surprising when taking into account the massive land mass of the corresponding administrative units.

The North Caucasus was the third largest "banishment" region (38.4 thousand families). In this case, the Urals prevailed as a destination region (26 thousand families), exceeding the intra-regional resettlement figure (12.4 thousand) more than two-fold. The Lower Volga Kray (30.9 thousand families), the Urals (28.4), the Central Chernozem Obl. (26) and the Central Volga (23 thousand) followed.

Figure 1. **"Kulak exile" in 1930–1931**

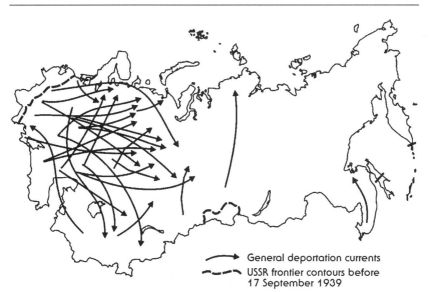

General deportation currents
USSR frontier contours before
17 September 1939

Apart from Ukraine and North Caucasus, the Urals proved to be the most prolific destination along with the West Obl., BSSR, Crimea, Ivanovo Industrial Obl., Tatar ASSR, and Nizhny Novgorod Kray. Besides, the Urals was a significant constituent of the deportation structure for Moscow Obl., lagging behind West Siberia only by a small margin.

Following the Urals, as a center of "kulak exile" gravitation, Kazakhstan was the second leading region in these terms. It prevailed among such regions of kulak destination as the Lower Volga, Central Chernozem Obl. (only a little ahead of the North Kray on this list) and Transcaucasia.

West Siberia proved the major recipient region not only for the Moscow Obl., but also for the Leningrad Obl. and Bashkir ASSR. The greater share of kulaks from Central Asia was distributed between Ukraine and the North Caucasus, which can largely be explained by stubborn attempts to develop cotton growing in these regions.

"KULAK EXILE" AND FAMINE REPERCUSSIONS
IN 1932–1934

On 20 July 1931, the Resettlement Bureau of the Communist Party Central Committee considered the question of mass resettlement and ruled that this strategic task of the party had been largely fulfilled. All further exiles were recommended to be carried out on a strictly individual basis. Nevertheless, mass banishment of kulaks continued in 1932, 1933, and even later, either as exceptional cases or as a matter of cleansing collective farms of kulak elements and saboteurs. Moreover, on 13 February 1933, the OGPU addressed the Communist Party Central Committee Politburo with a proposition that the additional resettlement of one million deportees to West Siberia, and one million to Kazakhstan, should be conducted. The resettled people would include representatives of the following groups: dekulakized peasants guilty of undermining bread provision or other campaigns; urban residents that refused to leave cities under the passportization regulations; peasants that escaped to cities and industrial centers seeking to avoid dekulakization and collectivization; those banned from frontier zones and sentenced to terms of three to five years by the OGPU. In response to this initiative, on 17 April 1933 the Communist Party Central Committee Politburo issued a resolution to begin the establishment of OGPU labor settlements, although the necessary funds were not allotted.

Although the plans for deportations (of newly uncovered kulaks) were limited, new economic development challenges kept surfacing while the struggle to achieve the old ones persisted: the Khibiny mountains, Karaganda, Aldan, and Narym (the Siberia Camp Administration), for example. While in the first three cases, development of large industrial deposits was the goal (apatites, coal and gold), in Narym it was 855 thousand hectares of arable land that were planned to be developed in order to render the kray self-sufficient in terms of grain, forage and vegetables within two years. For agricultural work it was planned to employ 55.7 thousand settlers (25 thousand of them able-bodied) residing in the Galkino, Parbigsky,[80] Toinsky, and Shegarsky *komendatura*s. Another 160.2 thousand persons (60 thousand able-bodied) were to be employed at timber harvesting jobs on vast territories from Vasyugan to Chulym.[81] However, these plans were shelved by May 1932, having been implemented only partially. Moreover, the deficit of labor in Kuzbass was the reason why some 2 thousand "specially resettled people" were returned from the Narym *komendatura*s.[82]

The predicament of kulak "specially resettled people" can be said to have begun to stabilize in 1932 (by 1933, virtually the entire contingent was made up of dekulakized peasants). While back in 1930 it was rather the lands and property of the dekulakized than the people themselves that were of interest to the state, in 1931–1932 these people became regarded as a "labor force" from which it was possible to reap benefit, to such an extent that certain measures were brought in aimed at their protection from arbitrary brutality from "employers." The very establishment of the Andreyev Commission, along with its regional counterparts (for example, the commission of Zakovsky in West Siberia Kray), was nothing else but an attempt to introduce economic rationality into the political spontaneity of the "kulak exile."

This was also reflected in the destination geography of the special settlements for dekulakized peasants. In this regard, a similar tendency appears to have been in place, namely, a shift from "politics" to "economics," from "super-extensiveness" to mere "extensiveness," and from the bold and hopelessly romantic plans cherished by Yago-da for the colonization of the North and other "remote areas" (some-times absolutely virgin lands, from whence there was absolutely no escape) through the use of the forced labor of prisoners and special settlers—to more localized, pragmatic and intensive projects aimed at regional development of a particular nature, which has more to do with tactical than strategic tasks (see below).

Consequently, the clear preference for the European North as a resettlement destination in 1930 was replaced by an orientation toward the Urals and Kazakhstan in 1931, and then West Siberia in 1931–1933. The latter tendency, though, may be also perceived as a recur-rence of the "extensive" approach. The following observation is of sig-nificance to our discussion: the north of West Siberia was developed mainly by kulaks from the kray's southern districts, while the "south-ern" komendaturas (which were more industrially oriented: Kuzbass, Kuznetskstroy and others) were populated with natives of the coun-try's European center.

In 1932, 71,236 persons[83] were transported to special settle-ments from other regions (i.e., without taking into account the intra-regional resettlement), a large portion of whom (39.4%) was quite unexpectedly transported to Central Asia, which surpassed Kaza-khstan (16.2%) and the Urals (14.2%) in its number of recipients. In 1933, the number of new resettlers reached 268,091, most of whom (140,697 persons, i.e., 52.5%) arrived in West Siberia;[84] 55,107 (i.e., 20.6%) in Kazakhstan; 33,920 (12.6%) in the Urals; 16,569 in the North Kray; 15,517 at the Belomorkanal [White Sea Canal] con-struction site; 3,927 in Gorky Kray and so on.[85] In 1935, another 4,711 families, i.e., 22,496 persons, were banished from the North Caucasus districts. The total of those resettled in 1933–1940 reached 418,586 persons.[86]

This figure, added to the number of kulaks deported in 1930–1932 (including the third category kulaks resettled in 1930, but with-out taking into account the intra-regional resettlement of 1932), pro-duces an immense total: approximately 2,540 thousand persons, with 81% of this figure amassed during the first two years.

In the winter of 1932–1933 another migration factor emerged. It was directly induced by collectivization, that had separated the most efficient land proprietors from their soil: deficient harvesting and the expropriation of "grain surpluses" eventually led to overwhelming starvation in the country's southern regions, namely in Ukraine, North Caucasus, and the Lower Volga region, in which at least 25–30 million people went without food. The party's Central Committee commissions sent to these regions kept uncovering "kulak sympathizers" and other culprits, expelling rank-and-file party and soviet activists[87] from the party, arresting peasants in hundreds of thousands—including cases falling under the shamefully notorious "law on gleaning" of 7 August 1932.[88] Entire settlements and villages were put on "black lists": for example, in December 1932, some 5 thousand households from a number of Kuban *stanitsa* settlements were banished mainly to North Kazakhstan and the Urals.[89] The vacated lands were forcefully repopulated with demobilized Red Army soldiers.[90]

In the period from the fall of 1932 to April 1933, the USSR population decreased by a chilling figure of 7.7 million, including 4 million in Ukraine and 1 million each in the North Caucasus, the Volga region, and Kazakhstan.[91]

Kazakhstan experienced a truly formidable situation in 1933, since collectivization and famine resulted in a 90% decrease of livestock. The "big leap" in stock farming (including measures aimed at the wholesale collectivization of livestock, even of small cattle holdings), and the policy of forced "settling"[92] [de-nomadization] of nomadic and semi-nomadic Kazakh people, not merely led to starvation and the deaths of 1 (by Zelenin's estimation) to 2 (according to Abylkhozhayev et al.) million people, but also engendered mass migration of Kazakhs [beyond the republic's borders]. According to Zelenin, this migration process embraced at least 400 thousand families, i.e., 2 million persons, while Abylkhozhin et al. estimate the figure as 1,030 thousand persons, 414 thousand of whom later returned to Kazakhstan while an approximately equal number settled in the Russian Federation and Central Asian republics, with the remaining 200 thousand settling abroad, in China, Mongolia, Afghanistan, Iran and Turkey. Obviously, this was a rather lengthy process, which started at the end of 1931 and gained momentum from spring 1932 through spring 1933.[93] The lands vacated by these people gradually fell into decay and dereliction.[94]

This factor was a likely key reason for the notable concentration of subsequently banished "special resettlers" and administrative deportees specifically in Kazakhstan and the republics of Central Asia.

The famine of 1932–1933 produced a wide range of repercussions and triggered a number of problems. One such problem was the necessity to populate those areas that had suffered the heaviest losses due to famine and dekulakization, which had directly led to labor force shortages. Among such regions were Ukraine, the North Caucasus (the Kuban region, first of all) and the Volga region. The natural birth rate in these regions (as well as in the Central Chernozem Obl.) was dramatically negative in 1933, in terms of both urban and rural population. The total deficiency of population reached 1,459 thousand persons in Ukraine alone, 278 thousand in the North Caucasus, and 175 thousand in the Lower Volga region.[95]

According to the information available as of December 1933, some 16 thousand families fell under the resettlement campaign within Ukraine, 3 thousand in the Central Chernozem Obl., and 300 Jewish families in the West Obl.[96] In other words, almost 100 thousand people were affected.

Simultaneously (in 1933–1934), a number of decisions were worked over concerning the transportation to the Kuban and the Black Sea coastline regions of Red Army resettlers inducted through military registration and enlistment offices. By the beginning of December 1933, a total of 31,458 persons, including 16,997 men, had been moved to these regions.[97] Another 50 thousand families were planned to be resettled to the regions in 1934.[98] In spite of the recognized high incidence of malaria in the regions in question, no preventive measures (quinine treatment) were undertaken, and no drugs were made available in case of sickness either. At the same time, even for "free" resettlers it was no easy task to leave.[99]

Nevertheless, a mass escape of Red Army resettlers from the Azov–Black Sea Kray started in the June of 1934. In autumn 1934 the number of escapees reached 30% (this phenomenon is labeled as "reversing" [obratnichestvo] in official correspondence).[100] As early as 27 September 1934, Azov–Black Sea Kray Communist Party committee member M. Malinov wrote to the CP Central Committee, to Stalin, Kaganovich and Zhdanov about the hardships that Red Army resettlers were experiencing, their unjustifiably high mortality and the large-scale escapes from the kray. The reasons for such a situation were not limited to malaria outbreaks and a negligent attitude on the part of the authorities. It was also the hostile disposition of the local residents, especially Cossacks, who treated the new settlers as unwelcome guests, that made the latter feel uncomfortable.[101]

In the period 1933–1937, the All-Union and NKVD Resettlement Committees moved 77,304 families, i.e., 347,866 persons. It is remarkable that 221,465 persons, i.e., 61%, were resettled to Ukraine, not simply anywhere! The Eastern Siberia, Azov–Black Sea Kray and Jewish Autonomous Oblast took fewer, having received only 38–39 thousand resettlers, not to mention the Far East and Buryat–Mongol ASSR, that hosted approximately 6 thousand people.

Almost 83% of the resettlement cases occurred in the period of 1933–1934, with more than half resettled in 1933. During those years, virtually all resettlers were sent to Ukrainian grain-growing regions: Odessa, Donetsk, Dnepropetrovsk, Kharkov Obls. (mostly from central Russia and the Upper Volga region, but also from the BSSR, and other Ukrainian regions such as Kiev, Vinnitsa and Chernigov Obls). Only around 2 thousand Moscow Oblast residents resettled to Stalingrad Oblast in 1934, constituting an exception, along with so-called Red Army families from various regions, or—in other words—demobilized soldiers forcefully (through military registration and enlistment offices) distributed to the North Caucasus in 1933 (over 36 thousand persons) and to the Far East in 1934 (only 1 thousand persons).

After 1935, Ukraine was no longer referred to as a resettlement destination in reports. From then onwards the currents of resettlers were divided between the regions of Eastern Siberia and the Far East. In 1937 Azov–Black Sea Kray joined the list, while the Tatar ASSR and Kursk Obl. became "donor" regions along with traditional donors (Voronezh and Gorky Obls.).[102]

One can build a picture of what was implied by the "figures" by reading a—rather typical—report, No. 800 "On planned resettlement from the Kursk Obl.," sent on 20 March 1938 by Kursk Obl. UNKVD chief, State Security Captain Boyechin to State Security Senior Major Zhukovsky, the people's commissar of internal affairs of the USSR.[103] Interestingly, in spite of the situation in the Kursk Obl., described in November of the same year by Captain Boyechin, State Security Junior Lieutenant Skorinkov, head of the UNKVD resettlement department in Chita Obl., addressed the head of the USSR NKVD resettlement department division, Commissary Pliner, with a proposition that the Communist Party Central Committee and Council of People's Commissars should request authorization for resettling an additional 1,000 households from the Kursk and Voronezh Obls. Such a measure was motivated, according to him, by the fact that "...re-cruitment of demobilized Red Army soldiers to *kolkhozy* has been undermined, and there is no one left to recruit any more".[104]

Apparently, some things never change, as Mandelshtam aptly wrote in his article "Humanism and modernity" (1923): "Egyptian builders treat the human mass as material that has to be sufficient and supplied in any quantity!"

It should be noted that the "special resettler" status stopped being the exclusive domain of dekulakized peasants, since, from March 1933, various "cleansing" measures targeting "socially dangerous" and "declassed" elements were launched and became increasingly pronounced in large cities (mainly in central and western regions) and in frontier zones. During these cleansing measures, sometimes reminiscent of raids, people were seized right off the streets and thrown into vans prepared for transportation to Siberia. According to Maksheyev, some 25 thousand residents of Moscow, Leningrad, Sochi and other cities appeared en masse in May 1933 in Tomsk. The new term "new target groups" [*novyye kontingenty*], denoting the "newcomers" as opposed to the "old" body of dekulakized peasants, started circulating among the locals.[105]

By 1935 all frontier zones were cleansed of kulaks and other unre-liable elements on a mandatory basis. On 17 January 1935 G. Yagoda wrote to Stalin about the "political undesirability" of the return of labor settlers whose rights had been restored in the places from where they had been banished. In particular, he suggested that a stipulation should be made that restoring citizens' rights did not entail the right to leave the settlement locations.[106]

An analysis of the data gathered by V. N. Zemskov demonstrates a high dynamism and structural heterogeneity among GULAG "spe-cial resettlers."[107] As of 1 July 1938, 1,741 labor settlements (later named "special" settlements) were registered at the Department for Labor Settlements of the GULAG of the NKVD of the USSR. The population of the settlements comprised 997.3 thousand labor set-tlers ("special settlers," to use later terminology), which made an average of 573 persons per settlement. The overwhelming majority of the settlers were former peasants, dekulakized in 1930–1933, and sev-eral dozens of thousands were made up of the "unreliable elements" banished from frontier zones and large cities in the mid-1930s, espe-cially after the assassination of Kirov.

Table 7 shows the macro-regional profile of the distribution of labor settlers. As we can see, the main current of pre-war labor settlers arrived in the European and Asian north of the USSR, i.e., to underdeveloped regions with harsh climatic conditions. The Urals and West Siberia, both of which took in the total of approximately 0.5 million settlers, in sheer numbers far outstripped the initial destinations, i.e., the European North, Kazakhstan and Eastern Siberia. At the same time, settlements in West Siberia were half the size as in the Urals, which demonstrates their different economic profiles—timber harvesting and industrial respectively. In terms of distribution in oblasts, there are two main concentration centers: the Novosibirsk and Sverdlovsk Obls. are clearly distinct, with 170–195 thousand labor settlers in each, with the Novosibirsk Obl. (then comprising today's Tomsk Obl. as its component, and in particular the notorious "Narym") embracing around 1/3 of the total number of labor settlements in the USSR.[108] Also of note is the scale of settlements in the North Caucasus and Kazakhstan.

It is remarkable and somewhat unexpected that in the period of 1932–1940, according to V. N. Zemskov,[109] the number of those who left special settlements (2,563,401 persons) considerably exceeded—

Table 7. **Territorial distribution of labor settlers** (1938)

Region	Number of settlements	Number of settlers (thousands persons)	Average settlement population size (persons)
The Urals	299	244.3	817
West Siberia	648	242.7	375
North of the European part	204	135.1	662
Kazakhstan	100	134.7	1,347
East Siberia	248	119.7	483
North Caucasus (Stavropol Kray)	10	45.5	4,550
Central Asia	56	35.2	629
Far East	128	29.3	229
Ukraine	44	7.5	170
Volga region (Kuybyshev Obl.)	4	3.3	825
TOTAL	1,741	997.3	573

Calculations made based on: Zemskov, 1994, p. 126, quoting GARF, h. 9479, r. 1, d. 48, l. 9–10.

by 0.4 million—the number of arrivals (2,176,600 persons).[110] The reverse pattern was only observed in 1935 (44,800 persons) and 1938 and 1939 (60,901 and 58,931 persons respectively), while in the other years the "outbound" number of settlers kept exceeding the "inbound" figures (by 174,938 persons in 1932; by 69,538 persons in 1933; by 98,835 persons in 1934 and so on). It was not merely high mortality rates and natural depopulation that conditioned such a situation. The birth rate exceeded the death rate in 1935 for the first time; in general in the period of 1932–1940, still however, the negative balance of the two values was significant—159,263 persons. "Escapes" constituted a significant drain: 629,042 persons (with only 235,120 persons, i.e., less than 2/5, registered as returned after escaping). There were also other categories of "dropouts": the convicted (53,212 persons), those released on various grounds (130,991, including 33,050 after reconsideration of their cases and being found "wrongly banished"[111]), those transferred to other people's care and responsibility (36,286 persons), those transferred to organizations (696,395 persons)[112] and "others," among whose number included those who married "free" local residents and who constitute a larger proportion (627,956 persons).

The proportion of labor settlers among the wider number of repressed people (prisoners and labor settlers) remained more or less stable in the late 1930s: 34.4% in 1937 and 31.6% in 1939. Within the same short space of time, the proportion of prisoners serving their terms in jail dramatically decreased (from 20.5% to 11.8%), while that of GULAG prison camp and reformatory inmates increased from 45.1% to 56.6%.[113]

In other words, the ideas articulated by Yanson in 1928 did not fall on deaf ears and remained influential throughout the following decade.

FRONTIER ZONE CLEANSING AND OTHER FORCED MIGRATIONS IN 1934–1939

It was not in the thirties that the inward-looking isolation of the Soviet Union began, but it dramatically increased during the period. During this decade, the barrier that was later to become known as the "iron curtain" was being forged. To use A. Roginsky's accurate observation, the state frontiers were increasingly reminiscent of a "front line." And this factor influenced Stalin's deportation policy to a great extent (see figure 2).

In the mid-thirties a series of actions, or rather carefully managed campaigns, were aimed at securing large cities, frontiers and border areas by means of their "cleansing" from "socially dangerous" elements, i.e., unreliable in the Soviet leadership's opinion, typically on the basis of social class membership, but even more often on grounds of ethnicity. We have already mentioned that the first decisions concerning "cleansing" operations near the western borders with Lithuania and Poland date back to 1929, and the operations themselves took place in 1930. It is essential to note that the first cleansing operations did not have class or ethnic implications.[114]

Figure 2. **Frontier zone cleansing and other forced migrations in 1929–1938**

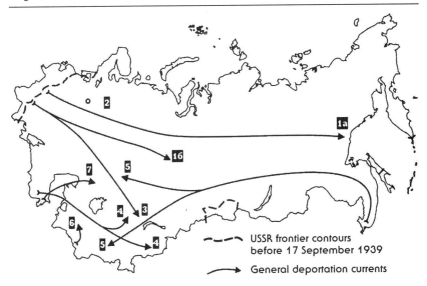

Deported groups:
1a: *Socially dangerous elements from the BSSR frontier zone* (1929);
1b: Socially dangerous elements from the UkSSR frontier zone (1929);
2: Ingermanland Finns from Leningrad locality (1935);
3: Poles and Germans from the UkSSR frontier zone (1936);
4: Kurds and other peoples from frontier zones and the Caucasus (1944);
5: Koreans from the Primorsky Kray (1937);
6: Iranian Jews from the Mary Obl. (1938);
7: Iranians from the Azerbaijani SSR frontier zone (1938).

It is also important to remember that the introduction of a passport system in the USSR on 27 December 1932 was motivated by the need to relieve Moscow, Leningrad, Kharkov and other large cities and industrial centers of counter-revolutionary, kulak, criminal and other anti-Soviet and "unnecessary" elements.[115]

A dramatic enhancement of various types of repression is commonly associated with the period between late 1934 and early 1935, the assassination of S. M. Kirov having been used formally to justify the change in campaign intensity. However, despite this, such repression as deportation was barely affected by this tendency. In this context, it is worthwhile mentioning the banishment of "the Déclassé" from Leningrad. This category included former nobility, industrial proprietors, landlords, bureaucrats, clerics, army and navy officers, gendarmes and policemen etc.

The operation in question, carried out only in Leningrad between late February and early March 1935, appears to be an extraordinarily mild measure, as compared to what was happening elsewhere: the affected citizens were simply banished from Leningrad for three years and allowed to enter other cities of their own volition. However, in reality they were sent away from Leningrad for ever: Leningrad was the second city on the "Minus Twelve" list, which comprised the 12 largest cities that were forbidden as places of residence in the future.

A circular "On the banishment of counter-revolutionary elements from Leningrad and its suburbs," issued by the NKVD chief department in the Leningrad Obl. on 27 February 1935, decreed that 5 thousand "former" families be made to leave Leningrad within one month.[116] The total of those tracked down—and ordered to be exiled by a Special NKVD Council[117]—constituted more than 11 thousand "former people," of whom 4,833 were "family heads," with 1,434 of them members of the nobility, 1,000 former tsarist military officers and 1,000 clerics. All these people were issued "trip" vouchers,[118] as NKVD officials put it.

As early as November 1929, Leningrad and the Leningrad Oblast were put on the list of places, where people that had been convicted by the Special Council were strictly prohibited from residing, even if they had lived there previously.[119]

A resolution of the Leningrad Oblast Communist Party Bureau on the banishment of Finnish population from the frontier zone (which was then adjacent to Leningrad on the northwest side), issued on 4 March 1935, was one of the first significant frontier "cleansing" measures. Some 200 thousand Ingermanland Finns (or Ingerians) were living in the oblast at that time. There was one Finnish national district (Kuyvazov) and scores of village councils, around 500 Finnish collective farms (that produced vegetables and milk for Leningrad residents), 322 Finnish schools, an agricultural technological college, a department of Finnish studies at the A. I. Gertsen Pedagogical Institute, and Finnish newspapers and publishing houses.

Almost all these organizations were liquidated in spring 1935. Finns residing within a 22 km-wide frontier zone (3,547 families) were the first to be banished. Those residing within a 100km-wide frontier zone in the Leningrad Obl. and within a 50km-wide frontier zone in Karelia were to be deported too, but as a matter of secondary importance. The "priority target group" was sent to Tajikistan (some 1,000 families), Kazakhstan and West Siberia (316 families from Karelia) between 1 and 25 April.[120] When it came to exiling the "secondary target group," 22 thousand people were banished from Kuyvazov district alone within 24 hours, thus bringing more than 100 villages to ruin (however, the destination was not particularly remote: the deportees were sent mainly to the Vologda Obl.).[121] The total number of the deported can be estimated at 30 thousand persons.

Significant deportation was also carried out in Ukraine in the spring of 1935 (between 20 February and 10 March): 41,650 persons, i.e., 8,329 families, were deported from Kiev and the Vinnitsa Obl. (that were adjacent to the border at that time) to the republic's eastern regions. Remarkably, Poles and Germans constituted around 60% of the resettled target group.[122] Approximately 1,500 additional families (almost all of them Polish) appear to have been banished in autumn 1935.[123]

Starting from January 1935, the Ukrainian and Kazakh NKVD leadership discussed plans to resettle another 15 thousand Polish and German households (approximately 45 thousand persons) from the Ukrainian frontier zone to Kazakhstan.[124] Germans and Poles (yet primarily all Poles) that resided within 800 meters of the then Polish state border were to be resettled, i.e., on the territory where the construction of military training grounds and fortifications was beginning. Apparently, the action was aimed at securing the building work from being observed by "undesirables," and yet the construction of an aircraft hanger, for example, was all but impossible to conceal as just on the other side of the border other Poles, often the locals' relatives, lived and looked on freely.

Judging by the date of the resolution (28 April), the target group in question was supposed to complete sowing their crops (it was stipulated that they be paid for the work), and they were not expected to produce a harvest at the place of destination. Apparently, it was presumed that they would have enough time to get prepared, move and settle at the new location during summer and early autumn.

The official idea was that the "resettled target groups" were not deprived of their citizenship rights. After all, it was only resettlement, nothing more drastic. They even retained the right to move around, but only within the boundaries of the destination administrative district. The destinations where they were settled followed the pattern of the existing NKVD labor settlements, and it was NKVD GULAG that was in charge of the arrangement of their housing, and the provision of employment (in agriculture) and initial bare essentials— which implied of course the resettlers' own contributions of finance and labor. In actuality, these were typically the true "special resettlers."[125] At destinations the resettlers were provided with land, collectivized livestock and equipment for establishing three MTSs (machine-tractor stations). Then agricultural cooperative associations were formed, exempted from all taxes and delivery plans for a three-year term. Privately owned livestock was allowed to be brought from home.[126]

In accordance with a resolution "On resettlers from Ukraine," of 16 February 1936, issued by the CP Central Committee and Council of People's Commissars of the Republic of Kazakhstan, 5,500 families were to be sent to the South Kazakhstan Obl., 3,000 families each to Alma-Ata and Karaganda Obls., 2,000 families to the East Kazakhstan Obl., and 100 to the Aktyubinsk Obl. The economic objectives that were pursued by this project included the expansion of areas used for sugar-beet harvesting, and the development of the sugar industry and tobacco-growing. A resolution on sugar-beet and tobacco-growing, adopted this time by the Council of People's Commissaries of the USSR, stipulated that Polish and German collective farm members be settled on the lands of three dairy and meat collective farms in Karaganda Obl.: Letovochnyi, Krasnoarmeysky, and Tarangulsky.[127] Apart from the Karaganda Obl., the reports also mention the North Kazakhstan Obl.

A letter from the deputy head of the NKVD GULAG of the USSR, I. I. Pliner, to people's commissar of internal affairs G. G. Yagoda, of 26 September 1936, concerned the resettlement of 15 thousand Polish and German families:

TO THE PEOPLE'S COMMISSARY OF INTERNAL AFFAIRS OF THE USSR, COMMISSARY-GENERAL OF THE STATE SECURITY G. G. YAGODA

Among the Polish and German families resettled from Western Ukraine to North Kazakhstan, 5,535 families, i.e., 26,778 persons, were resettled in June of the current year; 7,440 families, i.e., 32,740 persons, were delivered in September; making a total of 12,975 families, or 59,518 persons.

As of 20 September of the current year, 7,910 families, i.e., 37,213 persons, including those resettled in June, have arrived at the destinations.

Another 5,063 families, i.e., 22,045 persons, are being transported.

There are occurrences of scarlet fever, measles and typhus among the delivered resettlers.

In connection with the infectious diseases among the resettlers, orders were given to the NKVD of the UkSSR and the UNKVD of North Kazakhstan regarding the necessity to take decisive measures aimed at reinforcing prevention procedures at the places of departure, during transportation and at destinations.

Deputy head of the NKVD GULAG of the USSR, I. I. Pliner.

[signature]
26 September 1936

[Handwritten remarks over the text]:

The operation having been completed, a report for the Central Committee must be submitted.

[signature of Yagoda]

In two phases, in June and September 1936, 14,048 families were resettled and 37 new settlements founded.[128] According to N. F. Bugay, the first group of deportees comprised 35,829 Poles, including 23,334 adults, which equaled 10% of the population from within each district of departure. Only several dozen of them (apparently *nomenklatura* members and secret agents) moved to the RSFSR, while the rest of the target group were sent to Kazakhstan "on a state assignment" (and not only to the Karaganda and North

Kazakhstan Obls., but also to the Alma-Ata, Kokchetav and Taldy-Kurgan Obls.).[129]

Following the resolution of the All-Union Central Executive Committee and Council of People's Commissars of 17 July 1937, special defense zones, or border zones, were to be introduced along the USSR frontiers. In order to organize the zones, 1,325 Kurds were resettled from the frontier districts in Armenia and Azerbaijan in 1937, 812 of them were sent to the Kyrgyz Republic and 513 to Kazakhstan (as additional manpower for the soviet and collective farms in the Alma-Ata and South Kazakhstan Obls.).[130]

It was at the same time, in July 1937, that the Central Committee recalled the "extraterritorial enemies," namely Trotskyites and "subverters" and their family members. The latter, however, were (for some reason) allowed to choose their new place of residence if they used to live in capital cities or resort towns.[131]

However, it was not the western border areas that constituted the principal domain of the deportation activity, but the Far East. And it was Koreans—the first ethnic group in the USSR subjected to total deportation—that fell victims to the operations.

The first Koreans settled along the rivers Amur and Ussuri as early as the 19th century. After the year 1917, many Koreans moved to Primorsky Kray, in particular fleeing the occupation of their homeland by Japan. Following the Soviet annexation of the Far East Republic on 22 November 1922 and the declaration of all its residents as Soviet citizens, their numbers were replenished by a combination of Koreans, Chinese and Japanese. These people resided in the Posyet and Suchan districts (later united into the single Vladivostok district) and Suyfun district, Far East Kray. The Posyet national Korean district with its 55 Korean village councils was one of the 15 national districts located in the Far East Kray. These districts supplied at least half of the agricultural goods produced in the kray.

According to the USSR census of 1926, 169 thousand (compared to the 56 thousand in 1917[132]) Koreans, 77 thousand Chinese, and around 1 thousand Japanese were residing in the Far East Kray. The agricultural grounds Koreans possessed were relatively insignificant in size as compared to those owned by the Russian population, which all too often sparked conflict between the ethnic groups. Undoubtedly this fact played its role in determining the subsequent initial plans to deport Koreans beyond 48.5 north latitude.[133]

In 1937, when the borders had already been "locked down" and frontier infiltration stopped, according to the census later rejected as "defective," 167,259 Koreans resided on USSR territory (all of them in the Far East), approximately the same number as in 1926.[134] However, neglecting economic interests and only taking into account political considerations, the authorities found that the Koreans living in the Soviet Far East in the second half of the 1930s represented a threat to the region, and had to be resettled. Even more so as the Japanese had already started deporting Koreans from their border zone (to Sakhalin and inland in the Korean peninsula)—although they had a somewhat differing motive, namely, they regarded the Koreans as a "nutrient medium" for Soviet espionage.

On 23 April 1937, the newspaper *Pravda* exposed Japanese espionage in the Far East: Koreans and Chinese were made out to be key agents of the Japanese. In August 1937, the kray NKVD was headed by a not unknown figure, G. S. Lyushkov, a future defector.[135] In fact, he brought the resolution of the Council of People's Commissars and Communist Party Central Committee "On the banishment of the Korean population from the frontier zone of the Far East Kray", of 21 August 1937, which stipulated that the operation be completed by 1 January 1938. Remarkably, one of the items of the resolution read: "No obstacles must be put in the way of those resettled Koreans that wish to leave the country, crossing the border may be facilitated in such cases." Simultaneously, all Japanese citizens, including ethnic Koreans, were being expelled to Japan.

The first batch, 11,807 persons, possibly under direct suspicion of espionage, were deported. The total number of persons transported from Spassk, Posyet, Grodekovo, Birobidzhan and other places during September constituted 74,500. On 27–28 September 1937, the number of districts subjected to cleansing from Koreans enlarged to include Vladivostok, the Buryat–Mongol ASSR, the Chita Obl. and Khabarovsk Kray. Thus the second stage of the deportation of Koreans was sanctioned. For example, for the Khabarovsk Kray, where 1,155 Koreans resided (virtually all of them living in North Sakhalin), the time period set down for conducting the operation was two weeks, from 5 to 20 October.[136]

The Far East bodies went about their task, although it had been amplified, long before New Year's Eve, namely, as early as 25 October 1937. But in that time frame, 36,442 Korean households, or 171,781

persons, were transported from the kray in 124 trains (only 700 Koreans, fewer than those needed to fill one train, still remained in the
kray, and not for long). The train's passengers were drawn up according to the principles of "economically established groups." Along with
Koreans, 7 thousand Chinese, several hundreds each of ethnic Germans, Poles and Baltic nationals, and some 1 thousand Harbin repatriates were "collected."

In 1937 the resettled families were still paid compensation,
although a minimal one. The average total paid to a family constituted 6 thousand rubles, which covered travel expenses, crops left
behind, buildings, equipment and other utensils, a loan for building
a house at the place of destination, and even expenditures to get settled at new locations![137]

The way was long (in average around a month) and exhausting.
The majority of resettlers disembarked in Kazakhstan (20,170 families, or 95,526 persons), mainly in cities and small towns. In particular 9,350 persons stepped off the trains in North Kazakhstan, in settlements populated by Polish and German resettlers from the USSR's
western borders. The rest remained in Uzbekistan (16,272 families,
or 76,525 persons), some in the Central Asian republics, and even a
small number in the Stalingrad Obl. Part of the group were still forced
to move within Uzbekistan, since navigation on the Amu-Darya and
Aral Sea was closed (as a result they were settled in 44 instead of
7 districts).

The resettlers were faced with continental frosts, negligence and
the irresponsibility of local authorities (for example, the 4 thousand
Koreans who arrived on 31 December 1937 in Kustanay spent about
one week in their carriages before there was any sign of activity from
local authorities). There was a lack of housing, water, food, medicines,
and often an absence of any employment in the early stages (even a
threat of starvation emerged in a number of places). Collective farmers (since they received some food products and money as a payment
before the resettlement) were in a slightly better situation as compared to urban employees and workers, who found themselves in dire
circumstances (their payments were to be delayed until spring, yet in
reality they had not been fully compensated by the fall of 1938). And
yet economic life gradually took shape: Korean collective farms were
engaged in rice and vegetable growing and fishing and to a lesser
extent in cotton growing and cattle farming, albeit on a less nomadic

basis (persistent and unsuccessful efforts were made to adapt them for this trade).

Entire districts in the Far East were thus deserted. The Red Army and border guard detachments appropriated the best buildings, schools. However, it was not easy to populate the deserted lands, in spite of the fact that a special Resettlement Department was founded within the local NKVD. Some people came from the European part of the country, some after the 1936 demobilization from the army. It was planned to resettle 17.1 thousand peasant households to the Far East, in particular 7.5 thousand to the Far East Kray (in 1938 the kray itself was divided into two: Primorsky Kray and Khabarovsk Kray). In reality, only 1,027 families moved there in 1938, and a total of nearly 3.7 thousand households over the period of 1937–1939. That being so, the authorities failed to compensate the demographic and economic damage caused by the deportation of Koreans. Nor was it done during the war years, when evacuated target groups arrived: almost 17 thousand out of the 27 thousand that had been transported there actually remained in the kray.

The resettlement of Koreans and their concentration in Central Asia was continued in the war and post-war years. Small numbers of Koreans were brought in from the Murmansk and Stalingrad (Astrakhan) Obls. On 10 January 1943, a State Defense Committee resolution was issued stipulating that some 8 thousand Koreans be demobilized from the army and subsequently recruited to labor battalions and transport convoys (the Koreans were sent to the mines of Mosbass). After the war, these and other Korean labor army [trudarmiya] members were resettled to locations where the majority of Koreans were concentrated. But it is not quite clear what happened to the Koreans that were left on the Sakhalin Island by the Japanese after the USSR annexed this territory.

The question concerning the status of the deported Koreans did and still does incite arguments. In fact, their way of living did not differ from that typical of "special settlements" at all. And yet, although it was precisely the term "special resettlers" that was often used in the correspondence between the NKVD and Council of People's Commissars when referring to the banished Koreans, they were not regarded as special settlers in strict formal terms. Besides, they were not considered exiled administratively either, since their banishment was not motivated by repression but resulted from "forced cleansing" of the territories adjacent to the border with Japan that had occupied Korea and Manchuria. Within the legal files that existed in the 1930s, any restriction on movement was illegal with regard to Koreans. Even an order circulated by L. Beria on 2 July 1945 within the NKVD, by which the Koreans were to be registered as "special resettlers" (for a term of five years with a special stamp in their passports), was not backed by a corresponding resolution of the Council of People's Commissars or a USSR Supreme Soviet Presidium decree. Subsequently, the issue of this absurd "formality" remained a hotly debated issue among NKVD-related circles until 1949. The matter was resolved on a practical level only when MVD minister S. N. Kruglov signed a directive on 3 March 1947 that provided for the issuing of new passports to Koreans, giving them the right to reside within Central Asia, with the exception of border territories.

Of course, apart from the "frontier cleansing" along the western and eastern borders of the USSR in 1937–1938, similar operations were carried out in the south, in particular on the territories adjacent to Turkey, Iran and Afghanistan. Special banned zones were organized in July 1937 in Central Asia and the Caucasus; and the population was to be driven out. A total of 40 border districts of Georgia, Armenia, Azerbaijan, Turkmenistan, Uzbekistan and Tajikistan were assigned to be cleansed of "unreliable elements." In particular, 1,325 Kurds that had resided in the frontier zone were resettled to Kyrgyz Republic and Kazakhstan.[138] At the end of 1937, 1,121 Kurd and Armenian families from Armenia and Azerbaijan arrived in Kazakhstan (Alma-Ata and South Kazakhstan Obls.).[139]

According to available data, the total number of the "new target groups" of those deported in 1933–1937 can be estimated as 260 thousand persons. The overwhelming majority of them were resettled in the course of "frontier cleansing" operations, with two-thirds falling under the operation on resettling Koreans.

In terms of forced migrations, the years 1938 and 1939 proved to be relatively quiet. On 19 January 1938 a decision was taken to resettle 2 thousand Iranian families (or 6 thousand persons) to the Alma-Ata and South Kazakhstan Obls. of Kazakhstan,[140] that had received Soviet citizenship from frontier districts of Azerbaijan. Another example concerns the Iranian Jews from the Mary Obl. of Turkmenistan, who were deported to the northern deserted part of the oblast in 1938, a barren zone scarcely fit for human habitation.

However, that was just a sinister respite. The situation changed dramatically when the Second World War began, and the geopolitical conspiracy played out between the USSR and Germany sealed the fates of the Eastern European countries and the populations living in them.

NOTES

1 Tsutsiyev, 1998, 49–50.

2 For example, in March 1919 S. I. Syrtsov, head of the Civil Department of the Donburo, demanded that all male Cossacks aged 18–55 should be sent to Voronezh Gub. and other regions to be subjected to forced labor. Simultaneously, the resettlement of peasants from Central Russia to the Don region was being planned—and carried out! As early as April 1919 first 700 settlers arrived from Tver, Cherepovets, and Olonets Gub., and were later apparently destroyed to a single person by White Cossacks.

3 Kokhanovskaya *stanitsa*, already destroyed at the time, is more likely to be meant here (see Tsutsiyev, 1998, 180).

4 See Bugay, 1994a.

5 See Bugay, 1994a. S. Aliyeva cites the figure of 70 thousand Cossacks as deported to Kazakhstan and the Urals (Aliyeva, 1993, vol. 1, 27, citing a publication by *Nezavisimaya Gazeta* dated 12 May 1991). At the same time, it should be noted that attempts to interpret the Cossack deportations as a component of the Bolshevik policy aimed at "resolving the Russian question" in the Caucasus, as "Russophobia," and even "genocide of the Russian people" (see, for example, Bugay, Gonov, 1998, 81–103) are not convincing enough. Nevertheless, such rhetoric is widely used for overtly chauvinistic provocations, which is not only regrettable but also precarious.

6 The practice of deletion of any geographic, literary or physical mention. The denial of the very existence of a people and nation.

7 In accordance with an order issued by the Central Executive Committee of the Gorsky Republic on 25 April 1922 (Tsutsiyev, 1998, 180).

8 See Genis, 1998, 44–58; see also Martin, 1998, 827, citing materials from GARF (h. 3316, r. 64, f. 177, 220; h. 1235, r. 140, f. 127).

9 The steamer "Oberbürgermeistr Chaken" with Moscow and Kazan scholars (30 or 33 persons, some 70 including the family members) onboard departed on 28 September 1922 and arrived at its destination on 30 September 1922; the steamer "Preussen" carrying Petrograd scholars aboard (17 persons, 44 including the family members) departed on 15 November 1922 and arrived on 18 November 1922. All the deportees had been arrested first (see Khoruzhiy, S. S., *Posle pereryva: Sledy russkoy filosofii* [After a Break: Traces of Russian Philosophy] (Saint Petersburg, 1994), 188–208; Geler, M., "Pervoye preduprezhdeniye: Udar khlysta" [The First Warning: A Lash], *Vestnik russkogo studencheskogo khristianskogo dvizheniya* (Paris, 1979), no.127, 187–232).

10 The personalized nature of this expulsion places it somewhat aside from the bulk of the depurations considered in this study.

11 See Zaytsev, 1993, 104–106. With regard to banishment and exile by a court decree, actions of convicts and the administration were administered under a special resolution issued by the USSR Central Executive Committee and Council of People's Commissars on 10 January 1930 (See ibid., 106–107).

12 See Martin, 1998, p. 825, citing Anosov, D., *Koreytsy v Ussuriyskom kraye* [Koreans in Ussuri Kray] (Khabarovsk, Vladivostok, 1928), 6–7; and GARF, h. 1235, r. 120, f. 60, sh. 17–20.

13 See Martin, 1998, p. 825 citing GARF, h. 3316, r. 16a, f. 384, sh. 41–42; h. 1235, r. 141, f. 1356, sh. 18–19, etc. (Since the exact date of this operation is missing, there is no reference to it in supplement 1.)

14 In particular, he addressed the cases of Jews, Gypsies, and Kalmyks. See Martin, 1998, 825 citing GARF, h. 1235, r. 128, f. 2, sh. 110, 166; r. 141, f. 1531, sh. 103.

15 See Martin, 1998, 829–832.

16 One can talk about a certain connection between this principle and such theoretical constructs of Bolshevism (or at least of its Trotskyite variety) as "instigating the world fire," or in other words, exporting the revolution beyond Russia's borders. It is not a mere coincidence that, as T. Martin himself remarks, the Comintern and national communist parties were the most ardent supporters of the "Principle of Piedmont" in their actual political activities.

17 Read more on this in the previous chapter and below (in this chapter).

18 The regions, the reclaiming of which was considered indispensable but impossible to carry out based on the "planned–voluntary" principle, were subject to overtly forced reclaiming (Kolyma is one classical example).

19 RGAE, h. 5675, r. 1, f. 2, 3, 4.

20 It should be noted that the entire urban industry of the country in 1926 had capacities sufficient to employ only 0.4 million of the countryside population.

21 See Kalinin, M. I. and P. S. Smidovich, *O zemel'nom ustroystve trudyashchikhsya yevreyev v SSSR* [On the settling of working Jews in the USSR] (Moscow, 1927).

22 See Abramsky, Ch., "The Biro–Bidzhan Project," in Kochan, L. (ed.), *The Jews in Soviet Russia since 1917* (Oxford, 1978), 74.

23 See Kurbanova, 1993, 61–64.

24 See Kurbanova, 1993, 66–67, citing TsGA RT [Central Archives of the Republic of Tajikistan), h. 18, r. 3, f. 14, sh. 9.

25 See Kurbanova, 1993, 73, citing AKPT [Archives of the Communist Party of Tajikistan), h. 3, r. 6, f. 306, sh. 10–11.

26 See Kurbanova, 1993, 75–77.

27 See Krasilnikov, 1991, 183–185. The only dissonant voice was that of A. Solts: "We punish for any trifle... The NKYust and NKVD aim at turning our confinement facilities into commercial enterprises."

28 RGAE, h. 5675, r. 1, f. 9, sh. 1–2.

29 It was the speech Stalin made at a conference of Marxist agrarians on 27 December 1929 that triggered the process. A resolution "On the rate of col-

lectivization and state assistance for the organization of *kolkhozy*" was issued by the Communist Party Central Committee Politburo on 5 January 1930 and legally adopted on 1 February 1930 by the All-Union Central Executive Committee and Council of People's Commissars of the USSR in the form of a resolution "On measures for the reinforcement of the socialist restructuring of agricultural production in the regions subject to blanket collectivization, and for fighting kulaks."

30 Following T. Martin, let us note that the very notions of "border" and "frontier" had various implications at the time. Different types, regimes and corresponding widths (500 or 800m, or 7.5, 16, or 22km) of frontiers were officially recognized in 1923. From the perspective of deportation policy, the most relevant type of frontier is the one with the width of 22km. i.e., the area where population was deported from within the strategy of "border zone cleansing." (See Martin, 1998, 830, citing GARF, h. 3316, r. 16a, f. 22, sh. 3–12; RGASPI, h. 17, r. 3, f. 339, protocol 53, item 6.)

31 RGAE, h. 5675, r. 1, f. 43.

32 See Martin, 1998, 840–842.

33 A special classified instruction dated 4 February 1930 was drafted by the All-Union Central Executive Committee and Council of People's Commissars.

34 Ivnitsky, 1996, 127.

35 Ivnitsky, 1996, 228, citing GARF, h. 393, r. 2, f. 1796, sh. 306. Approximately this number of kulaks (around 55 thousand families) were transported to the North Kray in 1930–1931 (ibid., 192–194)

36 The dekulakization and banishment of the kulaks of the third category was postponed until fall (Ivnitsky, 1996, 130).

37 Ivnitsky, 1996, 69–70.

38 Ivnitsky, 1996, 133.

39 At first the OGPU asked for up to 100 thousand households to be received. The North Kray committee agreed to receive 50–70 thousand under a number of conditions, in particular that the resettled be put in scarcely populated areas that were experiencing shortage of labor force and that "hunger rations" be provided to them at the initial stage. (See the letter to L. M. Kaganovich by S. A. Bergavinov of 14 January 1930, cited by Ivnitsky, 1996, 132.)

40 Kazakhstan and Siberia were included in the list following Stalin's personal order.

41 Ivnitsky, 1996, 227–229.

42 In Parabel district or Chae-Parabel territory, with the rivers Vakh, Tym, and Ket.

43 See a report note by Siberian GPU deputy director Nikitin to Ryndin, USSR NKZ department for settlements, dated 7 February 1930 (RGAE, h. 5675, op.1, f.43. sh. 26–27). Cf. also a letter by Tomsk Okrug Communist Party committee secretary, Nusinov and Tomsk Okrug executive committee chairman, Reshchikov to West Siberia Kray Communist Party Committee secretary, R. I. Eikhe and kray executive committee chairman Klimenko, dated 7 March 1930 mentioning 20 thousand kulak households, i.e., 100 thousand people subject to transference from various Siberian regions to the Narym

region in 1930 (Maksheyev, 1997, 15–16, citing GANO, h. 47, r. 5, f. 104, sh. 153–154). The Center had also insisted on the settling of 18.5 thousand families expelled from the border areas of Ukraine and Belorussia to Siberia, and recommended that they be settled in the northern areas of the Yenisei and Ob river basins (Ivnitsky, 1996, 230).

44 Ivnitsky, 1996, 235.

45 Ivnitsky, 1996, 133–134. Further on, Kazakhstan was included in the plan again, and some regions were added.

46 The commission also included OGPU deputy chairman S. A. Messing, People's Commissar of Internal Affairs V. N. Tolmachev, S. S. Lobov (Supreme Soviet for People's Economy), A. I. Muralov (Narkomzem) and others. The commission was also assigned to deal with the question of central budget financing of the resettlement of the third category of kulaks, which was soon resolved negatively (Ivnitsky, 1996, 231–232).

47 Ivnitsky, 1996, 233–234. Cf. a somewhat different figure for inter-regional deportees: 342, 545 persons (Ivnitsky, 1996, 140).

48 All special settlements were transferred under the OGPU charge on 20 May 1931. On 25 Oktober 1931, G. Yagoda and OGPU prosecutor Katanyan issued a "Tentative resolution on the rights of settlement administrations in the special settlement districts." In particular, the document stipulated that OGPU *komendatura*s exercise administrative control of the settlements, and of organizing labor and everyday activities of the settlers. Settlement *komendatura*s were subordinated either directly to special resettlement departments at the plenipotentiary OGPU agencies or district *komendatura*s (depending on the local administrative structure). Apart from their special and economic functions in special settlements, *komendatura*s were also in charge of routine administrative duties pertinent to *selsovety*, i.e., common Soviet authority bodies; in this case they were working under the supervision of district *ispolkomy* [executive committees].

49 Ivnitsky, 1996, 242–243.

50 In the North Kray, the established upper limit for the size of settlements equaled 120 households (Ivnitsky, 1996, 232).

51 Ivnitsky, 1996, 142–146.

52 Although, some parameters were defined regarding the settlements belonging to this category: they were to comprise 20 through 100 households structured similarly to *khutor*s; and—expectably—lands allotted to them were to be of worse quality (See Ivnitsky, 1996, 237–241).

53 See Ivnitsky, 1996, 238.

54 See Ivnitsky, 1996, 240.

55 See Ivnitsky, 1996, 149.

56 This made 1/5 of all those dekulakized in 1930 (in spring the resettlement was halted due to the start of crop sowing and the "extremes" of the process of collectivization and dekulakization).

57 See Ivnitsky, 1996, 146–147, 240–241.

58 See Ivnitsky, 1996, 180–181.

59 See Ivnitsky, 1996, 242.

60 Krasilnikov, 1991, 188. In 1931, the OGPU GULAG embraced nearly the entire technological cycle of labor employment, having founded a three-layer contract system efficient in its own way (at the upper level, GULAG concluded contracts with corresponding top bodies, at the middle level it was government agencies and trusts that signed contracts with territorial GULAG branches, and at the lower level special *komendaturas* made deals with enterprises, such as timber-production plants or mines).

61 See Ivnitsky, 1996, 186–188. In Central Asia, the majority of *bai* [kulaks] were to be resettled within their districts but on lands of poor quality.

62 Meaning 350 and 450 kulaks belonging to the first and second categories respectively that were banished to Kazakhstan. (See Ivnitsky, 1996, 189.)

63 For example, 100 kulak households of German colonists were to be resettled from the Prigorodnyi district of Leningrad Obl. Apart from 5 thousand families that were to be deported to the Urals, another 4 thousand families were planned to be resettled within the oblast, in particular to turn their labor to extracting apatite at the Khibiny mountains and working at Nivstroi. Simultaneously, settling in the 150–200km frontier zone was strictly prohibited, for example, at Sinyavinsky peat fields near Schlisselburg (See Ivnitsky, 1996, 185, 190.)

64 The commission convened weekly. Among other members of the commission were Communist Party Central Committee Secretary P. P. Postyshev and OGPU Deputy Chairman Yagoda. On 5 October 1931 Andreyev's position in the Commission was taken over by Ya. E. Rudzutak, deputy chairman of the Council of People's Commissars and USSR Labor and Defense Council [*Sovet truda i oborony SSSR*], and head of the Communist Party Central Committee and People's Commissar of Workers and Peasants' Inspection of the USSR. It was only in March 1932 that the Commission was dissolved.

65 Kargasok, Parabel, Kolpashevo, Chainsky, Krivosheino, Baksinsky, Novo-Kuslovsky, Zyryansky and other districts (see Ivnitsky, 1996, 182–183; Adibekov, 1994, 153). Interestingly, the kray OGPU branch did not stop when the planned 40 thousand households were delivered to the destination by 1 June. It continued to resettle an additional 47 thousand households, without even asking for Moscow's authorization, which induced an "angry bark" from Moscow (see OGPU letter from Yagoda and Yevdokimov to Zakovsky OGPU plenipotentiary in the West Siberia Kray from 4.07.1931, in Krasilnikov, Kuznetsova, 1993, citing GARF, h. 9479, r. 1, f. 3, sh. 60). Nevertheless, some 10 thousand families (kulaks of the second category, and first-category kulak family members were deported from Bashkiria and the Moscow Obl. in July. All of them were employed in Kuzbass, namely, in Kuznetskstroy, Prokopievsky and the mines of Anzhero-Sudzhensk (ibid., citing GARF, h. 9479, r. 1, f. 3, sh. 66).

66 Danilov, Krasilnikov, 1993, 4.

67 Adibekov, 1994, 146–155.

68 Adibekov, 1994, 158. Interestingly, the resettlement of 4 thousand kulak families from Leningrad Obl. to Kazakhstan was cancelled. Instead they were sent to northern parts of the oblast to be employed at the Nivstroy and apatite

mines at the Khibiny mountains (Adibekov, 1994, 159, citing RGASPI, h. 17, r. 162, f. 10, sh. 68, 74).

69 Danilov, Invnitsky, 1989, 39.

70 It was planned to move 55 thousand families to the Urals in 1931: 30 thousand from Ukraine, 15 thousand from the North Caucasus and 5 thousand each from Belorussia and the Ivano-Voznesensk Obl. (see Ivnitsky, 1996, 191–192).

71 See the "Protocol of the sitting of A. A. Andreyev's Commission" of 15 May 1931 (Adibekov, 1994, 155, citing RGASPI, h. 17, r. 162, f. 10, sh. 51–54). The commission addressed Soyuzlesprom, Tsvetmetalzoloto and lumber enterprises pointing to the "inadmissible situation with regard to the economic use of the 'special resettlers,' ...with their placement and accommodation, supplies and wage payment..." as a "result of entire negligence" (ibid., 161–164).

72 The annual balance in hand between the salary deductions and expenditures on administrative apparatus and administrative services for labor settlers was quite a significant one (See Zemskov, 1994, 119–120).

73 Adibekov, 1994, 146.

74 Adibekov, 1994, 160. The completion of the mass kulak banishment was also specified by an "Instruction on the procedure of further banishment of kulak households" of 23 August 1931 (Adibekov, 1994, 171–172, citing RGASPI, h. 17, r. 162, f. 10, sh. 176, 180–181. Adopted by the Communist Party Central Committee Politburo on 30 August 1931).

75 Ivnitsky, 1996, 194–195.

76 Ivnitsky, 1996, 194.

77 Zemskov, 1994, 118, citing GARF, h. 9479, r. 1, f. 89, sh. 205 (in his earlier research, Zemskov refers to a somewhat different figure: 384,334 families; see Zemskov, 1990, 3). The number of those who arrived at destinations always was lower than the initial number of deportees, due to the high mortality rate during the transportation and escapes.

78 See the summing-up table "Deportations of peasants in 1930–1931" (Ivnitsky, 1996, 192–194).

79 RGANI, h. 89, op. 16, f. 1. sh. 7. See also: Ivanova, 1997, 87, citing Zemskov, 1994, 146. As of 1 March 1940, the GULAG supervised 53 camps (including camps engaged in railway construction), 425 IPL [correctional labor camps] or correctional labor colonies (including 170 industrial ones, 83 agricultural and 172 "counter-agent" ones, i.e., with labor force employed at the enterprises or construction sites of other ministries and organizations), and 50 reformatories for underage offenders. In addition, there were BIRs ("Bureaus for Correctional Work") that provided "employment" for prisoners rather than their "isolation." By this time, the total of GULAG prisoners had risen more than six times as compared to the corresponding figure of 1932, to reach 1,668.2 million persons, including 352 thousand IPL inmates, with 192 thousand of the latter kept in industrial and agricultural IPLs. Remarkably, the total number of the USSR population in 1940 equaled 194,077 thousand persons, in other words, GULAG prisoners made up 0.86% of the country's population, which means that almost every hundredth citizen was deprived of citizen's rights! No doubt not all of them were "political" prisoners, yet it was

"counter-revolutionary" activity that took first place in the crime structure making up 28% of the total (another 5.4% of criminal "violators of the established authority" should be added to this).

80 It was in this *komendatura* that a spontaneous rebellion of special settlers flared up in late July 1931 (See Danilov and Krasilnikov, 1993, 8).

81 See corresponding resolutions of the Communist Party Central Committee Politburo of 28 December 1931 (Maksheyev, 1997, 17–18).

82 Danilov, Krasilnikov, 1993, 4.

83 Ivnitsky, 1996, 196.

84 It is not quite clear whether the "local" western Siberian kulaks are included in this estimate. Voices advocating their resettlement to more remote okrugs and imposing the status of special resettlers on them were especially insistent in 1933 (see Maksheyev, 1997, 47, quoting TsDNI TO, h. 206, r. 1, f. 15, sh. 7).

85 Interestingly, Central Asia did not host a single resettler in 1933!

86 Ivnitsky, 1996, 202. Among them were 999 kulak families, i.e., 5,317 persons from Daghestan and Checheno-Ingushetia, who were transported to *sovkhozy* in Kirgizia and Kazakhstan as special labor settlers (see a letter by the deputy head of the NKVD GULAG, I. I. Pliner, to people's commissar of internal affairs, Yezhov, and his deputies Agranov and Berman, of 07 November 1936: GARF, h. 9479, r. 1, f. 36, sh. 33).

87 All former Communists convicted for undermining grain procurement were banished to northern oblasts on a par with kulaks (Ivnitsky, 1996, 215).

88 See Ivnitsky, 1996, 203–225. Among the punishments, the law specified a firing squad execution and did not provide for amnesty.

89 See Zelenin, 1989, 11; Ivnitsky, 1996, 211. N. V. Palibin (possibly mistakenly) presents a somewhat different list of *stanitsa* settlements included in the black list: Temirgoyevskaya, Umanskaya and Poltavskaya. While describing the process of resettlement from the *stanitsa* of Poltavskaya, which he had witnessed, the researcher stressed that *kolkhoz* members—middle-income and poor peasants—were subjected to banishment too, under the threat of being shot at that. See order No.1 of 17 December 1932 by Kabayev, the commandant of the *stanitsa* of Poltavskaya, Slavyansky district, North Caucasus Kray, on the banishment of all *stanitsa* residents—excepting "those that have actively demonstrated their faithfulness—for sabotaging economic measures carried out by the Soviet authorities" (Palibin, 1988, 152–153, 193–196). The same operation appears to be referred to by T. Martin, but he writes about some 60 thousand Kuban Cossacks banished in January 1933 (Martin, 1998, 946–947, quoting RGVA, h. 9, r. 36, f. 613, sh. 6, 46; and Oskolkov, Ye. N., *Golod 1932–1933: Khlebozagotovki i golod 1932–1933 v Severo-Kavkazskom kraye* [Famine 1932–1933: Grain procurement and famine in 1932–1933 in the North Caucasus Kray] (Rostov-on-Don, 1991), 55–60).

90 Forced resettlement of demobilized soldiers had already been practiced—at least in 1929–1930, when the idea of establishing "Red Army collective farms" along the USSR frontiers was being worked over. For example, in 1931 the Communist Party Central Committee and the Central Asian Bureau of the Communist Party Central Committee adopted a resolution on sending two

regiments of demobilized soldiers to Tajikistan for the construction of the
Vakhshsky irrigation system (Kurbanova, 1993, 59).

91 Ivnitsky, 1996, 224.

92 It would be more appropriate to use the word "saddling"!

93 Abylkhozhayev, Kozybayev, Tatimov, 1989, 67–69.

94 In 1926–1939, the number of Kazakhs dropped by 867.4 thousand to constitute only 3,100.9 thousand persons (see Zelenin, 1989, 6). Cf. another
estimate: 1,321 thousand persons, in Abylkhozhayev, Kozybayev, Tatimov,
1989, 65–67.

95 See Osokina, 1991. Interestingly, the data on the natural birth rate in Kazakhstan did not appear in the central statistics agencies at all.

96 RGAE, h. 5675, op. 1, f. 57, sh. 29.

97 The transportation was organized poorly, which was the reason why many
resettlers arrived at the destination points suffering pediculosis or scabies
(RGAE, h. 5675, op. 1, f. 43, sh. 23–25).

98 See the letter of the North Caucasus Kray Resettlement Committee to Comrade Rud, Central Resettlement Committee, of 28 November 1933 (RGAE,
h. 5675, op. 1, f. 56, sh. 41).

99 For example: "We wanted to cancel our registration, but we were not given
permission. They say we are now local residents, but we do not want to be.
We decided to leave, took our registration cards, but then we were detained,
all our documents were taken from us, and we were told that we could not
go anywhere. We said we are not going to live here. Then we were arrested
and they told us they would prosecute us. They threatened they would
deprive us of all political rights. They say they do not care that we served in
the army. In general, we are unhappy..." (A letter to the people's commissar
of the army and navy from Red Army service members I. S. Krynin,
N. P. Strafilov and N. A. Agapov, of 10 November 1933, *stanitsa* Novo-Mal-
orossiyskaya, Tikhoretsk district (RGAE, h. 5675, op. 1, f. 56).

100 See a letter of the plenipotentiary of the Kray Resettlement Committee of the
Communist Party Central Committee, O. Shadunets, to Communist Party
Central Committee Secretary Zhdanov of 25 September 1934 (RGAE,
h. 5675, op. 1, f. 55, sh. 32–34).

101 RGAE, h. 5675, op. 1, f. 55, sh. 35–37.

102 RGAE, h. 5675, op. 1, f. 185.

103 See supplement 2.

104 RGAE, h. 5675, op. 1, f. 196, sh. 26. The nature of such "recruitment" is
revealed, for example, in the report of 9 August 1938 submitted by inspector
D. N. Yankov to the assistant of the NKVD Resettlement Department Head
Grinberg: "Regarding the recruitment of Red Army soldiers from the Transbaykal military district, an address was written by me, signed by the assistant
of the UNKVD Resettlement Department Head Comrad Slyusarenko, and
sent to the Political Department of the Transbaykal military district on 20
July this year. On 28 June this year, before leaving Chita, I had spoken to
Comrade Leonov, division commissar of the Political Department, who told
me that military unit commissars were given the task to carry out recruit-

ment. He cannot shorten the terms for recruitment, he alleges he does not know himself. He cannot release soldiers before they complete their military training either. It is regiment commissar Comrade Sorokin, deputy head of the Political Department, who is in charge of recruitment issues" (RGAE, h. 5675, op. 1, f. 196, sh. 136). The same report refers to poor preparedness of Chita Obl. districts for receiving resettlers: "Many district Executive Committee chairmen took to deceiving us instead of implementing concrete measures in order to insure timely housing and dependency repair work... In many collective and soviet farms resettlers occupy leading positions. In some districts a number of resettlers were banished from frontier zones as people's enemies on the charges of espionage. In order to reveal the reasons for reversing the economic status of resettlers, it is necessary that resettlers be subjected to indiscriminate investigation and the issue be specifically raised in the oblast organizations. Without undertaking these steps and examining the roots of reversal, it will be difficult to carry out further resettlement, and the government expenditures on these purposes will not be justified. In essence, what we have today is a human conveyor system: some resettlers leave *kolkhozy* and then we place other resettlers into their houses."

105 Maksheyev, 1997, 52–65. There is also a reference to a letter written by Velichko to Stalin, Secretary R. I. Eykhe, and Narym Okrug Communist Party Committee secretary K. I. Levits, on 22 August 1933, which evoked a response in the form of a report by a commission of the West Siberia Kray committee concerning the horrendous fate of 6,114 persons transported as declassed elements by two trains from Moscow and Leningrad on 29 April 1933 and 30 April 1933 and brought via Tomsk and then by barges to the island of Nazino on the Ob river opposite to the estuary of the Nazina river on 18 May 1933 and 26 May 1933 respectively (no more than 2 thousand people survived the transportation, and the island itself was nicknamed Death Island or the Island of Cannibals). The report confirmed the facts rendered by Velichko and provided the following statistics in addition: the commission received 914 notifications regarding those banished erroneously. Some 174 out of 840 living people that underwent examination by the commission were immediately released, and 231 persons were sent to Novosibirsk for additional check-up; 240 inquiries were submitted for a check-up in the Siblag apparatus, 51 of them were declined. There is an enclosed list of 22 typical cases of wrongly banished persons. Among them are both Moscow residents and people who came from other cities, who were on their way for vacations or visiting Moscow on business. They would be seized while getting off a tram, or at their work places, at a bakery shop, at a railway station, or simply out in the street after watching a theatre performance; as a rule, they had passports or collective farm identification cards on them (GANO, h. 3-P, r. 1, f. 540a, sh. 89–100, 132–151).

106 Bugay, 1992, 42, quoting GARF, h. 3316, r. 2, f. 1668, sh. 1.

107 One department, whose title underwent constant changes, was "in charge" of these resettlers. The NKVD Resettlement Department was first established on 22 July 1936 under the supervision of the Council of People's

Commissars-controlled All-Union Resettlement Committee (it was chaired by I. I. Pliner in 1937–1938); on 9 August 1939 the department was transferred from under NKVD supervision to that of the Council of People's Commissars Resettlement Committee. The services for special settlers were organized by an NKVD Department for special settlements founded on 28 August 1941 and dissolved on 14 November 1942 (headed by I. V. Ivanov); its functions were taken over by an NKVD GULAG department for labor and special settlements. The NKVD–MVD department for special settlements was restored on 17 March 1944 and subsequently it was named the 9th MGB department—from 16 November 1950; MVD "P" department—from 14 March 1953; and the MVD 4th special department—from 30 October 1954. The department was dissolved on 27 March 1959, and its functions were taken over by the MVD chief militia department (see Kokurin, Petrov, 1997).

108 Gradually the significance of these "two powers" declined, as by 1 October 1944 the number of labor settlers in Novosibirsk Obl. constituted 170,645, or only some 5 thousand more than in Kazakhstan, while the total of labor settlers in Sverdlovsk Obl. was only 86,640 persons (Zemskov, 1994, 18).

109 See Zemskov, 1994.

110 Statistically this group consisted of two: arrivers from the regions and from organizations (for example, former GULAG prisoners transferred to settlements after serving their terms in camps), the data concerning the latter group though are available only starting from 1934 (see Zemskov, 1994, 124–125).

111 Apparently the remaining share consisted of "lumber," i.e., non-working women with young babies, the elderly and disabled. The NKVD regarded them exclusively as "*komendatura* dependants" and proposed that they be "dispersed" before their release from exile (see, for example, the order by the deputy head of the OTP of the UNKVD of East Siberia Kray, Anastasenko, and first department chief, Gladyshev, to Narym Okrug Communist Party Committee secretary, K. I. Levits of 2 January 1935, in Maksheyev, 1997, 76–77).

112 As a rule, this implied a transfer, a merely formal and temporary one, of a part of a special contingent from under OGPU control to another agency's supervision (for example, Narkomles [commissariat for timber harvesting]).

113 Zemskov, 1991b, 74–75.

114 Nonetheless, one cannot help admitting that T. Martin was right to note a closer—than it is generally perceived—link between the dekulakization and ethnicity. Particular peoples, especially Germans or Poles, were treated as kulaks almost indiscriminately, and even Russians, when judged against Koreans or Kazakhs, appeared kulak. Among those banished as kulaks from Belorussia or Ukraine, the number of Poles was disproportionately high, and some anti-kulak operations targeted Poles almost exclusively (Martin, 1998, 837–840).

115 See, for example, draft resolutions of the All-Union Central Executive Committee and Council of People's Commissars of the USSR "On the introduc-

tion of a universal passport system in the cities of the USSR" (RGANI, h. 89, op. 48, f. 25. sh. 1–2).

116 Ivanov, 1998, 118–119.

117 The mere fact of "individual" decision-making is supposed to situate this category apart from those repressed that can be considered forced migrants, however all other attributes, including the "list nature" of the repression are perfectly in place in this case.

118 Ivanov, 1998, 119.

119 Ivanov, 1998, 130.

120 See Bugay, 1991e.

121 See Kiuru, 1992; also see Martin, 1998, 249–250.

122 In particular, 2,886 Polish and 1,903 German families. Simultaneously, Polish and German national districts Marchlewski and Pulin (both located in Volyn) were liquidated. See Martin, 1998, 848–849, quoting GARF, h. 5446, r. 16a, f. 265, sh. 14. See also Brul, 1999, 97, quoting Yevtukh, V. and V. Chirko, *Nimtsi na Ukrayini (1920s–1990s)* [Germans in Ukraine (1920s–1990s)] (Kiev, 1994), 47. Unlike T. Martin, V. Brul writes about deportation to Siberia, not to eastern Ukraine.

123 See Martin, 1998, 848–849, quoting GARF, h. 5446, r. 16a, f. 265, sh. 14–15.

124 See Eisfeld, Herdt, 1996, 25–27. According to some sources, 63,976 persons were resettled in actuality (see Brul, 1999, 98, quoting *Iz istorii nemtsev Kazakhstana (1921–1935)* [From The history of Germans of Kazakhstan (1921–1935)] [Alma-Aty—Moscow, 1997], 85).

125 Their status as "special resettlers" was confirmed in 1952 by an order of the MGB and GP No. 001871164cc of 20 March 1952 (Bugay, 1995, 11, quoting GARF, h. P-9401, r. 1, f. 4475, sh. 74).

126 Things were destined to get worse, albeit in an unexpected way. On 20.07.1937 the Political Bureau of the Communist Party Central Committee adopted a resolution "On proposing to T. Yezhov that all Germans working at defense industry plants be arrested" (a corresponding order No. 00439 was issued by Yezhov on 25 July 1937). In August, a similar resolution and order were issued with respect to Poles, and then concerning Koreans, Latvians, Estonians, Finns, Greeks, Chinese, Iranians, Romanians, etc. It is worthwhile mentioning the mass arrests of Soviet citizens and Polish political emigrants within the campaign of Great Terror, namely, a so-called Polish operation was carried out by the NKVD in 1937–1938, which provided a form of link between the banishment of 1936–1937 and that of 1940–1941. For details see Okhotin, Roginsky, 1999.

127 See Eisfeld, Herdt, 1996, 27–29. Interestingly, the USSR Committee for Resettlement contributed funds to this resettlement.

128 See Eisfeld, Herdt, 1996, 30–31.

129 Bugay, 1995, 11–12.

130 Bugay, Gonov, 1998, 104, quoting GARF, h. 9401, r. 1, f. 3144, sh. 65.

131 Bugay, 1995, 18.

132 See Martin, 1998, 833–835. He also says that only 32.4% of Koreans that lived in the Far East Kray in 1922 had Soviet citizenship.

133 See above.

134 See Bugay, 1992; Bugay, 1994.

135 See details about him in Papchinsky, A. A. and M. A. Tumshis, "Ya schastliv, chto prinadlezhu k chislu rabotnikov karatelnykh organov," ili istinnyye prichiny pobega chekista Lyushkova za kordon" ["I am happy to belong to the penal bodies," or the true reasons for Cheka member Lyushkov's flight abroad] (Novyi Chasovoy, 1998), no.6–7, 132–146. Lyushkov was decorated for conducting the operation in question by the USSR Supreme Soviet Presidiumorder "On rewarding the Far East Kray UNKVD and NKPS staff," of 6 February 1938.

136 At the end of October, all Koreans from the North Sakhalin were transported to Vladivostok. See Pashkov, Dudarets, 1994, 15, quoting Khabarovsk Kray State Archive, h. 2, r. 1, f. 1316, sh. 148–150.

137 See Pashkov, Dudarets, 1994, 15, quoting the Far East Central State Archive of the RSFSR, h. P-2413, r. 2, f. 804, sh. 183–184.

138 See Bugay, 1995, 17.

139 Bugay, 1994c, 150–153.

140 Bugay, 1994c.

Forced Migrations during and after the Second World War (1939–1953)

SELECTIVE DEPORTATIONS FROM THE ANNEXED TERRITORIES OF POLAND, THE BALTIC REPUBLICS AND ROMANIA IN 1939–1941

It is widely accepted that 1 September 1939, the day when Germany attacked Poland from the west, was the first day of the Second World War. By attacking Poland in the east on 17 September, the Soviet Union entered the war as well.

In September 1939, after the Red Army occupied eastern provinces of Poland, which were immediately declared western territories of the "reunited" Ukraine and Belorussia, "cleansing" operations on these territories were swiftly launched. This time it was Polish, Ukrainian, Jewish and other "nationalists" that were to be introduced to this new form of nation building.

The dark shadow of the Molotov–Ribbentrop Pact loomed over the actions of the Soviet authorities in Poland. At least the main target groups earmarked for deportation were promptly interned, and some of them even convicted. Among them were: firstly, soldiers and officers taken prisoner (the Soviet side did not regard them as prisoners of war); secondly, all residents of the frontier zone between Wilno and Lvov, along with forest rangers, railway workers, and even prisoners; and thirdly, "socially alien" elements that failed to hide in time, such as province governors, public officials, police members, land proprietors, industrialists and traders. They were prosecuted by *troikas*[1] and sentenced to prison terms of 8 to 20 years under Criminal Code articles 54 or 58.

The rumors about the imminent deportations of Poles began to circulate as early as November 1939. However, it was only in 1940

that the wheels of mass banishment began to turn (it can be suggested that the Soviet–Finnish war was a hindrance to any earlier implementation[2]). The operations lasted into 1941. According to A. Guryanov, four successive and thoroughly rehearsed operations were carried out. Each of them was executed in fact within 24 hours. Three
operations were completed in 1940—10 February,[3] 13 April (more
precisely 9 and 13 April), and 29 June, and one in 1941 (in May–June).
The transportation by train of deportees inland into the USSR took
from two to four weeks. Guryanov, who studies the matter at the
transport logistics level (the number of trains required reached 211),
evaluates the total of those banished in the course of the three operations of 1940 as 275 thousand persons, 139–141 thousand of them
deported in February, 61 in April,[4] and 75 in the summer.[5]

The preparation for the first deportation started as early as 1939:
on 2 December 1939 Beria addressed Stalin with a proposition that
all *osadniki* (one can regard the group as a Polish equivalent to the
Cossacks) and their family members be banished from the annexed
districts before 15 February 1940.[6] And the official title of the first
deportation target group was precisely "special resettlers—*osadniki*"[7]
(or, more accurately, *osadniki* and forest rangers). According to the
official Soviet version, *osadniki* were "the bitterest enemies of the
working people": former military service members distinguished in
the Polish–Soviet war of 1920, who were rewarded by their grateful
motherland with strips of land in eastern districts populated mainly
by Belorussians and Ukrainians (Poles made up 85% of *osadniki*, but
there were also Ukrainians and Belorussians among them).

The operations were carried out at night, between 2 and 6 a.m.
But it was hardly possible to miss the signs of preparation, since one
could not disguise thousands of carts driven by local coachmen, hundreds of lorries and railway cars. Those that were not caught in the
raids were often listed as unavailable and left alone.

As early as 29 December 1939, the Council of People's Commissars adopted a decree "On the special settlement and labor
employment of *osadniki* banished from western oblasts of Ukraine
and Belorussia." In order to employ the resettlers, it was intended to
found special settlements under the supervision of the Narkomles in
timber-harvesting areas, primarily in the northern European part of
the country, in the Urals and Siberia: in particular, in the Komi
ASSR, in Kirov, Perm, Vologda, Arkhangelsk, Ivanovo, Yaroslavl,

Sverdlovsk and Omsk Obls., and in Altay and Krasnoyarsk Krays.[8] Taking into account the fact that forest rangers, who appeared to be naturally intended for the Narkomles, were included in the target groups at the "prompting" of Belorussia's Communist Party Central Committee first secretary, P. K. Ponomarenko,[9] Beria suggested that a part of the *osadniki* be used within the Narkomtsvetmet system for mining gold and copper ore, which was ratified by a Council of People's Commissars decree of 14 January 1940.

A section of the *osadniki* inevitably found themselves in camps and prisons rather than special settlements. All those *osadniki* family members, POWs' family members, prostitutes, and refugees present on the territory of eastern Poland after 1 September 1939, who expressed the wish to leave for the territory occupied by Germans but were rejected by Germany, were subject to resettlement to the USSR inland. On 10 April 1940 a Council of People's Commissars decree was adopted and a special instruction was issued concerning the procedure of resettlement: family members of those repressed and POWs were to be sent to Kazakhstan for 10 years, refugees to northern regions, to special settlements specializing in timber harvesting, and prostitutes to Kazakh and Uzbek SSR.

Notwithstanding the deteriorating road conditions, another mass raid on "liberated" Poles and their subsequent banishment was carried out on 13 April 1940: this target group was assigned the category of "administratively exiled." Among these were family members of repressed Polish officers, policemen, gendarmes, state employees, land proprietors, industrialists and members of insurgent organizations; among them were also teachers, petty traders, and even better-off peasants, the infamous "kulaks." Interestingly, on the eve of 9 April 1940, prostitutes were given the honor of being deported separately from the others.[10]

Khrebtovich-Buteneva recalled that one or two carts were transported every day, as a rule convoyed by two soldiers. They would knock at the doors, compare name lists, take away passports; they did their best to keep polite, even helped to pack and load luggage on the carts: it was allowed to take up to 100kg but in fact it was possible to take more than this. The carts were transported to the station and unloaded into railway freight cars. In the cars there were iron stoves, three levels of plank beds, and a place for luggage by the back wall. An NKVD member from Aktyubinsk said: "One cannot convert a

Pole to Communism, at least not the current generation. All of them are our enemies, no matter how many of them there are!"[11]

The convicted were transported to North Kazakhstan (namely to Aktyubinsk, Kustanay, North Kazakhstan, Pavlodar, Semipalatinsk and Akmolinsk Obls.), typically for a ten-year term; prostitutes were sent to Kazakhstan and Uzbekistan; all the others to northern Russia.[12]

As far as the deportation of refugees was concerned (this target group was termed "special resettlers—refugees"), it was postponed until summer. It would not be until 5 June 1940, the date of departure of the German commission considering citizens' applications for resettlement to the German-controlled territory, that the issue would come up again.[13] For the most part, these were Polish citizens that had fled to the east from the advancing Wehrmacht, the overwhelming majority of whom (85%) being Jews. In this case, it should be noted again, the refusal of the Germans to accept them and the subsequent deportation saved their lives.

Those belonging to this target group were not regarded as bitterest enemies (unlike *osadniki*[14]), but as "interned emigrants." However, some of them of their own volition and with German consent (and sometimes at their demand), were handed over to Germans. A corresponding joint decree was issued on 14 May 1941 by the Council of People's Commissars and the Communist Party Central Committee. Simultaneously it provided for the arrest, and 20-year settlement exile to remote areas of the USSR, of family members of "activists of Ukrainian and Polish counter-revolutionary nationalist organizations" (it was planned to address this issue in western Belarus too, in the future).

As a matter of fact, the deportations from the annexed Polish territories were going on up until Hitler's very attack on the USSR. According to calculations by A. Guryanov, the number of Poles deported from February 1940 to June 1941 amounted to a total of 309–312 thousand persons.[15] According to Zemskov's data, the total of the banished Polish "*osadniki*" and refugees reached 380 thousand, although in this case the estimate of the number of deportees as of 1 April 1941—210,559 persons, 134,491 of them *osadniki* and 76,008 refugees—appears to be surprisingly low. The largest target groups of former Polish citizens were located in the Arkhangelsk Obl. (some 54 thousand persons) and Sverdlovsk Obl. (around 24 thousand), along with the Novosibirsk Obl., the Komi ASSR, Krasnoyarsk Kray, and

Vologda, Ivanovo and Molotov Obls. (from 10 to 20 thousand persons).[16]

By some Polish estimates, the total of those expelled from prewar Poland to the USSR reached 1.6–1.8 million persons, without taking into consideration Belorussians, Lithuanians and Jews. In quantitative terms this evaluation is definitely exaggerated, but qualitatively it is unmistakable: Polish administration, the Polish army and Polish intellectuals ceased to exist.

Nevertheless, it must be mentioned that soon after Hitler's attack against the USSR and the establishment of official relations with the London-based Polish government, USSR Supreme Soviet Presidium decrees of 12 July and 17 August 1941 provided for many Poles[17] to be amnestied and released from special settlements: they were allowed to choose their place of residence unless it was located in frontier, restricted zones or restricted towns. Out of 389,382 repressed former Polish citizens, 120,962 persons were convicted and 243,106 were subjected to special resettlement. Of the above-mentioned total number, 119,865 persons, Anders army members, were evacuated to Iran in 1942, while the remaining 269,176 Poles were transported to districts located to the south of the previous places, and were thus concentrated in Kazakhstan, Central Asia, the Altay and Krasnoyarsk Krays, and in the Sverdlovsk and Chelyabinsk Obls. In January 1943, former Polish citizens were issued with Soviet passports, most of them (more than 165 thousand persons) were granted Soviet citizenship, while some 26 thousand retained their Polish citizenship. By the agreement between the Soviet and Polish governments of 30 June 1943, the amnesty was extended to all former Polish citizens on the territory of the USSR, after which another Polish army was gradually established on USSR territory.[18]

In summer 1940, the shadow of the Molotov–Ribbentrop pact hovered over the utmost northern and southern sectors of the USSR European border: it should be noted, the *new* European border. The focus on the western borders remained in place, but—apart from Poland—deportations were now carried out in the Baltic republics, Bessarabia, and North Bukovina.

On 14 June, the USSR delivered an ultimatum to Lithuania, and then, on 16 June, to Latvia and Estonia. The conditions of the ultimata were accepted by these countries' governments on 15, 16 and 17 June respectively; and new pro-Soviet governments[19] were promptly set up in these states, namely on 17, 20 and 21 June, in the same order. On 27–28 June, similar events took place in Romania, with the only difference that only a part of it was annexed; this included Bessarabia and North Bukovina. Soon (on 2 August) Bessarabia was united with Left-Bank Moldavia to form the Moldavian SSR.

On 23 June 1940, Beria issued an order stipulating the resettlement of "citizens of foreign nationalities" from the city of Murmansk and the Murmansk Obl. between 5 and 10 July. The target group was not limited to representatives of neighboring countries' nationalities, Finns, Swedes and Norwegians (2,540 families, i.e., 6,973 persons of these nationalities were resettled to the Karel–Finn ASSR), but also included Chinese, Germans, Poles, Greeks, Koreans etc. (altogether 675 families, i.e., 1,743 persons). They were sent to Altay.

Additional time was required for organizing deportations in the Baltic republics and Moldavia, and therefore the operations here were launched somewhat later. It was not until the late May of 1941, only one month before the beginning of the war, that a new—short, but extremely intense—wave of deportations started.

However, the preparations had been well laid beforehand. I. Serov signed an instruction concerning the conducting of the deportation of anti-Soviet elements from the Baltic states as early as 11 October 1939; and then for nearly a year and a half the crackdown was held up, and the region held its breath.[20] In mid-May 1941, Beria agreed with Stalin on a draft decree of the Council of People's Commissars and the Communist Party Central Committee "On taking action on cleansing the Lithuanian SSR of anti-Soviet, criminal and socially dangerous elements" (the Latvian and Estonian Republics were added to Lithuania at this stage of coordination).[21] This time the measure targeted former members of various nationalistic parties, police members, gendarmes, land proprietors, industrialists, high officials, officers and criminals involved in anti-Soviet activities and employed by foreign intelligence services for spying. Such persons were to be arrested, their property confiscated and they themselves sent to camps for terms of 5 to 8 years with a subsequent 20-year settlement in remote areas of the USSR. There, their families would be waiting for them on their release[22] (except for those of criminals), along with the families of those who were sentenced to capital punishment or who evaded justice by hiding (besides, this group included persons that had arrived from Germany under repatriation procedure and Germans that had applied for repatriation but later refused to leave). It was suggested that special camps be organized for internees where Stalinist justice would be exercised (or, as the draft decree read: "Special Council's decision-making"). Traditionally, registered prostitutes constituted a somewhat unusual target group; they were transported to northern regions of Kazakhstan for a 5-year term.

At first sight, the Moldavian operation appeared more random. However, its preparation had started long before its official initiator, S. A. Goglidze, the Central Committee and Council of People's Commissars plenipotentiary in the Moldavian SSR, addressed Stalin with a request to allow the banishment of some 5 thousand active counter-revolutionaries with their families (bourgeois party activists, land proprietors, policemen and gendarmes, officers of the White, Tsarist and Romanian armies, major traders, landlords, province foremen).[23] The operation preparation was completed by the beginning of June, and Beria's directive of 14 June in fact summed up the events that had already taken place.

The Directive was titled "Plan of NKVD measures on transporting, settling and employing special target groups [spetskontingenty] banished from the Lithuanian, Latvian, Estonian and Moldavian SSRs." The plan stipulated arrest and banishment of 30,885 former industrialists, land proprietors and members of bourgeois governments of the Baltic republics and Moldavia (as a rule, all of them were ascribed the status of "exiled settlers" [ssylnoposelentsy]) along with 46,557 family members. The intended routes were: from Lithuania to the Komi ASSR, from Latvia to Krasnoyarsk Kray, from Estonia to Altay Kray and South Kazakhstan Obl., from Moldavia (the largest target group in this case) to Kazakhstan (Aktyubinsk, Karaganda, Kustanay and Kzyl–Orda Obls.) and the Novosibirsk Obl.

The following is a concise "schedule" of the actual pre-war deportations conducted in 1941. Counter-revolutionaries and nationalists were banished from Western Ukraine on 22 May, from Moldavia, Chernovtsy and Ismail Obls. of the Ukrainian SSR on the night of 12–13 June, from Lithuania, Latvia and Estonia on 14 June, and from Western Belorussia on the night of 19–20 June.

Some 11 and 21 thousand persons were banished from Western Ukraine and Western Belorussia respectively (the destination in the former case was the South Kazakhstan Obl., Krasnoyarsk Kray, Omsk and Novosibirsk Obls., and in the latter case the Krasnoyarsk and Altay Krays and Novosibirsk Obl.).[24]

More than 30 thousand persons were resettled from Moldavia and Chernovtsy and Ismail Obls. of the UkSSR to Kazakhstan, the Komi ASSR, Krasnoyarsk Kray, Omsk Obl. and Novosibirsk Obl. With regard to Moldavia, more detailed data is available. In particular, 8–8.5 thousand local counter-revolutionary activists were assigned to be arrested there and subsequently banished: 5 thousand were sent to the Kozelshchina camp and 3 thousand to the Putivl camp. Their family members (33 thousand persons) faced banishment, primarily

Figure 3. **Forced migrations from regions annexed by the USSR, 1940–1941**

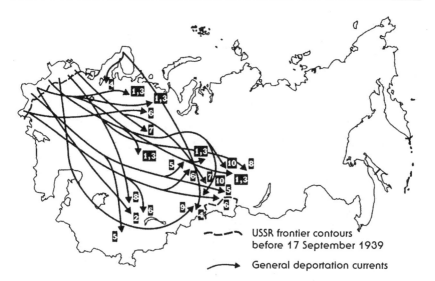

– – – USSR frontier contours
       before 17 September 1939

→ General deportation currents

Deported target groups:
1. Special resettlers—*osadniki* from former Eastern Poland (10 February 1940);
2. Administrative deportees from former Eastern Poland (9–13 April 1940);
3. Special resettlers—refugees from former Eastern Poland (29 June 1940);
4. Citizens of foreign nationalities from the Murmansk Obl. (5–10 July 1940);
5. Exiled settlers from Western Ukraine (22 May 1941);
6. Exiled settlers from Moldavia, and the Chernovtsy and Ismail Obls. (12–19 June 1941);
7. Exiled settlers from Estonia (14 June 1941);
8. Exiled settlers from Latvia (14 June 1941);
9. Exiled settlers from Lithuania (14 June 1941);
10. Exiled settlers from West Belorussia (19–20 June 1941).

to Kazakhstan and West Siberia. Some 11 thousand were sent to the South Kazakhstan, Aktyubinsk and Karaganda Obls., 10 thousand to the Novosibirsk Obl., and another 6 thousand to Kustanay and the Kzyl–Orda and Omsk Obls. (the Kirov Obl. was assigned as a reserve destination intended for another 6 thousand).[25]

The operation was commenced at 2.30 a.m. on 13 June (according to some sources on 12 June); only two hours were allowed for packing. Notwithstanding the unexpectedness, far fewer people were arrested and banished than had been planned (in particular, 22,848 persons were banished from Moldavia as of mid-September 1941, as compared to the total of 85,716 persons resettled in the course of this last pre-war operation). Incidentally, the actual destination geography in this case differed from that intended: 9,954 resettlers were registered in Kazakhstan, and 6,085 and 5,787 in the Omsk and Novosibirsk Obls. respectively. In the Krasnoyarsk Kray 470 persons and in the Komi ASSR 352 persons were added to the initial list.[26]

Deportees from Lithuania (17.5 thousand persons) were sent to the Novosibirsk Obl., Kazakhstan and the Komi ASSR, from Latvia (some 17 thousand persons)[27] to Krasnoyarsk Kray, Novosibirsk Obl. and Kazakhstan's Karaganda Obl., and from Estonia (some 6 thousand persons) to the Kirov and Novosibirsk Obls.

Therefore, the total of deportees from the new western regions of the USSR reached around 380–390 thousand persons.[28] The North of the European part of the USSR, the Urals, Western and Eastern Siberia, Kazakhstan and Uzbekistan became the key destinations (see figure 3).

The bulk of the deportation plans was not meant to be limited to these.

However, a war precluded their full implementation. This time—from the moment the Germans crossed the Bug on the dawn of 22 June 1941—the Great Patriotic War changed everything.

TOTAL PREVENTIVE DEPORTATION OF SOVIET GERMANS, FINNS AND GREEKS IN 1941–1942

The fact that the beginning of the main war coincided with one of the, by then routine, operations on deporting citizens to remote areas of the great motherland is highly significant. Unlike the border guards, Cheka members were not taken unawares by the war and managed to complete their tasks successfully and almost without loss.

As early as 22 June a Supreme Soviet Presidium decree "On martial law" was issued, which provided for local military authorities to have the right to banish all persons recognized as socially dangerous by administrative procedure. Beria circulated a corresponding directive on 4 July 1941. It should be noted, however, that the directive mentioned that discretion must be observed while resettling the persons in question, available information must be checked and no persons older than 60 or disabled should be banished.[29] However, the idea implied in the decree—to remove all those perceived as dangerous or unreliable as far as possible—proved to be rather a popular and effective one during the harsh war-time environment.

Under order No. 017 of the Military Council of the Western Front, a 5km-wide *combat operational zone* (subsequently expanded to a width of 25km) was established, from which all civilian population was to be resettled.[30]

On 17 November 1941, order No. 0428 was issued, signed by I. Stalin and B. Shaposhnikov, chief of the General Headquarters, which read in particular:

"1. All settlements in the rear of the German troops, 20–60km deep behind the front line and 20–30km to the right and to the left of the roads, must be destroyed and burned to ashes. [...] In case of necessity of withdrawal of our detachments in a particular locality, all Soviet population must be taken away too, and all settlements without an exception must be destroyed lest the enemy should use them."[31]

In relation to the USSR, the years of the Great Patriotic War were distinguished for not merely the unprecedented strain of every component of the state and people in a deathly but victorious fight against a merciless and powerful enemy, but also for the large number of acts of injustice, discrimination and repression toward a part of the Soviet population.

So-called punished peoples represent one example of the mentioned phenomenon. Subjecting particular peoples to total deportations was officially justified as retribution for the treason allegedly committed by these people, or so as to deny them the temptation to commit it. As a matter of fact, the "preventive deportations" were not even a punishment for potential treason, but rather for "having the ethnic background of a foreign nation that is at war or may join the war on the enemy side."[32] This constitutes a key difference between the situation characteristic of the Second World War as compared to the First World War, when exclusively "hostile countries' nationals," i.e., only citizens of the states that were participating in the war on the enemy side, were subject to deportations. This time, the countries' own citizens of the same ethnic background as the titular nationalities of the hostile states were targeted not only in the USSR, but in the USA too.[33]

However, it is a well-known fact that both heroism and selflessness on the one hand, and cowardice and disloyalty on the other, were manifested equally by representatives of all USSR nationalities, by those that were subsequently deported and by those that were not affected. For example, in the very first months of the war, more than 17 thousand Chechens and Ingushetians were mobilized into the army,[34] 40 thousand Meskhetian Turks (almost the entire adult population) left for the front, and 26 thousand of the latter were subsequently killed.[35] Out of 137 thousand Crimean Tatars drafted into the army, 57 thousand had been killed in the war by 1944.[36] Among those awarded the title Hero of the Soviet Union were ten Chechens and Ingushetians,[37] nine Germans,[38] eight Kalmyks,[39] and one Balkar.[40]

That is why charges of treason were both unfair and hypocritical, since the total number of Soviet citizens who found themselves on the territories occupied by the enemy and—due to this mere fact alone—had to be in contact in some way with the occupational authorities, reached some 60–65 million. More than one million people did actively collaborate with the occupying forces (and many even demonstrated real enthusiasm), staining themselves with the mark of treason and shedding the blood of so many innocent compatriots by betraying them to the occupying forces. Each of them perhaps deserved an individual charge of disloyalty and collaboration with the enemy, court prosecution, and severe punishment preceded by thorough fact-finding. There is no doubt that among the latter individuals were representatives of the peoples that were "punished" later, however the overwhelming majority of the "traitors" were made up of Russians and Ukrainians, which nevertheless did not lead to total punishment of these peoples, as is well known.

However, that these peoples were not subjected to collective punishment is not the true injustice. What is, the very fact of punish-

ing an entire people as surrogate for the legal prosecution of particular individuals. Irrespective of any statistics, collective charges and
collective punishments on the basis of ethnic background in themselves constitute a grave crime against humanity comparable to the
taking and shooting of hostages and the like.

Let us examine the chronology of forced migrations in the
USSR during the Great Patriotic War.

The very first blow came with the round-up of Soviet Germans
that were regarded as potential "collaborators" merely due to their
ethnic background being identical to that of the titular nationality of
the hostile state. Some 1.2 out of 1.5 million Soviet Germans had to
be subjected to resettlement. According to the results of the 1939 census, 1,427,222 citizens of German nationality were residing in the
USSR, only 1/5 of them in cities and towns. Germans were scattered
across the country rather extensively, however the larger German
colonies emerged in Russia (862.5 thousand), in Ukraine (392.7
thousand), in Kazakhstan (92.7 thousand), in Azerbaijan (32.1 thousand) and in Georgia (20.5 thousand). Within the RSFSR border,
they were concentrated in the German ASSR (366.7 thousand) in the
Volga region, in the Omsk Oblast (59.8 thousand), in the Crimea
(51.3 thousand), and in the Ordzhonikidze (45.7 thousand) and
Krasnodar (34.3 thousand) Krays. As we see, the only larger German
colonies located to the east of the Ural mountains were in Kazakhstan, the Omsk Obl. and Altay.

The problem of resettling Germans apparently emerged during
the course of the war rather than before. Otherwise it would be difficult, for example, to explain why, on 31 June 1941, the Supreme Court
of the Volga German ASSR sentenced I. Belousov, the chief of the
Kuybyshev *kolkhoz* sheep-trading farm in the Old Poltava canton, to a
six-year imprisonment term, putting the following statement of charge
against him: "for delivering chauvinistic abuses against Germans
residing in the USSR." As elsewhere in the country, the formation of
the people's defense guard detachments were underway in the republic between 13 July and 15 August: 11,193 persons, including 2,635
women joined this force. The oblast party committee held rallies all
over the republic, at which appeals to the German people were adopted; weekly reports were sent to Moscow about "examples of patriotic
and labor enthusiasm demonstrated by the working people of the
ASSR of Volga Germans."[41] On 3 August, a defense foundation was

set up in the republic, to which citizens sent their contributions. Possible hopes that counter-propaganda using the supportive German community, who enjoyed unrepressed freedom within Soviet borders, would undermine the morale of the Wehrmacht cannot be ruled out as a possible reason behind certain "delay" in the deportation of such Germans. And yet, neither the Soviet commander-in-chief personally nor his loyal political bodies deserve to receive the benefit of the doubt that they were naïve and unaware ("we did not know," "were not able to imagine" and so on) of what was to happen later.

Delay in the deportation due to economic motivations, i.e., expectations of bringing in the harvest, sound more feasible: the ASSR itself was a well developed agrarian region, and its plan for the 1941 grain deliveries was determined only on 27 June 1941. Had the Wehrmacht advance been less speedy, Stalin would have made sure the harvest was first collected prior to their deportation.

However, of course, the German rate of advance was not determined in Moscow. On the day when the defense foundation was set up in Engels (3 August), Stalin received a cryptographed message from the Southern Front military leadership, which read in particular: "1. The military actions by the Dniester river revealed that the German population shot at our withdrawing troops from windows and vegetable gardens. It was also established that on 1 August 1941 residents of a German village greeted the entering German fascist troops with bread and salt. There are a number of settlements populated by Germans on the front territory. 2. We solicit for a directive to be delivered to the local authorities for the immediate banishment of unreliable elements: [signatures of] Tyulenev, Zaporozhets, Romanov."

Stalin's reaction was instant and straightforward: "To Comrade Beria. We must smash them into oblivion."[42] Comrade Beria accepted this principle eagerly, and expanded the scope of the destruction required. It is true, however, that the decision may still have been made as early as at the end of July in the course of Beria and Molotov's clandestine visit to the republic.[43] After this the KGB allegedly organized a provocative landing of "airborne" troops wearing German uniforms, and republican newspapers and magazines came under pressure and began to close down one by one.

It was not until 12 August 1941, when a joint Communist Party Central Committee and Council of People's Commissars of the USSR decree on resettling Germans residing in the Volga region and

Kazakhstan was adopted, that preparations for the deportation were launched in actuality. Nonetheless, even at this time there were obstacles that slowed progress, which, in our opinion, were connected with the necessity to reap at least a portion of the harvest.

However, the fact remains that practical orders regarding the operation were not delivered until 26–27 August. Beria commanded the operation to be carried out between 3 and 20 September, and established an executive headquarters chaired by his deputy I. A. Serov. The Volga German ASSR was integrated into the Saratov and Stalingrad Obl., into a single region from the perspective of the deportation of Germans. A special force led by brigade commander Krivenko and comprising 13,100 militants—NKVD members (some 1.5 thousand persons), militiamen and Red Army members—was sent to the region. All the three oblasts were informed about the decision immediately, and one day later the oblast Communist Party Bureau took up implementing the deportation in strict accordance with the Center's directives.

A section for special settlements was set up within the NKVD central apparatus on 28 August 1941; it was to take up responsibility for the reception and settlement of the banished Germans at destinations.[44] On the same day (28 August), the well-known order "On the resettlement of the Volga Germans" was issued by the USSR Supreme Soviet Presidium: the order was nothing more than a mere token of parliamentary procedure that legitimized and confirmed the decision already taken at Lubyanka and in the Kremlin.

It would be interesting to compare this order with the statements made by the innocently convicted I. Belousov, the former chief of the former Kuybyshev *kolkhoz* sheep-trading farm in the former Old Poltava canton. At any rate, the order was remarkable for its novel approach in terms of providing grounds for state decisions: the charges that had been earlier applicable to particular individuals, for example non-reporting, were now administered with regard to an entire people:

"According to reliable data received by the military authorities, there are scores and thousands of agents and spies among ethnic Germans residing in the Volga region, who are to carry out explosions in districts populated by the Volga Germans following a signal delivered from Germany.

No Germans residing in the Volga region have informed the Soviet authorities about such a large number of agents and spies among them. Therefore, the German population of the Volga region is hiding enemies of the Soviet People and Soviet Authorities in their midst.

If any subversion commanded from Germany and implemented by German agents occurs in the republic of the Volga Germans, or adjacent regions, and bloodshed takes place, the Soviet Government will have to impose martial law and take punitive measures against the entire German population of the Volga region.

In order to forestall such undesirable phenomena and prevent mass bloodshed, the Supreme Soviet Presidium of the USSR finds it necessary to resettle the entire German population residing in the Volga region to other regions, where the resettlers will be allotted land and offered necessary state support in order to get established at their new places of residence.

Regions rich in arable land in the Novosibirsk and Omsk Obls., Altay Kray, Kazakhstan and other neighboring areas are to be used as places for new settlements.

In connection with the above, the State Defense Committee is appointed to carry out the resettlement of all Volga Germans, and provide the resettled Volga Germans with land at the new areas."

Excerpt from the NKVD instruction for resettling Germans residing in the Volga German ASSR and in the Saratov and Stalingrad Obls. (GARF, h. 9401)

"APPROVED"

PEOPLE'S COMMISSAR OF THE INTERIOR OF THE USSR
(L. BERIA) *[signature]*
27 August 1941

INSTRUCTION

FOR CONDUCTING THE RESETTLEMENT OF GERMANS RESIDING IN THE VOLGA GERMAN ASSR AND IN THE SARATOV AND STALINGRAD OBLASTS

All ethnic Germans residing in the Volga German ASSR and in the Saratov and Stalingrad Obls. are subject to resettlement.

Communist Party and Komsomol members are to be resettled simultaneously with all the others.

Germans residing in the mentioned regions are to be resettled to the territory of the Kazakh SSR, Krasnoyarsk and Altay Krays, and the Omsk and Novosibirsk Obls.

Family members of both rank-and-file and high-ranking Red Army servicemen are to be resettled within the general procedure. At the places of destination, they are to be given priority, first of all with regard to economic and domestic arrangements.

PREPARATION MEASURES

Oblast executive troikas established by the NKVD of the USSR order shall form and set up district executive troikas, which will comprise: the chief of the NKVD district department, chief of the militia...

[...]

Several days before the operation, after receiving orders from the oblast executive troikas, chiefs of the executive district groups shall inform the would-be resettlers about the necessity of resettlement and deliver explanations regarding the resettlement procedure. While doing this, no gatherings or collective discussions of the issues concerning the resettlements are to be permitted by any means.

PERSONS STAYING WITH GERMAN FAMILIES, WHOSE RESETTLEMENT IS NOT MANDATORY

[*The following item 1 is crossed out by Beria, the following document items 2 and 3 are changed to 1 and 2 respectively.*]

Family members that are not ethnic Germans are not subject to resettlement, but may follow other family members if they wish.

For example, a Russian [female] citizen married to a German shall not be subjected to compulsory resettlement, but may choose to follow her husband voluntarily.

In the case of families in which the head of the household (husband) is not an ethnic German, but the wife is German, the family shall not be resettled. [*The last clause of the sentence is handwritten by Beria, the previously printed phrase, crossed out by Beria, read "the wife may stay."*]

In cases when some family members are not available at the moment of transportation (are in hospital, on business trip etc.) such families shall be registered by NKVD bodies in order to ensure their subsequent resettlement to the new place of residence.

Following I. Serov's order, the decree was published on 30 August by the republican newspapers the (Russian-language) *Bolshevik* and (German-language) *Nachrichten*. This publication allowed first secretary of the oblast party committee S. Malov to address Stalin with a report stating that a large part of the German population manifested a critical attitude toward the decree, especially to the part asserting that enemies of the Soviet order were hiding within the German environment. On 5 September, Volga German ASSR high-ranking ethnic German officials—the chairman of the republic's Council of People's Commissars A. Gekman, the chairman of the Supreme Soviet K. Gofman and third secretary of the Oblast Communist Party G. Korbmacher—were dismissed from their posts,[45] and the existence of the Volga German Autonomous Republic itself was terminated on 6–7 September (interestingly, officially this termination was not declared!). The territory of the former Volga German ASSR was distributed between the Saratov (the city of Engels and 15 cantons) and Stalingrad (7 cantons) Obls. (the renaming of the cantons and settlements having German names followed on 19 May 1942).

It had already been a long time (29 August) since NKVD units occupied the initial locations. The organizational scheme of the deportation that they were to carry out was as follows (we will consider it in detail, since approximately the same scheme was used through the course of other operations).

Secret troikas, approved by NKVD orders, were formed in regions (consisting of the local NKVD chief, militia chief and party committee chairman). These, in their turn, formed district executive troikas, drew up schedules for railway car supply, and organized the reception and dispatch of the resettlers.

In order to put together the lists of those to be banished, the district executive groups visited collective farms, villages and towns and filled out registration cards for each family to be resettled comprising information about all its members. German women that were married to men of other ethnic backgrounds were not subject to deportation.[46] In cases when some family members were temporarily absent, NKVD bodies registered such families in order to ensure their subsequent resettlement to their new places of residence. In each case, the family head was warned that he was responsible for all family members that were to be resettled: if any one of them went into hiding, the family head and other family members would face prosecution under criminal law. Based on the data received from district troikas, the regional troikas drew up schedules for supplying railway cars so that rolling-stock standing time could be avoided.

Apart from executive troikas, commissions for taking over the property of resettling collective farms and assessing Germans' personal possessions were founded.[47] These commissions comprised the chairman of the district executive committee, the head of the district land department, representatives of the People's Commissariat of Production Deliveries, department of cattle deliveries, the district financial department or a State Bank office (in each district at least 50 clerks were recruited for public service in assisting the commissions). The property of the collective farms and MTS that were resettled was registered and taken over: collective farm buildings; agricultural equipment; draught and productive livestock; both reaped and standing agricultural crops; auxiliary enterprises with their available equipment, manufactured goods and raw materials; collective farms' cash assets etc.[48] Besides, representatives of the Commissariat for the Meat and Dairy Industry of the USSR accepted goods from collective farms and collective farm members as amortization of the deliveries to the state due in 1941, of the penalties for previous years' defaults in meat deliveries, and as the substitution of other agricultural products with meat.[49]

With the purpose of reinforcing the security of collective farm property in the course of the operation, groups assisting the executive groups and comprising members of Komsomol, party and soviet bodies were formed. Persons from adjacent regions or those evacuated from the immediate battle area were recruited by way of labor duty to form groups that would ensure the subsequent security of collective farm property, take care of livestock and harvest until new collective farms were organized and new settlers arrived.

The assessment of the private assets of the departing Germans was carried out by a special Assessment Commission comprising a plenipotentiary of the Narkomzem of the USSR, a collective farm chairman and a bank representative, with the resettling collective farm member participating in the procedure. Those leaving their property received a certificate stating the money value that was to be compensated to them at the new destination through construction work in the form of construction materials.[50]

Registration card of the head of a family of German special resettlers (from the collection of A. Eisfeld, Guttingen)
[Copies of the cards originally in Russian and their German translation presented]
[Page 1]

To be filled out per a family head	Alh.
Last name: Horn	Oblast
First name, second name: Josef, Wilhelm	
Year of birth: 1896	Rayon
Place of birth: Village of Yost,	
Kukkus canton, VG ASSR	Village
Nationality [ethnic background]: German	
Residence (precise): Village of Yost,	Date of arrival
Kukkus canton, VG ASSR	
Occupation: Collective farm worker	The card is drawn up by
Ground Decree of the Government of the	[Signature]
USSR of 28 August 1941	31 August 1941

[Page 2]
Family members

Last name, first name, second name	Year of birth	Relation
Horn, Lydia, Wilhelm	1896	wife
Horn, Pauline, Rudolf	1921	daughter-in-law
Horn, Alexander, Josef	1922	son
Horn, Pauline, Josef	1924	daughter
Horn, Wilhelm, Josef	1926	daughter
Horn, Irma, Josef	1930	daughter
Horn, David, Josef	1938	son
Horn, Heinrich, Heinrich	1939	grandson

Train No. 883 12.09.41 Barnaul
Special remarks: Son drafted to the Red Army

The departing Germans were allowed to take personal belongings, small items of agricultural and domestic equipment, one-month food supply; the total weight of the luggage was not to exceed 1 ton per family. The time allocated for packing was extremely short; resettlers had opportunity to prepare only minimal food supply (they slaughtered livestock, made sausages, and baked bread).

Despite individual lapses, the operation was a general success in terms of meeting the plan and schedule envisaging its completion within the period of 3–20 September. The total number of resettled persons amounted to 438.7 thousand, including 365.8 thousand from the Volga German ASSR, 46.7 thousand from the Saratov Oblast and 26.2 thousand from the Stalingrad Oblast (see figure 4). They were transported primarily to Kazakhstan, but also to Krasnoyarsk and Altay Krays, and to the Novosibirsk and Omsk Obls.: planned figures constituted respectively (with the exception of Kazakhstan) 21.5, 27.2, 28.6 and 24.3 thousand families. As a rule, the new settlements were located in rural areas regardless of the nature of the previous place of residence, but still there were exceptions (for example, the city of Tomsk, which then belonged to the Novosibirsk Oblast).[51]

Yet it is the Crimean rather than Volga Germans that appear to have been the first Soviet Germans to be physically deported. It was as early as the end of August that they were being transported from the Crimea to the Rostov Oblast and to the Ordzhonikidze Kray.[52] In pure legal terms, this deportation had the semblance of an evacuation, although a somewhat extraordinary one: based on ethnic criterion. Later, they were banished again, this time from the Stavropol Kray.

In fact, immediately after the decree of 28 August was issued, the authorities launched analogous operations in other regions of the country. The operation on the speedy deportation of Germans and Finns from the Leningrad Obl. became the first one in this "regional" series. Finns made up an overwhelming majority in this case (89 out of 96 thousand persons[53]). They were resettled to Krasnoyarsk Kray and the Novosibirsk Obl. (24 thousand persons per destination), the Omsk Obl. (21 thousand persons), Kazakhstan (15 thousand persons) and Altay Kray (12 thousand persons). A corresponding report to Stalin was dated 29 August,[54] and the NKVD directive on 30 August, after which the surge and scale of anti-German operations rolled yet further.

In September, another three decrees of the State Defense Committee followed: the first one (6 September) dealt with the resettlement of Germans from Moscow and the Moscow Obl. (8,617 persons) and from the Rostov Obl. (21,400 persons) to Kazakhstan,[55] urban residents settled in towns with a maximum status of district center. This operation was carried out almost simultaneously with the banishment from the Volga region, i.e., between 10 and 20 September.[56]

The decree of 21 September concerned Germans from the *North Caucasus* and *the Tula Obl*. It stipulated that the following target groups be resettled in the period from 25 September to 10 October: 95,489 persons from Ordzhonikidze Kray (to Krasnoyarsk Kray), 34,287 from Krasnodar Kray (to the Novosibirsk Obl.), 5,327 from the Kabardian–Balkar ASSR, 2,929 from the North Ossetian ASSR, and 3,208 from the Tula Obl.[57]

The decree of 22 September targeted the *Zaporozhye Obl.* (63 thousand persons), *Stalino Obl.* (41 thousand) and *Voroshilovgrad Obl.* (5,487 persons). All resettlers were to be moved to Kazakhstan: first from the Zaporozhye Obl. to the Aktyubinsk Obl. between 25 September–2 October (on the way, they were left in the Astrakhan Obl. to build a road), then to the Kustanay Obl. between 25 September and 10 October.[58] In addition, on 8 September 1941 Stalin issued an order to "withdraw" all ethnic German *army service members* from the front-line forces.

Figure 4. **Forced migrations during the Great Patriotic War, 1941–1945**

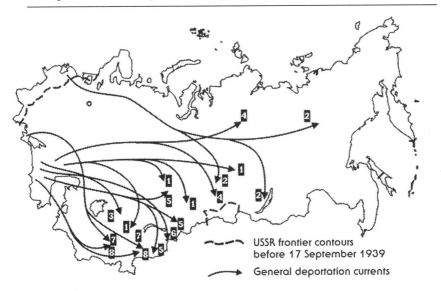

— — — USSR frontier contours
before 17 September 1939

⟶ General deportation currents

Deported target groups:
1. Germans (1941);
2. Finns (1941, 1942);
3. Karachais (1943);
4. Kalmyks (1944);
5. Chechens and Ingushetians (1944);
6. Balkars (1944);
7. Crimean Tatars (1944);
8. Meskhetian Turks (1944).

Another three State Defense Committee decrees were issued in October, two of them dated 8 October. The first one concerned Germans to be resettled from the Voronezh to the Omsk and Novosibirsk Obl. (5,125 persons) between 15 and 22 October, the second one dealt with Germans from Transcaucasia that were to be moved to Kzakhstan and the Novosibirsk Obl. between 15 and 30 October (these included 23,580 Germans from Georgia, 22,741 from Azerbaijan and 212 from Armenia). A separate decree of 22 October 1941 was devoted to *Dagestan* and *the Chechen—Ingush ASSR*: respectively 4 thousand and 547 Germans were to be resettled from these republics to Kazakhstan between 25 and 30 October.[59]

Two more Council of People's Commissars directives of similar content were issued in November 1941; they dealt with the resettlement of Germans from *the Kalmyk ASSR* (2 November) and *the Kuybyshev Obl.* (21 November) to Kazakhstan, and from the frontier districts inland within *the Chita Obl.* (21 November).[60] In March 1942, Germans were banished from the *Kharkov, Crimean, Odessa, Dnepropetrovsk* and *Kalinin Obls.*[61]

Therefore, Germans were banished from almost everywhere within the USSR, where they had resided or where it was possible to reside under the war-time conditions. The entire German population, with the exception of those that fell into the hands of the enemy, was forced to concentrate to the east of the Urals. Out of 873,578 Germans that were to be resettled in compliance with the "state assignment," 256,168 persons, i.e., 98%, had been actually banished by 25 October 1941. At the beginning of 1942, a total of 1,031.3 thousand Germans were registered at special settlements, 800 thousand of them banished from the European part of the USSR (they were distributed between Kazakhstan and Siberia in almost equal proportions), and 231.3 thousand "local" Germans (those not subjected to banishment)[62] who were not embraced by physical resettlement but merely transferred to the category of "special settlers." The number of Germans registered in 1941 and 1942 equaled 1,209,430 persons: 856,340 were resettled "on state assignment," 48,001 drafted to the armed forces, and 203,796 repatriated (yet it seems to be logical to think that they were "local").[63] Approximately 36.7% (444,005 persons) were stationed in Kazakhstan, 333,775 of them "on state assignment"[64] (mainly on Kazakh collective farms, more rarely on Russian and Ukrainian ones). Therefore, a rough estimation of the actual number of banished Germans thus amounts to 905 thousand.

The employment of labor of Germans at their new places of residence was an issue of significance. One option for a "rational resolution" of the issue was the labor mobilization of Germans into a so-called labor army[65] to meet war-time needs, whose members were dispatched as a labor force to areas that were, as a rule, remote from their family's place of settlement registration. The labor army members were arranged into worker battalions that followed camp-like regulations and received the GULAG rations. From the very beginning this organization was remarkably similar to the one that came about later, when the labor of other Germans was used, namely that of POWs and internees. The death rate among labor army members was higher than at special settlements proper, although elderly German people and children left to fend for themselves on food-strapped collective farms faced harsh conditions too.[66]

The labor army started to be formed as early as September 1941, when the NKVD construction battalions were rearranged into units of workers stationed in barracks and following camp regulations. It was with these formations that the term "labor army," used as an official term nowadays, first became associated. The first Germans to be "mobilized" into this army were German Red Army servicemen withdrawn from active duty. First they were registered as special settlers, but instead of being demobilized they were drafted into the labor army, which combined elements characteristic of military life with labor employment and camp conditions.[67]

By early 1942, the labor army comprised as many as 20.8 thousand Germans. Special State Defense Committee decrees of 10 January, 14 February and 7 October 1942 (along with those of 26 April, 2 and 19 August 1943)[68] on drafting the resettled German population into the labor army imparted a new dimension into the process and virtually led to the indiscriminate "mobilization" of able-bodied German resettlers into the labor army. While the two former decrees only dealt with men aged from 17 to 50 years (deportees and "locals" respectively), the latter decree concerned men aged 15 to 55 and women aged 16 to 45, with the exception of pregnant women and those having children younger than three years old. Non-appearance following a call for mobilization, refusal to work and sabotage led to severe punishment, including the firing squad.

In practice, for many labor army service represented another deportation in a short space of time.

The first "mobilization" wave (that was carried out from 10 to 30 January) was intended to embrace 120 thousand persons (45 thousand of them were to be used for timber harvesting, 40 thousand for constructing railways, and 35 thousand for building the plants of Bakal and Bogoslovka). The second wave applied to 40–45 thousand persons, and the third one to 123.5 thousand, including 52.7 thousand women. German women were sent on assignments of the People's Commissariat for oil, while men (naturally 15 or 16-year-old boys and men aged 51–55 were prevalent among them) to the enterprises of Chelyabugol and Karagandaugol coal trusts.[69] The fourth wave (May–September 1943) gleaned a mere 5.3 thousand men and 9.8 thousand women, sweeping up anybody in a fit of desperation, including pregnant women, children aged 14 and old men.

Around 222 thousand German labor army members were registered at the NKVD work units by the beginning of 1944. Some 101 thousand of them were used at the NKVD construction sites, while other peoples' labor was employed by other People's Commissariats. A total of 316.6 thousand Soviet Germans had been employed at labor units by January 1946,[70] when these establishments (along with the camp regime) were abolished. Based on the assumption that at least one-third of them were demobilized Red Army servicemen and "locals," i.e., did not fall into the category of forced migrants, one can come up with an estimated total number of banished Soviet Germans amounting to 1.05 million.

As far as the status of Soviet Germans as special settlers was concerned, it was confirmed again by a Council of People's Commissars decree of 8 January 1945 "On the legal status of special settlers" and by a USSR Supreme Soviet Presidium directive of 26 November 1948 "On criminal liability for escaping from the places of compulsory and permanent settlement of persons banished to remote areas of the Soviet Union during the Patriotic War" (a deliberate escape was punishable by 20 years of hard labor). The labor army was disbanded at the beginning of 1946, however the "released" labor army members remained at the disposal of the enterprises where they had worked, having only received the right to settle in dormitories beside the camp zone and bring in their families.

It should be noted that, apart from Germans, the labor army also incorporated Finns, Romanians, Hungarians and Italians, i.e., Soviet citizens of the same ethnic background as the titular nationalities of hostile countries. Their total number reached around 400 thousand persons, with 220 thousand used within the NKVD system and 180 thousand within other People's Commissariats' domains.[71]

Besides Germans, Ingermanland Finns were also subjected to preventive deportation. The first time, as was mentioned above, was in 1935 when they were banished from the Leningrad Obl. and Karelia, and then in September 1941, when they were resettled from the Leningrad Obl. along with Germans. However, not all Finns were banished at that time, and the rest of them were banished from Leningrad and its locality in March 1942 by a resolution of the Leningrad Front Military Council. In particular the resettlement was carried out on 9 and 26 March. The total of 3.5 thousand families, or 9 thousand persons, were resettled on 27–29 March 1942.[72] They were transported mainly to remote areas, such as the Irkutsk Obl., Krasnoyarsk Kray and Yakutsk ASSR, many were used in fishery collective farms on the Lena river and its tributaries. Finns were regarded as "administratively" resettled, and it was not until 29 December 1942 that they were registered as special resettlers.[73] On 3 April 1942, the State Defense Committee decreed that the front-line army be purged of Finns and the latter be transferred to the NKVD labor units.

Greeks were included in the number of preventively deported peoples too, although for far from obvious reasons.[74] A directive issued by Beria on 4 April 1942 stipulated that the Crimean and Caucasian towns and districts that traditionally contained Greek population—Kerch, Temryuk, the Taman Peninsula, Anapa and Novorossysk—be purged of foreign subjects and "anti-Soviet, alien and suspicious elements." A State Defense Committee decree of 29 May 1942 extended the list by adding Armavir, Maykop and a number of districts and *stanitsa* settlements of the Rostov Obl. and Krasnodar Kray. Besides, it built up the target group of those to be banished (under administrative procedure) by including foreign citizens of Greek nationality, Romanians and the Crimean Tatars in the list along with Germans.[75]

Taking into account the above-mentioned target groups, the Finns banished in 1941 and non-German labor army members, one can estimate the total number of persons preventively banished in 1941–1942 as 1.2 million.

At the same time, it should be taken into consideration that the war-time state border is identical to the front line. This is why the preventive deportations of Finns, Greeks, Romanians, Tatars (and Germans to a far lesser extent) may be regarded as operations for cleansing frontier zones, meant to prevent any temptation of compromise with the enemy.

"RETRIBUTIVE" TOTAL DEPORTATIONS OF THE PEOPLES OF THE NORTH CAUCASUS AND CRIMEA IN 1943–1944

Subsequent operations were not of a preventive nature but represented actions of "retribution" for the crimes actually or allegedly committed during the war to the detriment of the Soviet state. These deportations directly affected another six peoples: Karachais, Kalmyks, Chechens, Ingushetians, Balkars and Crimean Tatars.[76]

Karachais and Kalmyks were the second and third (after Germans) to come under the punitive onslaught of NKVD/MGB bodies, as early as 1943, in November and on the New Year's Eve respectively.

Karachais suffered because they (the directive reads "many Karachais") behaved "...traitorously, joined units organized by Germans for fighting the Soviet authorities, handed over honest Soviet citizens to Germans, accompanied and provided terrain guidance to the German troops advancing over the mountain passes in the Caucasus; and after the withdrawal of the enemy they resist measures carried out by the Soviet authorities, hide bandits and secret German agents from the authorities thus providing them with active support."[77]

The guilt of Kalmyks lay in the fact that they "...betrayed the Motherland, joined units organized by Germans for fighting the Red Army, handed over honest Soviet citizens to Germans, seized and handed over to Germans cattle evacuated from the Rostov Oblast and Ukraine; and after the Red Army drove out the enemy, they resist measures carried out by the Soviet authorities in order to restore the ruined German economy, launch bandit assaults against collective farms and terrorize local population..."

According to the 1939 All-Union census, 75,763 Karachais resided on the territory of the Karachai Autonomous Oblast (incorporated into Ordzhonikidze Kray). The oblast was occupied in the period from August 1942 through the end of January 1943. The anti-German underground movement was suppressed with the support of the so-called Karachai national committee (in January–February 1942, even after the German withdrawal, the committee organized a rebellion against the Soviet authorities in the Uchkulan district).

After the Mikoyan-Shakhar (contemporary Cherkessk) and other districts of the oblast were liberated, Beria's deputy I. Serov personally led the operations against anti-Soviet guerillas (in particular against the "Balyk army" near the upper reaches of the Malka river). On 15 April 1943, the NKVD and Prosecutor's Office of the USSR issued a joint directive that stipulated the banishment of 110 families (472 persons) of the Karachai "gang leaders" and "active bandits" beyond the oblast boundaries.[78] Judging by this specifically targeted action directed against particular enemies of the Soviet regime and their families, the issue of total deportation of the people was hardly on the agenda until later in autumn.

In September, however, the situation changed, according to A. S. Khunagov. A plan for the total deportation of Karachais to Kazakhstan's Dzhambul and South Kazakhstan Obl. and to Kyrgyzstan's Frunze Obl. was already under consideration in Moscow.[79]

And eventually, in October the first instances of targeted banishment received a "creative" impetus, and it was tactfully expanded to the to the entire Karachai people. A directive and a decree on the indiscriminate banishment of Karachais, the abolition of the Karachai Autonomous Oblast and the administrative structure on its territory were issued on 12 and 14 October 1943. The territory of the oblast (9 thousand square kilometers) was distributed between Stavropol Kray (the Zelenchuk districts, part of the Mikoyani and Pregradnensky districts, Ust-Dzhegutin and Malo-Karachai—later renamed Kislovodsk—districts), Georgia (the Uchkulan and part of the Mikoyani districts) and Krasnodar Kray (a part of the Pregradnensky district). On 6 November 1944, a Council of People's Commissars decree on the procedure of populating the former Karachai Autonomous Oblast was adopted. Subsequently the Karachai place names were changed.[80]

Armed units numbering 53,327 servicemen provided back-up through the course of the deportation.[81] Since the plan was to round up 62,842 persons, only 37,429 adults among them, there were nearly two armed Cheka members per each unarmed adult Karachai (including women).

Most of them were to be transported to Kazakhstan and Kyrgyzstan. The deportation itself took place on 2 November 1943. Taking into account additional persons found, the plan was actually over-fulfilled, the number of the resettled persons reaching 69,267. Kazakhstan received 12,342 families, i.e., 45,501 persons, 25,212 and 20,285 persons brought to South Kazakhstan and Dzhambul Obl. respectively. Another 22,900 persons were transported to Kyrgyzstan, and a few small target groups to Tajikistan, the Irkutsk Obl. and the Far East.[82] The following "statistics" sound utterly ridiculous: among the deportees were only 53 officially categorised as dangerous criminals [bandity], 41 deserters, 29 draft dodgers and 184 gang abettors.[83]

Following the deportation, another 329 Karachais were found in the oblast and 90 in other parts of the Caucasus, all of them were banished. Besides, 2,543 persons were demobilized from the Red Army, but they too found themselves in special komendaturas rather than back home.[84]

What kind of threat Karachai children and Red army servicemen posed for the Soviet regime remains unknown, but one of the most respected experts on peoples' deportations regards the NKVD multi-stage operation of deporting Karachais as a "manifestation of the administrative-command system" and a "tough form of controlling national groups and entire peoples".[85] In our opinion, the action rather represented a monstrous disregard of law and a crime against humanity, similar to those that were examined by the Nuremberg International tribunal, all too far from the Dzhambul Oblast.[86]

Decree of the Presidium of the Supreme Council of the USSR "On the disbandment of the Karachai Autonomous Oblast and on the administrative arrangement of its territory" of 12 October 1943

DECREE
OF THE PRESIDIUM OF THE SUPREME COUNCIL OF THE USSR

*On the disbandment of the Karachai Autonomous Oblast and
on the administrative arrangement of its territory*

Due to the fact that during the period of occupation of the Karachai Autonomous Oblast territory by the German fascist aggressors, many Karachais behaved traitorously, joined units organized by Germans for fighting the Soviet authorities, handed over honest Soviet citizens to Germans, accompanied and provided terrain guidance to the German troops advancing over the mountain passes in the Caucasus; and after the withdrawal of the enemy they resist measures carried out by the Soviet authorities, hide bandits and secret German agents from the authorities thus rendering active support to them [bandits and agents], the Presidium of the Supreme Council of the USSR *decrees:*

All Karachais residing on the territory of the Karachai Autonomous Oblast shall be banished to other regions of the USSR, and the Karachai Autonomous Oblast shall be abolished.

The Council of the People's Commissars of the USSR shall provide them with land lots at the destinations and with necessary state support for settlement arrangements

In connection with the abolition of the Karachai Autonomous Oblast:

The districts of Zelenchuk, Ust-Dzhegutin and Malo-Karachai of the former Karachai Autonomous Oblast shall remain within Stavropol Kray, under the jurisdiction of the Stavropol Kray executive committee of the soviets of workers' deputies. The Malo-Karachai district shall be renamed the Kislovodsk rural district.

The Pregradnensky district of the former Karachai Autonomous Oblast shall be incorporated into the Mostovsky district of Krasnodar Kray, its southern, eastern and western borders remaining unchanged, while the northern border shall be designated along the line starting from the village of Kunsha, Krasnodar Kray, via heights 1194, 1664, except for the village of Krugly, further via heights 1274, 1225 reaching the boundary of the pasture lands of the Circassian Autonomous Oblast near the height of 1918.[87]

The remainder of the territory of the Pregradnensky district, including the *stanitsa* of Pregradnensky shall be incorporated into the Zelenchuk district of Stavropol Kray.

The Uchkulan and a part of the Mikoyani districts of the former Karachai Autonomous Oblast shall be incorporated into the Georgian SSR; a new Klukhori district with its center in the town of Mikoyan-Shakhar shall be formed instead.

The town of Mikoyan-Shakhar shall be renamed Klukhori.

The following border between the RSFSR and the Georgian SSR shall be established in the district of Klukhori: in the west—along the current boundary of the former Mikoyani district, further to the east—to the north of the town of Klukhori and further on along the Mara river, around the village of Lower Mara coming up to the boundary of the former Uchkulan district to the south of the village of Higher Mara and further south along the current boundary of the former Uchkulan district.

The remaining territory and settlements of the former Mikoyani district shall be incorporated into Stavropol Kray's Ust-Dzhegutin district.

Chairman of the Presidium of the Supreme Council of the USSR
(M. Kalinin) [signature]
Secretary of the Presidium of the Supreme Council of the USSR
(A. Gorkin) [signature]

Moscow. Kremlin.

[Document] No.803/1.   12 October 1943

Kalmyks were the next to face their cruel fate. According to the census of 1939, the total Kalmyk population of the USSR numbered 134,402 persons. Apart from the Kalmyk ASSR, many Kalmyks resided in the Stalingrad Oblast and Stavropol Kray. Primarily they led a nomadic life and were engaged in animal husbandry.

By the early August of 1942, most of the districts of the Kalmyk ASSR including its capital city Elista were occupied. Some 25% of the population with all their cattle migrated to those districts behind the Volga river that were not occupied. The Kalmyk republic was liberated at the beginning of 1943.

The decision on the Kalmyk banishment as a "means to settle an inter-ethnic conflict" was further provoked by allegations concerning the surrender of the 110th Kalmyk cavalry division. On 27–28 December 1943, a USSR Supreme Soviet Presidium decree "On the disbandment of the Kalmyk ASSR and establishment of the Astrakhan Oblast as a part of the RSFSR," and a Council of People's Commissars decree on the banishment of Kalmyks to Altay and Krasnoyarsk Krays and Omsk and Novosibirsk Obl. were issued. A larger part of the former Kalmyk ASSR was changed into the newly-founded Astrakhan Oblast,[88] two *uluses* [districts] were transferred to the Stalingrad Obl.,[89] two others to the Rostov Obl.,[90] and one *ulus* to Stavropol Kray.[91] Another 211 hectares of pasture lands ("black earth") were handed over to Daghestan's collective farms. Elista itself was renamed the town of Stepnoy. Later, districts populated by Kalmyks were dismantled in other localities too, in particular the Kalmyk district in the Rostov Oblast (9 March 1944), Priyutninsky district delivered to Stavropol Kray after the disbandment of the Kalmyk ASSR (15 May), and 4 districts in the Astrakhan Oblast (25 May). Their territories were divided between the adjacent districts, and the Kalmyk names of most of the village councils were changed to Russian ones.

The deportation itself was conducted on 28 and 29 December 1943, within the operation under code name "Ulusy." The operation was implemented by 2,975 NKVD officers and the 3rd NKVD vehicular regiment that had been previously involved in resettling Karachais. Ivanovo Obl. regional NKVD chief, State Security Major General Markeyev, supervised the operation.

In the first sweep, 91,919 persons were transported, many elderly people and children among them. Another 1,014 persons joined them in January 1944. They were distributed in almost equal measure among the destination areas (the data are presented as of January 1944): 24,352 persons were placed in the Omsk Obl., 21,164 in Krasnoyarsk Kray, 20,858 in Altay Kray, and 18,333 in the Novosibirsk Obl. In the Omsk Obl., more than half of the Kalmyks were settled in its northern okrugs: the Yamal–Nenets, Khanty–Mansi and Tobolsk Okrugs.[92] Since the resettlement was carried out in winter time, the casualties in the course of transportation were extremely high.[93] In addition, epidemics (of typhoid fever) often broke out at the destinations.

In 1944, the Kalmyk deportation continued with the resettlement of those Kalmyks that had resided outside of the Kalmyk ASSR. In March, they were collected in the Rostov Oblast (2,536 persons were sent to the Omsk Obl. on 25 March 1944), in April in the Stalingrad Obl. (1,178 persons were transported to the Sverdlovsk Obl. on 2 to 4 June 1944). Those demobilized from the army were delivered in sections, the total amounting to 4,105 (poet David Kugultinov was one of them).[94]

Kalmyks were employed in agriculture, timber harvesting, but most often in industrial fishery. Their centuries-old experience in animal husbandry, especially distant-pasture, remained untapped.

In 1934, the Chechen AO and Ingush AO were united into a single Chechen–Ingush ASSR. Its territory virtually avoided occupation[95] completely, which made it rather difficult to accuse its peoples of direct treason. This is why the official charges this time included "...active and almost universal involvement in terrorist activities directed against the Soviets and Red Army." In particular, the existence of a mass rebel association under the title "United party of Caucasian brothers" led by Kh. Israilov (Terloyev) was alleged.[96]

In October 1943, deputy people's commissar of internal affairs B. Kobulov visited the republic in order to examine the local situation. In November of the same year, V. Chernyshov (apparently in the middle of the Kalmyk "affair") held a meeting with the heads of the NKVD departments in those districts where Kalmyks were placed. Among the matters he discussed with them were questions pertaining to an intended operation "Chechevitsa," i.e., the deportation of some 0.5 million Vainakhs (Chechens and Ingushetians). The plan provided for 200 thousand persons to be settled in the Novosibirsk Obl. and 35–40 thousand persons in each of the Altay and Krasnoyarsk Krays and the Omsk Obl.[97] However, these regions avoided this responsibility when a new plan, presented to Beria in the middle of December, envisaged a totally different location pattern, reminiscent of that used in the case of the Karachais: highlanders were distributed among Kazakhstan and Kyrgyzstan's regions.

On 29 January 1944, Beria approved an "Instruction on the procedure of resettlement of Chechens and Ingushetians." And on 31 January, the State Defense Committee issued two decrees at the same time, both implicitly concerning Chechens and Ingushetians but not referring to them directly: "On measures for the placement of special settlers on the territory of the Kazakh and Kyrgyz SSR" and "On the order of taking over cattle and agricultural products in the North Caucasus."

On 17 February 1944, Beria reported to Stalin that the preparation for the operation was coming to an end, and 459,486 persons were registered as subject to resettlement, including those residing in Vladikavkaz and Daghestan.[98] Some 310,620 Chechens and 81,100 Ingushetians were to be transported away in the course of the first mass operation (a so-called first train phase).

On 20 February 1944, Beria came to Grozny accompanied by I. Serov, B. Kobulov, and S. Mamulov and personally supervised the operation conducted by extraordinarily powerful forces: up to 19 thousand NKVD, NKGB and SMERSH executive staff members and some 100 thousand NKVD troops drawn up from all over the country for participating in "highland exercises" (even some frontline operations would involve fewer numbers of participants!).[99] On 22 February, Beria held a meeting with the republic's highest officials and spiritual leaders. He warned them about the operation planned to be conducted next day, early in the morning, and suggested they carry out necessary preparatory work among the population.[100]

Unlike the preceding one, this operation cannot be said to have been followed through without excesses: the figures such as 2,016 arrests and 20,072 confiscated guns are eloquent to this. The choice of season can be regarded as an "excess" too: snow in the mountains delayed the resettlement from the highland areas. In the district of Galanchzhoy in particular, the deportation proceeded until 2 March.

Nevertheless, 333,739 persons were evicted during the first day (23 February), and 176,950 of them were bundled onto traines. By 1 March, 478,479 persons were dispatched, 387,229 Chechens and 91,250 Ingushetians among them (in this target group there were also some 500 representatives of other peoples that had been banished by mistake); around 6 thousand Chechens got stuck in the mountains of the Galanchzhoy district due to the snow.

However, no one was to be left behind. That is why in a number of villages, the NKVD troops liquidated virtually the entire civilian population, using in particular burning as their barbaric method of choice.[101] It was not until relatively recently that the operation in the Galanchzhoy district's *aul* of Khaybakh received publicity: not being able to carry out the transportation of its residents, the NKVD troops under the command of Colonel General M. Gvishiani drove some 200 (according to other sources 600–700) persons into the collective farm stable, locked the doors and set the building on fire. Those who tried to make an escape were shot by automatic fire. Residents of the surrounding khutors were shot too.[102]

The Chechen–Ingush ASSR national political elite members were the last to leave their homeland: they were sent to Alma-Ata by a separate train.[103]

The principal State Defense Committee decree on the resettlement of Chechens and Ingushetians is dated 31 January, a corresponding NKVD directive was issued on 21 February 1944. The Chechen–Ingush ASSR itself was abolished by a USSR Supreme Soviet Presidium order of 7 March 1944, and a new okrug of Grozny was established within Stavropol Kray in the stead of the districts formerly populated by Chechens. However, the okrug contained only 2/3 of the former republic's territory. It included Stavropol Kray's northeastern districts populated by Nogays, Dargins, Kumyks (until 1937 these lands were parts of Daghestan) and Russians. Later the

Grozny Okrug was transformed into the Grozny Oblast (when the incorporation of the former Kizlyar district took place).

The parts of the former Chechen–Ingush ASSR that were not integrated into the Grozny Okrug included the former republic's western and some southern districts (i.e., Ingushetia proper) that were handed over to Georgia and North Ossetia, as well as eastern and southeastern districts (in particular, Vedeno, Nozhay-Yurt, Sayasan, Cheberloy within their effective boundaries, and parts of the Kurchaloy, Sharoy and Gudermes districts) that were transferred to Daghestan.

Most of the districts formerly populated with Ingushetians were incorporated into the North Ossetian ASSR, except the Sunzheno and Galashki (the Assino valley) districts that were included into the Grozny Okrug, and the southern part of the Prigorodnyi district (the Dzherakhov valley) handed over to Georgia (incidentally, a part of the Kabardian–Balkar ASSR's Kurpsky district, earlier populated by Ingushetians, was also integrated into North Ossetia; even earlier Stavropol Kray's town of Mozdok with its largely Russian population was incorporated into North Ossetia too). The lands "vacated" after the deportation were peopled mainly by Ossetians from Georgia (in the Prigorodnyi district)[104] and Russians (in the Sunzheno district).

Correspondingly, all Ingushetian toponyms were abolished and replaced by Ossetian and Russian ones. For example, the districts transferred from the Chechen–Ingush ASSR to North Ossetia were renamed by a USSR Supreme Soviet Presidium Directive of 29 April 1944, as follows: the Psedakh district—the Alan district, Nazran–Kosta-Khetagurovo, Achaluk–Nartovsky (the administrative center in the village of Achaluk transferred to the village of Nartovskoye, former Kantyshevo). Another USSR Supreme Soviet Presidium directive (of 30 August 1944) stipulated that all Grozny Oblast's districts and their centers be renamed.

A great majority of the Vainakh resettlers were delivered to Kazakhstan (239,768 Chechens and 78,470 Ingushetians) and Kyrgyzstan (70,097 Chechens and 2,278 Ingushetians). In Kazakhstan, Chechens concentrated primarily in the Akmolinsk, Pavlodar, North Kazakhstan, Karaganda, East Kazakhstan, Semipalatinsk and Alma-Ata Oblasts, and in Kyrgyzstan in the Frunze and Osh Oblasts.[105] Hundreds of special resettlers that had been employed in the oil industry at home, were sent to work at the deposits in the Guryev Oblast.

Gradually, additional target groups of Vainakh special resettlers were arriving at the destinations. Among them were prisoners (transferred from the North Ossetian ASSR to the Karaganda camps), demobilized[106] army servicemen that had resided in the European parts of the USSR, individuals located in the Caucasus,[107] "dodgers," repatriates[108] and others.

Having completed the Chechen–Ingush operation, Beria and his cronies were in no haste to leave the Caucasus alone. It was no accident that Kabardian Z. D. Kumekhov (the first secretary of the Kabardian–Balkar Oblast party organization) went to Grozny on 25 February 1944, where he saw L. Beria, I. Serov and B. Kobulov. The Kabardian–Balkar ASSR, namely its southern part—the Elbrus region—populated by Balkars, was next in line.

Beria failed to come up with more concrete charges against this people than the accusation of their inability to defend Elbrus[109] and the allegation of a conspiracy to unite the Balkar and Karachai ASSRs. In August 1942, a short-lived German occupation of a part of the Kabardian–Balkar ASSR began. The entire republic was, however, liberated from the Germans on 11 January 1943.

It was 24 February 1944 when Beria proposed to Stalin that Balkars be banished, and as soon as 26 February he issued an NKVD order "On the measures for evicting of the Balkar population from the Kabardian—Balkar ASSR."[110] The operation was carried out by 4 thousand NKVD executives and 17 thousand NKVD troops, under the control of Major General I. I. Piyashev. Major General M. I. Sladkevich and two local People's Commissars (of state security and of interior affairs) S. I. Filatov and K. P. Bziava were Piyashev's deputies. The area of the planned banishment was divided into five sectors: Elbrus, Chegem, Khulam-Bezengi, Cherek and Nalchik.

On 2 March, Beria (accompanied by B. Kobulov and S. Mamulov) visited Nalchik and the Elbrus locality. He informed Z. D. Kumekhov of the intention to banish Balkars and transfer their lands to Georgia in order for the latter to have a defensive line along the northern slopes of the higher Caucasus; and he promised that Kabardian would be "compensated" by receiving the former Karachai and Circassian lands.

A State Defense Committee decree on the banishment from the Kabardian–Balkar ASSR was issued on 5 March. The tenth of March was appointed the day of the beginning of the operation, but it was in fact conducted sooner: 8–9 March. This operation was apparently executed without much effort; after the banishment from Chechnya and Ingushetia anything else would appear a walkover. As early as 11 March Beria reported to Stalin that the eviction of 37,107 Balkars had been completed; the report to the Politburo of the Communist Party Central Committee was presented on 14 March, after which, incidentally, Z. D. Kumekhov was dismissed.

On 8 April 1944, a USSR Supreme Soviet Presidium order for the resettlement of Balkars and the renaming of the Kabardian–Balkar ASSR into the Kabardian ASSR was issued. The vacated lands were to be peopled with "collective farm members from the Kabardian ASSR's districts experiencing land shortages," i.e., with Kabardians. The southwestern areas of the republic (some 2 thousand square kilometers against the total area of 12.5 thousand square kilometers.) were handed over to the Georgian SSR.

Following the administrative–territorial crackdown, toponymic repression was customarily the next procedure to be carried out. On 29 May 1944, the RSFSR Supreme Soviet Presidium issued an order that stipulated that: a) the Khulam–Bezengi district be renamed the Sovietsky district, and the village of Kashkatau—its center—the village of Sovietskoye; b) centers of the following districts be removed: the Nagornyi district (from the village of Kamennomostskoye to the village of Sarmakovo), the Urvan district (from the village of Old Cherek to the worker settlement of Dokshukino, presently the town of Nartkala), the Chegem district (from the village of Old Chegem to Chegem-1); c) the Cherek district be abolished (its territory handed over to the Sovietsky and Leskensky districts). Later (in December 1944), a similar directive was issued by the Georgian SSR Supreme Soviet Presidium; it envisaged the renaming of five settlements in the Zemo–Svan district, which had also been founded on former Kabardian–Balkar ASSR's lands that were transferred to Georgia.

The total number of the deportees registered at destinations— in Kyrgyzstan (around 60%) and Kazakhstan—equaled 37,044 (562 persons deceased in the course of transportation are not taken into account). By October, there remained only 33,100 people. Apart from the presence of casualties, the difference can be explained by the fact that there was a considerable number of Kabardians brought to the destinations along with the Balkars by mistake (they were sent back, as a rule).

In the period of 5–10 May 1944, two scores of Balkar families that had resided on the former Karachai territory (then belonging to the Klukhori district of Georgia) were also banished.

In May and June, the clouds grew darker over the Kabardians too. In exact compliance with the Balkar "script," the banishment to Kazakhstan of 2,492 members of the families of "active German accessories, traitors and betrayers" from amongst Kabardians and, to a lesser extent, Russians was carried out. After members of the families of Red Army servicemen and people older than 70 years were exempted from the resettlement, the remaining 1,672 Kabardians were banished to the Dzhambul and South Kazakhstan Obl. of Kazakhstan.[111] However, no mass deportation of Kabardians followed.

As far as the issue of the Crimean Tatars was concerned, which was an ongoing process that started in the Caucasus[112] from as early as April 1944, it was to be resolved utterly and thoroughly.

The occupation of the Crimea by Germans lasted from the end of October 1941 (only Kerch and Sevastopol held the defense until May and July 1942) until April–May 1944. During this period, the Germans annihilated some 92 thousand, or 10%, of the peninsula's population. Both collaboration and underground resistance took place on a considerable scale in the Crimea, with many Crimean Tatars fighting on both sides.[113]

On 13 April, immediately after the Crimea was liberated, the NKVD and NKGB launched a campaign for cleansing its territory of anti-Soviet elements. In practice, this implied a threat of indiscriminate banishment of the Crimean Tatar population. On 10 May, Beria addressed Stalin with a written proposal regarding the banishment "taking into account the treacherous activities on the part of Crimean Tatars and due to the undesirability of Crimean Tatars further residing in the border zone of the Soviet Union."[114] Soon a plan of the operation to be conducted on 18 to 22 May was drafted by Serov and Kobulov. There had been no instance before that the period between the end of the occupation and deportation was that short: only a little over one month.

The State Defense Committee adopted decrees on the banishment of the Crimean Tatar population from the territory of the Crimean ASSR on 2 April, 11 and 21 May 1944. A similar decree on the banishment of the Crimean Tatars and, surprisingly, Greeks from the territories of Krasnodar Kray and the Rostov Obl. was issued on

29 May 1944. All operations in the Crimea were conducted by 32 thousand NKVD executives, officers and servicemen.[115]

The principal operation was launched at dawn on 18 May and carried out within three days. By 4 p.m. on 20 May, as many as 180,014 persons had been evicted, 173,287 of them already aboard trains and dispatched.[116] The final data show that the total of Crimean Tatars evicted from the Crimea reached 191,014 (more than 47 thousand families). As a result, by summer 1945 only 379 thousand of population remained in the Crimea as compared to the pre-war 875 thousand.

Some 37 thousand Crimean Tatar families (151,083 persons) were transported to Uzbekistan: the most numerous "colonies" settled in the Tashkent Obl. (around 65 thousand persons), Samarkand Obl. (32 thousand), Andizhan Obl. (19 thousand) and Fergana Obl. (16 thousand). The rest of the deportees were distributed in the Urals (the Molotov and Sverdlovsk Obls., and Udmurt ASSR) and the European part of the USSR (the Kostroma, Gorky, Moscow and other oblasts, and the Mari ASSR).

Interestingly, initially Uzbekistan agreed to receive only 70 thousand Crimean Tatars,[117] however later it had to "revise" its plans and conformed to the figure of 180 thousand. This required a republican NKVD department for special settlements to be established and given the task of preparing 359 special settlements and 97 *komendaturas*. Although Crimean Tatars were resettled in a more favourable season as compared to other peoples, they still had to undergo considerable ordeals judging by the incidence of disease and the high death rate among them: some 16 thousand in 1944, and another 13 thousand in 1945.[118]

"Toponymic repression" was not launched in the Crimea until the end of the year. On 20 October 1944, the Crimean Oblast party committee issued a decree that stipulated that all settlement, mountain and river names of Tatar, German or Greek origin be renamed. And then, on 14 December,[119] another decree was issued by the RSFSR Supreme Soviet Presidium, which envisaged that Tatar, German and for some reason even Krymchak names of 11 districts and district centers of the Crimean Oblast were to be replaced by Russian names. It was even later that the administrative status of the Crimea itself was dealt with: a USSR Supreme Soviet Presidium decree of 30 June 1945 ruled that the Crimean Oblast be renamed the Crimean ASSR within the RSFSR.[120] Another 327 and 1,062 Crimean Tatar villages and towns were renamed under the RSFSR Supreme Soviet Presidium decrees of 21 August 1945 and 18 May 1948 (marking the deportation anniversary!) respectively.[121] As a result, even Yalta temporarily became Krasnoarmeysk [derived from "Red Army"] and Ay-Petri turned into the Peter Mountain!

The echo of the "repressive toponymy" reverberated even later: for example, a USSR Supreme Soviet Presidium decree was issued on 14 January 1952, which provided for the railway stations on the territory of the Crimean Oblast to be renamed with Russian names.

PREVENTIVE FORCED DEPORTATIONS FROM TRANSCAUCASIA, AND OTHER DEPORTATIONS DURING THE LAST STAGE OF THE WAR IN 1944–1945

The mass banishment from the Crimea, which took place in spring, can be regarded as a "border zone cleansing operation" along with total ethnic deportation, since the Crimea represented a border zone. It was precisely about the undesirability of the presence of people of Crimean Tatar ethnic background *"on the border outskirts of the country"* (italicized by P. P.) that Beria wrote to Stalin on 10 May 1944.[122]

Evidently, Stalin did not dispute the point, and delivered a thorough crushing blow to the peoples of the Crimea and Caucasus, which were named in many official summaries simply as "other." Among those that fell into disgrace were Crimean Bulgarians that resided between Simferopol and Feodosia. They were guilty of merely having lived and worked under occupation by Germans ("they took an active part in the German-led campaign for delivering grain and food products for the German army").[123]

During the period of May through June 1944, an additional 66 thousand persons were banished from the Crimea and Caucasus. In particular, 41,854 persons were deported from the Crimea, including 15,040 Soviet Greeks, 12,422 Bulgarians, 9,620 Armenians, 1,119 Germans, along with Italians, Romanians and others (they were sent to the Bashkir and Mari ASSR, Kemerovo, Molotov, Sverdlovsk and Kirov Obl., and to the Guryev Obl. in Kazakhstan). The number also comprised some 3.5 thousand foreigners with expired passports—3,350 Greeks, 105 Turks, and 16 Iranians among them—who were transported to the Fergana Obl., Uzbekistan.[124] Besides, 8.3 thousand persons (only Greeks) were deported from Krasnodar Kray,[125] and another 16,375 (only Greeks) from the three Transcaucasian republics.[126] Because of their small number, Karaims avoided this "scoop," apart from those that were banished along with Crimean Tatars.[127]

Stalin's own motherland, Georgia, was to fall the next victim to the geopolitical concepts of Stalin, who did not differentiate between the state border and front line.

Having started with resettling 608 Kurdish and Azerbaijani families (3,240 persons in total), former residents of Tbilisi, to the districts of Tsalkini, Borchalini and Karayaz within the republic, Stalin set about handling the "Muslim peoples" of Georgia that populated the Soviet–Turkish border zone. If Turkey, which permanently kept some 30 military divisions along the Soviet border, did cause certain concerns as a potential aggressor, it was not the case at that time. Nevertheless, yet another "objective note" [spravka-ob'yektivka], submitted by Beria to Stalin, Molotov and Malenkov on 28 November 1944, stated that the population of Meshketia that "...had relatives among Turkey's residents were engaged in smuggling, manifested emigrant sentiments and served Turkish intelligence agencies as a contact medium for recruiting spy elements and implanting bandit groups."[128]

The issue of population banishment from the Turkish–Soviet border zone would come up as early as spring 1944. At that time, the discussion embraced some 77.5 thousand persons that were intended to be resettled within their, one might say, neighborhood, namely to districts of eastern Georgia. However, in his letter to Stalin of 24 July 1944, Beria suggested that 16.7 thousand households of "Turks, Kurds and Khemshins" be resettled from the border districts of Georgia to the Kazakh, Kyrgyz and Uzbek SSR.[129] And a decision to banish 76,021 Turks (later another 3,180 persons, those who "fell behind,"[130] were added to this number), 8,694 Kurds and 1,385 Khemshins was adopted. These target groups were to be replaced with 7 thousand peasant families from the land-poor districts of Georgia and 20 thousand border guards. On Beria's order, the entire operation was carried out under the direction of A. Kobulov and Georgian People's Commissars of State Security (Rapava) and of Internal Affairs (Karanadze).

Turks (later they were referred to as Azerbaijani) implied Meskhetian Turks in this case. They populated a historical region of

Meskhet–Dzhavakheti in Georgia. They and their neighbors (also Turkey-oriented), namely Khemshins (Muslim Armenians) and Kurds were banished from the Akhaltsikhe, Adigen, Aspindzi, Akhalkalaki and Bogdan districts of the Georgian SSR, only partially bordering Turkey. Meskhetian Turks resided on the territory annexed by Russia under the Andrianopol peace treaty of 1829. While descending from the same background as Georgians (Meskhi tribes), they had been under Turkish control for a long time, which resulted in their Turkish self-consciousness and their adopting Turkish rather than Georgian names, speaking the Turkish language and practicing Sunni Islam. They had already been subjected to repression on ethnic grounds back in 1928–1937, when they were forced to change their nationality and adopt Georgian surnames.

A decision concerning their deportation was made as early as July, possibly with the intention of completing its implementation before the onset of winter. However, it was impossible to carry out the operation on schedule due to the impassability of roads, and the completion of the Borzhomi–Vale railway required additional time—this was subsequently used for transporting Meskhetians. Besides, the Kazakh leaders, assigned to provide reception for the resettlers, virtually pleaded with the central authorities to delay their arrival insisting on their being overloaded with other target groups, but failed to find any compassion from the Center (although the "planned figure" for the Turks was cut for Kazakhstan[131]).

However, it was not until late fall, i.e., as many as three and a half months after the decree was adopted and two months after the NKVD instruction on the resettlement was issued, that the operation itself took place. It was launched on the morning of 15 November 1944 and went on for three days: two hours were allowed for preparations in each settlement. Only 4 thousand NKVD executives were appointed to carry out the operation. By 4 p.m., 17 November, 25 trains with forced migrants were dispatched from Georgia, with two railway cars of Gypsies among them for unclear reasons.[132]

According to various sources, some 90 to 116 thousand persons were banished in the course of three days. A figure of 91,095 is cited in Beria's report submitted to Stalin on 28 November, while summaries sent to Beria himself by Chernyshev and Kuznetsov refer to 92,307 resettlers, including 18,903 men, 27,399 women and 45,985 children younger than 16 years. More than half of the resettlers

(53,133 persons) arrived in Uzbekistan, another 28,598 persons in Kazakhstan,[133] and 10,546 persons in Kyrgyzstan.[134] The resettlers were primarily employed in agriculture.

Transportation from Georgia to Asia took at least three weeks. At the destinations the resettlers faced a totally foreign environment, filthy water and sometimes (usually in Uzbekistan) breakouts of (typhoid) epidemics. The fact that the operation was carried out in wintertime only contributed to the high mortality rate among the resettlers too. According to unofficial sources, the mortality rate reached 1/3, while official documents cited a figure of 11.8% (as of June 1948). Remarkably, the total number of that target group was continuously decreasing until the end of the 1940s.

Since the state border passed through the territory of Adjaria too, the republic did not avoid "cleansing" operations either. On 9 August 1944, the Georgian authorities ruled that 113 households, located in the proximity of border zone fortifications, be resettled. The resettlement was carried out between 25 and 26 November. And then something highly improbable happened to some of the resettled people, namely to Laz Georgians (numbering around 70 people). Following a petition of writer-minister M. Vanlishi and the subsequent order issued by Beria, they were tracked down and returned to their houses which had been abandoned in their homeland![135]

The political motivation behind the operation was the usual, single and transparent: "frontier zone cleansing," i.e., conducting special measures in preparation for the field of war (as a rule, an offensive was implied). The presence of unnecessary eyes and ears in the course of the troop deployments and construction of fortifications was never considered advisable. Deportations from South Georgia actually made little pragmatic sense for the state, while the economic disarray caused by the banishment of people who were working the lands was quite obvious.

As far as fighting the OUN activists (OUN stands for the "Organization of Ukrainian Nationalists") and other rebels in Western Ukraine was concerned, which started in 1944 immediately after the territory in question was liberated by the Red Army, this represented a border zone "cleansing operation" merely in appearance. A meaningful resistance was also put up in Western Belorussia and Baltic republics, especially Lithuania. These were true military operations in every sense with their share of victories and defeats, with thousands of casualties sustained; and the deportation of OUN members' families, which took place on 31 March 1944, was just one of the measures (albeit one of the most significant) used in this confrontation.

It was as early as April 1944, i.e., even before the deportation of Crimean Tatars was conducted, that the first train intended for 200 OUN members' families was prepared for their transportation to the Minsk district and Sovietsky district of Krasnoyark Kray. According to some sources, the number of deportees from Western Ukraine exceeded as many as 100 thousand in the year of 1944.[136]

On 21 March 1944, A. Veyner, the chairman of the Council of People's Commissars of the Estonian Republic, addressed his Moscow bosses with a suggestion that 700–750 family members of hostile elements be banished from Tallin.[137] On 16 June, Beria issued an order concerning the first banishment from the Baltic republics since 1941: this time 323 family members of "gang leaders and active bandits" were to be expelled from Lithuania,[138] along with 6,320 chiefs and members of rebel groups (the latter were banished to the Komi ASSR, and the Molotov and Sverdlovsk Obls.).[139]

Apart from the "punished" deported peoples, the total number of citizens resettled within the USSR in 1944–1945 amounted to some 260 thousand.

COMPENSATORY FORCED MIGRATIONS IN 1941–1946

The expulsion of entire peoples from their homelands destroyed their centuries-old way of life in terms of economy and social relations. One can imagine the experiences German, Caucasian or Kalmyk peasants had to go through in an alien climate and hostile social environment to assimilate into the new economic reality at the destinations, which was centered around such industries as timber harvesting, coal mining and other mining operations. However, no less tragic was the destiny of their homelands that had been developed through the labor of so many generations. These lands virtually fell out of productive economic use, and it was hard to maintain or re-develop them from scratch, especially in wartime.

The authorities had to settle the so-called legal population in the vacated areas, often by almost equally forceful measures. As a rule, these new settlers originated from neighboring districts. The instruments used for their recruitment included planned resettlement, evacuation and internal district resettlement. In other words, these were the forced compensatory migrations mentioned in the first chapter.

Although in their essence these—voluntary in formal terms—migrants actually represented forced migrants, we still should not consider them on an equal basis with those deported, but we cannot ignore them in this context either. If we assume that this "legal population" made up only 40% of the banished special target groups, the number would reach an additional 840 thousand persons merely in the case of "punished peoples" alone.

It is important to stress that virtually all deported peoples had primarily populated rural areas and been predominantly employed in farming. As of 1 January 1939, the Crimean Tatars and Germans were the most "urbanized" among the deported peoples, with the shares of their urban population reaching 28 and 20% respectively, while with others the figure never exceeded 3–8%. That is why it was an agricultural labor force that was required to maintain the economic profile of the lands left in such haste without proper care, and to take on the abandoned (practically expropriated by the state) houses, construction sites, cattle and working appliances.

This problem was first encountered before the war in connection with the deportation of Koreans, and during the war in the Volga region. The regions from which the German population was banished—mainly in the middle of the harvesting campaign at that—experienced a significant decrease of grain production. As early as September 1941, the Communist Party Central Committee drafted a plan for allotting the vacated territories with residents of neighboring districts and evacuees from the country's western regions (this also allowed for a decrease in resettlement costs). Resettlers and evacuees mixed; German peasants' property was transferred to newly founded collective farms in haste, but instances of looting were not rare.

Initially, it was planned to settle 17.4 thousand Russians from neighboring villages to the places left by Germans so they could take care of the cattle and property of the deportees.[140] Later another 52 thousand persons evacuated from the front-line zone were to be settled there. In March 1942, resettlement of an additional 6 thousand families from the Tambov, Voronezh, Orel and Penza Obls. to the abandoned areas was sanctioned. By summer, 4/5 of the required human resources had been "supplied," however the harvest of 1942 did not reach even 1/3 of the planned quantity, and the winter of 1942–1943 went foodless. In 1943, when the front line started rolling west, a mass withdrawal of the resettlers to their old locations began. In March 1944, a decision to resettle an additional 19,600 families to the region was made, out of which eventually only 4,200 families remained. The total of 18 thousand households was resettled to the territory of the former Volga German ASSR in the period of September 1941 through May 1945, but only 37% of the households laid roots and stayed. In economic terms, the experiment proved an utter failure.[141]

The Karachai, Chechen and other peoples' lands were "developed" in a similar way (only former Balkar settlements, at least those located in highland areas, remained largely abandoned[142]). In particular, in December 1943 a total of 2,115 Georgians were resettled to the territory of the Klukhori district founded within the Georgian SSR by way of uniting the former Uchkulan district and a part of the Mikoyani district that used to belong to Karachai.[143]

In the case of the former Chechen–Ingush ASSR, it was the neighboring population, primarily Ossetians, Daghestani and Russians (from Kizlyar and the Rostov Obls.) that was called to action. Nevertheless, the process of populating the lands was not effective; the abandoned houses and construction were falling into ruin. As many as 42 villages remained (fully or partly) empty. According to average estimates, the number of new settlers made up 40% of the number of the banished population. However, on the territory of the former Chechen–Ingush ASSR this proportion was even lower: by May 1945, some 10,200 new households were accommodated there, as compared to the 28,375 households before the banishment.[144] Grozny Oblast party committee chief Cheplakov asked Moscow to deliver another 5 thousand families to the region, mainly from the Volga area.

Agriculture, especially distant-pasture cattle husbandry and highland terrace farming, sustained large damage. The cattle that belonged to deportees remained behind[145] until they were deported as well, but this time in another direction, into the possession of collective farms of such regions as the Ukrainian SSR, Stavropol Kray, the Voronezh, Kursk and Orel Obls. Naturally, this operation was accompanied by large losses of livestock.

The Chechen banishment had a negative impact on both the

agriculture and industry of the former republic. As N. Bugay demonstrated, the non-fulfillment of the plans by the oil trust Malgobekneft,
and the reduction in oil production in 1944, was a direct consequence
of the deportation of the Chechens.[146]

Let us have a closer look at the compensatory resettlement currents from Daghestan. Four new districts with new names (except
one of them) were formed on the territory of the former Chechen–
Ingush ASSR (an area of 2.7 thousand square kilometers) and incor-
porated into Daghestan: Andalaly (with its center in the village of
Andalaly), Vedeno (the village of Vedeno), Ritlyab (the village of
Ritlyab) and Shuragat (the village of Shuragat). Also, the areas of the
Botlikh and Tsumada districts of the Daghestani ASSR were enlarged
owing to the integrated territory. Within the previous borders of
Daghestan, the Aukhov district (which had been populated by Akkin
Chechens) was renamed the Novolaksky district (with its center in
the village of Novolakskoye); while a part of its territory (two village
councils) was transferred to the neighboring district of Kazbek.

The Council of People's Commissars of the Daghestan ASSR
was assigned to resettle 6,300 peasant households to these abandoned
districts of the Daghestani highland areas by 15 April 1944.[147] Households of the resettling collective farm members were exempted from
state taxes, insurance payments and deliveries of all agricultural products to the state until the year 1946, inclusive.[148]

The republic's leadership fulfilled the plan within the space of
the first five days of the resettlement period (25–30 March 1944), i.e.,
in less than one month after the banishment of the Chechens. A total
of 16,100 households, or some 62 thousand persons, were resettled
(in particular from the Avar settlements of Georgia) by 10 August.
The resettlement covered 21 highland districts of the Daghestani
ASSR, with 144 *auls* resettled in their entirety and 110 partly. In addition, 700 Avar households that had resided on Georgian territory
were resettled to the area.[149] Therefore, the resulting number of
Daghestani people moved into the former Chechen lands reached at
least 65 thousand, which actually made around 1/5 of the then population of Daghestan's highland territory. Historically, this was the first
migration of this scale of representatives of the Daghestani peoples
beyond the traditional borders of their ethnic areas.

Around 55 thousand Daghestani resettlers were placed in four
districts incorporated into the Daghestani ASSR, and some 10 thou-

sand in the piedmont and plain lands within the republic's old borders. In three districts (the Vedeno, Andalaly and Ritlyab districts) on the territory integrated into Daghestan, the newly settled population comprised (alternately located) Andiys, Godoberins, Chamalals, Tindals, Khvarshins, Tsezs, Beshtins, Ginukhs, Akhvakhs, Katarins and Avars from the Botlikh, Tsumada, Tsunta, Akhvakh, Kakhib, Tlyarata, Gumbet, Charoda, Khunzakh, Gunib, Buinaksk and Untsukul districts (over 40 thousand persons). Beshtins, Ginukhs and Avars, who had resided in the Kvarel district of the Georgian SSR before 1944, were also settled in the above-mentioned districts (more then 3 thousand persons). Eventually, the fourth district (of Shuragat) was populated with Dargins from Akushin, Sergokala, Levashi, Dakhadaev and Kaytag districts (more than 10 thousand persons).[150] As far as the 10 thousand internal (within the republic's borders) resettlers were concerned, these included 7 thousand Laks from the Kuli and Laksky districts who were moved to the territory of the former Aukhov district, and some 3 thousand Avars from the Kazbek district who were placed in villages of two village councils transferred to the Kazbek district from the former Aukhov district (starting from 1957, they would have to endure pressure from the Chechens whose houses they occupied).

The Vainakh names of the places populated by new resettlers in the new districts were changed. As a rule, the new names were the same as the names of the *aul*s from where the new resettlers originated (Kidiri, Shapikh, Khushet, Khvarshi, Aknada, Bezhta, Ratlub, Sulevkent, Mulebki, Gerga and others, often with the prefix "New"). However, sometimes the settlements were given completely new names (Kirov-Aul, Pervomaysk, Krasnoarmeysk etc.). The ethnic composition of many new settlements was mixed, but the processes of assimilation within these communities developed fast, with Avars and Dargins consolidating the core ethnic groups in most cases.

Notwithstanding the impressive figures, the resettlement of Daghestani people to new places was far from voluntary. District council representatives and the military would arrive at the *aul*s, gather a common village meeting and declare the decision concerning the movement to other villages, where the collective farm members were expected to "prosper and thrive." And on the very same day, a long chain of carts and wagons would carry the resettlers along mountain paths and roads to the neighboring former Chechen–Ingush ASSR, and into the Chechen *aul*s that had been assigned to them well beforehand.

After the resettlement, Daghestani highlanders (especially those placed in the plain zone of Chechnya) found themselves in a new natural, geographic, social, cultural and ethnic environment. Their traditional lifestyle was destroyed; and the climatic conditions were different. The mortality rate was very high due to sickness and epidemics (mainly malaria and dysentery): according to oral testimonies, around 1/4–1/5 of resettlers died within the first two years after the relocation). The Daghestani people had difficulties adapting themselves to the new conditions, and a section of them tried to make a return, but they were detained and transported back. Some old *aul*s were destroyed in order to stop the flow of the "returnees" (the Tsunta district was especially notable for the number of destroyed *aul*s). Nevertheless, in 1957, when Chechens and Ingushetians returned to their homelands, most of the new settlers had to resettle for a second time in haste (as a rule, if not to towns on the plain, then to their original but partly destroyed *aul*s). Indeed, the short period of their sharing the land with the returning Chechens (who were temporarily unemployed and often behaved aggressively) was hardly a bloodless period of non-conflict.[151]

The appeal "to take part in the reconstruction of the Crimean health resorts" was put out immediately after the liberation of the Crimea from occupation. The deportation of Crimean Tatars, Greeks, Bulgarians and Armenians placed a certain economic urgency into this call. As soon as September–October 1944, more than 17 thousand collective farm members arrived there primarily from Ukraine. However, the animal husbandry, viticulture, tobacco cultivation and other types of economic activities that had thrived in the Crimea at the time of the Tatars required specific skills that the new settlers lacked. By the spring of 1945 the well-being of the 65 thousand new Crimean residents came under critical threat, which caused a massive out-flow of the resettlers. So, by April 1946, some 11,381 families had left the Crimea, while the number of families that moved in reached one thousand (in spite of the fact that a decree was adopted stipulating an unconditional pay-back to the state of all received credits and loans by the "reversers"). By 1 July 1948, 52.5% of families that had been brought there since 1944 had moved away from the Crimea. Other similar cases of economic vacuum emerged in the fashion in

places of one-time settlement of large and small ethnic groups. Therefore, it is no mere coincidence that it was the Saratov and Crimean
Obls. where the largest mechanic out-flow of population was registered at the beginning of 1950.[152]

The Kaliningrad Oblast, a part of Eastern Prussia annexed by
the USSR and incorporated into the RSFSR, also turned out to be
among such depopulated areas. The need for a labor force and popu-

Table 8. **Number of "voluntary" resettlers to the Kaliningrad Oblast**
(as of 1 September 1946 and 1 October 1946)

Region	Number of families	
	Actual	*Planned*
Belorussian SSR	1459/0	2,500
Voronezh Obl.	621/151	900
Kursk Obl.	511/199	900
Bryansk Obl.	466/152	500
Ulyanovsk Obl.	400/135	400
Novgorod Obl.	400/130	400
Kirov Obl.	394/263	400
Velikiye Luki Obl.	386/100	400
Vladimir Obl.	339/156	400
Gorky Obl.	334/143	400
Mordovian ASSR	319/122	300
Pskov Obl.	300/145	300
Kalinin Obl.	282/130	400
Penza Obl.	280/109	500
Ryazan Obl.	275/136	400
Moscow Obl.	273/106	400
Yaroslavl Obl.	260/121	300
Tambov Obl.	260/128	400
Chuvash ASSR	252/156	400
Kostroma Obl.	229/108	300
Orel Obl.	214/120	300
Kuybyshev Obl.	207/111	200
Kaluga Obl.	186/96	300
Mari ASSR	139/70	200

Remark: In the "Actual" column the first figures apply as of 1 October 1946; the
second as of 1 September 1946.
*Source: GARF, h. 9401, r. 2, d. 139, l. 104–105, 194–197. See also: M. G. Shenderyuk.
"Kto oni—pervyye pereselentsy v samuyu zapadnuyu?" [Who are they—the first resettlers to the very West?] Abstracts of presentations of the 4th Conference of the History
and Computer Association (Zvenigorod, 26 March–29 March 1998), Information Bulletin No. 23, March 1998, Moscow: Mosgorarkhiv, 1998, 142–144.*

lation as such was particularly critical there. A special resolution concerning voluntary resettlement of 12,000 collective farm members' families to the Kaliningrad Oblast was issued by the USSR Council of Ministers. On 8 September and 14 October 1946, S. Kruglov sent Stalin, Beria and Zhdanov reports on the resolution implementation. As of 1 September, 2,990 families had been resettled, and by 1 October the figure reached 8,795 families of collective farmers (see table 8). The accomplishment of Belorussia in October 1946 in supplying "volunteers" is remarkable.

ETHNIC AND OTHER DEPORTATIONS AFTER THE SECOND WORLD WAR, 1949–1953

Remarkably, even after the war, when all reasons and grounds used to justify deportations seem to have been exhausted, repressive migrations were persistently adhered to, although their intensity decreased.

However, the first one and a half to two years turned out to be, as it were, a respite. But let us not forget that it was precisely during this period that the main bulk of work had to be done with regard to the target groups "delivered" as a result of the war—namely POWs of hostile armies, the Westarbeiter, as well as German civilians, and of course Soviet repatriates[153]: after "filtration" many of them were assigned and transported to special settlements.

The idea of "repatriation" appeared attractive within the Soviet Union too: initiatives with regard to remedying the "excesses" of the past and returning certain categories of the deportees to their places were evident at the union level of the republics in 1946. For example, in their letter of 16 March the chairman of the Council of People's Commissars of the Latvian SSR, Latsis, and the secretary of the Central Party Committee of the Latvian SSR, Kalnberzin, addressed Molotov proposing that Latvians that had served in the Wehrmacht be returned home from exile. Kruglov supported the initiative suggesting that it should be extended to include Lithuania, Estonia and Moldova, and prepared a corresponding draft resolution of the Council of Ministers.[154] On 9 July, the secretary of the Georgian SSR CP Central Committee, Charkviani, addressed Beria too with a request that Georgian, Armenian and Azerbaijani repatriates be transferred from camps in remote parts of the USSR to Georgia, Armenia and

Azerbaijan, where their labor could be effectively employed. A relevant draft resolution of the Council of Ministers was prepared by 14 August,[155] however, it seems that Beria did not support all these initiatives.

Repressive policies, and particularly forced resettlements, were mounted once again in 1947 and were dramatically enhanced in 1948. The USSR Supreme Soviet Presidium decree of 21 February 1948 "On the post-confinement assignment of dangerous special state offenders to settlement in remote areas of the USSR" was of great consequence. Persons that were still serving their terms in special prisons and camps were to be subjected to an additional matter-of-course punishment: banishment to settlements in such "resorts" as Kolyma, Siberia (Krasnoyarsk Kray and the Novosibirsk Obl., but no further to the south than 50 km from the Transsib) and Kazakhstan (with the exception of the Alma-Ata, Guryev, South Kazakhstan, Aktyubinsk, East Kazakhstan and Semipalatinsk Obls.).

Crucially, the law was retrospective and applied to those who had already been released from prisons and camps in the period from the end of the war through the moment of the decree enactment (decisions concerning such persons were made by the Special Council of the MGB). It was this decree that brought about second terms for many repatriates that seemed to have already served their time for the motherland. Repeated arrests were launched as early as autumn 1948.[156]

The decree of 22 February 1948 adopted by the Council of Ministers envisaged another banishment of those who had been deported to a number of regions in the European part of the USSR, but this time from these regions.[157] A total of 82.5 thousand persons were to be transported to Siberia and Kazakhstan, the largest target groups residing in the Tula (17,906 persons), Vologda (10,297 persons), Kostroma (9,055 persons) and Moscow (8,297 persons) Obls. At the same time, some 80 thousand persons settled in the Bashkir, Mari and Udmurt ASSR, and in the Arkhangelsk, Kirov and Chkalov Obls. were not subject to a second resettlement. However, the decision faced a certain resistance at the local level: first a number of delays in its fulfillment occurred; and by summer 1948 the operation, one might say, broke down.[158] There is no doubt that after a long interval there emerged more clashes of interest between the Center and regions, the latter being nervous about the possible loss of qualified labor force and deterioration of their economic situation (judging by the documents, the leadership of the Karel–Finn ASSR was most assertive in defending its interests, as compared to others[159]).

It was in June 1948 that persecution of "spongers" was launched, the term applied to collective farm members who failed to fulfil the mandatory minimum of work-day units, which was interpreted as dodging farming labor duties. According to the USSR Supreme Soviet Presidium decree of 2 June 1948 "On the banishment to remote areas of individuals persistently avoiding their labor duties in the agricultural industry and leading an anti-social parasitic life," the right to pass sentences on offenders was granted to simple majorities of such "bodies" as collective farm general meetings or village gatherings; then the village council would submit the community decision to the district executive committee for approval. Merely in the course of 1948, over 27 thousand collective farmers were banished to special settlements (usually to the east of the Urals) for the term of eight years, with no investigation or trial carried out.[160] The total of the so-called decree resettlers made up 33,266 in the period of 1948—1953.[161]

As is well known, the population of the territories annexed by the USSR after the war opposed the sovietization policy, often taking up arms. Suppression of armed resistance to the Soviet authorities in the post-war years was bound to involve such well-tested measures as deportation of the rebel family members. Naturally, Western Ukraine and Lithuania, where the resistance was especially violent, were the starting point. In particular, deportations of OUN members from western Ukrainian regions continued. Some 75 thousand persons were deported from there by the mid-November of 1947.[162]

Under the Supreme Soviet decree of 21 February 1948, families of Lithuanian bandits and nationalists in hiding, along with those assisting them and kulak families were subject to banishment to special settlements. The planned number of those destined to be exiled constituted 12,134 families, or some 48 thousand persons. The projected destinations included Krasnoyarsk Kray, the Irkutsk Obl., the Buryat–Mongol and Yakut ASSR; and the timber-harvesting industry was to be the principal area for the deportees' labor application. The operation under code name "Vesna" [Spring] was carried out on 22 May, starting at midnight in Vilnius and Kaunas, and at 4 a.m. in the *uyezdz*. The total number of those deported reached 49,331 persons.[163]

A decree adopted by the Council of Ministers on 29 January 1949 sanctioned a new operation for the banishment of some 100–150 thousand "bourgeois nationalists" and their families, which was disguised as routine military exercises. This operation, exceeding the "Spring" operation of the previous year three-fold in scale, was to embrace the entire territory of the Baltic republics. It was given a no less romantic code name than "Priboy" [The wash of the waves]. The 76-thousand-strong body of MGB personnel and party activists involved in its implementation points to the magnitude and scope of the operation (it appears that this was the first instance since the banishment of Chechens and Ingushetians when such a large number of deporting forces were employed).[164]

The operation was conducted everywhere simultaneously, on 25 March 1949. By 6 p.m. that day 29,687 families, i.e., 89,874 persons, had already been arrested.[165] The total number of those banished in March 1949 (including those additionally banished) amounted to 30,630 families, or 94,779 persons, including 25,708 men, 41,987 women and 27,084 children. The distribution of the deportees among the republics went as follows: 13,624 families (42,149 persons) were banished from Latvia; 7,488 families (20,173 persons) from Estonia; and 9,518 families (31,917 persons) from Lithuania.[166] They were transported to the Irkutsk (25,834 persons), Omsk (22,542 persons) and Tomsk (16,065 persons) Obls., to Krasnoyarsk Kray (13,823 persons), the Novosibirsk (10,064 persons) and Amur (5,451 persons) Obls. and other destinations.[167]

So, 203,590 persons altogether, including 118,599 from Lithuania, 52,541 from Latvia and 32,540 from Estonia were banished from the Baltic republics to special settlements in the period of 1940–1953.[168]

In accordance with a resolution adopted by the Council of Ministers on 29 December 1949, so-called former Baltic residents—namely kulaks and alleged bandits (with families), and those repressed for anti-Soviet activities—were transported from the Pskov Oblast's Pytalovo, Pechora and Kachanovsky districts to Khabarovsk Kray in the first half of the year 1950. The official statement specified the banishment term as "for ever": the indicated districts had been parts of Estonia until 1940.[169]

Somewhat earlier, under a resolution of 6 October 1948, another 1,100 persons from the Ismail Obl. were included among the "kulak" target group of the Tomsk Obl.[170] And at the end of 1948, a new wave of deportations approached Moldavia.

On 12 October, moldavian minister of interior affairs, F. Ya. Tutushkin, addressed the Soviet government with a suggestion that 15 thousand kulak families, or at least 5 thousand families of especially hostile kulaks, be banished to remote areas. By 2 December, lists of the 33,640 persons, including 9,259 household heads, to be banished were prepared and split into categories. By mid-February 1949, the number of people put on the lists in question reached 40,854, including 11,281 household heads. Following these measures, in mid-March, the bureau of the Communist Party Central Committee of Moldavia, the CP Central Committee and the Moldavian SSR Council of Ministers sent a joint request to the Center in order to receive a permission to resettle kulaks, former landowners, major merchants, active collaborators with German occupying forces and activists of pro-fascist parties, numbering 39,091 persons altogether. The request was attended to: on 6 April 1949, the Politburo of the Communist Party Central Committee approved the Council of Ministers resolution concerning the banishment of 40,850 persons, i.e., 11,280 families from the territory of Moldavia. Eight executive sectors were founded for conducting the operation named "Yug" [South] by the leadership of the MVD of the USSR.[171]

On 11 June, the MVD issued an order on the procedures of reception, transportation, settlement and employment of the individuals banished from Moldavia. Operation South, that involved more than 21 thousand personnel, started at 2 a.m. on 5 July and was completed at 8 p.m. on 7 July.[172] Rain showers that occurred on those days hindered the operation's implementation, but they failed to flush away the Center's order. The target group was gathered and placed into 1,573 railway cars, split into 30 trains. These "passengers" comprised 11,253 families, or 35,796 persons (including 9,684 men, 14,033 women and 11,899 children). In about two weeks they were delivered to their destinations: the Kurgan, Tyumen, Irkutsk and Kemerovo Obls., Altay and Khabarovsk Kray, and the Buryat–Mongol ASSR.[173]

On 17 May 1949, the Communist Party Central Committee made another decision concerning Greeks (Greek citizens, stateless former Greek citizens, and former Greek citizens granted Soviet citizenship). The decision was motivated by the need to cleanse the

Black Sea coastline belonging to the RSFSR and Ukraine, and that pertaining to Georgia and Azerbaijan from "politically unreliable elements." It was proposed that they be exiled for permanent resettlement and employment in the South Kazakhstan and Dzhambul Obls. of Kazakhstan under MVD supervision.[174] The resettlement was executed in June 1949; 57,680 persons altogether, including 15,485 *Dashnaks*, were deported.[175]

At the same time, in summer 1949, small groups of Armenian Dashnaks, Turk and Greek nationals, stateless Turks and Greeks and former Turk and Greek citizens granted Soviet citizenship were banished from the territories of Georgia, Armenia and Azerbaijan, as well as from the Ukrainian and Russian (North-Caucasian) Black Sea coast.[176] In general, Osman Turks would mix with Meskhetian Turks at their destinations (Uzbekistan, Kazakhstan, Kyrgyzstan) and eventually were virtually absorbed into the latter ethnic group.

According to V. N. Zemskov, the total number of the special resettlers permanently banished from the Baltic republics, Moldavia and the Black Sea coast exceeded 170 thousand persons by mid-1949, and constituted respectively 91,204, 34,763 and 57,246 persons, as of 15 July 1949.[177]

Deportations continued into the 1950s. For example, 2,795 *Basmaches* and their family members were banished from Tajikistan to Kazakhstan's Kokchetav Obl. in March 1951.[178] In early 1951, the "cleansing" process of Georgian territory, in particular of Iranians, continued: they were sent to the Dzhambul and Alma-Ata Obls. Somewhat later (at the end of the year), Assyrians and other representatives of "hostile elements" were subjected to expulsion from Georgia too.[179]

The annexed territories were not neglected either. For instance, resolutions adopted by the Council of Ministers in January–March 1951 envisaged further resettlement of kulaks with families from Western Ukraine and Western Belorussia, along with the banishment of former Anders Army military servicemen, repatriated from England, from Lithuania to the Irkutsk Obl.

In addition, so-called sect elements, whose religious practices and propaganda were perceived as anti-Soviet by the authorities, were ejected from all annexed territories. The state security bodies were particularly consistent and thorough when dealing with members of the "Jehovah's Witness" sect that became yet another collective target of the agencies in question. Then minister of interior affairs, Abakumov, expressed his views regarding the deportation of sect members in his report to Stalin in October 1950; he suggested that the relevant operation be scheduled for March–April 1951. A corresponding resolution was adopted by the Council of Ministers on 3 March, and a suitable order subsequently issued by the MGB of the USSR on 6 March. On 24 March, the CM of the Moldavian SSR passed a decree "On the confiscation and selling of the property of individuals banished from the territory of the Moldavian SSR."[180] Operation "Sever" [North] was launched at 4 a.m. of 1 April 1951 and completed on 2 April. It was executed by approximately 2,600 personnel; and incidentally the number of the deportees was almost identical: 732 families, i.e., 2,619 persons, with women and children

Figure 5. **Forced migrations in 1947–1952**

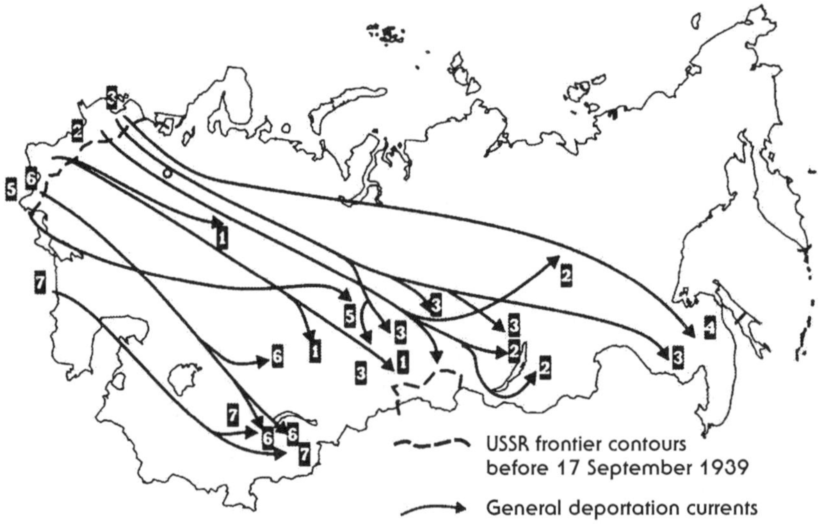

USSR frontier contours before 17 September 1939

General deportation currents

Deported target groups:
1. The OUN members from the Western Ukraine (1947–1948);
2. Lithuanians (1948);
3. Residents of the Baltic republics (1949);
4. Banished from the Pytalovo district of the Pskov Obl. (1949);
5. Banished from the Ismail district (1948);
6. Banished from Moldavia (1949);
7. Banished from the Black Sea coast (1949).

making up 2/3 of them. The Tomsk Obl. was assigned as their destination. Apart from the Tomsk Obl., Jehovists from other western
regions of the USSR were sent to the Irkutsk Obl.

Under a resolution of 5 September 1951, tens of thousands of
newly dekulakized peasants from the Baltic republics (16,833 persons), Right-Bank Moldavia (9,727 persons), Western Ukraine and
Western Belorussia (5,588 persons) arrived in the Tyumen Obl.,
Krasnoyarsk Kray, Kazakhstan and Yakutia for special settlement.[181]
Special resolutions were issued in spring 1952 with regard to kulaks
from Western Belorussia: under one of the resolutions, some 6 thousand persons were resettled to the Irkutsk Obl. and Kazakhstan in the
course of an operation conducted on 18–22 April 1952.[182]

Apparently, those resettled under the USSR Supreme Soviet
Presidium decree of 23 July 1951 for "vagrancy and begging" can be
included into the same category as the "spongers." An alleged projected deportation of Jews from central and western regions was to
have taken place somewhat later, however, on all accounts, it was
forestalled by Stalin's death. Notably, no direct evidence of this plan
has been discovered so far.[183]

Consequently, according to the available data, the total number
of the deported in the post-war years can be estimated as some 380–
400 thousand persons. The general geographic pattern of the banishment regions is reminiscent of that which evolved during the two final
war years, with the principal stress somewhat shifted from Transcaucasia to the western border zones warranted as USSR territory under
the Potsdam peace treaty. At the same time, a certain shift regarding
the destination geography occurred too: in particular, East Siberia
and, especially, Krasnoyarsk Kray were gradually brought to the forefront thus replacing, to a large degree, Kazakhstan and Uzbekistan,
whose role as destinations became far less significant.

NOTES

1 A *troika* was an "arbitrary" court system of three people to accelerate arrests
  and prosecution on a local level, abolished in fall 1938.
2 The Soviet–Finnish war started on 30 November 1939.
3 Interestingly, the starting date for issuing passports to the annexed territories'
  local population was set for the mid-February (See Filippov, 1997, 56–57).
4 N. F. Bugay cites a different figure: 22–25 thousand (Bugay, 1995, 13).

5 Guryanov, 1997a, 115.

6 Guryanov, 1997a, 117.

7 According to the official Soviet version, *osadniki* were "the bitterest enemies of the working people": former military service members distinguished in the Polish–Soviet war of 1920, who were rewarded by their grateful motherland with strips of land in eastern districts populated mainly by Belorussians and Ukrainians.

8 Bugay, 1995, 12.

9 It was he that suggested on 23 December 1939 that so-called forest rangers or forest security guards be included into the resettled target group.

10 Filippov, 1997, 53.

11 Khrebtovich-Buteneva, 1984, 48–53.

12 Bugay, 1995, 13.

13 Guryanov, 1997a, 120, quoting: GARF, h. 9479, r. 1, f. 57, sh. 40–41. It was this target group that was later addressed by the USSR Supreme Soviet Presidium decree of 17 August 1941 concerning exempting Poles from special settlement and the NKVD decree allowing them to reside on USSR territory with the exception of frontier and restricted zones along with places under martial law and restricted towns.

14 This difference in attitude was logically reflected in the fact that the death rate among *osadniki* was several times higher than among refugees (see Zemskov, 1990a, 5; Guryanov, 1997a).

15 Guryanov, 1997a, 116.

16 Zemskov, 1990a, 5–7. Out of the 177,043 Polish "special resettlers" as of 1 April 1941 (without taking into account 35,539 persons that resided in Kazakhstan, Krasnoyarsk Kray and Vologda Obl.) some 97 thousand (54.6%) were ethnic Polish, Jews made up 59 thousand (i.e., 33.3%), and there were 9 thousand each of Ukrainians and Belorussians (5.1—5.3%). See Zemskov, 1990a, 8.

17 Exceptions were those deported before 17 September 1939, deserters and criminals (Bugay, 1995, 192–193).

18 Bugay, 1995, 194–195.

19 Headed by Yu. Paletskis, A. Kirchenstein and I. Vares. V. Dekanozov, A. Vyshinsky and A. Zhdanov respectively were Soviet representatives in the governments.

20 Its text, that had leaked to the Germans, became disclosed in 1941 (see *These Names Accuse*, 1982, XVIII, XXXVI–XXXXI).

21 See the corresponding draft resolution of 16 May 1941 (RGANI, h. 89, op. 18, f. 3, sh. 2–5).

22 Interestingly, family heads subjected to arrest were supposed to initially spend some time there too. They were not informed of the upcoming separation of the families in order to avoid possible revolt on their part. As in the case of Poles, the weight of bare essentials and food that they were allowed to take was not to exceed 100kg (see Maksheyev, 1997, 106–108).

23 Passat, 1994, 23.

24 Here and beyond we will use approximate data first presented by Guryanov based on his "train-by-train" analysis (Guryanov, 1997b).

25 Passat, 1994, 24–25.
26 See Passat, 1994, 25–26.
27 Some 30 thousand names are listed in the Passional of the Latvian victims of the Stalin repression of 1941, which was first published in Stockholm in 1951 and then updated and republished in 1982. The list includes those executed and confined in prisons and camps (see *These Names Accuse*, 1982).
28 According to S. Parsadanova, 1,173,170 persons were deported from the regions in question; 318,564 of them had been employed in industry and 418,569 in agriculture. The death rate among those resettled reached 16% (Parsadanova, 1989, 36).
29 Zaytsev, 1993, 112.
30 The order was to be fulfilled by local authorities and "osobisty," i.e., members of the special departments of army units and detachments.
31 *Hidden Truth*, 210–211, quoting: TsAMO, h. 353, r. 5864, f. 1, sh. 27.
32 Bugay, 1995, 136.
33 Remarkably, in Germany itself, only USSR citizens were subjected to internship, while the first-wave Russian emigrants did not face any repression or restrictions.
34 Bugay, 1990b, 33.
35 Broydo, Prokhorov, 1994, 343.
36 Alekseyeva, 1992, 93.
37 Gakayev, 1997, 98.
38 Auman, Chebotareva, 1994, 45.
39 Bugay, 1995, 67.
40 Mukhazhir Umayev (Azamatov, Temirzhanov et al., 1994, 8).
41 German, A., 1996, 135–142.
42 Kriger, 1997.
43 No documentary evidence proving the visit did take place is available.
44 I. V. Ivanov was appointed to take the lead of the section. The body did not last long, and was dissolved on 14 November 1942; its functions were taken over by the department for labor and special settlements under the jurisdiction of the NKVD GULAG (see Kokurin, Petrov, 1997, 31, 270–271).
45 On 16 September, A. Gekman and G. Korbmacher were expelled from the party "for discrediting the decree" of 28 August 1941.
46 The same principle was followed in the course of all other deportations. According to other sources, this principle was first applied to Germans from Transcaucasia in October 1941 (Bugay, 1995, 41, quoting instruction No. 001487 passed by the NKVD on 11 October 1941).
47 A corresponding instruction was issued by the CNK on 30 August 1941 in connection with the deportation from the Volga region, and was subsequently used without amendments all over the USSR territory.
48 Notwithstanding the virtual total dismantling of German collective farms, the state expected to receive all due deliveries of goods from them. The resettlers employed at collective farms were promised to be allotted 3% of the agricultural products remaining after the completion of the compulsory plan, taking into account fulfilled work-day units. The grain that remained, after delivering

the compulsory plan supplies to the state and allotting the amount due to the departing resettlers, was sold to the state at the purchase rates by representatives of the NKZem of the USSR. A part of the grain supplies stayed in the collective farms to form the forage and seed fund for the collective farms' members to come. In cases of collective farms having debts, the debts were transferred to the new farm created on the same territory. Unharvested grains were purchased at a 30% discount for covering expenditures for its harvesting, storage and transportation. The means received from product realization were used for repaying all state loans (irrespective of the repayment terms), taxes, duties and insurance payments. Cash assets of the collective farms were transferred to the possession of the local authorities for subsequent reinforcement of newly formed local collective farms.

49 The livestock received from collective farms in excess of the state plan to be fulfilled was documented in records in three copies listing the number of the livestock and its live weight. Having produced the records at the destinations, the resettling collective farms were supposedly entitled to receive livestock. Every livestock head received from private owners was paid for, and the owners were given a receipt. The former livestock owners were assured that on producing the receipts at the destinations, they would be in a position to purchase workstock at the equivalent rates.

50 According to the testimonies given by Germans that had resided in Kanovo, Karlsfeld (khutor Zelenaya Roshcha), on the lands of collective farms Leninfeld, Rote-Fahne, Rot-Front (the village of Kochubeyevskoye) and the city of Stavropol, the takeover of private property was a formal procedure (documented by T. N. Plokhotnik).

51 Chebykina, 1999, 120–121.

52 Bugay, 1995, 39–40.

53 See Eisfeld, Herdt, 1996, 58.

54 See report of 29 August 1941 by V. M. Molotov, G. V. Malenkov, A. N. Kosygin, A. A. Zhdanov, to I. V. Stalin (Izvestia CPSU Central Committee. 1990, no.9).

55 According to other sources (Bugay, 1995, 44–45, table 2), Germans from the Rostov Obl. were also transported to the Novosibirsk Obl. and Altay Kray.

56 See Auman, Chebotareva, 1993, 161–162, 164 (according to T. N. Plokhotnik, between 15 and 20 September). The luggage restriction was 200 kilos.

57 See Auman, Chebotareva, 1993, 164–165. The destination is not indicated.

58 See Auman, Chebotareva, 1993, 165. See also Bugay, 1995, 44.

59 See Auman, Chebotareva, 1993, 166–168 (according to other data, between 22 October and 10 November 1941).

60 Bugay, 1995, 45.

61 Bugay, 1995, 45.

62 Around 226 thousand Germans had resided on these territories before the war, most of them in Kazakhstan (92 thousand persons), in the Omsk Obl. (59 thousand) and in Altay (29 thousand). See Eisfeld, Herdt, 1997, 45–46.

63 By the end of the war, 949,829 Germans were registered at special settlements, and 120,192 repatriated persons were added to that number in the post-war period (Zemskov, 1990a, 8).

64 Bugay, 1995, 42, quoting GARF, h. P-9479, r. 1, f. 641, sh. 76; f. 83, sh. 148.

65 The term "labor army" was not in official use, which was the ground used by member of the Collegium of the Ministry of Justice of the USSR O. V. Boykov, in his "Certificate" of 20 September 1990, in which he did not recognize the widely used term "labor army member" as a category falling under the status of special target group workers (Auman, Chebotareva, 1993, 333–334).

66 See Vyltsan, 1995, 32–33, quoting GARF, h. P-9479, r. 1, f. 641, sh. 76; f. 83, sh. 148.

67 See Chebykina, 1999; Malamud, 1999.

68 See Auman, Chebotareva, 1993, 168–175.

69 Germans were also employed in fishery under the resolutions of the Council of People's Commissars of the USSR and Communist Party Central Committee "On development of coastal fishery in the White Sea and Barents Sea" and "On development of fishery in the basin of Siberian rivers and in the Far East" (October 1942).

70 See NKVD order No. 30–39 of 5 January 1946 on the dismantling of residence zones of the settlers mobilized for work in the oil industry (Bugay, 1995, 55, quoting GARF, h. P-9479, r. 1, f. 148, sh. 162).

71 Kokurin, 1995, 64. Let us note that labor army members were nominally registered with the GULAG, and not the NKVD department for special settlements.

72 According to other sources, the figure amounted to some 40 thousand Finns (see Kuraptseva, N., "...I. Mukhin, syn Suokasa" [... I. Mukhin, a son of Suokas], Smena [Leningrad, 1991], 26 June).

73 Bugay, 1995, 192.

74 Zemskov, 1990a, 16.

75 See Kotsonis, 1997, 83–88.

76 At this point it seems to be appropriate to mention, at least in a footnote, one more plan that was allegedly considered by the NKVD and dating back to 22 June 1944, namely the plan to resettle all Ukrainians that had lived on the occupied territories, and not from the western Ukrainian regions, but from the Kiev, Poltava, Vinnitsa, Rovno and other obls. (see Aliyeva, 1993, vol. 3, 140–141, quoting TsDAGOU, h. 1, r. 70, spr. 997, ark. 91; unfortunately it proved impossible even to establish the exact name of the archive). There has been, however, no public response to this document which appears sensational. In any case, the plan was never implemented.

77 Such "grounds" seemed to be insufficient to some respected researchers dealing with the problem of deported peoples, and they came up with additional far-reaching factors of their own, namely the need to prevent desertion from the Red Army by Karachais. Another "eloquent" argument used is alleged activities of a German agent network numbering, according to some sources, up to 1,234 persons on the entire territory of the North Caucasus: even among the 302 enemy paratroopers registered by the NKVD, Karachai made up around 200. (See Bugay, Gonov, 1998, 121.) It makes one shudder to think of what would have happened, had Stalin and Beria found out that there were representatives of the Russian people among "deserters" and "spies" too!

78 Bugay, 1995, 61.

79 See Bugay, Gonov, 1998, 127.

80 For example, Mikoyan-Shakhar was originally renamed Mikoyani, and then Klukhori, which was its name until it was changed to Cherkessk on 8 January 1957.

81 Bugay, Gonov, 1998, 128.

82 Bugay, 1995, 62–66.

83 Bugay, Gonov, 1998, 128, quoting GARF, h. 9478, r. 1, f. 229, sh. 70.

84 Bugay, Gonov, 1998, 129

85 Bugay, Gonov, 1998, 130. The researchers are inclined to believe that "… the banishment of citizens of Karachai nationality was grounded on the opposition manifested by a part of the population toward the party's fundamentals, and their refusal to accept collectivization, along with their partial support of the fascist occupation regime." Even 55 years after the events as described, the impeccability of the Soviet authorities has not been called into question!

86 Crimes which have been all too often overlooked in contemporary Russian society, yet which were of a scale appropriate for a Nuremberg-style prosecution.

87 These are Russian cartographic labelling terms for hills denoted by their altitude.

88 It was formed by the former Ketchenerovsky, Chernozemelsky, Troitsky, Bstinsky, Privolzhsky and Kaspiysky *uluses*.

89 Former Moloderbent and Sarpinsky *uluses*.

90 Former Zapadny and Yashaltin *uluses*.

91 Former Priyutninsky *ulus*.

92 Bugay, 1995, 65–74, 88.

93 Bugay, 1995, 79–80.

94 Bugay, 1995, 74–77.

95 With the exception of the district of Malgobek in the north of the republic, which was liberated on 3 January 1943.

96 Bugay, Gonov, 1998, 135. See also Sidorenko, 2000, 57–76.

97 Bugay, 1990b, 38.

98 Bugay, 1995, 104, quoting: TsKhDRCh, h.1, r. 2, f. 64, sh. 167. Some districts populated by Akkin Chechens had been incorporated into the Daghestan ASSR as early as 1922.

99 Bugay, 1995, 103–107. V. P. Sidorenko cited the exact figure of 93,073 (2000, 78, referring to RGVA, h. 38650, r. 1, f. 607, sh. 37–41).

100 Those party and soviet bosses and spiritual leaders that conformed to the decision were granted a "bonus," namely an increased standard of the amount of luggage allowed for transportation (see Vyltsan, 1995, 37). The standard in these cases constituted 500kg per family (Bugay, 1990b, 38).

101 Bugay, Gonov, 1998, 147.

102 The first commission assigned to investigate the "operation" was established as early as 1956. Incidentally, M. Gvishiani was conferred to a second-rank order of Suvorov. (See "Kazn v kolkhoze imeni Berii" [Execution in the Beria collective farm], *Obshchaya gazeta*, 25 February–3 March 1999, no. 8, 15).

At the same time, an official report on the operation submitted by Gvishiani mentioned only a few score of those killed or deceased while being transported (Sidorenko, 2000, 79–80, citing RGVA, h. 38660, r. 1, f. 1, sh. 15).

103 Bugay, Gonov, 1998, 147.

104 The total of those banished from Georgia's Ossetian districts on the order amounted to 25–35 thousand persons. Those who had worked on the lots received for more than five years were given the state-owned land as their own private possession (Tsutsiyev, 1998, 72–73, referring to: *Materials on the resettlement of Ossetians* [Vladikavkaz: North Ossetian State Research Institute, 1991], 7–9).

105 Bugay, 1995, 107–108. The numbers of those resettled to other Central Asian republics, East Siberia and to the Far East were negligible.

106 All former army servicemen were deprived of their military identification cards and issued temporary certificates. They were transported to Alma-Ata and placed under the control of the NKVD department for special settlements of the Kazakh SSR, which decided on their further destinations. However, in May 1944, some 11 thousand reservists—Chechens, Ingushetians and Karachais—were delivered to the discretion of the NKVD departments of the Ivanovo and Yaroslavl Obls. (Bugay, 1995, 109–111). The total of former army service members belonging to the "punished peoples" that were received at special settlements reached around 157 thousand, including 5,943 officers, 20,209 sergeants and 130,691 rank-and-file servicemen (Bugay, 1990b, 41).

107 Including 2,741 persons from Georgia, 121 from Krasnodar Kray and so on (Bugay, 1990b, 42).

108 See chapter 5.

109 After the liberation, Elbrus was even renamed Ialbuzi (Georgian) for a while.

110 Its full text is quoted in: Shabayev, 1994, 47–51.

111 Bugay, 1995, 216.

112 This is confirmed in particular by an instruction of 5 April 1944 issued by Major General Golovko, the chief of the North Caucasus military district, and his Headquarters commander, Colonel Tabakov, and sent from Pyatigorsk to Major General Vetrov, the commander of the first rifle division of the NKVD interior forces stationed in Krasnodar (the division was assigned to be relocated in the Crimea). The document deals with the organization of Cheka military operations and combat tactics used to liquidate banditry on highland terrain. In essence it represents an attempt at summarizing the experience gained in the Caucasus in order to employ it under the conditions of the mountainous Crimea effectively. See also a draft of the "Instructions for the troops participating in the operations for banditry liquidation in the mountainous areas of the North Caucasus," dated July 1944 and signed by the NKVD interior force chief Lieutenant General Sheredega ("Bandity stremilis sokhranit fashistsky poryadok" [Bandits sought to maintain the fascist order], Publication by V. B. Veprintsev and I. A. Mochalin. VIZh. 1999, no. 5, 83–89, quoting RGVA, h. 38650, r. 1, f. 129, sh. 1–8, 71–86).

113 See Nekrich, 1978, 24–40.

114 Bugay, 1991d, 107.

115 Bugay, 1991d, 110.

116 Bugay, 1995, 216.

117 See in the cable of 22 February 1944 sent to V. Chernyshev by A. Kobulov (Bugay, 1995, 151).

118 Bugay, 1995, 156, 159. According to other sources (Nekrich, 1978, 97), the figure reached 13,592 (in the period of May 1944–January 1945).

119 According to Nekrich, on 21 August 1946 (Resolution No. 619/3).

120 One year later, on 25 June 1946, the RSFSR Supreme Soviet adopted a decree on the disbandment of the Crimean AO and its transformation into the Crimean Oblast (S. M. Chervonnaya writes about a decree issued by the Supreme Soviet of the USSR on 26 June 1946; see Chervonnaya, 1994, 15).

121 See Chervonnaya, 1997, 164–165.

122 Bugay, 1995, 149–150.

123 An excerpt from Beria's letter to Stalin of 29 May 1944 (Bugay, 1991d, 109). Bulgarians appear to have been the only people of the Soviet Union additionally "accused" of having let themselves be deported to Germany as a source of labor!

124 Principal deportation operations took place on 27–28 June 1944 (Bugay, 1995, 198–199).

125 Foreigners or stateless persons (Bugay, 1995, 198).

126 Bugay, 1995, 197–199.

127 See Bugay, 1995, 201.

128 Bugay, 1991d, 110.

129 Bugay, 1995, 169, citing GARF, h. R-9401, r. 2, f. 66, sh. 19.

130 Bugay, 1995, 169, citing GARF, h. R-9479, r. 1, f. 573, sh. 286.

131 Bugay, Gonov, 1998, 214–215.

132 Bugay, 1995, 175.

133 Interestingly, the Kazakh government, normally obedient but obviously failing to accommodate all other target groups as it was, addressed the Moscow authorities with a request to halt the "deliveries of other peoples for special settlement," the response to which was a considerable cut of the target group (only 6 thousand persons instead of 28 thousand) but not a total cessation of resettlement.

134 Bugay, 1995, 178.

135 See Bugay, 1995, 179–182.

136 Bugay, 1995, 204–209.

137 Bugay, 1995, 219.

138 Bugay, 1995, 215.

139 Bugay, 1995, 219.

140 The resettlers were given receipts for the property that was transferred to them. They appropriately called these receipts "filkina gramota" [a useless scrap of paper]. See a sample in: Auman, Chebotareva, 1993, 163.

141 See Silayeva, 1991; Bugay, 1995, 258–259; Bugay, 1999.

142 Nekrich, 1978, 117.

143 Nekrich, 1978.

144 Bugay, 1990b, 43, quoting: The Archives of the Chechen–Ingush CPSU Oblast Committee, h. 220, r.1, f. 21, sh. 4ob., b, 9, 14, 22–23, 76.

145 Instead of cows and sheep, new settlers received receipts stating the number of the submitted cattle. However, there were insufficient resources at the locations to which they moved, and their hopes of receiving the "goods" to which they were entitled were in vain.

146 Bugay, 1990b, 43–44.

147 In accordance with the Council of People's Commissars' resolutions of 9 March 1944 and 11 March 1944 adopted by the Council of People's Commissars. According to other sources, it was planned to resettle 5,000 households from Daghestan, 3,000 from North Ossetia and 500 from Georgia (Bugay, Gonov, 1998, 202).

148 TsGA of the Daghestani ASSR, h. R-168, r. 35, f. 25, sh. 318.

149 See a summary note of the Daghestani ASSR Council of People's Commissars to the chairman of the RSFSR Council of People's Commissars and to the People's Commissar of Agriculture (TsGA of the Daghestani ASSR, h. R-168, r. 35, f. 21, sh. 89, 191, 150; the information was conveyed to us by Sh. Muduyev).

150 Estimations are made by Sh. Muduyev based on the materials from TsGA of the Daghestani ASSR, h. R-168, r. 35, f. 22, sh. 51, 53; h. R-411, r. 3, f. 1, sh. 29, 93; f. 47, sh. 61).

151 See Prozumenshchikov, 1997, 48–52.

152 Silayeva, 1991.

153 See details about this target group in chapter 5.

154 See *"Special file" of Beria*, 1996, 31, with reference to: GARF, h. 9401, r. 2, f. 145, sh. 386–392. We have no information concerning whether the resolution was adopted.

155 See *"Special file" of Beria*, 1996, 91, with reference to: GARF, h. 9401, r. 2, f. 149, sh. 200–207.

156 Ivanova, 1997, 66–67. For the text of the decree see in: Zaytsev, 1993, 46.

157 Bugay, 1995, 224, with reference to: GARF, h. 9479, r. 1 f. 371, sh. 4.

158 Bugay, 1995, 224, with reference to: GARF, h. 9479, r. 1 f. 436, sh. 38–39. Nevertheless, individual operations did take place, for example, resettlement of a few hundred Crimean Tatars from the Gorky Oblast to Uzbekistan in April 1951 (Bugay, 1995, 245).

159 See, for example, objections to the planned resettlement of 600 "Vlassovists" from the republic to the Kemerovo Obl. (February 1947): *"Special file" of Beria*, 1996, 165, with reference to: GARF, h. R-9401, r. 2, f. 176, sh. 48–54.

160 Bugay, 1995, 235. According to other sources: 23 thousand persons (Ivanova, 1997, 63, quoting TsAODM, h. 203, r. 1, f. 116, sh. 10). With regard to peasants, one can also mention those convicted under a decree of 4 June 1947 concerning thefts of state and community property. In purely formal terms, these convicts cannot be regarded as deportees, however their proportion in the total number of convicts (1/4–1/5 of the annual figure) as well as their sheer number (117,641 persons in 1950; 97,583 in 1951; 103,161 in 1952) speak for themselves (Ivanova, 1997, 62).

161 Bugay, 1995, 236.

162 Bugay, 1995, 236.

163 Bugay, 1995, 226–229, quoting GARF, h. R-9479, r. 1, f. 427 and 569; h. R-8131, r. 32, f. 7351; h. R-9401, r. 1, f. 2949.

164 Chief of the MGB interior force central department, P. Burmak, was charged with the task of general planning and control of the operation (see detail in Strods, 1999; Chebrikov, 1996).

165 Strods, 1999, 133, with reference to RGVA, h. 38650, r. 1, f. 408, sh. 124.

166 Bugay, 1995, 230–231, quoting GARF, h. R-9401, r. 2, f. 235, sh. 27, 35. According to the summary submitted on 23 September 1988 to the CPSU Central Committee Politburo commission for repression of 1930–50s by KGB chairman Chebrikov, the number for the period of 1941–1953 was 195,707 persons (Chebrikov, 1996).

167 Bugay, 1995, 231–232; Strods, 1999, 134.

168 According to the information note of 16 December 1965 written by deputy chief of the 2nd department of the MVD of the USSR, Kardashov (see Bugay, 1995, 232, quoting GARF, h. R-7523, r. 109, f. 195, sh. 52, 53).

169 GARF, h. R-9479, r. 1, f. 641, sh. 386 ob. N. F. Bugay cites a different date: the first half of 1949. Bugay, 1995, 243, 244.

170 Bugay, 1995, 236.

171 Passat, 1994, 38–39; Bugay, 1995, 236.

172 The number included 4,495 special executives, 13,774 MGB military servicemen and 4,705 party activists (Passat, 1994, 42).

173 Passat, 1994, 41–45. Subsequently, the results of the operation were debated on many occasions and found unsatisfactory due to the "banditry" persisting in the republic. Even on 9 June 1952, L. I. Brezhnev, the then first secretary of the CP Central Committee of Moldavia, addressed the center pointing to the necessity to banish another 3 thousand persons, however no permission was given this time.

174 See Kotsonis, 1997, 85–87. It was allowed to take personal belongings, goods and food on the basis of a one-ton restriction per family.

175 Bugay, 1995, 241.

176 Bugay, Gonov, 1998, 222.

177 Zemskov, 1990a, 12.

178 Bugay, 1995, 244–245.

179 Bugay, 1995, 244.

180 Passat, 1994, 52–53.

181 Bugay, 1995, 234, 245.

182 Bugay, 1995, 249.

183 See one sample of rather logical indirect pieces of evidence in: Bar-Sella, Z., T. Shraiman, Ya. Toporovsky, "Poslednyaya tayna rezhima" [The Last Secret of the Regime], Okna, 1995, 7–13.12?, 4–6. The publication aroused intense feedback among the audience, in particular in the form of the readers' numerous letters containing analogous indirect substantiation.

Patterns of Deported Peoples' Settlement, and Rehabilitation Process

A prevalent majority of deportees were ascribed the status of "special resettlers," which implied their strict administrative subjection to the network of so-called special *komendatura*s in their new places of residence. In April 1949 the number of the *komendatura*s numbered 2,679.[1] One *komendatura* was designed to supervise an average of 700 families.[2]

On 8 January 1945, the Council of People's Commissars passed two important documents—"Provision on the NKVD special *komendatura*s" and "On the legal status of special resettlers"—that mitigated the special settlement regime. Apart from the freedom of movement and freedom in choosing residence, a number of special resettlers' civic rights were restored; they were to follow all directives of special *komendatura*s, to report any changes of their family composition within a three-day period and not to leave the zone controlled by a corresponding *komendatura* without its special sanction (arbitrary leave was regarded as an offence equal to escape and was prosecuted).[3] On 28 July 1945, a resolution "On benefits for special resettlers" dealing primarily with agricultural taxation was issued.

In January 1946, there were instances of cancellation of special settlement registration for ethnic groups. Finns, deported to the Yakut ASSR, Krasnoyarsk Kray and the Irkutsk Obl., were the first to be struck off the register. They were to remain in the same location, but their status of special settlers was changed to that of residents.[4]

Many people opted for escape: 24,324 attempts were recorded in the period until 1947, with only 9,917 fugitives, i.e., less than one half, detained.[5] According to other data (as of 1 October 1948), out of the total of 2,104,751 special settlers registered at that time, 77,541 escaped, with 20,955 of them remaining in hiding. Germans made the largest group among fugitives (22,235), however in proportional terms this number constituted 2.2% of the entire ethnic group, against 3.5% among the North Caucasus natives, 4.4% among former Crimean residents, 9.3% among the Vlasov army members [Vlasovtsy] and as many as 13.4% among the OUN members![6]

Under a resolution "On resettlers" issued by the Council of People's Commissars on 24 November 1948, punishments for escaping were aggravated to a significant extent.[7] Special *komendaturas* started administering both family and individual registration of special settlers; while in the Yakut ASSR and Krasnoyarsk Kray several strict-regime settlements were founded for those allegedly "strongly predisposed" to escaping. Special MVD inspections and fugitive-retrieval executive groups were constantly at work seeking runaways at their homelands, the supposed break-out destinations.[8]

However, it was later—when in writing they were made aware of the content of the USSR Supreme Soviet Presidium Decrees of 26 November 1948 and 9 October 1951—that special resettlers faced truly dark times. The decrees stipulated the term of their banishment as eternal, without the right of return to their native places. Escape was now to be punished by 20 years of penal servitude instead the previously envisaged 8 years of prison confinement.[9]

Apart from the seven "totally deported" peoples, the decree of 1948 targeted Crimean Greeks, Bulgarians and Armenians, Meskhetian Turks, Kurds and Khemshins, along with those banished from the Baltic republics in 1949. All these categories were ascribed a new status designation of "evictees": and MVD personnel were to get each evictee to produce a written acknowledgement of their familiarity with the decree content.

Over 1.8 million, or 80%, out of the 2.3 million registered special settlers fell under the category of "evictee."[10] As far as the Vlasov army members were concerned, and other special settlers employed at the construction enterprises to which the decree's stipulations on "eternal settlement" did not apply, their affiliation with these enterprises before the completion of their industrial and capital construction projects turned out to become something of a "gift" for them.[11] Besides, after 11 March 1952 special target group composition was replenished with those representatives of repressed ethnic and social groups that had served their terms in the GULAG work camps up until that time.[12]

A break in the clouds of the Stalin "eternity" opened only after the death of the "peoples' father." In the mid-1950s a series of USSR Supreme Soviet Presidium decrees was issued, which envisaged cancellation of restrictions pertaining to the legal status of deported special settlers (however, the wording used was remarkable: "since there is no necessity for further maintaining the restrictions in question," which was an indication of the state's firm conviction of the righteousness and legitimacy of the actions it had taken in the past).

The year 1954 brought about the first true relief: on 5 July the Council of Ministers passed a Decree "On the abolishment of some restrictions with regard to special settler legal status." The decree stated in particular that there was no further need to apply legal restrictions on special settlers in the view of the effective establishment of Soviet authority and the involvement of large masses of special settlers, employed in industries and agriculture, in the economic and cultural life within the districts of their new residence. Although officially the registration was not cancelled, the obligation to report to *komendaturas* every third day was replaced by a symbolic annual visit.

"Special settlers' " children that were either under 16 years of age, or older ones under the following conditions—admitted or sent for studies—were exempted from special settlement restrictions. Those remaining in special settlements were granted the right of residing and moving within the oblast they were ascribed to, and even beyond its boundaries, and all over the country in cases of business trips. However, the decree did not apply to all special settlers. The following categories did not come within the provisions of the decree: individuals convicted for committing "special dangerous" offences [*osobo opasnyye prestupleniya*], who were exiled after serving their confinement terms; violators of regime and social order; Ukrainian nationalists, bandits, bandit accomplices and their family members, who had been banished from western regions of Ukraine and Belorussia and from the Baltic republics in 1944–1952; former Anders army members banished from Lithuania and western regions of Ukraine and Belorussia; and, for some reason, Jehovists (again from the Baltic republics, and western regions of Ukraine and Belorussia and Moldavia).[13]

On 13 August 1954, the Council of Ministers issued another consequential decree: "On lifting special settlement restrictions relative to former kulaks, Germans registered at the place of residence and Germans mobilized for work in industry during war-time without being resettled."[14] The kulaks resettled as early as 1929–1933, along with Germans belonging to the target groups "local" and "mobilized" (labor army members) and not subjected to resettlement, were recognized as now stably established in the places of their new residence. In other words, first of all the cancellation of special settlement regime logically affected those that had been subjected to this regime for longer periods (with some kulaks having been in this situation for as long as a quarter of a century!), and those that had not been resettled at all. A total of 118 thousand people came within the decree stipulations at that time.[15]

Another two Council of Ministers decisions followed in 1955: "On issuing passports to special settlers" (10 March) and "On the cancellation of the registration for some categories of special settlers" (24 November). The well-known USSR Supreme Soviet Presidium decree "On the amnesty for Soviet citizens that collaborated with occupiers in the time of the Great Patriotic War" was issued 17 September 1955.

The first resolution affecting specifically a "punished people" (apart from Finns) appeared in 1955. That was a decree by the USSR Supreme Soviet Presidium of 13 December 1955 "On lifting restrictions relative to the legal status of Germans and their family members assigned to special settlements."[16]

In 1956, USSR Supreme Soviet Presidium decrees on lifting the restrictions continuously followed each other: on 17 January—relating to the Poles banished in 1936; 17 March—concerning Kalmyks; 27 March—regarding Greeks, Bulgarians and Armenians; 18 April—the Crimean Tatars, Balkars, Meskhetian Turks, Kurds and Khemshins; 16 July—Chechens, Ingushetians and Karachais (not all of them were allowed to return to their homelands). Apparently, one more decree can be added to the same list, namely the decree of the USSR Supreme Soviet Presidium of 10 March 1956 abolishing the decree of 12 February 1948, i.e., canceling administrative banishment and allowing for the Baltic "nationalists" that had served their punishment terms to make their way to special settlements in order to unite with their families residing there.[17] Interestingly, the wave of these decrees was launched before (not after) Khrushchev delivered his famous "secret" speech at the CPSU 20th Congress (24–25 February 1956).

The autonomy of five of the totally repressed peoples that used to possess their self-government systems was restored. However, it was not returned to two peoples, namely Germans and the Crimean Tatars (which has still not been done).[18]

Nevertheless, there still was large distinction between lifting the restriction on rights and actually exercising those rights. The decrees provided for neither mandatory restitution of the property confiscated in the course of resettlement, nor opportunities for returning to native places and homes, while a number of restrictions were still virtually valid until the early 1990s.

To use the style of wording common to Cheka personnel officials: due to the above-mentioned circumstances, it cannot be regarded as possible to consider the process of the rehabilitation of forced migrants, as it was executed in the USSR and is being carried out in Russia and other CIS countries at present, as being satisfactory.

PATTERNS OF DEPORTED PEOPLES' SETTLEMENT AT THE DESTINATIONS

By the end of 1945, a total of 967,085 families, or 2,342,506 persons, were registered at special settlements.[19] In the period from 1938 through 1945, the number of special settlers (including exiled settlers, exiles and evictees) increased 2.2-fold, chiefly due to the deliveries of the "punished peoples" distributed mainly between the republics of Central Asia and Kazakhstan, where the registered number of such new settlers grew 6–9 times. The total number in question reached 2.2 million persons thus exceeding 1% of the country's population, while in 1950 the proportion grew to approach the 1.5% threshold (precisely, 1.47%).

Table 9[20] and figure 6 show the dynamics and regional distribution of the target groups.

However, instead of the eagerly expected liberalization of the regime, the first post-war years brought about its further toughening, and consequently produced a half-million increase of the special settlement population. It was at that moment—1 January 1953—that the largest simultaneous number of special settlers ever was registered in the country: 2,753,356 persons.[21] (As of the same date and according to the official data, the population of the GULAG camps and

Table 9. **Regional distribution of special settlers**
(1938, 1945, 1953 and 1958, thousands of persons)

Region	1938	1945	1950	1953	1958	1945 to 1938	1953 to 1945	1958 to 1953
The Urals	244.3	238.0	264.3	236.6	9.7	0.97	0.99	0.04
West Siberia	242.7	456.2	605.6	634.0	47.7	1.88	1.39	0.08
USSR European North	135.1	79.6	91.3	87.6	8.3	0.59	1.10	0.09
Kazakhstan	134.7	846.1	893.1	988.4	6.7	6.28	1.17	0.01
East Siberia	19.7	173.5	222.7	275.7	65.7	1.45	1.59	0.24
North Caucasus	45.5	24.6	0.7	0.3	—	0.54	0.01	—
Central Asia	35.2	324.4	358.3	380.7	0.3	9.22	1.17	0.00
Far East	29.3	19.6	107.3	64.2	15.8	0.67	3.28	0.25
Ukraine	7.5	5.2	5.2	0.7	–	0.69	0.13	—
Volga region	3.3	22.0	22.0	23.0	0.0	6.67	1.05	0.00
Center	—	22.4	22.4	26.3	—	—	1.17	—
TOTAL	897.3	2,212.1	2,607.9	2,753.4	154.3	2.22	1.24	0.06

Estimates made based on: Zemskov, 1995 (the data given as of 1 July 1950; GARF, h. 9479, r. 1, d. 641, l. 372–380).

colonies constituted a marginally smaller number, namely 2,472,247 inmates.[22])

During the period of 1945–1953, the number of special settlers in Trans-Ural regions grew dramatically: 1.39 times in West Siberia, 1.59 times in Eastern Siberia, and 3.28 times in the Far East. Their common proportion in the country's total constituted 35.4%, as compared to 29.4% in 1945. The absolute values remained the same in the Urals, the European North and the Center. At the same time, the corresponding increase in the Central Asian republics and Kazakhstan dropped remarkably to 17%, which was comparable to the natural population growth of the banished peoples placed in these regions. Nevertheless, the dynamics of the proportion the special settlers of Central Asia and Kazakhstan made up in the country's total is impressive: 17.2% in 1938, 49.7% in 1945, and 52.9% in 1953.

By 1958, when the majority of the deported peoples had been freed from special settlement restraints, the total share of Central Asia and Kazakhstan in terms of the number of special settlers residing there fell as low as 0.5%, while the proportion of special settlers residing in the harsh Trans-Ural territories (with more than one half of them in Western Siberia) grew to 83.7%: traditionally, the target groups not affected by the rehabilitation waves were located there.

The first wave in question affected kulak special settlers: their rehabilitation was continuously carried out during the course of the 1940s. By the beginning of 1949, their number still remaining on register exceeded 130 thousand persons by a small margin; and it was only in the Tomsk and Kemerovo Obls. that they still made the majority target group among special settlers.

By that time, deported Germans came to be the most significant target group in the structure of special settlement population. By the end of the war, there were nearly 1 million (949.8 thousand) Germans registered at special settlements, without taking into account deceased and escaped. The number included (in thousands): 446.5 (47%) natives of the Volga German ASSR; 149.2 (15.7%) Germans from the Northwest Caucasus and Crimea; 79.6 (8.3%) from the Zaporozhye, Stalino and Voroshilovgrad Obls. of the Ukrainian SSR; 46.7 (4.9%) from the Saratov Obl.; 46.4 (4.9%) from the Trans-caucasia, 38.3 (4%) from the Rostov Obl.; 26.2 (2.8%) from the Stalingrad Obl.; etc.[23]

In the post-war period, the structure of the German special settlement population, which had incorporated several different deportation waves, and complex as it was, became even more elaborate.

Figure 6. Republics, krays and oblasts of the USSR with the indication of the number of special settlers registered there as of 1 July 1950

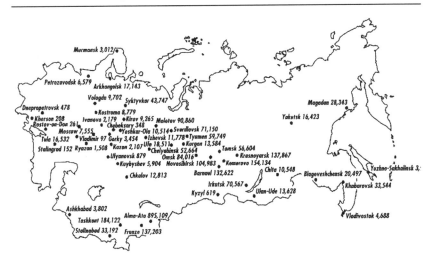

Source: GARF, h. 9479, r. 1, d. 641, l. 400

Apart from the "banished" Germans (from the Volga region and other European regions), "local" Germans (those that had lived on the Trans-Ural territories before the war), and "mobilized" Germans (drafted to the labor army and until 1945 ascribed to the special zones pertaining to their work places[24]), two new categories emerged. The first one, the *Volksdeutsche*, included Germans from the western regions of the USSR (chiefly from southern Ukraine) that had managed to avoid the deportation at the beginning of the war, but were seized by the Red Army in the course of the liberation of regions that had been under occupation.[25] These people were interned, their property confiscated, after which, as a rule, they were transported to the Chernogorsky special camp in Krasnoyarsk Kray. In addition, by the beginning of 1949, 120.2 thousand German "repatriates," i.e., those returned by repatriation commissions from Germany and Austria, were registered at special settlements.

While there were 1,012.8 thousand Germans registered at special settlements as of 1 October 1948, by 1 January 1953 their number grew to reach as many as 1,224.9 thousand, including (in thousands) 855.7 banished Germans, 208.4 repatriates, 111.3 "locals" and 48.6 "mobilized" individuals. In 1953, Germans constituted 44.5% of the total number of special settlers, while the second largest category—the Chechens—only made up around a quarter of that number.

What does the more specified geographic pattern of settlement of the "punished peoples" and ethnic special resettlers in general look like?

There is a unique map preserved in the archive of the NKVD department for special settlements: a 1:4,000,000-scale map of the USSR with indicated territorial division as of 1954 and with demarcated scaled letter-punches of seven colors denoting seven "punished peoples."[26] In each oblast of the RSFSR and Kazakhstan, the letter-punches are placed in a row in a way reminiscent of a cardiogram, while in the case of the Central Asian republics the data are given for each entire republic, without taking into account their inner administrative division. A hand-written note on the map dates it back to June 1956, which implies that the data represent what can be called a summary of the total deportations of the "punished peoples" produced on the threshold, or in the process, of abolishing special settlement restrictions.

Examining the map (where it was possible, we supplemented it with data pertaining to the peoples omitted by the map, such as Koreans, Finns and Meskhetian Turks) throws up some remarkable observations and conclusions. Special settlers were absolutely absent on a significant part of the territory of the USSR, namely in its western regions (Ukraine, Belorussia, Moldavia, the Baltic republics, all oblasts of the RSFSR to the west of Moscow), in a number of border zone regions (the Murmansk and Kamchatka Obl., Primorsky Kray), and in the regions where these peoples had been banished from (the North Caucasus, the Lower Volga region).[27]

In other regions, there is a combined representation of "punished peoples" in one way or other. Strikingly, German settlers are present nearly everywhere. There are regions in the European part, in which there are no members of other ethnic groups, apart from Germans (for example, the Vologda, Ryazan or Ulyanovsk Obls.), or other "punished peoples" target groups are negligibly small (for example, the Komi, Karel, Udmurt, Tatar, Buryat ASSRs, the oblasts of Arkhangelsk, Kirov, Chelyabinsk, Kurgan, Chita and Irkutsk, and Amur and Khabarovsk Krays in the RSFSR; along with the Urals Obl. in Kazakhstan and the entire territory of Turkmenistan). However, a more precise picture arises taking into consideration Ingermanland Finns, who were placed in the country's European part too, in particular in the Vologda Obl. or the Karel ASSR (the Crimean Tatars who were also settled in the European part in 1944, which is dealt with below).

In terms of the number of German special settlers, most prominent are the regions of the European North, the South Urals, and southern territories of the Far East, where no deportation of the German population took place (apart from mobilization into the labor army and insignificant internal regional resettlements, as, for example, in the Chita Obl., where Germans were "moved aside" from the border). The share of the later resettlement to the west, motivated by particular industrial needs (for example, to the mines of Mosbass in the Moscow and Tula Obls.), was of no substantial consequence. It was the German target group in the Chelyabinsk Obl. that gave the largest group in the regions of German special settlers' numerical *predominance*.

Rarely do the German population not constitute one of the three leading groups among the deported peoples' target groups in particular regions. If Germans are not predominant, they are *leading*, with a very large margin at that. In combination with the Crimean Tatars,

Germans make leading groups in a number of other oblasts of the European part, Volga region and the Urals (the oblasts of Moscow, Tula, Kostroma, Ivanovo, Gorky, Kuybyshev, Sverdlov, the Chuvas and Bashkir ASSRs), as well as in Yakutia, the Magadan and Kemerovo Obls., and Tajikistan. A reverse combination (with Tatars ahead of Germans) is encountered only in two cases: in the Mari ASSR and Uzbekistan, with Crimean Tatars *predominant* in the latter case (133 thousand, as compared to 8.5 thousand Germans who are also numerically inferior to Koreans and Meskhetian Turks).

In six regions of West and East Siberia (the Tyumen, Omsk, Tomsk and Novosibirsk Obls.), Germans are followed by the settled Kalmyks, as a rule, in colonies numbering 0–15 thousand persons, while in Sakhalin (a region generally untypical of both groups) Kalmyks are even more numerous than Germans.

Germans and Chechens make the leading "duet" in five Kazakh oblasts (of Karaganda, Semipalatinsk, North Kazakhstan, Aktyubinsk and Guryev). In another four oblasts located in North Kazakhstan (the Kustanay, Kokchetav, Akmolinsk and Pavlodar Obls.) the following combination of target groups is in place: Germans, Ingushetians and Chechens.

According to the map, in one case (the East Kazakhstan Obl.), Chechens are prevalent over Germans, in others their combination is supplemented with another people: for example, Kalmyks in the Karakalpak ASSR, and Balkars in the Alma-Ata and Taldy–Kurgan Obls. in southeastern Kazakhstan. In another two southern Kazakhstan oblasts, the following combinations are encountered: Karachais + Germans + Chechens (in the Chimkent Obl.) and Chechens + Karachais + Germans (in the Dzhambul Obl.). The most complex combination—Chechens + Karachais + Germans + Balkars—is in place in Kyrgyzstan.

Therefore, there were only ten exceptions to the German numeric leadership, with Chechens in the lead in six of these exceptional instances, the Crimean Tatars in two, and Kalmyks and Karachai each in one case.

Figure 7 depicts the space pattern of settlement of the deported peoples. We shall stress again that it was their nearly universal presence that made the key feature of the deported Germans' settlement pattern. Their biggest concentration sites (with their numbers making up at least 70 thousand persons) were situated in Altay, Tajikistan, and in the Karaganda, Novosibirsk and Akmolinsk Obls. An equally numerous concentration existed in the case of only three other peoples: the Crimean Tatars and Koreans in Uzbekistan, and Chechens in Kyrgyzstan.

Chechens, the second most numerous repressed people, were predominant in Kyrgyzstan and in the adjacent southeastern oblasts of Kazakhstan, along with the Karakalpak ASSR. They formed representative colonies (5 thousand persons or more in each) all over Kazakhstan, save its very western oblasts (however, even the relatively numerically insignificant Chechen population in the Guryev Obl. bore a highly responsorial assignment: as a rule, these were oil industry workers from Grozny).

The Crimean Tatars were highly concentrated in Uzbekistan, and simultaneously formed large colonies in the regions of Russia, making, along with Germans, a significant presence in its central European part (apart from them, Ingermanland Finns were present in large numbers too). Possibly, it was the highest original level of

Figure 7. **Key settlement patterns of deported peoples (the mid-1950s)**

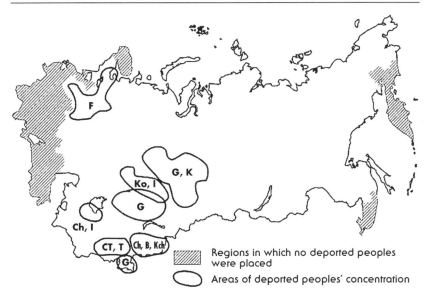

Regions in which no deported peoples were placed

Areas of deported peoples' concentration

B—Balkars; I—Ingushetians; K—Kalmyks; Ko—Koreans; CT—the Crimean Tatars; Kch—Karachais; G—Germans; T—Meskhetian Turks; F—Finns; Ch—Chechens

urbanization among Crimean Tatars, as compared to the rest of the seven repressed peoples, that constituted the key factor that contributed to the formation of the space pattern.

The principal area of Kalmyk settlement was shifted furthest to the east, namely to Siberia (especially its western part). Their numbers exceeded 8–10 thousand persons in each of the following regions: Altay and Krasnoyarsk Krays and the Novosibirsk, Omsk, Tomsk, Tyumen Obls. As far as Central Asia was concerned, the Kalmyk presence was considerable only in the Karakalpak ASSR, whose climatic conditions were reminiscent of those in the former Kalmyk ASSR, and very different from those in Sakhalin where their numerical leadership appears to have been rather accidental (in both cases it must have been the Kalmyk's fishery expertise that had come to be the crucial deciding factor). Notably, the major share of the Finn population deported at the beginning of the war was based virtually in the same regions (Krasnoyarsk and Altay Krays and the Novosibirsk and Omsk Obls.).

Ingushetians, a people related to Chechens that used to live next to them in the Caucasus, followed a similar pattern of banishment too: next to Chechens but still separate. It was the northern areas of Kazakhstan where Ingushetians were concentrated and consistently made second largest groups among the deported peoples.

In the case of Karachais and Balkars, their settlement patterns were similar to each other's and, in turn, to that typical of Chechens. Their largest concentrations were located in Kyrgyzstan and adjacent Kazakh oblasts (Karachais even made the most numerous group in the Chimkent Obl.).

The settlement pattern of Meskhetian Turks was largely reminiscent of that of the Crimean Tatars: they were concentrated in Uzbekistan and Kyrgyzstan, in particular in the Fergana Valley located in both republics. With regard to Koreans, their main settlement areas were located in North Kazakhstan and Uzbekistan (and in this sense, it was mirroring the original placement of a part of the Poles, in particular the target group of "administrative exiles" of 1940; most of them were released in 1941).

Taking into consideration the number of kulaks, as well as Germans, Koreans and North Caucasian peoples that Kazakhstan absorbed during the years of deportations, it appears that the demographic chaos that befell the republic in 1932–1933 following the starvation and migration of Kazakhs to China was largely compensated and overcome.

Over one-half (52.4%) of the Soviet Germans turned out to be placed in Kazakhstan as a result of their mass deportation. Large groups of German population (from 50 to 100 thousand persons) were settled in the krays and oblasts of Siberia. In 1959, Germans made the fourth largest people in Kazakhstan, and came to be the third one in 1989 (when their number exceeded that of Ukrainians) and yet their share still fell from 7.1 to 5.8% in the process. Simultaneously, cultural and linguistic assimilation was taking place: while, according to the census of 1970, 67% of Soviet Germans considered German their native language, that number fell to 57%, as registered by the 1979 census.

According to the USSR population census conducted in 1989, a total of approximately 2.1 million Germans resided in the country. During the period of 1953–1989, their number grew significantly in Kazakhstan, Kyrgyzstan and Uzbekistan (from 448.6 up to 957.5, from 15.8 to 101.3, and from 8.4 to 39.8 thousand persons, respectively). Only 842 thousand Germans resided in Russia at the time, including 17 thousand in the Saratov Obl. and 14 thousand in the Volgograd Obl., which made in total no more than 1.5% of the Soviet German population.

Kazakhstan became the main destination for Chechens (77.2%), Ingushetians (96.8%), Karachais (56.4%) and Balkars (50.6%) too. As it was already mentioned, there was no German "monopoly" in Uzbekistan: it was the Crimean Tatars, Koreans and Meskhetian Turks that constituted the prevalent groups there, while in Kyrgyzstan it was Chechens, Germans, Karachais and Meskhetian Turks.

The list and sequence of the largest repressed peoples on the USSR scale differed from those in place in the Russian Federation. In the former case, the list went as follows: Germans, Chechens, Koreans, Crimean Tatars and Ingushetians; while the latter list was: Chechens, Germans, Ingushetians, Kalmyks and Karachais (see table 10).

The table illustrates the fact that, while living in alien parts, most of the repressed peoples managed to overcome the demographic crisis caused by the deportation and their populations grew significantly. There were a few exceptions, however, in particular Balkars, whose total number in 1959 was a little lower than in 1939, and, especially,

Table 10. **Population sizes of the repressed peoples of the USSR (1939–1989)**
(thousands of persons)

Peoples	1939	1959	1970	1979	1989
Germans	1,427.2	1,619.7	1,846.3	1,936.2	2,038.6
Karachais	75.8	81.4	112.7	131.1	150.3
Kalmyks	134.4	106.1	137.2	146.6	173.8
Chechens	408.0	418.8	612.7	755.8	899.0
Ingushetians	92.1	110.0	157.6	186.2	237.4
Balkars	42.7	42.4	59.5	66.3	85.1
Crimean Tatars	218.9	No data	No data	No data	271.7
Koreans	182.3	313.7	337.5	388.9	438.7
Meskhetian Turks	No data	No data	No data	No data	207.5
Finns	144.7	92.7	84.8	77.1	67.4
Greeks	286.4	309.3	336.7	343.8	358.1

Sources:Vsesoyuznaya perepis naseleniya 1939 g.: Osnovnyye itogi [All-Union Popu-lation Census of 1939: Main Results], M., 1992, 80; Naseleniye SSSR. 1987 [USSR Population. 1987], collection of articles, M., 1988, 98–100; Natsionalnyi sostav nase-leniya RSFSR. Po dannym Vsesoyuznoy perepisi naselaniya 1989 g. [Ethnic Composi-tion of the Population of the USSR. Based on the Data of the 1989 All-Union Census], M., 1990, 8–16.

Kalmyks: their population of 1959 made up merely 78.9% of that reg-istered in 1939. It was Kalmyks among all repressed peoples that suf-fered the highest mortality rate: a total of 44,125 of them had died by 1 August 1948.[28]

REHABILITATION AND INTERNAL REPATRIATION OF KALMYKS AND PEOPLES OF THE NORTH CAUCASUS

The miserable existence the deported peoples led in alien lands was dragged out for over more than a decade. They hardly had any oppor-tunities to defend their rights, which brought about such extraordi-nary action as the delivering of a memorandum on the situation of the Kalmyks to UN Secretary-General D. Hammerscheld by a Kalmyk delegation headed by D. Burkhinov on 13 December 1953.[29]

The lifting of the special settlement restrictions became the first step in the political and civil rehabilitation of the "punished peoples." The imposition of the restrictions was indiscriminative and collective in nature, such as their abolishment which was enacted in the period from May 1955 through July 1956. The first people to be affected by the rehabilitation measures was the one that was first to be repressed, namely Germans. Germans made 695 thousand out of the 740 thousand persons released from "supervision" following the USSR Council of Ministers decree "On striking particular categories of special settlers off the register," issued on 24 November 1955.[30]

At that time, none of the "punished peoples" had yet been granted the right to return to their native lands, and therefore, none of them was privileged over others.

The beginning of 1957 was remarkable for the next step taken: the restoration of the statehood and autonomy lost by five of the "punished peoples" during the war years. The corresponding procedure took an unusual form: the USSR Supreme Soviet Presidium recommended to its RSFSR counterpart that the autonomies be restored. Therefore, although the abolishment of the autonomies was executed by the union Center, their restoration was transferred to the jurisdiction of one of the union republics (the RSFSR).

Soon some repressed peoples were allowed to return to their native lands in the North Caucasus and Lower Volga region: on 25 January 1957, deputy minister of internal affairs, Tolstikov, signed the order "On the sanctioning of residence and registration of the Kalmyks, Balkars, Karachais, Chechens, Ingushetians and their family members, banished in the period of the Great Patriotic War."[31]

Below is the text of a certificate on removal from a special settlement register (from the collection of A. Eisfeld, Guttingen).

[English translation of the Russian original, hand-written parts are italicized]

Ministry of Internal Affairs of the Tajik SSR is not equivalent to residence permit

Certificate No. 3282

10 February 1956
city of Stalinabad
Citizen *Schefer Ivan Heronimovich, of 1922*
year of birth, native of the *village of Zultz*
of the Veselinov district, the Nikolayev Obl.
nationality *German*, was registered

at a special settlement, and from *13 February* 1956
is removed from the register.

The certificate is issued for submission to passport-issuing authority

Chief of the Department of Internal Affairs
[Stamp]   [Signature]

The party and government carried out a rather discriminatory policy, there was no equal treatment of different target groups. With regard to Germans, Crimean Tatars, as well as Meskhetian Turks and other deported natives of Transcaucasia, the restoration of civil rights did not imply the possibility of physical return to the homelands.[32] This was the first occasion when a group of totally deported peoples was split.

In the cases of those peoples that were allowed to go back home, the process of returning started immediately after their statehood was restored. However, in these cases discrimination occurred too. So, *Autonomous Republic* status was granted to the territories belonging to Balkars, Chechens and Ingushetians at the very beginning, while the homelands of Kalmyks and Karachais were merely ascribed *Autonomous Oblast* status. And whereas for Karachais the status remained the same as before the banishment, for Kalmyks there was an evident "lowering" of status, and they had to wait until 29 July 1958 for the return of the "republic" status, i.e., another one and half years. Karachais' rights were infringed in another way: while before the war a separate Karachai Autonomous Oblast existed, this time they had to share autonomy with Circassians.

It only appears that another wedge was driven between the "privileged" Chechens, Ingushetians and Balkars, on the one hand, and the "discriminated" Kalmyks and Karachais, on the other. In reality, it was between these peoples that a real, and far deeper, split emerged. It was actually the *Chechens, Ingushetians*, and *Kalmyks* that proved truly discriminated against, since their state-administrative rehabilitation (the restoration of their ethnic statehood) was not confirmed by territorial rehabilitation (i.e., by the restoration of the boundaries of their national autonomous republics as of the date of the deportation),[33] which means that the rehabilitation was in theory and practice incomplete. In other words, although Chechens and Ingushetians were allowed to return to their previous territorial administrative unit, the form and boundaries of the unit were partially restored, and differed from those that had been in effect before the banishment: the new make-up contained ominous omissions and land deletions that foreshadowed the bloody conflicts of the future. At that time, under the authoritarian and unitary Soviet order, the dangers lurking behind these changes may not have been realized in their entirety. However, nowadays, when Vladikavkaz and, especially, the Prigorodnyi district have become plain symbols of bloodshed, the unambiguous implications of those territorial nuances can be clearly discerned.

As a result, the eight "punished peoples" (we have supplemented the "seven" with Meskhetian Turks, a people that, although it had not possessed an autonomous territorial status before the deportation, exceeded Balkars and was comparable to Ingushetians and Kalmyks in terms of population, and—most importantly—was and still is separated from its homeland) ended up divided into three groups.

The first group included *Karachais* and *Balkars*, i.e., fully rehabilitated peoples (their rehabilitation was satisfactory at least as far as all formal criteria were concerned). The second group comprised *Chechens, Ingushetians* and *Kalmyks*, i.e., partially (or inadequately) rehabilitated peoples (rehabilitated with regard to their civil rights and state-administrative status, but not in terms of territory). The third group embraced *Germans, Crimean Tatars* and *Meskhetian Turks*, i.e., non-rehabilitated peoples, whose rehabilitation was reduced to nothing more than restoration of their political and civil rights, but involved no renewal of their state-administrative or, all the more, territorial status.

From the perspective of their conflict-generating potentials, the second group constituted a far more powerful hotbed of resentment than the third one, due to the mere fact that the "unsatisfied" ethnic grouping was consolidated and structured in administrative terms.

Let us conduct a concise analysis of the developments pertaining to particular "punished peoples," in the order corresponding to their categorization. Each case distinctly reveals both common and individual problems that the peoples in question faced.

Let us start with the first group, i.e., rehabilitated peoples.

Balkars. The special settlement restrictions were lifted on 18 April 1956 (under the same decree that affected the Crimean

Tatars, Meskhetian Turks and others), however the right to return to
their native land was not stipulated. On 9 January 1957, the Kabardian ASSR was transformed into the Kabardian–Balkar ASSR, with
the territories incorporated into Georgia reverted and their former
names restored. In addition, the restriction on returning to the previous places of residence was lifted. The return of the Balkars to their
homeland was like a tide: some 22 thousand people had come back
by April 1958. Nearly 81% of the population returned by 1959, over
86% by 1970, and around 90% of all Balkars had made their way
back by 1979.[34] Nevertheless, the return to at least four settlements
in the Cherek Gorge—the villages of Dumala, Kunyum, Sautu and
Upper Cherek—never took place.[35]

   Karachais. The special settlement restrictions were abolished on
16 July 1956 (simultaneously with Ingushetians and Chechens), however their right of return to their native land was not provided for. On
9 January 1957, the Circassian AO was transformed into the
Karachai–Circassian AO (let us note again that a separate Karachai
AO had existed before the deportation). The territories, integrated
into Krasnodar Kray and the Georgian SSR after the deportation,
were returned under the autonomous oblast's jurisdiction, and the
former Balkar toponyms were restored on the territories reverted
from Georgia. The ban on return to former residence places was cancelled, and a new administrative territorial division was established.
The return of Karachais was almost as "intense" as that of Balkars
(see table 11).

Table 11. **The returning of the repressed peoples of the USSR to their homelands**
(1959–1989) (population size; thousands of persons)

Peoples	1959	1970	1979	1989	1959–1989
Karachais	84.3	86.1	83.3	83.0	−1.3
Kalmyks	61.2	80.4	83.3	84.2	+23.0
Chechens	58.2	83.1	80.9	76.8	+18.6
Ingushetians	45.3	72.1	72.4	69.0	+23.7
Balkars	81.0	86.3	90.0	83.2	+2.2

Sources:*Vsesoyuznaya perepis naseleniya 1939 g.: Osnovnyye itogi [All-Union Population Census of 1939: Main Results], M., 1992, 80; Naseleniye SSSR. 1987 [USSR
Population. 1987], collection of articles, M., 1988, 98–100; Natsionalnyi sostav naseleniya RSFSR. Po dannym Vsesoyuznoy perepisi naselaniya 1989 g. [Ethnic Composition of the Population of the USSR. Based on the Data of the 1989 All-Union Census],
M., 1990, 8–16.*

The table demonstrates that Karachais and Balkars were leading in terms of rapidity of homecoming, over 80% of them having returned by 1959, while Kalmyks (correspondingly, 61.2%), Chechens (58.2%) and, notably, Ingushetians (45.3%) were in no hurry. In the case of Ingushetians (and Kalmyks too) their incomplete territorial rehabilitation produced a slowing effect on returnee numbers. The maximum concentration of the ethnic group in its republic fell in 1970 in the case of Chechens, 1979 in the case of Ingushetians, and 1989 in the cases of Balkars and Kalmyks.

Now let us turn to the partially rehabilitated peoples.

Kalmyks. The special settlement restrictions were lifted on 16 July 1956, with no right of return to the native land provided. On 9 January 1957, a Kalmyk AO was formed within Stavropol Kray. The former republic's territory, with the exception of the Nariman and Liman districts remaining under the jurisdiction of the Astrakhan Obl., was returned to the AO; and the old place names, although not all of them, were restored. The ban on coming back to the homeland was cancelled too. Eventually, on 29 July 1958, Stavropol Kray's Kalmyk AO was transformed into a Kalmyk ASSR. In the case of the Kalmyk ASSR, the fact that two of its former districts (where the Kalmyk population used to make up 2–11%) were not transferred back induced no subsequent dramatic repercussions or mass resentment.

Chechens and Ingushetians. Chechens and Ingushetians were freed from the special settlement restrictions on 16 June 1956 (concurrently with Karachais), but were not granted the right to return home. The Chechen–Ingush ASSR was restored on 9 January 1957, three districts—Kargali, Shelkovo and Naursky—withdrawn from Stavropol Kray and populated with Cossacks and Nagays in the first place, were transferred back to the republic. The Chechen lands taken over by Daghestan and Georgia were returned in their entirety, with most districts ascribed their old Chechen and Ingushetian names.

However, a number of highland districts remained under a ban for Chechens to reside in, under the pretext of their unsuitability as agricultural areas. The former residents of the areas in question (the districts of Itum-Kale, Galanchzhoy and Sharoy, whose pre-deportation population had made up 75 thousand persons) were placed in Cossack *stanitsa* settlements and *auls* located on the plain. It was precisely in order to compensate for the lack of lands caused by these restrictions that three districts formerly included in Stavropol Kray were incorporated into the republic. Akkin Chechens, who had resided in Daghestan's districts of Khasavyurt, Novolaksky and Kazbek, were forbidden to return to their native *auls*: a special resolution, issued by the Council of Ministers of the Daghestani ASSR on 16 July 1958, postulated the introduction of a special passport regime for them.[36]

Besides, approximately 1/6 of the former Ingushetian territory was not returned, in particular the Prigorodnyi district adjacent to Vladikavkaz (the district had been among the five Ingushetian districts transferred to North Ossetia following the deportation, with its territory somewhat cut down); a narrow strip on the right-hand side of the Daryal Gorge from the Georgian border along the river Armkhi (this area, along with the Dzherakhov Gorge, had been part of Georgia in 1944–1945); and a part of the former Psedakh district, a 5–7km-wide strip linking the main territory with the district of Mozdok (the so-called Mozdok Ossetian corridor). The Ossetian population was resettled from the districts of Nazran, Psedakh and Achaluk in 1957–1958—not to Georgia, where it had been brought from under the authorities' ruling—but to the Prigorodnyi district instead (naturally, those Ossetian resettlers that had settled down in the Prigorodnyi district itself were allowed to stay there). Apparently, the idea of their repatriation to Georgia was perceived as a more menacing threat, and this may, as A. A. Tsutsiyev suggests, constitute the answer to the question of why the Prigorodnyi district was not returned to the Ingushetians (according to the official explanation, that was the case since "the district had become closely attached to Vladikavkaz in economic terms").[37]

At the same time, Ingushetians were not prohibited from returning to and residing in the Prigorodnyi district, which was designated to become, and gain the reputation of, an exemplary "district of friendship between Ossetians and Ingushetians." However, the returnees had to arrive to their villages occupied by other people. They had to build their homes in the outskirts in an atmosphere of mistrust and hostility, and sometimes on completely clear sites (this was how the new Ingushetian settlement of Kartsa emerged, to give one example). Consequently, the Prigorodnyi district came to be an area densely populated by two territorially interchanged or merged ethnic groups, whose mutual relations were fairly tense, which made for a simmering district prone to conflict.

Whereas 140 thousand persons returned home in spring 1957 (with the plan envisaging 78 thousand persons), by the end of the year, the number grew to reach as many as 200 thousand persons.[38] No more than 60% of Chechens and 50% of Ingushetians resided in the native land in 1959 (taking into account the Prigorodnyi district). By the year 1970, the respective proportions amounted to 90% and 85%.[39] However, the general intensity of the Chechens' and Ingushetians' return to their native lands was lower, as compared to the other "punished peoples" (in the case of Ingushetians the reluctance was, to a large extent, conditioned by the incompleteness of territorial restitution[40]).

REHABILITATION OF GERMANS

So, when the majority of the "punished peoples" were allowed to return home and their statehood was restored in the mid-1950s, "exceptions" were made in the cases of the Crimean Tatars, Germans and Meskhetian Turks. They were acquitted of all charges, but they were not granted a legally formulated right of return to their homelands for a long time after, while Meskhetian Turks have not received it even today.

Demographically asserting that Germans and the Crimean Tatars had "rooted down" in their new locations better than others, in reality the authorities were extremely wary of any disturbance to the status quo that may have developed with the absence of these peoples. Having examined the geography of German settlement over the USSR and learned that they, as it turned out, were scattered and numbered 60–80 thousand only in 9 regions, minister of internal affairs of the USSR, N. P. Dudorov, came to the conclusion that restoration of the German Autonomous Republic would have been pointless.[41] In 1956, the same minister found it most logical to create an autonomous republic for Crimean Tatars in Uzbekistan, since its "climatic and environmental conditions approximate the conditions in their previous place of residence."[42]

Instead of returning to their native lands and reintegrating into the contemporary local reality, the peoples in question had to choose between resigning themselves to the authorities' decision or struggling for their rights. The need to assert their rights produced specific forms of struggle and bodies, for example "delegations" and "congresses" of the Soviet Germans, "congresses" of Meskhetian Turks, *kurultays* of Crimean Tatars, along with *samizdat* and dissident movements tinged with national motifs (especially typical of Crimean Tatars), which, despite this, were closely linked to such significant centrally based figures as A. Sakharov, P. Grigorenko and A. Nekrich. Illegal repatriation came to be one of the forms that the struggle would take; people would move into their native places without permission and, in spite of the bans, seize lands, houses, etc.[43]

In the late 1980s, the Supreme Council of the USSR established commissions to examine the specific problems of each of the three peoples: Soviet Germans, Crimean Tatars and Meskhetian Turks.

Let us go over the rehabilitation fate of each of the three non-rehabilitated peoples one by one.

As far as Germans are concerned, they were the first repressed people that was acquitted of the groundless indiscriminate accusations and legal restrictions, as early as 13 December 1955. However, the key assignment of the ruling was to legitimatize Germans further residing at the places to where they had been banished ("taking into account the fact that the German population took deep root at the new places of residence [...] and their native places are occupied"). The abolishment of the special registration by no means implied subsequent right to property restitution and, most importantly, the right to return to their native land.

Interestingly, the Decree issued by the USSR Supreme Soviet Presidium on 28 August 1941 was not officially cancelled until 29 August 1964. However, having been acquitted of the "crime," the punishment remained in effect: neither Germans' right to return to the Volga region, nor restoration of their autonomy were envisaged.

The first and second delegations of Soviet Germans visited Moscow at the beginning of January and in June–July 1965, petitioning for their right to return to their homeland. And although both delegations were received by the chairman of the USSR Supreme Soviet Presidium, A. I. Mikoyan (on 12 January and 7 July 1965), they failed to achieve their primary goal. As a matter of fact, on both occasions they were promised support for their ethnic and cultural autonomy, but denied the key right to administrative and territorial rehabilitation, under the pretexts of unsuitability, inappropriateness of timing, unavailability of necessary vast funds and impossibility for agriculture to be successfully developed in the virgin lands without the German settlers' contribution.[44] Another reason referred to was the alleged overpopulation of the territory of the former Volga German ASSR, which incidentally was not the case at all: population growth there was evident only in urban areas, while the number of countryside residents constituted 20–30% of the pre-war level.

The legal restrictions imposed on Germans with regard to returning to the Volga region were not lifted until November 1972. In 1979, an unsuccessful attempt to establish a German autonomous oblast in Kazakhstan was made, and even corresponding draft decrees were prepared by the USSR Supreme Soviet Presidium and Kazakh SSR Supreme Soviet Presidium. However, after demonstrations, unprecedented in their anti-German hostility, were staged by Kazakh youth in Tselinograd and Atbasar on 16, 19 and 22 June 1979, even this half-measure was quietly shelved.[45]

The third, fourth and fifth delegations of Soviet Germans visited Moscow in April, July and October 1988. The third delegation addressed M. S. Gorbachev and A. A. Gromyko (the then chairman of the OVS of the USSR) with a letter on 13 April 1988. However, neither Gorbachev, nor Ryzhkov, nor even A. Yakovlev received the delegates; the meetings took place at the CPSU Central Committee and USSR Supreme Soviet. Germans also appealed to the 19th CPSU conference that was held at the end of June 1988 (the document was titled "The way we conceive the restoration of the Volga German ASSR"). Here is an excerpt from the appeal: "In order to forestall the slightest grievance or misunderstanding between the local population and Soviet Germans arriving in the Autonomous Republic, necessary consciousness-raising activity should be carried out... By no means the local population is to suffer any damages in connection with the restoration of the Autonomous Republic. All those willing should and must stay where they are currently residing. Soviet Germans have been subjected to a severe experience of injustice; and they will not allow any injustice to befall other people, their would-be neighbors and colleagues. Soviet Germans will not reclaim any houses, property and other assets confiscated from them in 1941, since such actions would lack any reasonable grounds and might inflict unfair damages on innocent people. Soviet Germans will only follow their single principal goal: the restoration of German autonomy."[46]

On 28–31 March 1989, the All-Union non-government cultural and educational society of Soviet Germans "Revival" (Wiedergeburt) held its constituent conference co-chaired by G. G. Grout and G. G. Wormsbecher in Moscow. And on 14 November 1989, a declaration "On the recognition as unlawful and criminal of the repressive acts against peoples who were subjected to forced resettlement, and on guaranteeing their rights" was adopted by the USSR Supreme Soviet.[47]

After the adoption of the declaration, a new promising situation emerged with regard to the possible restoration of the German Autonomous Republic in the Volga region, within the boundaries of the Saratov and Volgograd Obls., which was supported by the Supreme Soviet of the USSR. Under such positive circumstances, the ultimatum put forward by the Revival society—"the Autonomous Republic within former borders or nothing"—(in combination with a number of tactless statements with regard to the local population) played a rather counterproductive role and to some extent played into anti-German hands.

In addition, the movement organized by Soviet Germans for the restoration of the Volga German Autonomous Republic faced resistance in the form of an organized campaign against such development. Rallies and gatherings of those opposed to the autonomy restoration were held in the Volga region. On 14 August 1990, the Saratov Oblast Executive Committee adopted a resolution "On high-priority measures for resolving the problems of the Germans residing in the oblast." A similar perspective was held by the state commission for Soviet Germans' affairs under the USSR Council of Ministers and by the department for inter-ethnic relations of the TSK KPSS (headed by V. Gusev and V. Mikhaylov), which was reflected in a number of memos issued by this body that premeditated state decisions.[48] The conclusion asserting the "absence at present of favorable circumstances for the restoration" of the German Autonomous Republic in the Volga region was traditionally based on the unconquerable postulate of "the unacceptability of the complication of inter-ethnic relations."

The Congress of Soviet Germans scheduled for 16 July 1990 was postponed until December 1990, and then until 12 March 1991, with a clear intention to promote—under CPSU supervision—certain documents that would virtually reduce to zero the chances of the restoration of autonomy. At this point, M. Gorbachev eventually found time for the Germans, however he met only with representatives of their conformist faction to discuss the possibilities for establishing a super-territorial body, thus virtually turning down the variant of authentic autonomy.[49]

Strange as it may seem, a visit of the president of the RSFSR B. Yeltsin to the Volga region proved to be the climax of the anti-German campaign. He came to Saratov on 8 January 1991: never before had the overt support for the opponents of German autonomy been expressed in such an unambiguous manner and at such a high level.[50]

No legislative acts issued subsequently contradicted this sentiment: neither the "Law on the rehabilitation of repressed peoples" of 26 January 1991, nor RSFSR presidential decrees "On high-priority measures for the rehabilitation of Soviet Germans" of 21 February 1992 and "On the establishment on the basis of agricultural industrial facilities of satellite settlements for Russian Germans in the Volga region, and on guarantees of the settlements' social and economic development" of 21 May 1992. The decree on the rehabilitation of Soviet Germans envisaged, in particular, the establishment of a German ethnic district in the Saratov Obl. and a national okrug in the Volgograd Obl. However, as soon as 18 June 1992 a session of the Saratov Obl. Engels district council expressed its opposition to the institution of any ethnic territorial units on its lands.

Only two such units were created on the territory of the RSFSR under the mentioned legislative acts: a German ethnic district in Altay Kray, which comprised 16 settlements with the total number of residents exceeding 20 thousand, and the Azov national district in the Omsk Obl. The following position was elaborated for these Siberian regions: "Ethnic districts are no alternative to a republic, but there is no alternative to ethnic districts available today." In 1991–1995, the FRG provided Altay Kray with financial support of 60 million German marks. A 3,000-number capacity automatic telephone exchange was built by Siemens in the district. Societies such as "Halbstadt GmbH" and "Brücke" were established; and free German language courses were organized (the latter fact is symptomatic, since neither local residents, nor even district leaders, used German for communication).

Residential houses for German settlers were constructed in the neighborhood of agricultural facilities in the Saratov Obl. districts of Engels, Marksovo, Krasnokut and Rovno, i.e., the central territory of the former Volga German ASSR. Germans were invited to move to the Ulyanovsk (village of Bogdashkino) and Leningrad Obls., and to the places in Ukraine in which they used to live before the war. The "Köningsberg" variant of autonomy restoration was debated in the mass media too.

After the unification of Germany, the FRG government proved to be a powerful supporter of the promoters of German autonomy, since Germany was no longer interested in further massive repatriation of Soviet Germans. An official statement was made by G. D. Genscher: "The FRG is supportive of the Germans' staying in the Soviet Union."[51] Logically, Russia and Germany signed a "Protocol on cooperation for the gradual restoration of Soviet German statehood."

The first congress of Volga Germans was held on 4–6 February 1993. An association of Volga Germans was established there. It was there that a factual rejection of the political struggle was declared, while the stress was to be shifted to solving the economic, social and cultural problems of the Volga Germans.

Nevertheless, the powerful movement against the gradual restoration of German autonomy persisted in the Volga region. Consequently, further developments relating to the restoration (or rather non-restoration) of the autonomous republic motivated Germans to produce the following ultimatum, publicly articulated by the Revival leadership: it is only total emigration to the FRG that can be an alternative to the Volga German Autonomous Republic.

And this is how the situation is developing in reality. Germans are voting with their feet and their truly "mass" emigration has been a reality since 1990.

The ghost of emigration has always been present in the political struggle of Soviet Germans for their legitimate rights. The concept of emigration as an alternative emerged immediately after the rehabilitation process started, but formally such a possibility came into being in 1951.

According to the FRG census of 1950, some 51 thousand Germans born on the territory within the Soviet borders of 1939 resided in the FRG at the time the census was conducted. This factor proved to be a consequential one in terms of stimulating immigration from the Soviet Union, since at the early stages of the process the Soviet side was supportive chiefly in the cases of family reunions. It was first in 1951 that a number of ethnic Germans (1,721) left the USSR for the FRG. After 22 February 1955, when the Bundestag ruled that the German citizenship granted during the war should be recognized, the provisions of the "Law on evictees" embraced all Germans residing in East Europe and subjected to persecution and deportations. As soon as May 1956, some 80 thousand Soviet Germans' applications for emigration to the FRG had been submitted to the German Embassy in Moscow.[52] The actual number of German emigrants in 1958–1959 amounted to 4–5.5 thousand persons.

At the same time, as in the case of Jews, the Soviet authorities hindered the German emigration from the country, allowing it with evident reluctance and exclusively in cases of family reunion. Germans, who were denied their right to repatriation, became more active in their efforts in the mid-1970s: their demonstrations—not very large-scale but frequent—were held, as a rule, in front of the buildings of the CPSU Central Committee and German Embassy.[53]

In some republics (Estonia, Latvia and Kazakhstan) emigration committees were established striving to consolidate efforts in order to receive emigration permissions. A samizdat collection "Repatria," elucidating the problems of the German repatriation movement, was published in January 1974.[54] At the end of 1976, around 300 Germans from Kazakhstan and Kyrgyzstan first employed such forms of protest as rejection of Soviet citizenship by handing in their passports to the authorities and simultaneous appeals to the governments of the USSR and FRG and to international organizations. Many of the "rejecters" were later repressed for the "violation of the passport regulations" and even for "libel upon the Soviet order."[55]

Incidentally, it was the emigration total of 1976 (9,704 persons) that remained the highest figure for a long time. It was not until 1987 that the 10-thousand threshold was overcome (14,488 emigrants), after which virtually each year saw the emigration figure accelerate (persons): 47,572 in 1988; 98,134 in 1989; 147,950 in 1990; 147,320 in 1991; 195,950 in 1992; 207,347 in 1993; 213,214 in 1994. The number remained almost the same in 1995 (209,409 persons), and started dropping in 1996 (172,181 persons).

The decrease can be ascribed to the toughened immigration regulations introduced by the FRG rather than by the emergence of more favorable conditions for Germans in Kazakhstan, Russia, etc. In particular, a so-called Law on assignation of place of residence was adopted by the Bundestag on 16 July 1989 as a supplement to the

"Law on evictees." In fact, taking into account its amendments of
1 March 1996 and 13 November 1997, the Law stipulates assignation
of immigrants to particular lands, or even specific towns, for the first
two years of their residing in Germany, while for those that entered
Germany after 29 February 1996 the period in question is increased
to four and a half years. The regulation is officially justified by the
necessity of the even distribution of the immigrants among regions,
however in practice it was dictated by the motivation to attach the
immigrants to the eastern lands, where only some 20% of resettlers
from the former USSR resided.[56]

At present, it is the German state itself that constitutes the major
obstacle for the emigration of ethnic Germans from the former USSR
republics, since the country experienced serious economic problems
in the second half of the 1990s and its subsequent internal political
situation has been unfavorable to any type of immigration. In the
period of 1995–1998, the immigration flow shrank more than two-fold
and eventually stabilized in 1999 having reached a number barely
exceeding 100 thousand persons. The requirement to pass a language
proficiency test (Sprachtest) while still in the CIS countries became
another powerful barrier for the potential repatriates (as a rule, at
least 1/3 of those admitted for taking the test fail it).[57]

Nonetheless, the 1990s proved to be notable for the massive
departure of Germans from the republics of the former USSR. The
total number of Soviet Germans that moved to the FRG in the period of 1951–1999 reached 1.9 million (see table 12). Some estimates
hold that Germans traveling "by passport" (i.e., those that entered
Germany on the basis of paragraph 4 of the "Law on evictees") make
approximately 4/5 of the immigrants, while the remaining 1/5 comprises their spouses, offspring and relatives (mainly of Russian and
Ukrainian descent).

By the time of the USSR break-up, some 15% of the German
population that had resided in Russia, Ukraine and Turkmenistan had
emigrated, while the corresponding number of those that departed
from Kazakhstan, Kyrgyzstan, Uzbekistan and Tajikistan reached
around 20–25% (even 35% in the cases of some Transcaucasian
republics).[58] These discrepancies are quite revealing with regard to
the various degrees of pressure driving the German population out of
the territory of the former USSR. Less than 1/3 of Germans that used
to live in Kazakhstan remained there by early 1997; while only 1/6 of

former ethnic German residents of Kyrgyzstan stayed put. Regarding Tajikistan, virtually the entire German target group there had departed by that time. The level of German emigration from Russia is significantly lower. Moreover, substantial migration from the Central Asian states to Russia is underway.[59]

In terms of the outflow of German repatriates from the former USSR as of 1996, Kazakhstan was in the lead (with an average of 56%), although simultaneously its share (along with those of the Central Asian states) was steadily decreasing, while the corresponding proportion from Russia, on the contrary, was growing to reach approximately 32.7% (see table 13).

Meanwhile, German autonomy no longer appears to be a subject for debate in either Russia or Kazakhstan. Russia watered down all relevant action to merely issuing another presidential decree "On additional measures for the rehabilitation of Russian Germans" and declaring the cultural autonomy of Russian Germans at the end of 1997. A special federal program "The development of social, economic and cultural bases for the revival of Russian Germans"[60] was

Table 12. Dynamics of German immigration to Germany
from the former USSR (1951–1996)

Time period	German immigrants from the former USSR (persons)	Their proportion out of the total number of German immigrants to Germany (%)
1951–1955	1,956	3.3
1956–1960	14,086	4.8
1961–1965	3,593	3.9
1966–1970	3,593	2.9
1971–1975	21,591	17.5
1976–1980	41,613	15.8
1981–1985	8,664	3.8
1986–1990	308,537	28.1
1991–1995	972,866	87.5
1996–1999	509,225	98.0
TOTAL during 1951–1999	1,886,534	48.0

Estimates made based on: Bundesaugleichsamt, Statistischer Bericht Az.: I/2 Vt 6838, 6. Dezember 1991; Info-Dienst Deutsche Aussiedler: Januar 1993. Nr. 38. S. 39; Januar 1994. Nr. 49. S.15; Januar 1995. Nr. 63. S. 4; Januar 1996. Nr. 75. S. 3; Bubdesverwaltuingsamt, Jahresstatistik Aussiedler 1996, 1997, 1998, 1999 (we express our sincere appreciation to Dr. B. Ditz for the original data he provided.—P. P.)

Table 13. Structure of German immigration to Germany from the former
USSR countries (1992–1996)

CIS country	1992	1993	1994	1995	1996	1992–1996
Kazakhstan	114,382	113,288	121,517	117,148	92,125	558,460
	58.5	54.6	57.0	55.9	53.5	56.0
Russia	55,875	67,365	68,397	71,685	63,311	326,633
	28.6	32.5	32.1	34.2	36.8	32.7
Kyrgyzstan	12,618	12,373	10,847	8,858	7,467	52,163
	6.4	6.0	5.1	4.2	4.3	5.2
Other Central Asian states	7,555	9,005	7,046	5,889	4,155	33,650
	3.9	4.3	3.3	2.8	2.4	3.4
Ukraine	2,700	2,711	3,139	3,650	3,460	15,660
	1.4	1.3	1.5	1.7	2.0	1.6
Other countries	2,446	2,605	2,268	2,179	1,663	11,161
	1.2	1.3	1.0	1.2	1.0	1.1
TOTAL	195,576	207,347	213,214	209,409	172,181	997,727
%	100	100	100	100	100	100

The upper figure contains the number of persons, and the lower figure indicates the percentage.

Estimates made based on: Bundesaugleichsamt, Statistischer Bericht Az.: I/2Vt 6838, 6. Dezember 1991; Info-Dienst Deutsche Aussiedler: Januar 1993. Nr. 38. S. 39; Januar 1994. Nr. 49. S. 15; Januar 1995. Nr. 63. S. 4; Januar 1996. Nr. 75. S. 3; Bubdesverwaltuingsamt, Jahresstatistik Aussiedler 1996.

developed by the public state foundation "Russian Germans"[61] and on the initiative of the Ministry for National Affairs and Federal Relations of the Russian Federation. It seems, however, that the opportunity for the restoration of German autonomy in Russia has been lost irretrievably.

REHABILITATION OF THE CRIMEAN TATARS

The Crimean Tatars had been banished from the RSFSR; one decade later the Crimea was transferred under the jurisdiction of another republic, Ukraine, under a decree issued by the USSR Supreme Soviet Presidium on 19 February 1954. By the USSR Supreme Soviet Presidium decree of 28 April 1956 the special settlement registration was lifted with regard to Crimean Tatars, and their civil rights were restored. However, the restoration was not complete. In particular, they remained deprived of the rights to *repatriation* and *restitution,* i.e., the rights to return to their homelands and be compensated for the property confiscated from them in the course of deportation. Even the indiscriminate accusations that had been brought against the Tatars were not repudiated until much later, namely under the Supreme Soviet decree of 5 September 1967 (the issuance of the decree was preceded by a meeting between KGB chairman Yu. Andropov and a Crimean Tatar delegation).

However, the Crimean Tatar movement for returning home dated back to their common petition campaign of 1956. Starting from 1968, the movement developed ties with the Soviet human rights movement which formed one of its major sections of interest within a short time.[62] Activists of the Crimean Tatar movement were always under the close surveillance of the state security and internal affairs bodies.[63] The arrests and prosecution of Mustafa Dzhemilev were especially salient (1969, 1974 and 1979).

In October 1966, the Crimean Tatars held mass rallies devoted to the 45th anniversary of the establishment of the Crimean ASSR, which were dispersed by the militia and troops with savagery. The secretary of the USSR Supreme Soviet, Georgadze, the minister of internal affairs, Shchelokov, KGB chairman, Andropov and the prosecutor general, Rudenko, received a Crimean Tatar delegation on 21 June 1967. However, the promise given at the meeting of prompt rehabilitation of Crimean Tatars and sanctioning their return home was never fulfilled. It was not until 5 September 1967—after rallies held (and subsequently dispersed) in Tashkent by thousands of participants on 27 August and 2 September—that two decrees were issued by the USSR Supreme Soviet Presidium. The first one had the expressive title "On citizens of Tatar nationality, former residents of the Crimea." This document did repudiate the indiscriminate charge against Crimean Tatars of treason. The other decree—"On the administering procedure with regard to chapter 2 of the USSR Supreme Soviet Presidium decree of 28 April 1956" (it was this chapter that confirmed the prohibition for moving to the Crimea)—allowed Crimean Tatars to reside all over the territory of the USSR but only "in conformity with the effective legislation pertaining to employment and passport regulations."

The practical implication of the decree was that the passport and *propiska* [residence permission] regulations would become new weapons of state defense used against the Crimean Tatars.[64] Nevertheless, it did not prevent the first returnees from coming back home almost immediately after the decrees were published. Some 1,200 families (6 thousand persons) arrived in the Crimea during the three months from September to December 1967, but only two families and three single persons were able to break through the vicious bureaucratic circle and receive legal *propiska*. Directors of enterprises were given orders to reject Crimean Tatar job applications, school headmasters were instructed not to admit Tatar children from families that did not have residence permission, and notaries were to deny Crimean Tatars legalization of real-estate purchases.[65]

The regulations pertaining to resettlement to the Crimea were toughened further in spring 1968, when it was ruled that *orgnabor*, a special work hiring scheme (by responsible officials sent from the Crimea to the Central Asian republics), be the only lawful way for Tatars to return to the homeland. Some 168 Tatar families returned to the Crimea in 1968 under the *orgnabor* regulations, 33 families followed in 1969, and 16 in 1970. Undoubtedly, the number of those that came back without authorization from the authorities was significantly higher, although they were denied residence registration as before, and even prosecuted for violations of the passport regulations (only 18 families and 13 single persons were issued *propiska*, and 17 persons were imprisoned in 1968). The total number of Crimean Tatars that received *propiska* in the period of 1968–1979 made up approximately 15 thousand.[66] It should be stressed that the majority of them were most active participants in the Crimean Tatar movement; thus the pursuits of those Crimean Tatars remaining in Central Asia were essentially undermined, and suppliant and even defeatist sentiments intensified among them.

Having encountered the insuperable obstacles erected by the authorities and the impossibility of legalizing their status in the Crimea, tens of thousands of Crimean Tatars chose to settle outside of the Crimea but at least in its close neighborhood, in particular in the western part of Krasnodar Kray (Krymsky, Taman and Novorossiysk districts) or in southern Ukraine (the Kherson and Nikolayev Obls., the towns of Novoalekseyevka and Melitopol, etc.).

Incidentally, the authorities' attempts to establish the Crimean Tatars in Central Asia or Kazakhstan persistently failed. For example, in 1974, when Crimean Tatar S. Tairov was appointed the first secretary of the Dzhezkazgan Obl. party committee, the population did not respond to his calls to resettle in the territory under his patronage. The samizdat Crimean Tatar magazine *Emel* wrote: "Deep in his heart, no Crimean Tatar, be he even a KGB agent or a movement provocateur, ever betrayed his desire to return home."[67]

The authorities delivered yet another—rather clumsy at that—blow upon the Crimean Tatars: these people were simply ignored when the All-Union population census was carried out in 1970. The Crimean Tatars were regarded as only one part of the entire Tatar population of the country. This stimulated Crimean Tatars to conduct their own alternative self-census in 1971, which produced the figure of 833 thousand persons.[68]

In the late 1970s the authorities launched a counterattack: on 25 April 1978 the secret directive No. 221 of the Uzbek Ministry of Internal Affairs came into force prohibiting the militia passport departments from cancelling Crimean Tatars' *propiska* in Uzbekistan unless the resettlers were able to produce certificates from their future place of residence confirming the availability of employment and housing there. No such practice was administered in any other republic, and in Uzbekistan itself the regulation applied exclusively to Crimean Tatars.

In the Crimea itself instances of the ousting and even the throwing out of Crimean Tatars became more frequent starting from October 1978 (dozens of families fell victims as a result). In order to legitimate the practice, the USSR Council of Ministers adopted resolution No. 700 "On additional measures for toughening passport regulations in the Crimean Obl.," of 15 October 1978. Consequently, no court decision was necessary for eviction: a ruling by the district executive committee was sufficient![69]

One instance of eviction drove carpenter Musa Mamut from the village of Besh-Terek (Donskoye) of the Simferopol district to self-immolation in June 1978. Neither this case, nor multiple appeals and delegations sent to the oblast and All-Union bureau on the initiative of Crimean Tatars, or even their address submitted to the UN in 1979, managed to produce any significant result,[70] apart from the inclusion of Crimean Tatars into the 1979 population census on equal terms with other nationalities.

A state commission for Crimean Tatar affairs (chaired by A. A. Gromyko) was created in 1987, however its suggestions did not go much further than improvement of the social and everyday living conditions and cultural development of the Crimean Tatar people: the

establishment of a Crimean autonomous oblast still did not appear
feasible. The above-mentioned Supreme Soviet declaration of 14
November 1989 failed to become a turning point in the Crimean
Tatar affair.

It is noteworthy that Crimean Tatars were persistent in fighting
for their rights during the entire period of their exile and under any
circumstances. Their preparedness to move to their homeland immediately and under any conditions was almost unanimous, and the
pogroms of Crimean Tatars in the Fergana Valley in June 1989 did not
dampen their decisiveness but merely advanced it yet further.[71]

A plenary meeting of the Crimean Obl. CPSU committee that
was held on 5–6 January 1990 was devoted to the problems of inter-
ethnic relations in the Crimea. It was here that Crimean Tatar representatives took part in such an event for the first time. In May 1990, a
policy document outlining the state program for the returning of
Crimean Tatars to the Crimea was formulated. It recognized their
right to settle in the Crimea, that is, in essence it merely accepted the
process that was already largely underway in reality, without state
approval and in spite of resistance on the part of the state (the state
still established the terms for the completion of the resettlement: first
1996, and later 1998).

The period intended for the implementation of the "State program for the adaptation and integration of the deported Crimean
Tatars and other ethnic groups into Ukrainian society, and for the
revival of their culture and education" expired in 1997. Then followed
a "Program of priority measures for the establishment of settlements
and facilities for the deported Crimean Tatars and citizens belonging
to other ethnic groups that returned and reside in the Autonomous
Republic of Crimea."[72]

Apparently, the Council for Productive Forces Research of the
Academy of Sciences of the Ukrainian SSR relied on the policy document mentioned previously while drafting the "Suggestions for the
rational settlement of Crimean Tatars and the development of the
social sphere of the Crimean Obl."[73] In particular, a key proposition
was made that approximately 60% of the expected returning Crimean
Tatars be placed in the Crimea's steppe areas (only 31% of the
Crimean Tatar population used to reside there before the deportation).
And the sea-side and mountain areas were claimed to be overpopu-
lated, which was not the case in reality. The proportion of the would-be

urban Crimean Tatar population was contemplated as even lower than before the deportation, although the share of urban residents among the people grew considerably higher during the years in exile.[74]

The first relatively large-scale inflow (around 5 thousand persons) of Crimean Tatars to the peninsula took place in 1977–1979. By spring 1987 approximately 17.5 thousand Crimean Tatars moved to the Crimea, and their number doubled by the middle of the same year.[75] The *propiska* of Crimean Tatars was sanctioned in 18 out of the oblast's 24 districts (in the steppe and piedmont zones) in December 1987. According to the 1989 population census data, 38.4 thousand Crimean Tatars resided in the Crimea at the time. Some 30 thousand persons repatriated during 1989, and another 40 thousand in 1990. The number of Crimean Tatar returnees reached 150 thousand by the end of 1991, with only half of them having official Ukrainian citizenship.[76] However, further inflows of Crimean Tatar population to the Crimea were less intensive (25 thousand persons in 1992; 17 thousand in 1993; 11 thousand in 1994; and 9 thousand in 1995). And yet the share of urban population among the returning Tatars was steadily growing.

In early 1996, the total number of Crimean Tatars residing in the Crimea reached 220.5 thousand, or approximately 240 thousand taking into account those unregistered. Thus, they made the third most numerous people (following Russians and Ukrainians) in the Crimea, with the proportion of Crimean Tatar population exceeding 1/4 in some settlements and even districts.[77] *Medzhlises*, Crimean Tatar self-government bodies (illegitimate from the perspective of the Ukrainian constitution[78]), were established in each Crimean administrative district or settlement where Tatars resided. During the period in question Crimean Tatars firmly established themselves in the peninsula's agricultural market, and, according to some sources, in the shadow economy too. But simultaneously, the unemployment rate among Crimean Tatars is menacingly high. Crimean Tatars' conflicts (and sometimes bloody clashes) with the authorities, on the one hand, and with the rest of the peninsula's population, on the other hand, represent another great danger.[79]

On 12 February 1991, the Ukrainian Supreme Soviet adopted a resolution on the transformation of the Crimean Autonomous Oblast into the Crimean Autonomous Republic under the jurisdiction of Ukraine; and on 26 February 1992 the Crimean Autonomous Repub-

lic was renamed the Republic of Crimea. The newly established
republic was in no official way associated with either its Crimean
Tatar, or the numerically predominant Russian, population (it is noteworthy that the Crimean Tatar community opposes pro-Russian sep-
aratism in the Crimea).

After the break-up of the USSR, the problem of repatriation of
the Crimean Tatars, along with Meskhetian Turks (see below), turned
into an international issue concerning a number of sovereign states,
first of all Uzbekistan, Ukraine, Georgia and Russia. Russia promptly distanced itself from participating in the repatriation process,
although Russia is a legal assignee of the USSR, the state that carried
out the deportation of Crimean Tatars. Russia's financial assistance
was minimized in 1992, and fully terminated in 1993. According to
S. Chervonnaya, Uzbekistan, in its turn, chose to turn the Crimean
Tatar repatriation process to its own advantage by establishing border customs and other obstacles on the path of the emigrants. And
even the means allocated for Crimean Tatar repatriates to settle down
at the new places were often spent unwisely and inefficiently.[80]

The Crimean Tatar population in Russia is relatively small. Those
Crimean Tatars residing in Krasnodar Kray, for example, have been
actively resettling to the Crimea in recent years, in a way "vacating"
the space for, and selling their houses to, Meskhetian Turks returning
to their homeland. At the same time, a significant share of the
Crimean Tatar people are still residing outside the Crimea.

REHABILITATION OF MESKHETIAN TURKS

The rehabilitation of Meskhetian Turks, a people that were employed
for developing the Hungry Steppe [*Golodnaya step*] in Central Asia for
many years, appears to be a particularly unsuccessful rehabilitation
process. After 1956, when the special settlement regime was cancelled
with regard to Meskhetian Turks, their routes, never leading home,
took them to Moscow and Tbilisi. Starting from 1956, dozens of delegations visited both capitals: in Moscow they were referred to Tbilisi, and in Tbilisi they were directed back to Moscow.

In 1956, Meskhetian Turks were declared to be. Azerbaijanis and
eventually sent to the Caucasus, not to Meskhetia. So, instead, they

wound up in the Kabardian–Balkar ASSR (from which they spread to Stavropol and Krasnodar Krays) and to Azerbaijan, where labor force was needed at that time for developing the dry Mugabi Steppe. While in the North Caucasus their contacts with the local population were rather limited (since Meskhetian Turks themselves perceived the North Caucasus as nothing more than a temporary base on their way home), in Azerbaijan, surrounded by a people ethnically related to them, Meskhetian Turks gradually grew increasingly assimilated into the host culture.[81] Moreover, a considerable number of Meskhetian Turks still remain in Central Asia, first of all due to their fairly stable (and quite often even thriving) economic situation, and, secondly, because of the as yet unresolved question concerning their repatriation to Georgia. All attempts to realize their right to repatriation unfailingly encountered resistance and firm rejection on the part of the Georgian authorities, which is justified by referring to social, economic and demographic difficulties.

In the early 1960s, Meskhetian Turk representatives residing in various parts of the country united to form a "Temporary Organizational Committee for Repatriation." The first universal convention of Meskhetian Turks was held at Lenin Yuli collective farm, in the Tashkent Obl., on 15 February 1964. The delegates elected schoolmaster Enver Odabashev as the committee's chairman, and authorized him and a delegation comprising 125 representatives to deliver an address to Moscow on behalf of the Meskhetian Turk people.[82]

In May 1968, the USSR Supreme Soviet Presidium issued a resolution that formally declared the rights of Meskhetian Turks equal to those of other peoples of the USSR. As soon as 24 July 1968, 7 thousand Meskhetian Turks arrived in Tbilisi and gathered in front of the government building demanding an audience. Indeed, Mzhavanadze, the then first secretary of the Georgian CPSU Central Committee agreed to receive them in two days. While talking at the meeting, he promised to annually place 100 families in a number of Georgia's districts, but did not live up to his word. The very first repatriates were provided with employment and housing, but soon they were dismissed from jobs and even evicted to Azerbaijan.

On 19 April 1969, E. Odabashev was arrested in the Azerbaijani village of Saalty, although he was soon released on the demand of the crowd of Meskhetian Turks that gathered in front of the district executive council building. The 33rd Meskhetian Turk delegation comprising 120 representatives sent to Moscow in August 1969 was received at the CPSU Central Committee by a certain Moralev, who articulated yet another rejection of the delegates' demands, and insultingly to boot. After all the delegates had cast away their passports in the reception hall and declared their renunciation of Soviet citizenship, they were detained and convoyed out of Moscow.

In desperation, a group of Meskhetian Turks appealed to the Turkish Embassy in Moscow in April 1970 for permission to immigrate to Turkey. The initiative received backing at the sixth peoples' convention of Meskhetian Turks, which was held in the Saalty district of Azerbaijan on 2 May 1970. Lists of Meskhetian Turks wishing to emigrate were submitted to the Embassy on 15 March 1971. At the same time, this measure caused a split in the movement, the majority of which supported the repatriation cause.

In August 1971 E. Odabashev was arrested and sentenced to a two-year camp confinement; and the arrests of both his deputies, M. Niyazov and I. Karimov, followed in a few months.[83]

In spring 1976, representatives of the Meskhetian Turks identifying with Georgians rather than Turks visited Tbilisi, where a dinner was given in their honor by the chairman of the Initiative human rights group of Georgia. Instead of E. Shevarnadze, the first secretary of the Georgian CPSU Central Committee, his assistant received the delegates: the meeting, however, brought about no productive outcomes either.

At their eighth convention, organized in the village of Erokko in the Kabardian–Balkar ASSR on 18 June 1976, Meskhetian Turks came up with an alternative program for stage-by-stage repatriation based on the renunciation of their restitution rights, and the intention of forming youth teams that would construct houses on their own. Then, as an unofficial but fundamental repatriation condition, the Georgian side put forward a demand that Meskhetian Turks recognize their Georgian descent and change their names correspondingly. This caused yet another split in the Meskhetian Turk camp between the pro-Georgian "conformists" that were prepared to accept the condition in their desperation, and the "uncompromising" that would take no such step under any conditions.

Numerically, the "uncompromising" faction was overwhelming, which was reflected in the decisions made at the ninth convention of

Meskhetian Turks that took place in the Kabardian–Balkar ASSR's village of Psykhod on 28 July 1988. The stance taken by the "pro-Georgian" faction was condemned. Nevertheless, the first Meskhetian Turk families started arriving in Georgia, and, in order to forestall the ethnic concentration, the authorities placed them in various districts of Georgia.

Below is the translated text of the decree of the Presidium of the Supreme Council of the USSR "On lifting the restrictions relative to the USSR citizens of Azerbaijani nationality that were resettled from the Georgian SSR in 1944" of 31 October 1957, No. 161/29,

DECREE

OF THE PRESIDIUM OF THE SUPREME COUNCIL OF THE USSR

On lifting the restrictions relating to the USSR citizens of Azerbaijani nationality that were resettled from the Georgian SSR in 1944

Due to the fact that during the resettlement from the Adjar ASSR, Akhaltsikhe, Akhalkalaki, Adigen, Aspindzi and Bogdan districts of the Georgian SSR, the citizens of Azerbaijani nationality that were subsequently subjected to special settlement restrictions proved to have been wrongly resettled, the Presidium of the Supreme Council of the USSR *decrees:*

All restrictions placed on the citizens of Azerbaijani nationality resettled in 1944 from the Adjar ASSR, Akhaltsikhe, Akhalkalaki, Adigen, Aspindzi and Bogdan districts of the Georgian SSR to the Kazakh, Kyrgyz and Uzbek SSR shall be lifted.

Taking into consideration the fact that the districts of the Georgian SSR, where the citizens of Azerbaijani nationality where resettled from, are currently settled, and, according to the Georgian SSR government, there is no adequate capacity for the placing and economic integration of these citizens in other districts of the republic, the citizens in question shall be granted the right to permanent residence in the Azerbaijani SSR.

Chairman of the Presidium of the Supreme Council of the USSR (K. Voroshilov) [signature]

Secretary of the Presidium of the Supreme Council of the USSR (M. Georgadze) [signature]

Moscow. Kremlin.

31 October 1957

This first "peaceful" inflow of resettlers was not statistically significant. The census of 1989 registered a total of 207.5 thousand
Meskhetian Turks in the USSR,[84] with only 9.9 thousand residing in
the RSFSR. The rest lived in Uzbekistan (106.0 thousand persons),
Kazakhstan (49.6 thousand persons), Kyrgyzstan (21.3 thousand persons) and Azerbaijan (17.7 thousand persons).

Today, at the beginning of the third millennium, A. Osipov estimates the number of Meskhetian Turks at some 290 thousand; and it
is in Kazakhstan that their majority is residing (from 80 to 100 thousand persons). The following on the list are Russia (50–70 thousand
persons), Azerbaijan (40–60 thousand persons), and Kyrgyzstan
(25–30 thousand persons); Uzbekistan (15–20 thousand persons)
only takes fifth position ahead of Ukraine (5–10 thousand persons)
and Georgia. In the Russian Federation, Meskhetian Turks are concentrated in Krasnodar Kray (13–16 thousand persons), the Rostov
Obl. (13–15 thousand persons), the Kabardian–Balkar Autonomous
Republic (5.0–5.5 thousand persons), the Chechen ASSR, Belgorod
and Volgograd Obls., Stavropol Kray and the Voronezh Obl. (from 2.5
to 5 thousand persons).[85] It is rather remarkable that wherever Meskhetian Turks reside, even today they adhere to the traditional centuries-
old rural lifestyle.

Such a dramatic change of geographical residence patterns was
caused by the tragic events of June 1989. A series of massacres of
Turks in the Fergana Valley aroused then a "second migration wave"
from Central Asia, which involved over 90 thousand persons. Incidentally, it was not until the gruesome events took place that a commission for Meskhetian Turk affairs was set up at the USSR Supreme
Soviet Council for Nationalities.

At that point, the USSR authorities issued an official ruling that
some 17 thousand Meskhetian Turks (i.e., virtually all the Turkish
population of the Fergana Valley, but no other regions) be transported to a number of the central regions of the European part of the
RSFSR.[86] Another 70 thousand persons from other parts of Uzbekistan pulled up their roots and followed the first migrants.

In central Russia, they found themselves in circumstances they
were not prepared for. Their arrival, as a rule, stirred a negative reaction on the part of local residents, who wondered why Meskhetian
Turks had not been sent back to Georgia, their native land.

As a result, Meskhetian Turks themselves started perceiving this resettlement as another forced migration, and subsequently a substantial number of them (about 2/5) moved to other regions located further to the south (Ukraine, the North Caucasus, Kazakhstan), this time on their own initiative.

Formal appeals for a sanction to receive the resettlers were delivered on the people's behalf to the authorities of a number of the North Caucasian regions, but commonly were confronted with negative responses, excepting the cases of Azerbaijan and the Chechen–Ingush ASSR. It was Azerbaijan that eventually received the "second migration wave": its lands in the Dzheyran–Choy Steppe were allocated for the new settlements.

Initially, Meskhetian Turks were received at approximately the same areas where the Crimean Tatars and Greeks used to reside before (the Krymsky district and Abinsk district in the kray's western part, and the Apsheron district and rural area in the neighborhood of the town of Belorechensk in the southwest). They were placed on special registration lists by the local administrations. However, after 26 August 1989, when the kray administration halted the permanent residence registration of citizens arriving in the kray and introduced tougher migration regulations (actually targeting Armenian refugees from Azerbaijan, apart from Meskhetian Turks), the migrants' status became rather undetermined and questionable.

The overwhelming majority of Meskhetian Turks (15–16 thousand persons, with 12–14 thousand of them de facto forced migrants[87]) are residing in Krasnodar Kray without residence permits, although often in their own houses purchased from the Crimean Tatars and Greeks returning to the Crimea.[88] Notwithstanding the fact that their legal status received a certain improvement in February 1992,[89] the situation for them remains discriminatory, and precisely on ethnic grounds. Even now they are deprived of the right to legalize real-estate purchases, to be officially employed permanently, and to receive pensions and social allowances. Their children are not admitted to Russian higher educational establishments (children older than 16 years were issued Russian passports only in the period from February 1995 to April 1996). Moreover, the range of discriminatory practices the kray authorities apply to Meskhetian Turks in order to force them out is expanding. In particular, the resolution "On measures for the mitigation of inter-ethnic tension in the areas of compact settlement of Meskhetian Turks temporarily residing on the territory of Krasnodar Kray," issued by the kray legislative assembly on 24 April 1996, imposes a regular and chargeable (one "official" minimum monthly salary installment every three months) registration procedure on every adult Meskhetian Turk.[90]

The massacres in the Fergana Valley and all subsequent events rendered the repatriation-related stance Meskhetian Turks adhere to even tougher and more determined. Their tenth congress, which was held in the village of Adigul in the Azerbaijani SSR's Saalty district, formulated an unconditional demand for repatriation to Georgia. If the demand is not satisfied, 70–80% of Meskhetian Turks intend to immigrate to Turkey.[91]

However, the German-like mass emigration model seems rather unlikely to work in this case, since the discrepancy between Germany and Turkey is too significant, in particular in terms of the legal and economic provisions needed for large-scale repatriation of the titular nationality population. Besides, the situation of Meskhetian Turks in the Azerbaijani environment is not comparable to the situation of Germans in Kazakh society. This raises a suggestion that the most likely development of the Meskhetian Turk situation—taking into account the radicalization of Krasnodar Kray authorities' discriminatory policies targeting the migrants—may involve their gradual moving to and consolidation in Azerbaijan, with prospective piecemeal assimilation into and absorption by the Azerbaijani ethnic environment.

Some 80 Meskhetian Turk families have already settled at different locations in Georgia. However, in spite of all the efforts (taken, in particular, by Georgian human rights activists) and even two special decrees issued by the Georgian government, which recognize the formal right of the evictees to repatriation, hopes for a mass return of Meskhetian Turks to Georgia remain virtually unthinkable.[92]

To conclude, starting from the 1950s, all the three non-rehabilitated peoples have been carrying on a peaceful, organized and generally—regarding the fulfillment of the key tasks—unsuccessful struggle. Admittedly, Germans and Crimean Tatars eventually received the personal right to reside in their native lands, while Meskhetian Turks are still deprived of this right and are dispersed in a number of Caucasian regions (Azerbaijan, the Kabardian–Balkar ASSR and Krasnodar Kray) and in Central Asia, to where they once were banished. Crimean Tatars, who have already consolidated themselves in the Crimea over the past decade and created an actual efficient system of intra-ethnic self-regulation (the *Medzhlis*es of different levels) are still far from achieving their ultimate goals, although much closer as compared to the others. As far as Soviet Germans are concerned, scattered, as before, they see their total emigration to the FRG as the only alternative to the restoration of the Volga German ASSR. Simultaneously, notwithstanding the existing precedents, emigration to Turkey represents no feasible alternative for either Crimean Tatars or Meskhetian Turks.

REPRESSED PEOPLES AND ETHNIC CONFLICTS ON THE TERRITORY OF THE FORMER USSR IN THE 1990s

Should one divert one's attention from the arbitrariness and violence that were associated with the deportations and resettlement, one might acquire a somewhat broader perspective and discern the positive aspects that contributed to the experience of the repressed peoples.

As Zh. Zayonchkovskaya shrewdly remarked, the people that were returning in the 1950s were fairly distinct and largely different from those deported in the 1940s.[93] For example, the overwhelming majority of the Caucasian peoples were poor and poorly educated peasants at the moment of deportation.[94] Only those most active and with the most initiative were able to survive under the harsh conditions they faced during their exile. At the same time, their new social environment in Central Asia and Kazakhstan comprised even more backward and socially inert population, which put the deported peoples in a favorable position with regard to their prospects and opened firm opportunities within the employment structure and the possibility to educate their children. Had they been delayed at the places of exile for longer periods, they would have been bound to form the local elite, as did happen in the cases of Meskhetian Turks and Crimean Tatars. However, since the return of the Caucasian peoples was more rapid and took place earlier, their social priority over the local population was not quite as obvious.

In addition, some representatives of the North Caucasian peoples (as a rule, members of mixed families, but others too) stayed in Central Asia, which led to the formation of what could be called an "internal diasporas" within the USSR. Simultaneously, their staying outside relieved the demographic pressure in their native lands, since each autonomous unit in the North Caucasus suffered agrarian over-population in one way or another, which added fuel to the fire of the conflicts that emerged.

In a sense, the break-up of the USSR brought about the disinte-gration of many "internal diasporas" and their separation by the newly established state borders. This hindered, and in some cases com-pletely blocked, ties within communities and even families: for exam-ple, there appeared Koreans of Russia, of Uzbekistan, of Kazakhstan, etc., with all too tangible state and customs barriers between them, rather than merely formal or transparent borders. Contrary to the trends observed in the 1980s, a further drift of nationalities to their titular native administrative units has typically occurred, leading to additional demographic pressure in the lands in question.

Within the past 10–15 years, the dramatic growth of nationalist sentiments in the Caucasus, Kazakhstan and Central Asian republics, Uzbekistan in particular, not to mention Tajikistan (by far the most volatile republic in the region), has on many occasions challenged the local communities of the deported peoples, seriously raising the ques-tion of what is to be done.

As a matter of fact, there are not many options: 1) to try to adjust oneself, to get accustomed and stay; 2) to move to other post-Soviet states (chiefly to Russia); or 3) to emigrate further abroad, especially in the cases of the peoples that have a "historic homeland," such as Germans, Greeks, Koreans, Finns, and partly Meskhetian Turks.

The risk and difficulties associated with the first way are fairly obvious. Except for Germans, the third possibility also turns out to be rather problematic to achieve in practice, since metropolitan coun-tries maintain different repatriation regulations (however, visible repatriation trends are confirmed statistically in the cases of other repressed peoples too).

For example, in South Korea (a country suffering harsh land deficit), the repatriation of Soviet Koreans is encountered with a cool reception, and—on the contrary—the emigration of its own citizens is actively encouraged. According to V. Tyan, repatriation is seriously considered chiefly by those Koreans that reside in Sakhalin (they were deported there by the Japanese in the past), know the Korean lan-guage and have relatives in South Korea. They have nearly no chances finding jobs in Korea, which is the reason why the two largest groups of emigrants are pensioners, who are subsequently placed in state homes for the aged (there are already several hundreds of such people), and students that have the right to a particular work-hour quota. Koreans from Central Asia—with their cultural and linguistic flexibility, education and primarily agrarian (vegetable growing) professional orientation—migrate to Russia most readily. There are favorable preconditions for the participation of Koreans in the economic development of such regions as the Central Non-Black-Earth Region and the Far East. Such migration, however, has been exclusively of a private nature today and is not encouraged or supported by the Russian state.[95]

In the Perestroika years—and, especially, in the period of the competitive co-existence of the USSR and RSFSR Supreme Soviets—there were certain grounds for the repressed peoples to cherish promised hopes and illusions. The Constituent Congress of the Confederation of Repressed Peoples, which was held on 24 November 1990 in Moscow, adopted a declaration of the rehabilitation and revival of the repressed peoples.[96]

Most of the peoples in question established their own organizations. For example, a "Union of Ingermanlandians" [Inkerin Littoo] of Leningrad was formed on 3 October 1988 to represent the interests of more than 18 thousand Ingermanland Finns residing in the city and oblast. The union is promoting the national revival, supported by the state of Finland and its Lutheran Church (e.g., in obtaining visas, language training, professional training, and seasonal work in Finland). A similar association, "Kheimo", is working in Moscow. The recognition of the Russian Finns as a repressed people, postulated in the Russian Federation Supreme Soviet resolution of 29 June 1993, was an outcome of the mentioned organizations' activities.

Sometimes, there emerged organizations competing with each other or representing different trends within a particular national group. For instance, an international Meskhetian Turk association "Vatan" [Turkish for "Motherland"], created in 1990, advocates unconditional repatriation that would restore the original cultural balance of the Alkhaltsikhi district of Georgia, while the "Khena" [Georgian for "Salvation"] organization unites those prepared to identify themselves as "Muslim Georgians" and to settle in various parts of Georgia. In addition, there is an "Umid" [Turkish for "Hope"] society, founded in 1994 by Meskhetian Turks adherent to the idea of emigration to Turkey.[97]

Nevertheless, as has already been shown, the process of the repressed peoples' rehabilitation (especially territorial rehabilitation) as such cannot be considered completed. The legislative acts recently adopted by the state—the RSFSR Supreme Soviet declaration "Of the recognition of the repressive actions against the peoples subjected to forced resettlement as unlawful and criminal, and securing their rights" (of 14 November 1989), its resolution concerning the cancellation of corresponding legislative documents in conformity with the declaration (of 7 March 1991), and the RSFSR law "On the rehabilitation of repressed peoples" (of 26 April 1991)—unfortunately have not dotted all the "i"s.

The list of ethnically motivated territorial claims and conflicts in the former USSR is not a short one. There is information pointing to nearly 300 instances of official or unofficial territorial claims[98] that have been put forward in the period of 1988–1996, with at least 140 of them remaining unresolved,[99] around 20 having developed into armed conflicts, and 6 into regional wars. It is important to stress that it was not the USSR collapse that brought the conflicts about; it merely exposed them, and rendered them more salient and ever more contentious.

The role the deported peoples played in the inter-ethnic conflicts of the later Soviet period (i.e., the Gorbachev Perestroika) may not have been principal or crucial, and yet it was fairly conspicuous. Regrettably, after the disintegration of the USSR and formation of new RSFSR borders, this role proved to be more consequential.

For instance, the Karachai autonomy has not yet been restored. As far as Ingushetians are concerned, a significant part of their former territory has not yet been returned to them. Neither administrative territorial arrangement, nor toponyms, have been fully reinstated in the cases of Balkars, Akkin Chechens and Kalmyks, and—most importantly—the autonomous administrative units of Crimean Tatars and Volga Germans have not been restored at all.

Some conflicts have already drawn streams of blood and tears. They were shed both in the alien lands into which the sufferers were thrown by the tyrannical will of the "Father of the peoples": the massacres and pogroms of Meskhetian Turks in the Fergana Valley in

June 1989 represent a conspicuous example; and on their native soil: for example, the Ingushetian demonstrations of 16–19 January 1973 demanding the return of the Prigorodnyi district,[100] or bloody clashes in the Sunzha district's *stanitsa* of Troitskaya in April 1991, when an actual Cossack pogrom occurred evidently provoking the Ingushetians' rapid departure.[101]

And yet, the most prominent event was the bloody eight-day conflict between Ossetians and Ingushetians that burst out in autumn 1992 (lasting from 30 October to 6 November), that was only extinguished through the intervention of Russian troops.[102]

Typologically, and in appearance, the conflict represented a case reminiscent of classic irredenta, i.e., a movement to reclaim parts of a historical homeland owned in the past and currently densely populated with compatriots but belonging to adjacent territorial formations.[103]

The historical factors of the old Ossetian–Ingushetian confrontation, which culminated in its bloody apogee in 1992, can be understood more profoundly in a broader Caucasian and all-Russian contexts. In legal terms, the arbitrariness comprising the deportation and unsatisfactory rehabilitation of the Ingushetian people did not constitute the exclusive root of the conflict. The situation was also a result of a critical contradiction between the Constitution of the Russian Federation and the RSFSR law on the rehabilitation of repressed peoples, of 26 April 1991.

As a reminder, after the dismantling of the Chechen–Ingush ASSR, a part of the former republic, including the Prigorodnyi district that was populated mainly by Ingushetians prior to the deportation, was transferred to North Ossetia. The district remained a part of North Ossetia even after the restoration of the Chechen–Ingush ASSR in 1957. The Ingushetians' spontaneous repopulating of the Prigorodnyi district began all the same; and gradually—due to intense differences between Ingushetians and Ossetians' demographic behavior[104]—Ingushetians caught up with Ossetians numerically, and even took the lead in the southern and northern parts of the district and in the capital's suburbs.

Simultaneously with the Ingushetians returning, Ossetians were gradually taking root in the new soil, and by the late 1970s they had already exchanged the old and alien Ingushetian houses for new ones which nearly every family built for themselves. From the perspective of the Ossetians, the handing over of the Prigorodnyi district to the Ingushetians—who dominated in the settlements (Kartsma, Redant, Terk, Dachnyi) that surrounded Vladikavkaz as it is—would present a direct threat to their capital. And the Ingushetians' claims for the right-bank part of Vladikavkaz with its industry and infrastructure multiplied these fears dramatically (the Mozdok corridor was a third territorial section on which Ingushetians' claims spread).

The overt confrontation between the two peoples started developing long before the events of 1992, from approximately 1981, when first clashes between Ingushetian rally participants and troops took place in Ordzhonikidze. At that time, the authorities were still strong enough to suppress the violence, however, directly before the USSR collapse, the situation gained a new momentum. The 2nd and 3rd congresses of the Ingushetian people that were held in September 1989 and October 1991 (i.e., before the establishment of the Republic of Ingushetia in June 1992) produced insistent calls for the forceful "territorial rehabilitation" of the Ingushetian people; by the beginning of 1992 nearly every Ingushetian family had firearms at its disposal.

In their turn, Ossetian extremists demanded that Ingushetians be ousted from the villages with mixed population and from Vladikavkaz. From 1990, Ossetian self-defense units started to be formed; and the North Ossetian Republican Guard was established in summer 1991.

Various clashes between Ossetians and Ingushetians, some of them with casualties, became more frequent in the early 1990s. It was the events of 20–22 October 1992 that eventually set off the conflict itself: an Ossetian militia armored vehicle ran over a 13-year-old Ingushetian girl in the village of Oktyabrskoye; and another two Ingushetians were killed in the village of Yuzhnyi (in a clash with Ossetian militia forces). A full-fledged armed conflict burst out on the night of 30–31 October. At the beginning, Ingushetians were predominant, seizing virtually all the villages with mixed population in the Prigorodnyi district. However, on 31 October the Russian army intervened in the struggle on the side of the Ossetians. Remarkably, an ancient saying about Ossetians as "faithful sons of Russia" was resurrected (read: Ingushetians are betrayers, which is why they were banished in the past).[105]

Both the Ingushetian attack and Ossetian counter-attack were carried out in a way consistent with all the most barbarous traits of ethnic war: with hostage-taking, murders, rape, pillaging and the destruction of homes. It was not until 2 November that Yeltsin issued a decree declaring a state of emergency on the entire territory of North Ossetia and Ingushetia,[106] and no sooner than 6 November the remaining hotbeds of armed confrontation were damped out. The Decree stipulated the establishment of a new administration, which was first to be chaired by Vice-Prime Minister G. Khizha. A new decree by Yeltsin on 12 November restricted the territory under the jurisdiction of the temporary administration to a narrow buffer zone along the border between North Ossetia and Ingushetia.[107]

The Ossetian–Ingushetian conflict produced the following tragic statistics: 600 persons killed (171 of them Ossetian and 419 Ingushetian), 315 missing, thousands wounded, 57 thousand refugees (7 thousand of them Ossetian and 50 thousand Ingushetian[108]) and 4 thousand ruined houses.[109] According to another official source, 546 persons were killed, 407 of them Ingushetian and 105 Ossetian.[110] Yet other sources cite the following numbers: 262 killed, including 12 Russian military service members, 120 Ingushetians and 130 Ossetians;[111] or 1,000 persons as the total number of casualties.[112] Eleven Ingushetian settlements were completely destroyed. According to the Ministry for Nationalities Affairs of the Russian Federation, the material damage sustained in the conflict zone amounted to some 20 million US dollars.[113]

It was not until January 1993 that the two sides launched a negotiation process (the "round table" in Kislovodsk). On 18–21 March 1993, a summit was held in the same city, where North Ossetia's president A. Galazov and newly elected Ingushetian president R. Aushev signed an "Agreement on the measures for the complex resolution of the problem of refugees and forced migrants on the territories of the Ingush Republic and North Ossetia." In particular, it was ruled that those citizens of the two republics that had officially resided in the Prigorodnyi district before the conflict and had not been involved in crimes be returned to their home settlements.

In December 1993, in the course of the 1993 election campaign, Yeltsin visited the North Caucasus and attended a meeting with the leaders of all North Caucasian republics, held in Nalchik. The discussion resulted in a decision that a new Ingushetian capital be founded in the town of Magas; and Ingushetian refugees be returned to four villages of the Prigorodnyi district (Chermen, Dongaron,

Dachnoye and Kurtat). On 13 December 1993, a corresponding decree on the return of Ingushetian refugees was issued by the president of the Russian Federation. Meetings of Galazov and Aushev took place in 1994; and agreements concerning the return procedure were signed on 24 June 1994 in Beslan. After the Russian troops launched their military operation in Chechnya at the end of 1994, the state of emergency in the Ossetian–Ingushetian conflict zone was cancelled, after which the Ingushetian side denounced the Kislovodsk and Beslan agreements as restricting the rights of citizens.

Next time Galazov and Aushev met without intermediaries on 11 July 1995 in Vladikavkaz. This was where they signed a treaty, which stipulated in particular the rejection of mutual territorial claims (which was disavowed by Aushev literally the next day).

Meanwhile, bloody encounters in the conflict zone persisted: from the assassination of temporary administration chairman V. P. Polyanichko on 1 August 1993 to a grenade attack on a bus carrying Ingushetian refugees on 17 July 1997 in the Prigorodnyi district. Later followed two acts of terror against Ossetian militiamen (29 July) and an offensive launched by some 1,000 armed Ossetians against an Ingushetian refugee camp in the village of Tarskoye (people were beaten indiscriminately, 83 "wagon" homes were burned down, the camp was utterly pillaged, and seven hostages were taken; the camp had to be evacuated to Ingushetian territory).

Consequently, the main conflict was little short of flaring up again; and the Ingushetian side proposed that direct presidential rule be introduced in the conflict zone. The Ossetian side opposed the suggestion demanding, yet again, that all territorial claims be rejected once and for all (the Ingush Constitution regards the Prigorodnyi district as an inalienable part of the republic). In its turn, the Federal Center performed the mediator role in the negotiations, but showed actual solidarity with the Ossetian side.[114]

As a consequence, the Ossetian–Ingushetian conflict proved to be on the threshold of a new undeclared war. During the meetings of Galazov and Aushev with Chernomyrdin and Yeltsin, held on 4, 7 and 9 August, Moscow demanded that a moratorium on armed actions be concluded for a period of 10 to 15 years. The "Agreement on conflict settlement and cooperation between the Republic of North Ossetia–Alania and the Republic of Ingushetia," signed in Moscow on 4 September 1994, was just a declaration in essence. On 15 October

1997, Aushev, Galazov and Chernomyrdin adopted a program of cooperative actions by the state authorities of the Russian Federation and two sides of the conflict for mitigating conflict repercussions, however the program failed to offer an effective breakthrough either.

From the Ingushetian perspective, the concept of moratorium was acceptable, seeing as a stage of the plan aimed at the returning of the lands alienated in 1944. The "Address to the Ossetian people," adopted on 27 September 1997 at a congress of the Ingushetian people, refers to common, good-neighbor multi-ethnicity in the Prigorodnyi district, but under Ingush jurisdiction.[115]

The process of the return of Ingushetian refugees to the Prigorodnyi district resumed: over 5 thousand persons had come back by the end of 1995, and some 11 thousand persons by the middle of 1997.[116] A. G. Zdravomyslov asserts that the Ossetian–Ingushetian conflict can be resolved exclusively on the grounds of compromise, for example, in the form of joint control over the Prigorodnyi district.

However, the emergence of new ethnic deportations and ethnic wars—and both phenomena were involved in the Ossetian–Ingushetian conflict—is extremely dangerous. Regrettably, these particular methods have come to be considered as practical methods of conflict "resolution" through the course of the ethnic–territorial conflicts that have spread and developed over the territory of the former USSR. Calls for such actions keep falling from the lips of radical nationalists, including representatives of the regions, from which their predecessors had been deported in the past (for example, in Western Ukraine).

And of course there is plenty of "practical experience" of such methods, which has not been territorially limited to the North Caucasus, but spread throughout Central Asia and Transcaucasia. In particular, 160 thousand Azerbaijanis were evicted from Armenia and Karabakh; and 250 thousand Armenians were thrown out of Azerbaijan during the years of the Karabakh conflict. The number of Georgian refugees from the Georgian–Abkhaz conflict zone mounted to 230 thousand persons. The Pamir Tajiks, who were forced down to the valleys in the past, now have to move back to Badakhshan.

Possible new instances of discrimination on ethnic grounds, in particular targeting representatives of the peoples repressed in the past, represent a serious hazard too. To refer to one example of such actions, an instruction issued by the Russian general staff that the mobilization into the army of reservists from amongst "citizens whose

rights were restored" (as they are termed in the instruction!) be carried out on an individual basis and after agreement with the local
security bodies of the Russian Federation—the very bodies whose
predecessors had planned and implemented the deportations in the
first place. However, no individual or agreement procedures were
needed in the cases of various sensitive military units (i.e., intelligence, airforce, radio-engineering and tank), inaccessible for members of the "indicated target groups."[117]

NOTES

1 Bugay, Gonov, 1998, 242.

2 See the "draft plan" for resettlement, dated as early as September 1943, discovered by A. S. Khunagov (Bugay, Gonov, 1998, 230). Interestingly, it was
proposed that representatives of the deported peoples make up half of the
komendatura personnel.

3 Zaytsev, 1993, 113–114. In settlements, commandants had the right to subject
special resettlers to punishments in the form of fines of up to 10 rubles or
arrest for a term of up to five days.

4 See details in a summary note of 17 January 1946 (GARF, h. 9401, r. 1,
f. 2410, sh. 178).

5 Bugay, Gonov, 1998, 237.

6 The estimation was made based on Bugay, Gonov, 1998, 241, referring to the
"Summary on forestalling escapes of special resettlers from the moment of
their placement" (GARF, h. 9401, r. 1, f. 31445, sh. 20).

7 Bugay, Gonov, 1998, 235. In particular, the USSR Supreme Soviet Presidium
Resolution No. 1481-730 of 03 June 1948, stipulating that a confinement term
of up to eight years for escaping became applicable.

8 Bugay, Gonov, 1998, 238–241.

9 Bugay, Gonov, 1998, 236.

10 Zemskov, 1990a, 9–10.

11 Zaytsev, 1993, 125.

12 Bugay, Gonov, 1998, 236.

13 Zaytsev, 1993, 126–127.

14 Zaytsev, 1993, 127–128.

15 Bugay, 1995, 260.

16 However, it was preceded by decisions concerning the cancellation of the registration regime for children of ethnic German citizens (5 July 1954) and providing for their mobilization for military service (23 August 1955), along with
the ruling on lifting the special settlement restrictions applying to Germans,
CPSU members and candidate members, and their family members (9 May
1955). See Bugay, 1995, 260.

17 Zaytsev, 1993, 119, 121–122.

18 Instead of these measures, a number of resolutions were issued later—in the mid–1960s, early 1970s and late 1980s—explaining the issues pertaining to the restoration of rights.

19 Bugay, 1995, 220.

20 Following are the dates for which similar data are available: 1 April 1945, i.e., right before the end of the war; 1 January 1953, i.e., on the crest of another wave of the Stalin repression, which was stopped only due to his death; 1 January 1958, when a large share of the "punished peoples" and other illegally deported population groups either returned to their native lands, as North Caucasians and some other peoples, or received civic rights to remain in their new residences, such as Germans and the Crimean Tatars.

21 Zemskov, 1990a, 16.

22 Ivanova, 1997, 77, with a reference to: TsAODM, h. 203, r. 1, f. 990, sh. 134.

23 Zemskov, 1990a, 8.

24 Registered at the department for special settlements of the NKVD of the USSR from 1946.

25 Under the Third Reich they had enjoyed all civic rights and corresponding privileges.

26 GARF, h. 9479, r. 1, f. 31.

27 In the regions in questions, settlers belonging to other categories are present, but rarely, for example the Vlasov army members (in the Murmansk Obl. and Primorsky Kray) or kulaks (in the Kherson Obl.).

28 Bugay, Gonov, 1998, 193.

29 Bugay, Gonov, 1998, 283.

30 Bugay, Gonov, 1998, 285.

31 Bugay, Gonov, 1998, 288.

32 A similar restriction was actually imposed on Koreans too, although they were not among special settlers.

33 See a definition of "territorial rehabilitation" in Zdravomyslov, 1998, 51.

34 The proportion dropped again down to 83.2% in the 1980s.

35 The information was provided by R. Kuliyev. The villages in question were directly involved in the events that occurred in the Cherek Gorge in 1942–1943, a distorted interpretation of which was used as one of the pretexts for the deportation (see Azamatov, Temirzhanov et al., 1994).

36 See Prozumenshchikov, 1995.

37 Tsutsiyev, 1998, 73–75. Naturally, there was no question of toponymic rehabilitation with regard to the Ingushetian settlements in the Prigorodnyi district. According to Tsutsiyev, the list of the settlements goes as follows (the pre-1944 names are bracketed): Mayskiy, Chermen (Bazorkino), Dongaron (Tsuroyurt), Kurgat (Gadaborshevo), Dachnoye (Yandiyevo), Kambileyevskoye (Galgay-Yurt), Oktyabrskoye (Sholkhi), Sunzha (Akki-Yurt), Komgaron (Tauzen-Yurt), Tarskoye (Angusht), Chernorechenskoye, Terk (Dlinnaya Dolina), Balta, Redant 1, Redant 2, Popov khutor (Metskhalsky), Yuzhnyi, Kartsma, Ezmi (Tsutsiyev, 1998, 81). Cf. the similar toponymic repression against the initial Russian names of some of these villages (former *stanitsa* settlements), described in chapter 2.

38 Bugay, 1995, Mejer 280–281.

39 At that time, 508.9 thousand Chechens and 113.7 thousand Ingushetians resided in the Chechen–Ingush ASSR (another 40 thousand Chechens lived in Daghestan, and 18.4 thousand Ingushetians in the North Ossetian ASSR).

40 A. A. Tsutsiyev estimated the proportion of those former residents that returned to the Prigorodnyi district as ranging between 30–50% (Tsutsiyev, 1998, 75).

41 Bugay, 1995, 260–261.

42 Bugay, 1995, 289. Incidentally, there is another interesting, although highly debatable, explanation as to why Soviet Germans were denied the right to "repatriate": mainly due to their own "fault," namely their strict discipline and hard-working nature, which were the reasons why it was they who were left to develop the barren lands! Simultaneously, rebellious peoples like Chechens and Ingushetians were allowed to return since they produced nothing but harm in the new areas (Tsutsiyev, 1998, 73).

43 Chervonnaya, 1997, 151–152.

44 The situation in general is perfectly summed up in the image described in a letter of 9 July 1965 submitted by the German delegates to A. Mikoyan. It turns out that a criminal, who has served 23 years in confinement, was convicted wrongly. And in this situation he is told: "You were punished by mistake, you are not guilty, you are a good guy. But you have got so used to being here, you have taken such 'deep root' that you shall stay here." (See Auman, Chebotareva, 1994, 21–41).

45 Auman, Chebotareva, 1993, 190–197.

46 Auman, Chebotareva, 1994, 69.

47 See supplement 4.

48 See memo "On the situation around the issue of Soviet Germans" of 24 September 1990 (RGANI, h. 89, op. 8, f. 60. sh. 3–11).

49 To a large extent this fostered a split among the leadership of the Revival society itself.

50 Speaking to workers that gathered holding up such slogans as "German autonomy is in Germany," Yeltsin literally "improvised" the following: "…I am going to make a responsible statement so that everyone will know. No German autonomy will be established on territories without compact German population, i.e., unless there is an overwhelming majority of Germans residing on this territory! I guarantee this to you as President! It is a completely different matter if we talk about, say, the vacant 300-hectare military testing ground in the Volgograd region [the military ground of Kapustin Yar is implied here—P. P.], and Marshal Shaposhnikov is prepared to hand it over. They can be settled there, let us say. And let them then develop that land filled with shells. And Germany will help [shortly before the meeting, Yeltsin was promised financial support during his visit to Germany—P. P.]. Maybe somewhere there, in some future time, there will be some sort of oblast like that— or maybe some sort of Volga German ethnic district—but only after there are 90% of Germans living there." (Quoted as in Auman, Chebotareva, 1993, 401–402.)

51 See *Izvestiya*, newspaper issue of 20 March 1991.

52 Kriger, 1997, 5.

53 During one of the demonstrations in front of the Central Committee building, L. Oldenburg chained herself and her children to a traffic lights post (see Alekseyeva, 1992, 138).

54 The collection was first designed as a periodical, but after the departure of its compilers (V. Grigas, L. Bauer and F. Ruppel) for the FRG, its publication was never resumed (see Alekseyeva, 1992, 138).

55 See Alekseyeva, 1992, 138–139.

56 Naturally, the Law is not of a prohibitive nature. However, immigrants leaving the place of residence assigned to them entails consequent deprivation of the integration allowance, free language courses, and the minimization of social benefits.

57 It is remarkable that related comments by Waffenschmidt, the federal commissioner for resettler affairs in the Kohl government, often sounded like victorious "front-line reports," as if he had been talking about fighting a flood or vermin hordes (A. L. "German newspapers on resettlers," in *The Eastern Express* [Ahlen, 1997] no. 9, 7).

58 Heinkel R., *Binnenintegration als Faktor für die Eingliederung Russlanddeutscher Aussiedler in die Bundesrepublik Deutschland—das Beispiel zweier Gemeinden in Rheinhessen. Festschrift für Erdmann Gormsen zum 65. Geburstag,* Mainz 1994, 445–458).

59 According to Kriger, 1997, 5. Incidentally, Germans from the Baltic states immigrate to Russia too.

60 The program was designed for the period of 1997–2006 (the make up of the program was to be completed as early as December 1996, however the deadline was not kept to due to the lack of necessary statistical data). The project itself is "specific" singularly in terms of its implementation mechanism (by way of directives imposed by the ministry) and related budget planning (see Petrov, N., "Prezidentsky ukaz nakonets-to vypolnen" [Presidential order fulfilled at last], *Inostranets,* 1997, no. 20, 4 June, 22).

61 The Russian Federation's foundation branch was chaired by V. Bauer (former State Duma deputy and former deputy minister for nationalities and regional policy in the governments of V. Chernomyrdin and S. Kirienko).

62 See Alekseyeva, 1992, 93–140. The movement established itself in 1956–1964. The first legal case was brought against Crimean Tatar activists in Tashkent in 1962. The climax of the movement activities—rallies, petitions, delegations and the publication of a bulletin (the predecessor of the "Khronika tekushchikh sobytiy" [Current Affairs Chronicle])—took place in 1964–1969. The movement began to decline in the 1970s.

63 See Nekrich, 1978 (about professor R. I. Muzafarov and others). In December 1973 a trial on their case was held in Simferopol.

64 Before the decrees were published, *propiska* was in effect only in the cities and resort towns of the Crimea; and in 1967–1968 it was introduced in all Crimean settlements. Residing without *propiska* was regarded as a criminal offence in the USSR (see Alekseyeva, 1992, 98–99). See also Council of Min-

isters resolutions of 15 August 1978, 24 December 1987, etc. Due to this, the migration balance in the Crimea turned out negative in 1987 (Chervonnaya, 1997, 145).

65 Alekseyeva, 1992, 98–99.

66 Alekseyeva, 1992, 100.

67 Alekseyeva, 1992, 109.

68 Alekseyeva, 1992, 103.

69 Alekseyeva, 1992, 107–108.

70 Alekseyeva, 1992, 106–109.

71 Only persons in mixed marriages constituted exceptions in this respect.

72 See Chervonnaya, 1997, 152–153, 156–157, 181–182.

73 At the time (26 November 1990), the author of this research was an expert invited to evaluate the suggestions (within the expert evaluation procedure of the State Planning Committee of the USSR).

74 According to the results of research conducted in 1989 by the Center for Independent Expert Evaluation of the Soviet–US foundation "Cultural Initiative" (chaired by E. I. Pain), urban residents constituted 62.1% among the Tatars that returned to the Crimea, 53.5% wished to reside in cities and towns, while only 26.6% managed to settle there. This naturally caused a number of complications that repatriates, and especially the Crimean Tatar intelligentsia, had to face.

75 Chervonnaya, 1997, 146.

76 Chervonnaya, 1997, 146. For a long time the problem of citizenship remained a stumbling block in the relations between the Crimean Tatar community and the Ukrainian state, which resulted in the boycott of the 1995 elections to the local councils by the Crimean Tatars (Chervonnaya, 1997, 159).

77 Chervonnaya, 1997, 147–149.

78 Vlasov, S., *Political aspects of migration-related problems in Ukraine*, Materials of the seminar "Ukraine—Russia: prospects for collaboration in the spheres of migration and citizenship," Moscow Carnegie Center, 30 September 1996, 6–8.

79 For example, the destruction of the Crimean Tatar tent camp in the village of Krasny Ray near Alushta on 10 July 1992 (Chervonnaya, 1994, 19).

80 Chervonnaya, 1994, 17–18.

81 See Panesh, Yermolov, 1991.

82 Alekseyeva, 1992, 111.

83 Alekseyeva, 1992, 112–113.

84 In accordance with the results of a census conducted by an initiative group, there are some 400 thousand Meskhetian Turks (see Broydo, Prokhorov, 1994, 342).

85 Osipov, 1998, 9.

86 See Council of Ministers Resolution No. 503 of 26 June 1989 and RSFSR Council of Ministers Resolution No. 220 of 13 July 1989.

87 As a rule, they are not recognized as such de jure, since they are not officially registered Russian citizens.

88 Osipov, 1997, 257–259. For details see Osipov, Cherepova, 1996.

89 Under Resolution No. 97, adopted by the Smaller Soviet of Krasnodar Kray, the settlers are issued temporary residence certificates, permits for temporary employment without *propiska*, and temporary registration of vehicles (Osipov, Cherepova, 1996, 5–6). Before the resolution was issued, Meskhetian Turks were even denied the right to marriage or childbirth registration, the possession of *propiska* by one of the newly married couples was not considered sufficient.

90 See Osipov, A., "Meskhetinskye Turki v Krasnodarskom kraye" [Meskhetian Turks in Krasnodar Kray], *SEMRPK*, 1997, no. 4, 19–21.

91 Panesh, Yermolov, 1991, 217.

92 See in Akhalkatsi, E., "From Georgia: on Meskhetians," *Nationalities Papers, Vosh*, June 1996, no. 2, 303–305.

93 Zayonchkovskaya Z., "Die Gesellschaftssituation als Spannungsfaktor im Nordlichen Kaukasus," in Dahlmann, Hirschfeld (eds.), 1999, 583–588.

94 See details regarding their actual level of elementary education in Zemskov, 1990a, 14, 15.

95 Tyan, V., "Koreytsy nadeyutsya byt poleznymi Rossii" [Koreans hope to be helpful to Russia], *Inostranets*, 1994, no. 23, 6 June.

96 In particular, the document contained draft definitions of the concepts of repressed people and rehabilitation: "A repressed people is a historically established community that was subjected to the state-imposed policies of forced resettlement, slander and humiliation of human dignity, infringement of its rights and lawful interests, destruction of political and economic structures pertaining to the national and territorial arrangement, obliteration of the traditional national culture and language. According to the commonly recognized international norms, the listed actions are qualified as genocide [...] 2. The rehabilitation of repressed peoples involves return of the national groups to their traditional native places of residence, restoration of their national administrative units within the former borders, compensatory measures in cultural and economic spheres."

97 Osipov, Cherepova, 1996, 15–18.

98 There are multiple classifications of ethnic territory and claims.

99 Streletsky, 1997, 226–227.

100 The rallies took place following the delivery of a collective letter "On the fate of the Ingushetian people" to the CPSU TSK in December 1972 (see Tsutsiyev, 1998, 80; Prozumenshchikov, 1997).

101 Tsutsiyev, 1998, 91.

102 For a detailed prehistory of the complex and conflictual interrelations between the two neighboring peoples see Tsutsiyev, 1998.

103 See Streletsky, 1997, 234, 235.

104 Among the large North Caucasian peoples, Ossetians also take the lead in terms of their urban population proportion (66% in 1989, as compared to the 38% among the Ingushetians).

105 According to a sound observation by A. G. Zdravonyslov, the key words of the conflict "aggression" and "sweeping" [zachishcheniye] later transformed into "ethnic cleansing" and "genocide," were first used by Russian

general G. Filatov in his speech on North Ossetian television (Zdravomyslov, 1997, 91).

106 The official period of validity of the decree—until 4 February 1995—was extended by the parliament on several occasions.

107 Zdravomyslov, 1998, 71–73.

108 With regard to the number of refugees, there is data ranging from 37.5 thousand to 40.3 thousand persons, with 31 thousand of them officially registered residents. See Dzadziyev, A., L. Dzugayev, "Bezhentsy i vynuzhdennyye pereselentsy iz Severnoy Osetii" [Refugees and forced migrants from North Ossetia], *SEMRPK*, 1997, no. 4, 16. For all that, the Ingushetian population of the Mozdok district and the village of Mayskoye of the Prigorodnyi district, along with some Ingushetian residents of the Prigorodnyi district's village Chermen and the town of Kartsma of the Vladikavkaz city council did not leave their settlements even after 31 October 1992.

109 Zdravomyslov, 1997, 91.

110 Tsutsiyev, 1998, 5, citing *Vestnik vremennoy administratsii v zone chrezvychaynogo polozheniya na chasti territorii Respubliki Ingushetiya i Respubliki Severnaya Osetiya* [Bulletin of the temporary administration in the state-of-emergency zone on a part of the territories of the Republic of Ingushetia and Republic of North Ossetia], 1993, 7 May, no. 37, 1.

111 Official data of the Russian Federation State Committee for Emergency Situations (see Aksenov, S., S. Gavrilov, "Aushev i Galazov dogovorilis uvazhat drug druga" [Aushev and Galazov agreed to respect each other], *Kommersant-Daily*, 1997, 5 September, 2).

112 Mukomel, 1997, 301–303, with reference to the North Ossetian diplomatic mission (546 killed and 261 missing—in 1993) and Human Rights Watch.

113 Mukomel, 1997, 308.

114 Zhukov, M., S. Aksenov, "Moskva poprosila Ausheva i Galazova pomiritsya" [Moscow asked Aushev and Galazov to make up their differences], *Kommersant-Daily*, 1997, 22 July, 3.

115 Dzadziyev, A., "Syezd narodov Ingushetii" [Congress of the Ingushetian people], *SEMRPK*, 1997, no. 4, 24–25.

116 See Zdravomyslov, 1998, 8, 92–93.

117 Instruction of the General Headquarters No. 315/1/00350 of 16 December 1993 (quoted in Aliyeva, S., "Repressirovannyye narody vse yeshche zhdut. Kontseptsii natsionalnoy politiki v Rossii poka ne sushchestvuyet" [Repressed peoples are still waiting. There is no concept of ethnic policy in Russia yet], *Nezavisimaya gazeta*, 1995, 21 May, 3).

PART II

INTERNATIONAL FORCED MIGRATIONS

Internment and Deportation of German Civilians from European Countries to the USSR

THE VICTORS' LABOR BALANCE AND "LABOR REPARATIONS"

It is a well-known fact that—apart from millions of German POWs— German civilians from both the Third Reich and territories that had never belonged to it worked on the territory of the USSR. Their actual status and the ways their labor was used reveal many common features with those typical of POWs, and yet there are certain related specific features. There is no doubt that the motivation and "pre-history" of the use of German civilian labor in the USSR represent such points.

The issue of the so-called internees (or—as they are often alternatively termed—mobilized and interned), that is, the issue pertaining to the deportation and labor use of German civilians in the USSR in the last months of the war and first post-war years, has its precedent and has been subject to much research.

The problem in question has been extensively dealt with in the Western academic literature, in particular in Germany. The target groups affected by the deportations are generally considered by the researchers as a part of the 14 million Germans forced out of their pre-war homelands and placed within the Allies' occupation zones in Germany. The first serious publications on the topic were published as early as the late 1950s–early 1960s. They were primarily based on statistical data and witnesses' testimonies.[1] A number of publications that appeared in the 1980s did not contribute much new, either in terms of related factual information or interpretation of the events.[2]

It was not until the second half of the 1980s and 1990s that research works largely relying on archive sources, apart from memoirs, were published.[3] Among such works, a thorough three-volume research titled "Deportation of the Transylvania Saxons to the Soviet Union in 1945–1949" stands out. It was prepared by a group of Münster historians led by G. Weber.[4] Since the problem of German civilian internees is inseparably linked with the issue of German POWs, it is always touched upon in the research devoted to the latter, for example in the well-known monograph "In the Archipelago GUPVI" by S. Karner.[5]

In the USSR, as in the other East European socialist countries, the deportation of civilian German workers remained a taboo topic for nearly half a century, until the mid-1990s; and access to related archives was restricted during the period in question as well. And although the first reluctant and cautious references to the issue fell from the lips of N. Ceauşescu as early as 1966 and 1971, no attempts at scientific analysis of the matter were even contemplated at the time. It was not until 1994–1995 that the first publications based on the data from the Romanian state archive located in Bucharest came out: first of all, the monograph "Deportation of ethnic Germans from Romania to the Soviet Union in 1945" by H. Baier and others.[6]

Approximately at the same period, i.e., in the mid-1990s, the first publications dealing with the topic appeared in Russia. In 1994 articles by V. B. Konasov, A. V. Tereshchuk, P. N. Knyshevsky, and M. I. Semiryaga were published.[7] And in 1995 a booklet *Interned Youth* by I. I. Chukhin was issued, which thoroughly reconstructed the history of camp no. 517 for interned German women at the station of Padoozero near Petrozavodsk.[8] The author of this research also made presentations on research dealing with the issue of interned and mobilized Germans on many occasions: his first related publications were issued in 1997–1998.[9] After a while, German publications based on the data originating from Russian sources came out, in particular the article by G. Klein.[10]

The issue of the internees involves multiple aspects. A sinister shadow was cast over the events by military expediency (the need to nip in the bud any threat of civilian armed resistance on the territory occupied by the Red Army), by politics ("reparation through labor" was presented as an essential triumph of justice, and—in a sense—retaliation for the use of the Ostarbeiter slave labor in Germany), and by justice (determining of the status of interned persons, legitimizing their labor use). But—above all other things—the situation was conditioned by economic circumstances (the exhaustion of resources, including human labor resources, during the period of war and the need to overcome the destruction, etc.).

From the perspective of international law, internment as a special (and particularly mild in its enforcement) type of freedom restriction applied to civilians did not contravene the Hague conventions of 1907 and other treaties. In the case of the parties of military conflicts, civilian citizens of the opposing side were acceptably subject to internment, while in the case of neutral countries, the legitimacy of internment applied to the conflict parties' military service members discovered on the neutral countries' territory. In its own draft "Enactment on POWs" of 1929, the USSR regarded as POWs citizens of the enemy state who took up arms (for all that, irrespective of whether they were organized into units), which contravened the Hague and Geneva Conventions (which the USSR refused to ratify).[11]

P. N. Knyshevsky took up the analysis of the economic aspect of the "operation for mobilization and internment." Apart from military and political spheres, the exclusive powers with which the State Defense Committee was endowed during war-time extended to purely economic matters, and—for all that—to both front-line and rear-area economies to an equal extent. In the period of its operation, i.e., during the 1,626 days from 30 June 1941 to 3 September 1945, the State Defense Committee issued 9,971 decrees and resolutions (in other words, it made approximately six important decisions a day!).[12]

The net population growth was somewhat lower than 640 thousand persons in 1945. In 1946, it rose almost three-fold; Lithuania was the only region with a negative population dynamics value.[13]

The Soviet labor legislation was formed before the war[14] and represented, as Knyshevsky defined it, an "accomplished system of barracks economy administered through the mechanism of total mobilization." Within the space of half a year starting from 26 June 1940, 2.09 million persons were convicted on the charges of unsanctioned absence from the workplace, along with non-attendance and poor punctuality, with over 1.7 million of them sentenced to a six-month term of reformatory labor at...their own workplaces. "Starting from 1941, the number of those subjected to punitive measures decreased, since the practice of coercion proved efficient, and the system firmly established itself, which predetermined the absence of the need for additional radical war-time alterations, except in effect for some individual amendments of the legislation."[15]

However, the rapid advance of the Wehrmacht required taking exigent measures towards the evacuation of enterprises and their stuff, and their subsequent establishment at new locations, which often involved such actions as forceful housing redistribution and resettlement of a part of the local population to other areas.[16]

The labor mobilization[17] comprised as its component the drafting into the, ironically termed, alternative labor service—through the system of military registration and enlistment offices—of reservists unfit the general military service (even individuals affected with tuberculosis) and some formally eligible conscripts (as a rule, "unreliable nationals," i.e., Koreans, Bulgarians, Greeks, Turks, etc.). Knyshevsky writes: "Drafting to the alternative labor service proved to be more efficient than the population labor mobilization carried out by civilian authorities; and it was in operation not only until the end of the war, but also during the first post-war years..."[18] So-called target demobilization, i.e., ascription of army servicemen, transferred to the reserve, to particular enterprises under the jurisdiction of the leading People's Commissariats, was another essential source of highly disciplined labor force. In addition, certain types of special troops were used as important labor units.[19] Notoriously, the GULAG system had substantial human labor resources at its disposal too.

Even so, the Soviet human resources were nearly exhausted by the end of the war; and the use of the enemy labor force appeared to be simply a matter of fact, reasonable and appropriate. Justifiable, especially taking into account that the defeated enemy had shown not the slightest hesitation or scruples over doing the same when the boot was on the other foot during the war.

The issue of the use of German labor was aired long before the completion of armed action.

In his written report of 31 August 1943, William Malkin considered German labor force as one of the most promising potential reparation types.[20] Nevertheless, the prevailing opinion among the British and American officials, with regard to reparations, was a theoretic acceptance but primarily in the form of restitution (i.e., the return of what was taken away and pillaged plus an equivalent compensation for that), rather than in cash. As far as "reparation through labor" was concerned, they denounced the idea in a fairly decisive way.

Interestingly, among the 16 UN members that submitted their claims for reparations it was only Poland that demanded that German qualified workforce be used for the reconstruction of the country's economy. It must be noted that—apart from delivering German workers to the winner states—the concept of "reparation through labor" at the time also implied using their unpaid labor at the enterprises of their own country placed under the orders of the victorious nations.[21]

The very first reference to the matter (among those that were available to us) is contained in a paper by M. M. Litvinov (at that time deputy people's commissar of foreign affairs) titled "On the treatment of Germany and other enemy countries in Europe" and compiled on 9 October 1943 (apparently, by way of preparation for the October meeting of the allied nations' ministers of foreign affairs that was to be held in Moscow, and for the November summit of Stalin, Churchill and Roosevelt in Tehran).

However, it was academic Ivan Mikhaylovich Maysky—the USSR ambassador to London and Molotov's deputy in the People's Commissariat of Foreign Affairs—that was the principal Soviet theoretician of the post-war world vision, and the reparation issue in particular. As early as November 1943 he was charged with the task of forming a commission for examining reparation-related issues and drafting a plan on how it would function. The plan was submitted as soon as 10 November; and in a couple of weeks the NKID "Commission for the compensation of the damage inflicted on the USSR by Hitler Germany and its allies" was established.[22] Needless to say, the commission was acting in cooperation with the "Extraordinary state commission for the establishment and investigation of the crimes committed by German fascist aggressors and their associates, and the damage inflicted by their actions," founded in November 1942.

Maysky departed from the idea that the participation of civilian Germans in the reconstruction of the economy destroyed by their armies was acceptable, fair and desirable. While asserting the idea, he appealed to the actual experience of Germany itself which successfully integrated tens of millions of foreign civilians as a labor force into its economy. However, such a measure was considered to be applicable only if Germany proved to be unable to pay its reparation liabilities in another form.

The commission chaired by Maysky was operating flat out. As early as 11 January 1944 Maysky submitted a paper titled "On the desirable foundations of the future peace." The document suggested "…charging Germany with reparations, in particular reparations in the form of labor, for a lengthy period (at least ten years)." It went on: "The matter in question has two sides to it. On the one hand, the reparations are to represent the soonest possible compensation for the damage inflicted on the USSR and other countries by Germany. On the other hand, the reparations, particularly reparations through labor, i.e., the annual withdrawal of a several-million strong labor force from the German national economy, are bound to weaken Germany's economy and its national military potential."[23]

On 3 March 1944, Maysky briefed the authority on the Commission's three-month operation period. The USSR's own reparation program was spelt out under his leadership by August 1944. In a document entitled "Reparations. Memo No. 1" and dated 27 July, submitted to Stalin, Molotov and a score of other addressees on 28 July, Maysky regarded "German labor" as a far more valuable reparation source, as compared to goods deliveries: "Provided the average annual number of labor force constitutes 5 million persons, the total reparation figure under this rubric will amount to 35–40 billion dollars within a ten-year period."[24] It is noteworthy that the total reparation amount to be paid within the mentioned period was estimated by Maysky's commission as some 70–75 billion dollars, which means that the "reparations through labor" were to make at least half of the entire figure!

On 9 October 1944—apparently as part of the preparation for Churchill and Eden's visit to Moscow—Maysky submitted an extensive paper titled "The position of the USA and Britain with regard to the reparation issue, and our possible counter arguments" to Molotov. In particular, he wrote: "Reparations in the form of German labor are considered acceptable, although the issue raises intense polemics within the USA and Britain.[25] It is unanimously recognized that the mentioned reparation form is thinkable exclusively as used by the USSR but not by the capitalist countries."[26]

(We would like to note in brackets that the truce treaties signed by the USA, USSR and Britain with Romania and Finland on 12 and 15 September 1944 touch upon the reparation issue, but by no means the question of "reparation through labor.")

At the end of January 1945, when the Soviet government was deep in the process of preparation for the Crimea conference of the three allied nations, Maysky sent Molotov a memo with the attached project "Formulae on the reparations to be made by Germany." The document envisaged general "...use of German labor force in the countries affected by the German aggression with the purpose of mending the economic losses inflicted on these countries by that German aggression," or—in other words—Germany's obligation to "...provide, for the period of ten post-war years, the reparation recipient states with the annual number of labor force (including highly qualified technical expertise) that the states in question will find sufficient for reviving their national economies... Exact figures with regard to the number and qualifications of the required work force will be determined later." Such provisions, according to Maysky, were to guarantee the USSR an annual approximate minimum of "5 million German workers of various qualifications (including highly qualified technical personnel) during ten years after the war's completion."[27]

As is well known, the conference was held in Yalta on 4–11 February 1945; and the Soviet side there continuously addressed the "German labor" issue with admirable persistence.

However, the program presentation on reparations, made by I. M. Maysky on behalf of the Soviet side during a meeting of the heads of government on 5 February, did not refer to the issue. And yet in the Soviet side's written proposition "The basic principles of payment of reparations by Germany," delivered by Molotov to Eden and Stettinius on 7 February read: "[...] 2. The issue of the use of German labor for reparation is put aside for the moment, it will be discussed later..."[28] The US secretary of state Stettinius used the same formula in his address to Molotov on 9 February 1945.[29] In its turn, the British address, handed over to Molotov by Eden on 10 February, appeared as if the Soviet proposition had been essentially accepted and was to be developed: "b) The use of German labor and truck deliveries."[30]

A separate "Protocol of the negotiations between the leaders of three governments at the Crimea conference with regard to the question of in-kind reparations by Germany," sent by Molotov to Eden and Stettinius the very same day (10 February) and proposed for signing by the heads of government at the conference, read: "[...] 2. Reparations shall be received from Germany in three forms: a) single confiscation, within two years of Germany's capitulation or cessation of organized resistance, of German national assets located both on German territory and beyond its borders [...]; the confiscation shall be carried out with the principal purpose of destroying German mil-

itary potential; b) annual deliveries of routinely produced goods after
the end of the war and during the period to be defined; c) use of German labor force."[31] At the same time, the British and American conference summary draft versions referred to the item using a cautious
formula as above,[32] while the final protocol omitted it altogether.[33]
But despite that, the mentioned protocol and the "Protocol of Pro-
ceedings of the Crimea Conference" retained the wording "use of
German labor force."[34]

After all, what did the Soviet side imply by the "use of German
labor force?" It appears the idea was similar to the German concept
of "Arbeitseinsatz im Dritten Reich." In other words, what was meant
was the deportation of a part of German civilian population (both
Reichsdeutsche and Volksdeutsche) to the USSR for subsequent use
as labor force (needless to say, this unconditionally applied to the
POWs). If something different had been meant, for example the use
of German labor force on German territory involving consequent
partial confiscation of the produced goods to the advantage of the
winner nation, what would have essentially distinguished item "c"
from item "b"?

The same approach can be detected in the materials of the
Berlin (Potsdam) conference. Below is the advice Generalissimo Stalin gave to Prime Minister Churchill on 25 July 1945 during the ninth
sitting of the heads of governments:

> Churchill: [...] *In Britain, this year, we shall have the most coal-less winter
> because we are short of coal.*
>
> Stalin: *Why? Britain has always exported coal.*
>
> Churchill: *That's because the miners have not yet been demobilized, there's
> a labor shortage in the coal industry.*
>
> Stalin: *There are enough POWs. We have POWs working on coal, it would
> be very hard without them. We are rehabilitating our coal reserves and are using
> POWs for the purpose. You have 400,000 German soldiers in Norway, they are
> not even disarmed, and I do not know what they are waiting for. There you have
> manpower.*[35]

Churchill, whose country had long before signed the Hague
treaties on POWs, avoided any discussion on such controversial
advice in a diplomatic way. Incidentally, by the end of the summer of
1945, the American stance with respect to the use of German civilian

labor force as a reparation element transformed too: from the US perspective, the practice was to be restricted exclusively to the use of convicted war criminals.[36]

It is remarkable though that, unlike in Yalta, the "German labor" usage issue was not raised in Potsdam, by the Soviet delegates in particular. Was it not a fact that the USSR had already—long before the Potsdam and Yalta conferences—resolved the question unilaterally?

INTERNMENT OF GERMANS IN SOUTHEAST EUROPE

There is a widely spread opinion represented in German-language academic literature that the deportation of the German minority from Romania was in one way or other stipulated as a condition in the unpublished appendices of the truce treaty between the USSR and Romania signed in Moscow as early as 12 September 1944.[37] Since the fact has been neither confirmed nor refuted so far, we will leave the clarification of the matter until (hopefully) the near future.

Today's point of departure comes at the moment when Stalin issued a related order, the precise date of which has not been established yet either. It is known that on 24 November 1944 People's Commissar of Internal Affairs Beria submitted a written report to Stalin which stated that—in accordance with the latter's orders—three groups of USSR NKVD executive officers were sent to the territories of the East European states, liberated by the troops of the 2nd, 3rd and 4th Ukrainian fronts, on assignment to carry out a preliminary registration of all ethnic Germans residing there.[38] The control over the operation was entrusted to Beria's deputy, A. N. Apollonov[39], and chief of the Central Department for the NKVD rear-security troops, I. M. Gorbatyuk.[40]

The purpose of the action was quite transparent: locating civilian candidates for labor mobilization and deportation to the destinations prescribed from Moscow, or—in other words—"reparation through labor!"

The NKVD executive groups were backed by 106 SMERSH counter-intelligence units (more than 800 servicemen). Apollonov and Gorbatyuk delivered a preliminary report to Beria on 5 December[41]; and on 15 December Beria briefed Stalin and Molotov on the results of the timely completed registration.[42] A total of 551,049 ethnic Germans, including 240,436 men and 310,613 women, were registered on the designated territory. The largest ethnic German population was located on Romanian territory: 421,846 persons, including 70,476 able-bodied men aged between 17 and 45 years. In addition, 73,572 persons were registered in Yugoslavia, 50,292 persons in Hungary, 4,250 persons in Czechoslovakia, and 1,089 persons in Bulgaria. The vast majority of them were subjects of the corresponding countries of residence. Part of the ethnic Germans from Yugoslavia and Romania— as a rule, "Reichsdeutsche" (German citizens numbering 24,694 persons)—had already been interned and were kept in camps (16,804 persons in 22 camps in Yugoslavia, and 7,890 persons in 15 camps in Romania). Even then the intention to use them as labor force was transparent: men constituted 82% of the camp inmates in Romania, and 59% in Yugoslavia, while persons of working age made up 79% in Romania and as many as 100% in Yugoslavia![43]

Initially it was suggested that the mobilization target group be restricted to males aged 17–45, who numbered a total of 97,484 persons (or 70 thousand persons with the deduction of the disabled). Beria requested Stalin's approval for the mobilization of the Germans subject to internment and their delivery to the USSR for working on the restoration of the coal industry in Donbass (up to 50 thousand persons) and ferrous metallurgy in the south (up to 20 thousand persons).

The proposition was duly approved, although with amendments stipulating the use of female labor force too. As soon as 16 December 1944 the State Defense Committee issued decree No. 7161cc.[44] Taking into account its critical importance for our study, we reproduce the document below in its entirety:

The State Defense Committee decrees:

1. *All able-bodied Germans—men aged 17–45 and women aged 18–30—located on the territories of Romania, Yugoslavia, Hungary, Bulgaria and Czechoslovakia shall be mobilized and interned to be subsequently transported to the USSR as a labor force.*

   Germans of both German and Hungarian citizenship, and German citizens of Romania, Yugoslavia, Bulgaria and Czechoslovakia shall be identified as subject to the mobilization.

2. *The control over the mobilization operation shall be entrusted to the NKVD of the USSR (Comrade Beria).*

   The NKVD shall be given the task of carrying out the arrangement of collection points, reception of the mobilized, and formation, delivery and convoy of the trains.

The mobilized shall be transported to the USSR by trains as frequently as required to deliver Germans gathered at the collection points.

3. *Comrades Malinovsky[45] and Vinogradov[46] in Romania, and Comrades Tolbukhin[47] and Biryuzov[48] in Bulgaria and Yugoslavia, shall be given the task:*

   a) *to document the mobilization and internment of the Germans, indicated in item 1, via the governmental bodies of the corresponding states;*

   b) *in cooperation with the USSR NKVD representatives, Comrades Apollonov and Gorbatyuk, to ensure that the relevant military and civilian authorities take necessary measures to guarantee the appearance of the Germans to be mobilized at the collection points.*

Comrades Malinovsky and Tolbukhin in Hungary, and Comrade Petrov[49] in Czechoslovakia, shall be given the task to announce corresponding orders on behalf of the Front Command and via military commandants with regard to the mobilization of Germans in conformity with item 1 hereby, and—in cooperation with the USSR NKVD representatives, Comrades Apollonov and Gorbatyuk— to ensure that the relevant measures be taken to guarantee the appearance of the Germans to be mobilized at the collection points.

1. *The Germans to be mobilized shall be allowed to take warm clothes, spare underwear, bedclothes, personal utensils and food, with the total luggage weight restricted to 200 kg per person.*

2. *Head of the Red Army rear zone, Comrade Khrulev[50] and Chief of the UPVOSO Comrade Kovalev[51] shall be appointed responsible for providing railway and motor transport for delivering the mobilized Germans and supplying them with food on the way.*

3. *All mobilized Germans shall be employed for working on the restoration of the coal industry in Donbass and in the south ferrous metallurgy.*

   Germans arriving at the destinations shall be organized into 1,000-person work battalions.

   The NKO (Comrade Golikov[52]) shall deploy 12 officers of the list of partially fit for the Red Army service to each battalion.

4. *The Narkomugol and Narkomchermet shall be charged to organize the reception of the German internees at the work places, along with their housing, food provision and other types of material support, and to arrange their distribution for work.*

   The Narkomugol (Comrade Vakhrushev[53]) and Narkomchermet (Comrade Tevosyan[54]) shall be appointed responsible for the preparation of living space for receiving the arriving German internees.

The Narkomvnudel, in cooperation with the Narkomugol and Narkom-
chermet, shall establish the regulations pertaining to the daily routine and the
conditions for the labor use of the German internees.

5. *Starting from the 1st quarter of the year 1945, the Gosplan of the USSR*
   (Comrade Voznesensky[55]) shall allot an additional amount of food supply and
   industrial goods for the Narkomugol and Narkomchermet in order for them to
   be provided to the arriving German internees in conformity with the worker
   norms, established at the enterprises of these People's Commissariats.

6. *The Narkomzdrav (Comrade Miterev[56]) shall organize the health care and*
   hygiene provisions for the German internees, arriving for work to the Narko-
   mugol and Narkomchermet enterprises; and the Narkomugol and Narkom-
   chermet shall provide the Narkomzdrav with necessary premises.

7. *The mobilization and internment of the Germans shall be carried out in the*
   period of December 1944 through January 1945; and the transportation to the
   places of work shall be completed by 15 February 1945.

Head of the State Defense Committee STALIN

On 22 December, three NKVD generals—Colonel General
A. N. Apollonov, Major General I. M. Gorbatyuk and Lieutenant
General M. I. Sladkevich[57]—submitted a report on their visits to the
Military Councils of the 2nd and 3rd Ukrainian fronts on 21–22
December 1944 to Comrade Beria[58]:

…Plans of the mobilization of Germans have been drafted and approved by the
Military Councils. Comrade Tolbukhin issued an order which charges all com-
manders of the armies to:

a) *announce the mobilization of Germans via the military commandants, with*
   the notification that those that fail to show up will be prosecuted by the Mili-
   tary Tribunal and their families repressed;

b) *organize the transportation of Germans to the collection points and departure*
   stations using the army resources.

   The order stipulates that the transportation of all the Germans beyond the
   front zone be completed by 3 January 1945.

   On 22 December, Comrade Tolbukhin cabled to Marshal Tito his request
   to carry out the complete set of urgent measures for mobilizing Germans on the
   territory of Yugoslavia.[59]

   Comrade Zapevalin,[60] assisted by a group of executive officers, has been
   appointed responsible for the mobilization of Germans in Yugoslavia and their

*transportation to the USSR. The same orders have been sent by Comrade Tol-
bukhin to Colonel General Biryuzov stationed in Sofia. Comrade Tolbukhin
deployed 50 Red Army officers to assist our executive groups.*

*…We prepared a draft decree to be issued by the Romanian government
regarding the mobilization of Germans, and a draft instruction of the Romanian gendarmerie department to its local branches on the practical implementation of the internment.*

*Today Comrade Vinogradov has fixed an appointment with Romanian
prime minister Radescu[61] in order to propose the draft documents to the latter
for signing.*

Apollonov   *Gorbatyuk*   *Sladkevich*

The same three—Apollonov, Gorbatyuk, and Sladkevich—submitted a "Plan of key measures for the preparation and execution of
the operation on the internment and deportation of Germans to the
USSR" to Beria on 26 December.[62] The plan established central
headquarters in Bucharest and ten operational sectors, six of them on
Romanian territory and two in each of Hungary and Yugoslavia[63]; the
territory of each sector was divided into districts under the control of
executive groups. Taking into account the small numbers of Germans
in Czechoslovakia and Bulgaria, the responsibility for the operations
was placed on the chiefs of the NKVD rear-security troops of the corresponding fronts. The operations were executed by NKVD forces
supported by the troops deployed for this purpose by the Front Command (interestingly, a Romanian regiment was selected among others for conducting the operation in Hungary). The convoy troops
were distributed in proportion to the deportees, based on an average
of 25 to 30 servicemen per train.

The following time limits were established: a) 28 December
1944–5 January 1945 for Yugoslavia and Hungary (within the territory of the 3rd Ukrainian front); 1–10 January 1945 for Hungary
(within the territory of the 2nd Ukrainian front); 10 January–
1 February 1945 for Romania and Transylvania[64]; 27 December
1944–1 January 1945 for Czechoslovakia. The internees were to be
assembled at the collection points, delivered to the departure stations, placed on the trains and dispatched to the destinations within
the indicated time limits.

Western researchers are unanimous in their belief that the selection of Christmas-time for the beginning of the operation was no

mere coincidence: it was possible to "trap" far more people on the days of the traditional family celebration.[65] It is noteworthy that such a tendency was apparent in the course of the deportations of the "punished peoples" in the USSR itself. And yet, it seems that it was not this particular nuance that determined the schedule of the operation in the first place: the plan was drawn up so that the same limited troops contingent might be employed on several occasions in the course of the campaign.

The internment mechanism did not alter from one country to another. The only "privilege" granted to Romania was that the announcement of the internment of Germans was made by the local gendarme officer, not by the Soviet commandant. The announcing body had already received name lists, drawn up in advance by the local authorities and police and agreed upon with the local Communist Party body. The German population of villages (preliminarily sealed off by mixed armed detachments) were summoned into the local authority premises, where they were informed about the mobilization and familiarized with the list of personal belongings and goods they were to take (with a total luggage weight not exceeding 200 kg per person).[66] After that they were allowed to return home and get prepared, and then they were sent to collection points.

The convoying of Germans to collection points was carried out by the local interior forces under the supervision of the Soviet executive officers, while the actual collection points were entirely administered by the Soviet side. The collection points had a supply of warm clothes and footwear, and food provision specified by form No. 4, sufficient for 15 days. It was at the points that those registered who were arriving were checked over to determine their working ability. Those recognized as being disabled (along with the sick, pregnant women, those with children under one and a half years of age, members of other ethnic groups, priests or monks) were exempted and returned to their places of residence, while those regarded as able-bodied were registered on the name lists compiled for each train[67] (however, in cases when a train was already at the station ready for departure, the checking procedure would sometimes be omitted). In accordance with the needs analysis, a total of 103 trains, or 5,677 railway cars, were to be made and delivered; the stations of Galaţ, Adjuj-Nau, Sokola and Foksani were assigned as transfer points for the broad-gauge rolling stock. Germans that evaded the mobilization were put on lists of names submitted to the local gendarmerie authorized to locate and arrest the dodgers and hand them over to the Romanian, Hungarian, etc. military tribunals.

There were no remarkable excesses in the course of the operation. There were instances of escape attempts though, but only a few such attempts proved successful (in particular, in cases when the escapees managed to bribe a Romanian gendarme before being loaded onto the trains). However, in Romania there were isolated instances of armed resistance on the part of Romanian military servicemen: in the town of Fegeres on 21 January (the incident resulted in the injury of State Security Lieutenant Astafyev) and in the village of Girbovo (a fire attack on the collection point).[68] An instance of severe poisoning (a suicide attempt) was registered in Hungary.

What caused far more serious damage to the operation's "successful implementation" was negligence with regard to classified information (so-called airing) on the part of the Romanian side, which allowed some Germans to hastily change their ethnic membership or place of residence and thus to avoid their fate. Disorganization (in Soviet terms) was also caused by multiple appeals for exemption of German women from mobilization on the grounds of their civil marriages with Romanians or men of other ethnic backgrounds (some Soviet officers' reports contain sarcastic references to the "marriages" contracted right at the collection points). In addition, the police inspectorate of the town of Galaţ, for example, sanctioned exemption from mobilization, based on special requests of enterprises, of German professionals that had resided in Romania before 1916 and had Romanian relatives.[69]

At the same time, there were instances of official complaints: for example, the Hungarian government denounced the "gross excesses" in the methods used in the course of the operation. On 5 January, Kuznetsov, Osokin and Zusmanovich met with Prime Minister Miklósi and two Hungarian ministers in order to discuss the matter. The discussion resulted in the release of ten Hungarians from collection points and the dismissal of the most active voice of complaint, the governor of the Gyula district Csige Varga Antal.[70]

On 6 January 1945, Vinogradov (apparently in the presence of the three above-mentioned officials) received Prime Minister Radescu and his ministers for foreign affairs and truce affairs. Referring to public opinion with regard to the upcoming mobilization and internment, they asked for an official address to the Romanian government on behalf of the Allied Control Commission for Romania, in one place, and additionally requested that women with children be exempted from the mobilization (it was proposed to compensate for the consequent shortage of labor force through raising the upper age limit for women from 30 to 35 years). First Vinogradov "agreed" to the latter proposition, yet limiting the age of the children that counted to one year! However, the 30-year age limit for women was eventually preserved. On the same day, the USSR sent the Romanian government note No. 031 on behalf of the Allied Commission demanding that all able-bodied Germans residing in Romania be mobilized as a labor force, irrespective of their citizenship. They were allowed to take personal belongings and a 15-day food supply, and granted the right to receive and send letters and parcels. People evading mobilization and those harboring them were subject to severe punitive measures.[71]

In practice, however, some "deviations" from the orders occurred. For example, as E. Klein (maiden name Weber) recollects, the order announced to the residents of her native village of Hodony applied to women up to 31 years of age. Both upper and lower age limits were not strictly adhered to. For example, one 16-year-old girl was deported on the mere ground that her father, whose name was on the list, was absent.

Heartrending outbursts of emotion would take place at the trackside before departures. Both men and women would be held in the same premises at the collection points for several days: "When we were heading for the station convoyed by armed soldiers, bell chimes were heard from a Catholic church, which I perceived as funeral chimes. Indeed, for many these chimes were the last ones they heard in their lives."[72] Later isolated "mistakes" by the convoy forces were revealed: for example, one Iulian Bors, an ethnic Romanian that happened to be at the railway station on 2 February, was seized, pushed into a train filled with interned Germans, and dispatched to the USSR.[73]

The trains comprised 40–50 cars, with each containing 40–45 persons: both men and women of different ages. A rectangular hole serving as a toilet was cut in the middle of the car floor. The trains were moved mainly at night, standing still on side tracks during the day.

It should be noted that Romania proved to become the principal location in Southeast Europe, where the operations for the mobilizing and internment of the able-bodied German population were carried out. At least 3/4 of the "special target group" was based in the country; it also accommodated the operation headquarters and comprised six out of the ten operational sectors. The entire operation comprised two chronological stages (11–26 January and 26 January–2 February) and three successive phases: first mobilization (by way of house-to-house check-ups) of the urban target group was carried out, then the rural population was subjected to the same procedure, and lastly the target group from the Romanian army (primarily but not exclusively the rank-and-file contingent) was seized.[74]

In the province of Timiş (operational sector No. 1), the special target group assembled at the collection points comprised 37,113 persons, men and women making up approximately equal proportions; 5,121 of them were subsequently exempted. Taking into account 852 men collected from the Romanian army, the total number of the dispatched members of the special target group reached 31,992 persons, with 16,455 males amongst them. Thus, the shortage, in relation to the evaluation figure presented by the Romanian authorities (51,537 persons), made up 14,213 individuals (or more than 1/4), with some 3/5 of the deficit number falling on the towns of Timişoara, Arad and Resita. This prompted the sector chief, State Security Colonel Korotkov, to administer mass "sweep operations" in these cities and villages with high concentrations of German population, which, as he wrote, "brought about good results." Finally 19 trains were dispatched.[75]

In the province of Mureş (operational sector No. 2), the preliminary check produced the figure of 28,292 able-bodied Germans, and 4,553 persons of so-termed reserve ages (men aged between 16 and 46–48, and women aged between 17 and 31–32), which were regarded as supplemental force, a secondary internment target group.[76] The operation in the sector in question was launched on 13 January, first in the town of Sibiu, and then in other districts. By 30 January, 25,488 persons were delivered to collection points, 2,927 of them subsequently exempted. The rest were loaded up, filling 735 cars that made up 13 trains. On 26 January an order stipulating internment amongst servicemen of the Romanian army was issued, which allowed the mobilization of an additional 1,007 persons.

In the provinces of Bucegi and Olt (operation sector No. 3), 49,448 Germans were registered, with 13,459 of them of working age eligible for mobilization. The mobilization and internment was administered by some 11 thousand personnel, including 1.5 thousand NKVD executives and 9.5 thousand Romanian gendarmerie, police, and "siguranta" staff (security bodies). Apart from the internee camps already operating in the sector, another five collection points were established.[77] In order to deliver internees to the points, both motor vehicles and horse-drawn carts belonging to the local population and Romanian army were "mobilized" too. The total number of the mobilized made up 15,880 persons, 1,657 of whom were exempted and released. As of 2 February 1945, 13,612 persons were dispatched to the USSR; the remaining 609 persons waited their turn in Ploiesti.[78]

Romanian operational sector No. 4 comprised the city of Galaţ and four adjacent districts. However, the German population on the territory was very scarce: only 608 persons were put on the special target group lists. Some 418 persons amongst those registered were collected as of 18 January 1945, including 353 men and 55 women.[79]

The schedule of the operation to be carried out in Hungary (and in the North Transylvania[80]) was altered to an extent. The campaign comprised two stages. First—in the period of 28 (according to some sources 20) December through 15 January 1945—11 executive groups were formed, which operated in cooperation with local administrations; and accordingly 11 collection points were set up.[81] After the lists were double-checked, the number of persons subject to internment was established as 15,428. The process of internment itself was commenced on 30 December; 12,137 persons were delivered to collection points by 5 January 1945, and by 15 January the number reached 14,352 persons. Exemption applied to 1,050 of them. A greater part of the remaining internees—14,352—were put on aboard nine trains and sent to the USSR (the principal destinations were Kishinev and Bendery, but also Cheboksary, Antropshino and Ust-Aba of the Perm Railway branch).

Only five executive groups (having experience of the previous operation) were formed during the second stage of the operation, carried out in the second half of January. They were stationed in Budapest, Kőbánya Alsó, Miskolc, Szerencs and Ceglédbercel. As of 31 January 1945, 454 out of the 7,115 registered Germans were exempted due to sickness. The rest, now termed as the "special target group," were concentrated at four collection points. All four trains dispatched in January were bound for Donbass. Taking into account the first stage of the operation, a total of 19,576 able-bodied Germans were mobilized and delivered to the USSR aboard 15 trains.[82]

The 3rd Ukrainian Front embraced the territory of Yugoslavia and a part of Hungary. There the operation was executed in the period from 23 December 1944 to 14 January 1945. The total number of those mobilized by the Front was 21,695 persons, including 9,747 men and 11,948 women. They were almost equally distributed between Yugoslavia and Hungary: 10,935 and 10,760 persons respectively. Altogether 17 trains, or 786 railway cars, were required for their delivery.[83] Following an order issued by Apollonov, the Front Command started mobilizing another 10 thousand people, but after "recruiting" only 879 people it had to drop the campaign due to a worsening situation at the front.

The operation comprising the mobilization, internment and delivery to the USSR of the German population of the Balkan countries was completed by 2 February, on which Apollonov, Gorbatyuk and Sladkevich briefed Beria. In the Balkans the number of internees constituted 124,542 persons, including 66,616 males and 57,926 females. Some 12,190 of them were exempted and released from the collection points. Therefore, 112,352 persons were sent to the USSR, according to the operation executives.[84] Other sources maintain an even larger number of people—namely 112,480 persons, 61,375 males and 51,105 females among them—were subjected to mobilization and internment in the Balkans with subsequent delivery to the USSR (see table 14). A third source cites a smaller figure: 111,831 in total.[85]

On 22 February 1945, Beria prepared a draft USSR Supreme Soviet Presidium decree "On awarding orders and medals to NKVD-NKGB personnel for successful completion of special government assignments."[86] The cover letter attached to the document by Beria summarized the results of the entire campaign carried out in the period of 25 December 1944–31 January 1945. The personnel engaged in the operation numbered 10,443 NKVD-NKGB officers and soldiers (Red Army rear-zone security troops, frontier troops and interior forces) and 664 NKVD-NKGB executive officers.

The Allies' reaction to the Soviet deportations conducted in the Balkans was intensely negative.[87] At the same time, the Germans themselves showed signs of serious concern in connection with the deportations undertaken by the USSR. According to Soviet intelligence data, one of the conditions set by Himmler in the course of talks

Table 14. Registration and internment of German population in the countries
of Southeast Europe

| Country | Registered | | | Interned | | |
	Men	Women	Total	Men	Women	Total
Romania*	186,509	235,337	421,846	36,590	32,742	69,332
Hungary	19,024	31,268	50,292	20,989	10,934	31,923
Yugoslavia**	32,966	40,606	73,572	3,692	7,243	10,935
Czechoslovakia	1,412	2,837	4,250	49	166	215
Bulgaria	524	565	1,089	55	20	75
TOTAL:	240,435	310,613	551,049	61,375	51,105	112,480

Remarks: *—including 484 from North Transylvania (357 men and 127 women).
    **—according to a summary of 7 September 1945 compiled by deputy
chief of the GUPVI NKVD of the USSR, Major General Shemena,
111,831 persons, including 12,364 from Yugoslavia, were dispatched
from the stations of Sokola-Galaţ and Adjuj-Nau to the USSR in
January–March 1945, which exceeds the table data to a degree.

Source: GARF, h. 9401, r. 2, d. 68, l. 144–147; TsKhIDK, h. 1/p, r. 13a, d. 5, l. 9.

conducted with the American and British representatives through the
mediation of the Red Cross in February 1945 was their placing pressure on the USSR so as to prevent it from deporting German civilians from the territories occupied by the Red Army.[88]

INTERNMENT OF GERMANS ON THE TERRITORY OF THE THIRD REICH

It is noteworthy that the above account embraced primarily civilian
ethnic Germans that were not German or Austrian subjects (or, to
use the Nazi terminology, the *Volksdeutsche*). The issue of the mobilization and internment of the *Reichsdeutsche*, that is, German nationals proper, was kept unresolved, although the combat actions conducted by the Red Army had spread onto the Reich territory long
before (from October 1944).

Apparently, some new rationale was needed in order to launch
mass internment within Germany itself. To find and formulate such
rationale, though, proved a relatively easy task: attacks against Red
Army servicemen, terrorist groups consisting of Wehrmacht soldiers
and officers disguised in civilian clothing, subversion aimed at the
disorganization of the Red Army front-line and rear communications,

etc. Taking into account their own partisan experience in the German rear zone, this time the Soviet leadership strove to nip in the bud any similar actions on the part of the enemy!

Order No. 0016 of the NKVD of the USSR "On the measures for cleansing the Red Army field force rear zone from the enemy element" constituted the first step of the campaign. By this order, Beria appointed NKVD representatives to all fronts, and delegated the command over the 60-thousand strong NKVD rear security troops for conducting corresponding Cheka and army joint operations (adequate camp premises were ordered to be allocated within three days).[89]

The next crucial step was State Defense Committee decree No. 7467cc of 3 February 1945, which postulated that "...persons caught in the act of committing terrorist or subversive acts be severely punished through merciless extermination at the scene of the crime."[90] With respect to other civilians, it was stipulated that on the territories of the 1st, 2nd and 3rd Belorussian and 1st Ukrainian fronts mobilization be applied to "...all male Germans aged 17–50 years, able-bodied and capable of bearing arms. Germans whose prior membership in the German army or the Volkssturm units has been established shall be convoyed to the NKVD camps for POWs. The rest of the mobilized Germans shall be organized into labor battalions, manned with 750–1,200 persons each, for subsequent use as a work force in the Soviet Union, in the Ukrainian and Belorussian SSR in the first place."

Taking into consideration the absence of legitimate authorities in Germany at the time, all necessary orders concerning mobilization were to be issued by the front commanders (correspondingly, by Zhukov, Rokossovsky, Chernyakhovsky and Konev), and the principal practical measures were to be implemented by the NKVD representatives appointed by Beria (respectively, I. A. Serov,[91] L. S. Tsanava,[92] V. S. Abakumov, and P. Ya. Meshik[93]). The NKVD tasks also included the distribution and conveying of the German population, who had been mobilized and subjected to the checking procedure, to the People's Commissariats and enterprises in the USSR, which were in need of work force and had capacities for receiving, housing and employing the workers in accordance with an earlier approved resolution.[94] Therefore, charging Beria to supervise the entire operation on mobilization and internment of Germans appeared fairly logical.

Based on the stipulations of the State Defense Committee decree of 3 February 1945, Beria issued internal NKVD order No. 0061 on 6 February 1945. The order supplemented the decree with particular details, for example: "...The order summoning the Germans subject to mobilization shall specify the procedure and time-limits for their appearance at the collection points. Mobilized Germans shall take: a complete set of winter and summer clothing and footwear, at least two changes of underwear, a set of bedclothes (blanket, sheets, pillowcase and mattress case), personal utensils (dishes, cutlery and a tea cup), and a 15-day food supply as the minimum. The order shall stipulate that those that fail to appear at the collection points be prosecuted by the Military Tribunal." The same order also specified that all NKVD representatives at the fronts were to compile daily reports on the progress of mobilization starting from 10 February 1945. Deputy people's commissars of the NKVD, S. Kruglov and V. Chernyshev[95], were appointed to oversee the implementation of the order.

As early as 22 February, Beria submitted the first report to Stalin with regard to the launch and progress of the mobilization of civilian German population. As of 20 February 1945, 28,105 men aged 17–50 were mobilized in the operational zones of the fronts referred to above, primarily in Upper Silesia and East Prussia. Due to the changes in the situation at the Baltic fronts, in the same letter Beria requested that the State Defense Committee Decree of 3 February 1945 be enacted on the territories of the 1st and 2nd Baltic fronts too.[96]

The total number of Germans mobilized and/or arrested on the territories controlled by the 1st, 2nd and 3rd Belorussian and 1st Ukrainian fronts constituted: 28,105 persons (apparently German citizens proper) as of 2 February 1945[97]; 35,988 persons as of 23 February; 58,318 persons as of 3 March,[98] 68,680 persons as of 9 March[99]; 75,759 persons as of 19 March[100]; 97,487 persons as of 10 April 1945.[101]

The people in question were rounded up in the course of cleansing operations in the rear zone of the affected fronts, where the "enemy elements" were of a fairly broad range of shades, and thus targeted by the NKVD executives. For instance, the aforementioned 35,998 "internees" registered as of 23 February made up merely a little over one-third of the total number of persons (92,016) detained by the NKVD by that time. Apparently the concept of "internees" included such variations as "agents and official personnel of the enemy intelligence and counter-intelligence services," "subverters and terrorists," "members of fascist organizations" (making the most numerous group of 31,007 persons), Volksdeutsche and, possibly, some others.[102] This concept certainly did not cover such categories as ROA [Russian Liberation Army] servicemen (Vlasov army members), betrayers of the motherland, traitors, accomplices and abettors of the occupants, and the Soviet Volksdeutsche.

The mobilization and internment of Germans—along with other actions taken to cleanse the Red Army rear zone of enemy elements—continued at least until mid-April–early May 1945. In his letter to Stalin of 17 April 1945, Beria reported that a total of 215,540 persons had been "seized" in the course of the operations in question by 15 April 1945, including (by "shades"): 8,470 "agents and official personnel of the enemy intelligence and counter-intelligence services, and subverters and terrorists"; 123,166 "members of fascist organizations"; 31,190 "senior and rank-and-file servicemen of the armies fighting against the USSR"; 3,319 "leading and executive personnel of the police bodies, prisons, concentration camps, and staff of prosecution and judicial bodies"; 2,272 "chiefs of large companies and administrative organizations, and press staff"; 17,495 "betrayers of the motherland, traitors, occupiers' accomplices and abettors that fled with the German fascist armed forces"; and 29,628 of "other enemy element." There were only 138,200 Germans among the total number of "seized" persons (215,540): the rest included Poles (38,660 persons)[103]; USSR citizens (27,880 persons); Hungarians (3,200 persons); Slovaks (1,130 persons), and Italians (390 persons).

Amongst the mentioned 215,540 people, only 148,540 were eventually delivered to the USSR. The rest of them either were held in custody in camps and prisons in the immediate battle area (62 thousand), or died during the operation or on the way to the destinations (5 thousand). According to Beria, most of these people were ordinary (read: of the lowest ranks) members of various fascist organizations (trade unions, labor or youth organizations, etc.); and their internment "...at a particular moment was dictated by the need for the promptest possible cleansing of the rear zones of the enemy elements."

Besides, due to the age and poor physical condition of the majority of the target group in question, their employment for manual labor was not possible. By the middle of April, only 25 thousand of the mobilized Germans were actually used as workers in the coal industry, non-ferrous metallurgy, peat extraction and the construction industry. This prompted the NKVD to propose that: first, the number of the categories of those subject to internment "by way of the rear-zone cleansing" be reduced; second, with the exception made for people representing the special interest of the state (scientific, military etc.) interest, the transportation to the USSR of those already interned be halted—instead, an adequate number of camps and prisons be established in Germany proper; and third, the data concerning the internees that had already been deported to the USSR be reviewed in order to identify the disabled for their subsequent delivery back to their native countries.

While drawing a draft for a corresponding NKVD order, Beria addressed Stalin requesting the latter's approval, which was received on the same day, judging by the following remark on the letter: "Was approved by Comrade Stalin after a private presentation. 17/VI 45 L. Beria."[104] Besides, the fact appears to be confirmed by the issuance of State Defense Committee decree No. 8148cc bearing the same date, 17 April 1945, and stipulating that further mobilization of Germans on the territories of the fronts and their delivery to the USSR be terminated.[105] The decree mentioned 97,487 German internees, already available, that were to be ascribed to the following People's Commissariats of the USSR (persons): Narkomugol [coal industry]—37,600; Narkomstroy [construction industry]—28,800 (including 20,000 employed for dismantling work at the fronts); Narkomchermet [ferrous metallurgy]—13,100; NKPS [communications]—5,700; Narkommesttopprom [fuel industry]—3,750; Narkompishcheprom [food industry]; and Narkomtankprom [tank production]—2,000 each; Narkomgrazhdanzhilstroy [civilian construction industry]—1,600; Narkomelektrostantsy [power plants]—1,550; Narkomstroymaterialov [production of construction materials] and Narkomsredmash [mechanical industry]—1,000 each; Narkomvooruzhenya [arms production]—250.

On 18 April 1945 (the next day), with a preliminary authorization by Stalin, the USSR NKVD issued internal order No. 00315 "On partial amendment of NKVD order No. 0016 of 11 January 1945".[106] Under the new order, the number of categories to which the "rear-zone cleansing" measures applied, was considerably cut down (most effective was the withdrawal of the largest target group: ordinary "members of various fascist organizations").

As before, arrest (and, in a number of cases, execution on the spot) remained applicable to members of the following groups: a) spies, subverters and terrorists belonging to the German intelligence services; b) members of all organizations and groups left behind by the German command for committing subversions in the Red Army rear area; c) those tuning into illegal radio stations and supporters of subversive groups; d) active members of the National-Socialist party; e) leaders of the regional, city and district youth fascist associations; f) members of the Gestapo, SD and other punitive bodies; g) heads of the regional, city and district administrative bodies, and editors and authors of anti-Soviet magazines and newspapers. The mass delivery of all arrested individuals was terminated; and the disabled, sick, elderly, and women were to be released from custody.[107] Persons from the same categories who had already been transported to the USSR, were to be subjected to a checking procedure and returned to their native countries, with the exception of...physically fit individuals that were to be transferred to industrial enterprises as a work force! There was probably no way back for these people: the door behind them, or maybe the coffin lid over them, had been slammed shut.[108]

For all that, this wave of internment and subsequent deportation affected a total of 155,262 persons, or nearly 2/5 more than the first, largely Balkan, wave.

SOME OUTCOMES OF THE OPERATION FOR THE INTERNMENT OF GERMANS

The two "waves" produced a total of some 267 thousand persons. There was one—but fairly essential—difference between the two "waves," which lay in the status of the internees. While the internees from Southeast Europe were regarded as "mobilized internees" (they were also designated to group "D"), the internees from the former Reich (or, rather, the majority of them) were termed "arrested internees" (and designated to group "B").

Let us clarify the point. The NKVD order No. 00101 of 22 February 1945 established the following categories of persons subject to filtration: "A"—POWs of the enemy armies; "B"—civilian members of various enemy organizations, heads of regional and district legislative and executive authorities, burgomasters, heads of large commercial and administrative organizations, editors of magazines and newspapers, authors of anti-Soviet publications and other hostile elements; "C"—Soviet citizens that had been held prisoner; "D"— members of the German work battalions, mobilized under the State Defense Committee decrees. Remarkably, such statuses as "daughter of a land owner," "trader," "exploiter," and others constituted sufficient grounds for being ranked under the "D" category.[109]

The NKVD produced the first quantitative summary by the beginning of the year 1946.

In January–March 1945, 111,831 German internees, including 61,375 men and 50,456 women, were transported to the USSR from the Balkan countries. Most of them were deported from Romania (67,332), Hungary (31,920) and Yugoslavia (12,579). In February–April 1945, another 77,741 persons, almost exclusively men (77,059), were brought from former Upper Silesia and East Prussia. Therefore, altogether 189,572 internees belonging to the "D" group (mobilized internees) were stationed in the USSR by the end of the war, arranged into work battalions and transferred to industrial enterprises. Taking into account the 18,667 persons that had joined the target group after filtration in the NKVD camps,[110] the total number of internees under the category was 208,239 persons.

However, the quantitative reductions (so-called withdrawals) in this group were impressive, even during the first year. As of 1 October 1946, these losses constituted 76,109 persons (40,331 of them, including 10,983 Poles, were repatriated; and another 35,775 "withdrew" due to their own deaths). Consequently, only 132,133 members of the category remained in the USSR as of the same date.

In addition, in March–May 1945 the USSR interned 94,601 persons of the "B" group (arrested internees), with subsequent "withdrawals" among them numbering as many as 79,546 persons. The structure of the "withdrawals" in this case looks as follows: 21,250 (including 15,597 Poles) were repatriated; 19,270 were transferred to labor battalions; 10,263 were handed over to the POW camps; 2,874 transferred to filtration camps; and 25,889 either died or "withdrew" for other reasons. The number of persons remaining in camps and camp stations, who were not subjected to "filtration," constituted 15,055.

To sum up, a "mere" 150–165 thousand people out of nearly 303 thousand (including Poles and Japanese) interned under one category or another were left in the USSR by February 1946, or, in other words there remained less than a half of the initial number![111]

The summary of the GUPVI work in 1946, prepared by GUPVI deputy chief, Major General Ratushnyi for Lieutenant General Krivenko on 15 January 1947, indicates the size of the registration card index of those interned and mobilized: there were 344,671 registration cards.[112]

NOTES

1 T. Schieder, *Dokumentation der Vertreibung der Deutschen aus Ost-Mitteleuropa,* vols. 1–5. Wolfenbüttel, 1953–196; *Die Deutschen Vertreibungsverluste. Bevölkerungsbilanzen für die deutschen Vertreibungsgebiete 1939/50* (Wiesbaden, 1958); Rhode, G., *Phasen und Formen der Massenzwangswanderungen in Europa: Die Vertriebenen in Westdeutschland,* vol. 1 (Kiel, 1959).

2 See: Ahrens, W., *Verbrechen an Deutschen. Dokumente der Vertreibung.* (Rosenheim, 1983); Mitzka H., *Zur Geschichte der Massendeportationen von Ostd- und Südostdeutschen in die Sowjetunion im Jahre 1945: Ein historish-politische Beitrag* (Einhausen, 1985).

3 *Vertreibung und Vertreibungsverbrechen 1945–1978. Bericht des Bundesarchivs vom 28.05.1974. Archivalien und ausgewählte Erlebnisberichte* (Bonn, 1989).

4 Weber, G., R. Weber-Schlenther, A. Nassehi, O. Sill, G. Kneer, *Die Deportation von Siebenbürger Sachsen in die Sowjetunion 1945–1949* (Cologne—Weimar: Böhlau Verlag, 1996) vols. 1–3

5 Karner, S., *Im Archipel GUPVI. Kriegsgefangenschaft und Internierung in der Sowjetunion 1941–1956. Kriegsfolgen-Forschung* (Vienna—Munich: R. Oldenbourg Verlag, 1995), vol.1. 269.

6 Baier, H., *Deportatea etnicilor germani din Romania in Uniunea Sovetice* (Sмbiu, 1994) (in Romanian). See also Zach, K., C. Zach, "Die Deportation Deutscher aus Romänien in die Sowjetunion 1945," *Südostdeutsche Vierteljahresblätter* (Munich, 1995), 5–17. At the same time, the documents belonging to the Romanian Council of Ministers were, and still remain, inaccessible to researchers, which, as G. Klein observes (see below), fuels persistent rumors and speculation, particularly among the German public, regarding the issue of Romanians "sacrificing" the German minority in order to save themselves from the deportation.

7 "They shall be immediately handed over to the military tribunal..." Introductory article and comments by Konasov, V. B. and A. V. Tereshchuk, *Russkoye-proshloye* 1994, no. 5, 318–337 (further: Konasov, Tereshchuk, 1994); Knyshevsky, P. N., "State Defense Committee: Methods of labor force mobiliza-

tion," *Voprosy istorii*, 1994, no. 2, 53–65 (further: Knyshevsky, 1994); "Semirya-ga, M. I., "The orders that we did not know about. Stalin wanted to bring all able-bodied Germans from Germany to the USSR," *Novoye vremnya*, 1994, no. 15, 56–57.

8 Chukhin, I. I., *Interned Youth. History of USSR NKVD camp No. 517 for interned German women.* Moscow–Petrozavodsk: Memorial, 1995, 64.

9 See in particular: Polian, P. M., "International meeting of researchers studying the Hitler and Stalin terror" (Report from a conference in Mülheim an der Ruhr, March 1995), *Izv. RAN*, Geography Series, 1996, no. 1, 152–153; Polian, P. M., "'Labor reparations': Motivation and prehistory of the post-war labor use of the 'interned and mobilized' German civilians in the USSR," *Problemy voyennogo plena: Istoriya i sovremennost* [POW Problems: History and Contemporaneity]. Materials of international practical and academic conference of 23–25 October 1997, Vologda, part 2 (Vologda, 1997), 59–67; Polian, P. M., "Geography of forced migrations in the USSR," abstract of dissertation for a doctoral degree in geographic sciences (Moscow, Geography institute of the Russian Academy of Sciences, 1998), 29–32.

10 Klein, G., "Im Lichte sowjetischer Quellen. Die Deportation Deutscher aus Rumänien zur Zwangsarbeit in die UdSSR 1945," *Südostdeutsche Vierteljahres-blätter* (Munich, 1998), no. 2, 153–162. It is not so much the republication of documents, well known to historians, that makes Klein's work valuable, but the introduction of a series of private documents pertaining to individual people's fates, in particular the lives of his family members (with their kind permission, on a number of occasions below we will refer to their memoirs, lent to us by G. Klein).

11 See: Konasov, Tereshchuk, 1994, 318. With reference to: AVP, h. 054, p. 293, r. 6160, sh. 33.

12 Most of the documents were signed by Stalin, as the State Defense Committee chairman, but some were signed by his deputies (by Molotov, and later also by Beria). Besides, the State Defense Committee comprised K. Ye. Voroshilov and G. M. Malenkov, and later (from February 1942) L. M. Kaganovich, A. I. Mikoyan, N. A. Bulganin and N. A. Voznesensky were admitted to the State Defense Committee as members too.

13 GARF, h. 9401, r. 2, f. 169, sh. 219–223.

14 See decrees of the USSR Supreme Soviet Presidium: "On the switch-over to the eight-hour work day and seven-day work week, and on the prohibition of arbitrary departure from enterprises or offices" of 26 June 1940; "On the prohibition of arbitrary departure from the workplace of tractor and harvester drivers employed at the machine-tractor stations" of 17 July 1940; "On the state labor resources of the USSR" of 2 October 1940; "On the procedure of the inter-enterprise mandatory transfer of engineers, technologists, foremen, executives and qualified workers" of 19 October 1940. During war-time, additional decrees came out: USSR Supreme Soviet Presidium decree "On the war-time work schedule of workers and employees" (which enacted from one to three overtime work hours daily) of 26 June 1941; USSR Council of People's Commissars and Communist Party Central Committee directive "Every-

thing for the front, everything for victory" of 29 June 1941. State Defense Committee resolution No. 903cc of 17 November 1941 authorized the NKVD to apply any sanctions, including capital punishment, to the "violators of the USSR ruling order."

15 Knyshevsky, 1994, 54.

16 See examples in Knyshevsky, 1994, 57–58.

17 Apparently, the use of the term "mobilization" with regard to citizens of other countries has the same semantic implication.

18 Knyshevsky, 1994, 58. The transport, construction and metallurgic industries were the biggest consumers of such labor force.

19 For example, they were employed for the dismantling, delivering and escorting of industrial equipment on the orders of a special committee established by State Defense Committee resolution No. 7590cc of 25 February 1945.

20 See: Weber, U. A., 1995, vol. 1, 77.

21 "SSSR i germansky vopros. 22 iyunya 1941 g.–8 maya 1945 g." [The USSR and the German Question: 22 June 1941–8 May 1945], Moscow, 1996 (further referred to as: *The USSR and the German Question*), 286–305, quoting: AVP (Foreign Policy Archive of the Russian Federation), h. 12, r. 9, p. 132, f. 4, sh. 178–209.

22 See: Kynin, G. P., "Germansky vopros vo vzaimootnosheniyah SSSR, SShA i Velikobritanii. 1944–1945 gg." [The German question in the relations of the USSR, USA and Great Britain: 1944–1945] *Novaya i noveyshaya istoriya*, 1995, no. 1, 117, with reference to: AVP, h. 06, r. 6, p. 20, f. 166, sh. 2–6. Apart from the NKID representatives (I. M. Maysky: chairman, and G. P. Arkadyeva: secretary), the commission included representatives of the Academy of Sciences (Ye. S. Varga), of the People's Commissariat for Foreign Trade (K. P. Babarin), and of the Gosplan (V. V. Kuznetsov, with M. Z. Saburov and N. M. Siluyanov having joined him in January 1944). The commission held its first meeting on 24.11.1943.

23 "Tak chtoby ni odnoy derzhave ili kombinatsii derzhav ne prihodila mysl ob agressii protiv SSSR" [So that no state or group of states might conceive the idea of aggression against the USSR]. *Istochnik*, 1995, no. 4, 127.

24 *The USSR and the German Question*, 506–516, quoting: AVP, h. 06, r. 6, p. 16, f. 164, sh. 1–69.

25 For example, in May 1944 the US State Department members found the use of the German work force within a three to four year period quite appropriate (Kynin, 1995 quoting: AVP, h. 012, r. 5, p. 56, f. 42, sh. 5–29).

26 *The USSR and the German Question*, 555–559, quoting: AVP, h. 06, r. 6, p. 16, f. 165, sh. 1–11. Incidentally, Maysky suggested that possible objections on the part of the Allies be contested with the following argument: mass deportation of German labor force to the USSR would mitigate the "threat of mass unemployment in Germany."

27 *The USSR and the German Question*, 601–605, quoting: AVP, h. 07, r. 10, p. 16, f. 212, sh. 7–14.

28 "Sovetsky Soyuz na Mezhdunarodnykh konferentsiyakh perioda Velikoy Otechestvennoy voyny 1941–1945 gg." [The Soviet Union at the internation-

al conferences in the period of the Great Patriotic War of 1941–1945], vol. 4: Krymskaya konferentsiya rukovoditeley trekh soyuznykh derzhav—SSSR, SshA i Velikobritanii. 4–11 fevralya 1945 g. [The Crimea conference of the leaders of the three allied nations: the USSR, USA and Great Britain, 4–11 February 1945]. Collection of documents (Moscow, Politizdat, 1984), 106.

29 Ibid., 156.

30 Ibid., 184.

31 Ibid., 214–215. See also: AVP, h. 0431/IV, r. 4, p. 5, f. 22, sh. 39–40.

32 Ibid., 226, 232–233. Here the following formula is alluded to: "Temporarily leaving aside the use of German labor force as a form of reparation, which will be addressed later..."

33 Ibid., 248. Published in *Izvestiya* on 13 February 1945.

34 Ibid., 253, 259. Published in *Izvestiya* on 17 March 1947.

35 "Sovetsky Soyuz na Mezhdunarodnykh konferentsiyakh perioda Velikoy Otechestvennoy voyny 1941–1945 gg." [The Soviet Union at the International conferences in the period of the Great Patriotic War of 1941–1945], vol. 6: Berlinskaya (Potsdamskaya) konferentsiya rukovoditeley trekh soyuznykh derzhav—SSSR, SShA i Velikobritanii. 17 iyulya–2 avgusta 1945 g. [The Berlin (Potsdam) conference of the leaders of the three allied nations: the USSR, USA and Great Britain, 17 July–2 August 1945]. Collection of documents (Moscow, Politizdat, 1984), 184. Interestingly, on another day and in another context—when Stalin needed to ground and justify the expulsion and deportation of the German population from the territories transferred to Poland and the establishment of Polish population on these territories—Stalin used completely different arguments: "...I also ask Mr. Churchill to consider the fact that the Germans themselves are short of manpower. The greater part of the enterprises we found in the course of our advance were manned by foreign workers—Italians, Bulgarians, Frenchmen, Russians, Ukrainians, etc. All of these workers had been forcibly driven from their homeland by the Germans. When the Russian troops arrived in these areas, the foreign workers considered themselves free, and went home. Where are the German workers? It turns out that most of them were drafted into the German army and were either killed during the war or taken prisoner. This produced a situation in which German industry was operating with the most insignificant number of German workers, and a great number of foreign workers..." (ibid., 116).

36 See TASS report of the press conference given by Pouly, the US representative to the Allied Reparation Commission (AVP, h. 0431/I, r. 1, p. 7, f. 48, sh. 20–22).

37 The information was, in particular, delivered by the German intelligence service as early as the end of July. And in its issue of 9 September 1944, the official government newspaper *Völkische Beobachter* wrote of some 1.4 million workers deported from Romania. See a related review in: Weber, 1995, vol. 1, s. 127–135. G. Weber himself does not share the opinion.

38 GARF, h. 9401, r. 2, f. 67, sh. 386.

39 Apollonov, Arkady Nikolayevich (1907—1978): colonel general; in 1941–1948—chief of the central department of interior troops; deputy people's commissar of troops; in 1948–1950—chairman of the committee for sports and physical culture affairs at the USSR Council of Ministers; in 1951—deputy state security minister for troops.

40 Gorbatyuk, Ivan Markovich (1903—1957): NKVD major general; co-headed the operations for the deportations of Chechens, Ingushetians and Karachais; from 1945—lieutenant general; chief of the central department for the NKVD rear-security troops (after the dissolution of the department, was appointed the chief of the Ivanovo Oblast NKVD department).

41 RGVA, h. 1p, r. 13a, f. 227.

42 GARF, h. 9401, r. 2, f. 68, sh. 144–147.

43 See in letter of 12 December 1944 by Apollonov to Beria (RGVA, h. 1p, r. 13a, f. 237).

44 APRF (Russian Federation President Archives), h. 3, r. 58, f. 500, sh. 108–110; TsKhSD, h. 89, r. 75, f. 1, sh. 1–3. Cf. reference to another source of the same document (RTsKhIDNI, h. 644, r. 1, f. 352, sh. 67) in Knyshevsky, 1994, 59. Another copy, along with the presentation of the document signed by Beria, is held in the so-called Stalin's special file (GARF, h. 9401, r. 2, f. 68, sh. 153–156).

45 Malinovsky, Rodion Yakovlevich (1898–1967): marshal of the Soviet Union (1944); commander of the troops of the 2nd Ukrainian front. Under his orders, the mobilization and internment of Germans was carried out on the territories of Hungary and Transylvania.

46 Vinogradov, Vladislav Petrovich (1899–1962): lieutenant general of the commissary service; from 1944—the chief of the SKK headquarters in Romania, deputy chairman of the SKK.

47 Tolbukhin, Fedor Ivanovich (1894–1949): marshal of the Soviet Union (1944); commander of the troops of the South and 3rd and 4th Ukrainian fronts; in 1945–1947—the commander-in-chief of the Southern group of troops.

48 Biryuzov, Sergey Semenovich (1904–1964): marshal of the Soviet Union (1955); chief of the headquarters of the South and 4th and 3rd (from May 1944) Ukrainian fronts; from October 1944—commander of the 37th Army and chief military advisor of the Bulgarian armed forces; in 1945–1947—the deputy commander-in-chief of the Southern group of troops, deputy chairman of the SKK in Bulgaria.

49 Petrov, Ivan Yefimovich (1896–1958): army general (1944); commander of the 2nd Belorussian and 4th Ukrainian fronts; chief of the headquarters of the 1st Ukrainian front.

50 Khrulev, Andrey Vasilyevich (1892–1962): army general (1943); in 1941–1945—deputy people's commissar of defense of the USSR; head of the Red Army rear zone (simultaneously—in 1942–1943—the people's commissar of communications of the USSR).

51 Kovalev, Ivan Vladimirovich (1901–1993): in 1944—chief of the UPVOSO (department for military communications); in 1944–1948—the people's commissar (minister) of communications of the USSR.

52 Golikov, Filipp Ivanovich (1900–1980): colonel general (from 1961—marshal); from 1943—deputy defense people's commissar of the USSR on personnel; chief of the central department for personnel of the People's Commissariat of Defense; in 1944–1952—chief of the repatriation department of the Council of People's Commissars (Council of Ministers) of the USSR. See: Polian, P., *Zhertvy dvukh diktatur. Ostarbaitery i voyennoplennyye v Tretyem Reikhe i ikh repatriatsiya* [Victims of two dictatorships. The Ostarbeiter and POWs in the Third Reich and their repatriation.] (Moscow, 1996),190–191.

53 Vakhrushev, Vasily Vasilyevich (1902–1947): in 1939–1946—People's Commissar of the coal industry of the USSR; in 1946–1947—people's commissar of the coal industry of the eastern territories of the USSR.

54 Tevosyan, Ivan Fedorovich (1902–1958): people's commissar of ferrous metallurgy of the USSR.

55 Voznesensky, Nikolay Aleksandrovich (1903–1950): academician of the Academy of Sciences of the USSR (1943); from 1938—chairman of the Gosplan of the USSR; from 1939—deputy chairman of the Council of People's Commissars (Council of Ministers) of the USSR; in 1942–1945—member of the State Defense Committee; author of the monograph "Military economy of the USSR in the period of the Great Patriotic War" (1948); executed and rehabilitated posthumously.

56 Miterev, Georgy Andreyevich (1900–1977): in 1939–1947—people's commissar (minister) of health care of the USSR.

57 Sladkevich, Moisey Iosifovich (1906—?): lieutenant general; from 1923—in the Red Army; from 1931—member of the Communist Party and OGPU troops; in 1945—deputy chief of the NKVD internal troops.

58 Quotation from: Konasov, Tereshchuk, 1994, 323, which refers to: RGVA, h. 1/p, r. 13a, f. 5, sh. 238–240.

59 In accordance with an agreement between Marshal Stalin and Marshal Tito, the head of the National Committee for the Liberation of Yugoslavia, the Red Army crossed the Bulgarian–Yugoslav border on 29 September 1944, but stayed on the territory of Yugoslavia only temporarily, until the end of 1944, when it essentially completed its operational assignment. Therefore, the entire procedure of internment, mobilization and deportation of Germans from Yugoslavia (right up to the collection and reception points) was carried out by the local Yugoslav authorities on their own, with their being given essentially the same powers administered by the Red Army fronts.

60 Zapevalin: we have no data at our disposal.

61 Radescu, Nikolae: general corps; chief of the General Headquarters of the Romanian army. From 2 December 1944 (after the resignation of the Sanatescu government) to 28 February 1945—prime minister and minister for foreign affairs of Romania. Subsequently emigrated to the USA.

62 RGVA, h. 1/p, r. 13a, f. 5, sh. 242–247. Males born in 1899–1927 and females born in 1914–1926 were subject to internment. See also the instructions issued by the commander of the Romanian gendarme corps for its local branches regarding the internment of Germans (RGVA, h. 1/p, r. 13a, f. 5, sh. 299–301).

63 Below are their official numbers and designations: 1) Timiş; 2) Mureş; 3) Olt
and Bucegi; 4) Mare and Lower Danube; 5) Prut; 6) Szomes; 7) Pest-Pilis,
Solt-Kiskun and Csongrád; 8) Jász-Nagykun-Szolnok, Békés, Heves, Hajdú,
Bihar, Satu-Mare; 9) Belgrade; 10) Sombor. See: RGVA, h. 1/p, r. 13a, f. 5,
sh. 356.

64 The Romanians themselves were geared up for an even more limited time
span (10–20 January 1945), which probably merely proved impracticable
(RGVA, h. 1/p, r. 13a, f. 5, sh. 299).

65 See, for example: Weber, U. A., 1995, vol. 1, 75–76.

66 RGVA, h. 1/p, r. 13a, f. 5, sh. 207–211, 304.

67 The trains were accompanied by convoy troops and medical staff.

68 See a report from operational sector No.2 (RGVA, h. 1/p, r. 13a, f. 5, sh. 69–70).

69 RGVA, h. 1/p, r. 13a, f. 5, sh. 40.

70 From a report of 5 January 1945 submitted to Apollonov by Kuznetsov and
Osokin. First referred to in: Konasov, Tereshchuk, 1994, 325–326, quoting:
RGVA, h. 1/p, r. 13a, f. 5, sh. 251–252 (correction: sh. 253–254).

71 Konasov, Tereshchuk, 1994, 324, with reference to: RGVA, h. 1/p, r. 13a, f. 5,
sh. 308.

72 Quotation taken from memoirs by E. Klein, written on 14 January 1995.

73 See: Konasov, Tereshchuk, 1994, 328, quoting: RGVA, h. 1/p, r. 12e, f. 27, sh. 62.

74 The total number of the target group members, belonging to the 3rd sector
only, amounted to some 2,000 persons.

75 RGVA, h. 1/p, r. 13a, f. 5, sh. 72–80.

76 It is remarkable that other documents examined by us do not mention the category "reserve age." Therefore, we are not in the position to judge whether
this "nuance" was envisaged in the assignments given from the Center, or it
represented an individual "initiative" on the part of chief of the 2nd operation
sector, Colonel Kozhevnikov (see his report: RGVA, h. 1/p, r. 13a, f. 5, sh.
63–70).

77 The collection points were located in the following towns (their capacities are
given in brackets, in persons): Braşov (10,000), Ploieşti and Bucharest (3,000
each), Caracal and Tîrgu-Jiu (300 each).

78 RGVA, h. 1/p, r. 13a, f. 5, sh. 29–35.

79 RGVA, h. 1/p, r. 13a, f. 5, sh. 36–40.

80 Or else: Satu-Mare province.

81 The collection points were located in the following towns (their numbers are
given in brackets (in persons): Sanisleu (7,000), Carei (8,000), Satu-Mare,
Balmazújváros (7,020), Polszta (1,060), Komplot (8,040), Zsedvernek (2,060),
Mezőberény (8,000), Gyula, Elek and Ceglédbercel (no data) (RGVA, h. 1/p,
r. 13a, f. 5, sh. 23–25).

82 RGVA, h. 1/p, r. 13a, f. 5, sh. 13–15. A significant portion of the internees
from Yugoslavia were sent to Donbass for work at the mines of the Stalinugol
and Voroshilovgradugol trusts (GARF, h. 9401, r. 2, f. 92, sh. 44).

83 The transportation procedure was hindered by natural conditions: since the
drifting of ice on the Danube impeded the process of river crossing, the

planned time-limit—3 January 1945—was not observed (RGVA, h. 1/p, r. 13a, f. 5, sh. 26–28).

84 RGVA, h. 1/p, r. 13a, f. 5, sh. 16–20.

85 Konasov, Tereshchuk, 1994, 330, with reference to: RGVA, h. 1/p, r. 13a, f. 5, sh. 12; see also RGVA, h. 1/p, r. 01e, f. 81, sh. 123–124.

86 GARF, h. 9401c, r. 2, f. 93, sh. 26–44.

87 See Weber, Weber-Schlenther, 1996.

88 See a memo of 11 April 1945 submitted to Molotov by KGB commissar V. N. Merkulov (*The USSR and the German Question*, 632, quoting: AVP, h. 06, r. 7, p. 14, f. 138, sh. 24–27).

89 Information provided by N. Okhotin.

90 APRF, h. 3, r. 58, f. 500, sh. 130–133. Other locations: RGANI, h. 89, op. 75, f. 3. sh. 1–4; RTsKhIDNI, h. 644, r. 1, f. 369, sh. 3 (Knyshevsky, 1994, 60, 65).

91 Serov, Ivan Aleksandrovich (1905–1990): colonel general; in 1941–1945—deputy Narkom, the NKVD of the USSR, state security commissar of the 2nd rank; in 1954–1959—chief of the KGB of the USSR; later was appointed military official in Tashkent; was later reduced in rank from army general to major general, and dispossessed of state awards for "lack of vigilance."

92 Tsanava, Lazar Fomich (1900–1953): lieutenant general; state security commissar of the 3rd rank; before the mentioned appointment was the deputy chief of the partisan movement headquarters, after—deputy minister for state security of the USSR and chief of the 2nd MGB department (co-supervised the operation on the liquidation of Mikhoels; died during the case investigation).

93 Meshik, Pavel Yakovlevich (1910–1953): lieutenant general; state security commissar of the 3rd rank; before the mentioned appointment was the deputy chief of the GUKR SMERSH NKO of the USSR, after—deputy chief of the 1st central department of the USSR Council of People's Commissars (Council of Ministers), minister of internal affairs of the Ukrainian SSR. Executed, without rehabilitation.

94 See State Defense Committee resolution No. 7252cc of 29 December 1944. Serov, Tsanava and Meshik were promoted on 2 May 1945 (See State Defense Committee resolution No. 8377cc of 2 May 1945. See: APRF, h. 3, r. 64, f. 799, sh. 19–20; RGANI, h. 89, op. 75, f. 6, sh. 1, 2.) Having become the front deputy commanders for civilian affairs from that point on, these officials were responsible for carrying out all measures postulated by the Soviet military command concerning the control over the German territory occupied by the Red Army. They were responsible for recruiting and appointing German population representatives to the local executive and judicial authorities, and supervising these authorities' operations. Their more habitual task—tracking down and punishing spies, subverters, etc.—also remained within their remit. The relevant vertical structure included local Red Army military commandants, and in some cases specially deployed envoys. Thus, it was the peacetime arrangements within the defeated state that constituted the new "operational mission" of the newly appointed front deputy commanders. This was

the departure point from which the would-be Soviet Military Administration in Germany originated.

95 RGVA, h. 1/p, r. 37a, f. 3, sh. 20–23. Chernyshev, Vasily Vasilyevich (1896–1952): colonel general; in 1941–1945—deputy Narkom, the NKVD of the USSR, state security commissar of the 2nd rank.

96 APRF, h. 3, r. 64, f. 799, sh. 7–8 (on an NKVD form). A copy is available in the "Stalin's special file" (GARF, h. 9401c, r. 2, f. 93, sh. 2–3). Bagramyan was the commander of the 1st Baltic front, were Tkachenko was NKVD representative.

97 GARF, h. 9401c, r. 2, f. 93, sh. 183.

98 GARF, h. 9401c, r. 2, f. 93, sh. 254.

99 GARF, h. 9401c, r. 2, f. 93, sh. 352.

100 GARF, h. 9401c, r. 2, f. 93, sh. 352.

101 GARF, h. 9401c, r. 2, f. 93, sh. 393, 394.

102 GARF, h. 9401c, r. 2, f. 93, sh. 184–185.

103 The Poles that resided in Germany were fairly soon (as early as summer 1945) repatriated to Poland.

104 APRF, h. 3, r. 58, f. 501, sh. 43–49. See other copies at: RGANI, h. 89, op. 75, f. 5, sh. 1–7; GARF, h. 9401c, r. 2, f. 95, sh. 253–255.

105 APRF, h. 3, r. 58, f. 501, sh. 50–51. See draft at: GARF, h. 9401c, r. 2, f. 95, sh. 37, 38 (ibid., sh. 36, the cover letter by Beria to Stalin, starting with the words: "Following your order, I present a draft project...")

106 APRF, h. 3, r. 58, f. 501, sh. 193–197.

107 State security commissars of the 2nd rank V. Chernyshev and B. Kobulov, Chief of the USSR GUPVI NKVD Krivenko, and chief of the department for check-up and filtration camps Shitikov were appointed responsible for carrying out the filtration and re-filtration of arrested individuals.

108 Moreover, corresponding directives—concerning the application of the State Defense Committee decrees of 16 and 29 December 1945 to all People's Commissariats and departments (initially the Decrees had affected two, and—later—three departments)—were also issued by Beria, but this time in the capacity of the State Defense Committee deputy chairman, instead of that of the people's commissar of internal affairs (directive No. GOKO-6255cc of 22 April 1945. APRF, h. 3, r. 58, f. 501, sh. 52).

109 Chukhin, 1995, 6, 7.

110 In accordance with USSR NKVD order No. 00315—1945.

111 RGVA, h. 1/p, r. 4a, f. 21, sh. 2.

112 RGVA, h. 1/p, r. 23a, f. 2, sh. 162.

Employment of Labor of German Civilians from European Countries in the USSR, and Their Repatriation

DESTINATION GEOGRAPHY AND EMPLOYMENT OF LABOR OF GERMAN INTERNEES IN THE USSR

The geographical pattern of the internees' destinations is remarkable. As we can see, the State Defense Committee kept their word: most of the internees—over 3/4—were transported to the Donbass and adjacent metal-production areas in southern Ukraine (see table 15 and figure 8).

Another 11% were "employed" in the Urals. Relatively small target groups were placed in the North Caucasus, Belorussia, Ukraine and the Moscow Obl. Among the 15 oblasts in which one labor battalion was stationed, only 2 (the Aktyubinsk and Kemerovo Obls.) were located to the east of the Urals, and another 3 in the north of the European part of the USSR (the Karel–Finn ASSR, Arkhangelsk and Murmansk Obls.). Interestingly, male workers were prevalent in the Donbass, while women made up the majority in the Urals.

As compared to the placement of the Soviet special resettlers at the time, this geographical pattern looks fairly privileged and "humane." In essence, it repeats the pattern of placement of the Soviet repatriates, a considerable number of whom were recruited for rehabilitation work in the Donbass mines. It is noteworthy that the Donbass population was most significantly affected by the German campaign of driving Soviet citizens to Germany as a labor force.

As early as 29 December 1944 (i.e., 13 days after the crucial decree No. 7161cc was issued), by way of elaborating on the matter the State Defense Committee adopted Resolution "On the use of interned Germans as a labor force" (No. 7252cc).[1] The People's Com-

missariats involved initially—the Narkomugol and Narkomchermet—
were joined by the Narkomtsvetmet (headed by People's Commissar
Lomako[2]): its enterprises were to host 20 thousand out of the projected total of 140 thousand labor force, or half of the force that was
to be at the Narkomchermet's disposal (40 thousand), and quarter of
that intended for the Narkomugol (80 thousand).

The majority of the internees were planned to be sent to the
Stalino (56 thousand), Voroshilovgrad (28 thousand) and Rostov (8.5
thousand) Obls., where they were to be employed mainly in the coal
industry. In its turn, ferrous metal production was the prevailing
sphere in the Dnepropetrovsk Obl. (22.5 thousand). The inclusion of
the Narkomtsvetmet [non-ferrous metal production] implied a significant extension of the geographic area where the internee labor
would be used: related enterprises were located in the Urals (the
Sverdlovsk Obl. was alone to receive 5 thousand people), in the Lenin-

Table 15. **Geographical patterns of the distribution of German internees within the USSR, as of 1 January 1946**

No.	Oblasts and republics	Number of labor battalions	Internees Persons	%	Proportion of male force %
1.	Stalino Obl.	63	49,452	37.4	55.8
2.	Voroshilovgrad Obl.	30	26,015	19.7	64.6
3.	Dnepropetrovsk Obl.	27	18,556	14.0	61.2
4.	Chelyabinsk Obl.	6	5,185	3.9	42.8
5.	Rostov Obl.	5	4,314	3.3	50.9
6.	Sverdlovsk Obl.	6	3,470	2.6	45.9
7.	Georgian SSR	4	2,972	2.2	88.8
8.	Chkalov Obl.	3	2,780	2.1	95.0
9.	Kharkov Obl.	4	2,409	1.8	69.6
10.	Molotov Obl.	3	1,946	1.5	41.7
11.	Zaporozhye Obl.	2	1,608	1.2	77.1
12.	Minsk Obl.	3	1,526	1.2	100.0
13.	Komi ASSR	2	1,357	1.0	22.3
14.	Chuvash ASSR	2	966	0.7	7.9
15.	Grozny Obl.	2	927	0.7	35.0
16.	Moscow Obl.	3	877	0.7	100.0
17.	Kurgan Obl.		788	0.6	7.7
18.	North Ossetian ASSR	2	762	0.6	63.1
19–33.	Others	14	6,243	4.8	
	Total	183	132,133	100.0	58.7

Source; RGVA, h. 1p, r. 4a, d. 21, l. 3.

Figure 8. **Placement of German internees in the USSR as of 1 February 1946**
(in thousands of persons)

Number of internees in oblasts
Over 25 [on the map the following oblasts, from west to east: the Stalino Obl.];
10–25 [on the map: the Dnepropetrovsk, Voroshilovgrad Obls.];
2–10 [on the map: the Georgian SSR, Kharkov, Rostov, Minsk, Chkalov,
   Chelyabinsk, Sverdlovsk Obls.];
1–2 [on the map: the Zaporozhye, Molotov Obls., Komi ASSR].

grad Obl., North Ossetia, as well as Kazakhstan, Uzbekistan and Tajikistan.

Special commissions, assigned to manage all relevant tasks, were established in the Stalino, Voroshilovgrad, Dnepropetrovsk and Rostov Obls. They comprised the secretary of the oblast party committee (the commission chairman), the chairman of the oblast executive committee, the chief of the NKVD department and representatives of the interested industries.[3] The commissions were authorized to use any premises under the control of the interested People's Commissariats, as well as any others, located close to the enterprises. The commissions were instructed to submit reports to the NKVD of the USSR as early as 3 January 1945. The reports were supposed to contain accounts of the undertaken measures, in particular of the enterprises' preparedness to receive internees, and to indicate the stations of destination and unloading of the trains carrying internees. The process of preparation and equipment of corresponding premises was to be completed by 15 January; the receiving People's Commissariats were supposed to deploy their representatives to the enterprises. The officers supervising the work battalions were regarded as doing active army service with all consequent rights, responsibilities and privileges.

On 21 February 1941, the State Defense Committee issued decree No. 7565cc "On the distribution of Germans, mobilized on the territories of the active Fronts, for work in industry."[4] The first target groups of mobilized Germans (85 thousand persons) were to be distributed among 12 All-Union and 2 republican (the BSSR) People's Commissariats: 67 thousand of them were intended for the Ukrainian SSR, and 18 thousand for the Belorussian SSR. Among the largest people "takers" were Narkomugol (25 thousand), Narkomstroy (11 thousand), Narkomchermet (10 thousand), Narkomles, NKPS, and the BSSR Narkomtopprom (5 thousand each).

The internees' status and life and labor conditions were stipulated in the specifically designed NKVD "Directive on the placement, management and employment of mobilized and interned Germans" of 27 February 1945.[5]

The document stipulated the deployment of interned and mobilized Germans from Southeast Europe for rehabilitation and construction work at the mines, and principal and satellite enterprises of the above-mentioned People's Commissariats; or, in other words, the directive envisaged a formal transfer of the internees from the sphere controlled by the central department for POW and internee affairs of the MVD of the USSR (the GUPVI). In practice, this implied much worse conditions for the internees, as compared to those provided to German POWs, since the People's Commissariats and their enterprises regarded the internees as an expendable work force and showed little concern over the workers' everyday living conditions or state of health.[6]

Labor battalions were routine units subordinated to corresponding People's Commissariats. Each battalion comprised three to five companies numbering up to 1,000 workers each; the companies were overseen by officers deployed by the NKO for this purpose.[7] Apart from supervising a number of other related matters, the NKVD exercised executive control over guard service and conformity with regulations and registration administration in the internee battalions.

Orders and requirements delivered by the NKVD were of paramount importance.

In other aspects, the internees were totally subordinated to and provided by "their" People's Commissariats. The People's Commissariats were responsible for delivering all necessary services to the internees, from supplying food to cultural and social facilities and health care measures. Under the regulations, the internees were to be accommodated in barracks, surrounded by a barbed-wire fence (embracing the inner yard too), and guarded by armed sentry service subordinated to the People's Commissariat (the residing of men and women in one zone was allowed, provided they were placed in separate barracks). Inner regulations established in the barracks were similar to those administered in the NKVD POW camps.

Violators of the regulations were punished under the provisions of the Red Army disciplinary statute. Repeated or gross violations, attempted escapes or refusal to work, were likely to entail confinement in the NKVD strict-security detention camps in remote or northern territories (therefore, these performed a role similar to that of the Third Reich concentration camps). Other types of violations were subject to account before the Military Tribunal.

All internees were grouped into brigades and shifts. The formation of brigades and shifts was carried out in accordance with the industry routine and the inner battalion structural divisions (companies, platoons). Internees' qualifications and health condition were supposed to be taken into consideration while forming brigades; however, in practice this principle was not always, and everywhere, observed. The workers were required to start for work in organized groups, and—although without the convoy—escorted by the battalion commanders or enterprise caretakers. Meals were provided in special canteens in accordance with the standards established for workers employed at the same enterprises, including bonus rations for good work performance.[8]

Payment of a monthly salary was envisaged too, depending on the production output.[9] However, deductions were made from the salary to reimburse the costs of meals, servicing of hostels and changing of bedclothes, the guard and remuneration for the personnel, and 10% centralized expenditures. The sick or incapacitated remained fully provided for by the enterprise until the question of their repatriation was resolved.

However, these were the formal regulations. The practical side
of the matter differed substantially. Below is another excerpt from the
memoirs by E. Klein:

*We arrived at the destination—the city of Stalino [now Donetsk]—on 5 Febru-
ary. We were detrained by a coal mine... The camp consisted of three large buildings. Women were placed in one block building, and men in another, opposite to
the first one. The third one contained the kitchen and canteen. What was absent
was toilets. That is why we had to relieve ourselves right behind our buildings.
Later, the men had to erect separating walls. The camp was surrounded with a
barbed-wire fence, with a lookout tower in each of the four corners. At the entrance
there was a small booth, in which a sentry party was always on duty.*

*During the first days there, we were just sitting on bare plank beds, doing
nothing... Soon a first group of men were sent to the mine. Then came the
women's turn. Previously, all of us had to undergo a medical check-up. For example, I was diagnosed by a "doctor" as having tuberculosis. I was more than happy
to hear this erroneous diagnosis, since it saved me from working in the mine itself.*

*As far as provision was concerned, those working in the mine were given a
better ration than the rest of us. They were supposed to get larger portions of bread
and porridge, which rarely contained pieces of horse flesh. As a rule, three times a
day we were offered cabbage soup or green pickled tomatoes boiled in water, which
were replaced by boiled beetroot leaves in spring. What kept us functioning was the
bread, but it also contained more of fiber than calories. At first we still had clothes
and underwear that we were selling to buy some cornflour to make corn porridge
to eat.*

*The first people to die were men over 40 years of age. They were not able to
cope with the difficulties and overcome the hunger. In camp no. 1064 near the village of Vetka, where I was kept from July 1945, seven to eight people, brought from
Silesia, Pomerania and other eastern regions, died every day. It was we, women
from camp no. 1021, that were supposed to fill the "openings" that had emerged.
Some were lucky to be assigned to work at the canteen or kitchen, or the infir-
mary. I was employed at a construction site, sometimes in the garden, and eventually at a brick plant open pit. The hygienic conditions of the camp were
appalling. Catching and squashing lice was our daily routine after work. There
was no other way to get rid of them. It was not until November, when the first
typhoid epidemics burst out, that some measures for lice prevention were taken,
like heat treatment of clothes and underwear.*

*All 70 women, my barrack-mates, got sick almost simultaneously. I was not
immune to sickness either. Suffering 40-degree fever and unable to even sit up on*

my own, I was lying on my plank bed right below the ceiling, with another two victims lying on their beds below mine. There were no medicines available. Hospital attendant Holtzman, a German from the Black Sea region, would come every morning, measure our body temperatures and inquire about our condition, whether that one on the upper level was still able to move her head or not. I survived solely on tea for two days. And when I felt a little better, I exchanged my bread portion for an apple. And, although I was able to "develop" some potatoes from November (at the time I was employed at the storehouse sorting out potatoes), I never recovered completely. At the same time, they started serving potatoes to us in the canteen too, instead of millet porridge. The potatoes were rotten because of the cold and had a disgusting taste.

At the brick plant, I was always given harder tasks. I had to carry up to 20 kilos of bricks at a time. My own weight was 42 kilos. On one occasion I fainted. When we came back to camp, there was a commission that sorted out the weak and sick to be sent back home. However, I did not yet "qualify." By September 1946 however, I had been so weakened that they sent me home with the next party to be dispatched.

To render the above description complete, one should mention typhoid epidemics, overt hatred of Germans in general on the part of some personnel members, and constant stealing by staff of food and other goods delivered to camps.[10] As I. I. Chukhin, a historian from Petrozavodsk, remarks, "...the fate of civilian internees turned out worse in many aspects, as compared to that of POWs confined in strictly regulated camps with centralized provision."[11] For all that, the local residents employed at the same enterprises as the "Westarbeiter" had to live under conditions comparable to those endured by the Germans,[12] while, unlike in the case of internees, the amount of food that the locals were able to get was directly dependant on their production output.

It must be noted that the POW and internee labor was not profitable, with very rare exceptions. It had to be subsidized constantly.

A selective inspection of reports from four camps, which was carried out by the finance department of the Belorussian NKVD in early summer 1945, revealed a camp financial sustainability range of 9–27%. The analysis of the situation in one of the camps (No. 168) exposed a series of acute internal conflicts: between the camp administration and health department, between the production department and employer (the enterprise). The administration was interested in acquiring labor force for its internal camp needs; the health department strove to maintain the health of inmates in a satisfactory condition; the enterprises wanted to gain the maximum possible number of work force retaining low net costs: and—since the payment was calculated based on an assignment order—the production output was not a matter of concern, which provoked mismanagement. Nonetheless, the situation presented the severest problem for the camp production departments, but foremost for the POWs themselves, who were denounced by the enterprise as nothing other than "spongers" and subverters.[13]

Such relations were duplicated in the "Westarbeiter" camps too. The following data were available concerning the use of labor of "B"-group internees in January 1946: 80% of workers were employed by the enterprises, while some 14% were not working at all due to sickness or absence of warm clothes. The proportion of people that fulfilled or over-fulfilled the mandatory production plan barely rose to reach 35%.[14] In February the proportion of those employed at the enterprises sank as low as 60%.[15]

Nevertheless, the summary report on the percentage of financial sustainability of POW labor use came up with the figure of 73% in 1945, 93.5% in 1946, and 61.7% in the first quarter of 1947.[16] These "decent" figures, however, may raise persistent doubts, should one take into account all said above. According to "target group" members' multiple testimonies, the overwhelming majority of able-bodied workers, leaving aside those disabled, sick and incapacitated in other aspects, were incapable of fulfilling the assigned production tasks. According to I. Chukhin, it was only in rare exceptional cases that the monetary value of the workers' production outcomes exceeded the cost of their meals.[17]

By 1 May 1945, there were 288,459 civilian internees in the USSR.[18] At the end of August 1945 the State Defense Committee addressed the issue of German internees again.[19] Judging by the fact that the largest numbers of the work force were ascribed to the Narkomugol, Narkomchermet and Narkomtsvetmet, the significant expansion of the circle of industrial consumers of the "Westarbeiter" labor, as it was envisaged by the April decree, remained merely on paper. The three People's Commissariats mentioned before were instructed to "eliminate all faults pertaining to the living conditions, servicing and supplying of internees" within a period of one month. This meant that the internees were to be provided with outfits, underwear and footwear, recreational goods, newspapers and movies and access to consumer goods stalls; and teams of caretakers were to be formed (with one caretaker intended for 30 internees). The Narkomzdrav was ordered to deliver health service and medicine supplies to the internees, while the NKVD was given the task to organize the transportation of up to 25 thousand incapacitated internees[20] home to Germany.[21]

However, the situation hardly changed with time, which can be deduced from the fact that the USSR Council of Ministers issued another decree on 7 May 1948.[22] Its mere title—"On the improvement of life and labor conditions of German internees"—indicates that the usual range of unresolved urgent problems remained in place. The BSSR Council of Ministers and 17 All-Union ministries were given strict orders to create acceptable living conditions for the internees belonging to work battalions (with a minimum living area of two square meters allocated per person); to repair and equip the living premises and adjust them for winter conditions; to improve the hygiene conditions in camps to meet adequate standards; to organize hygiene, health care and disease-prevention services for the internees and in particular to have 5 thousand people placed to special POW hospitals by 1 July 1948. In order for those whose health had deteriorated to recover, it was allowed to employ them exclusively for light types of field work within camps during spring and summertime. The last item of the decree permitted the ministries to change the status of those internees who expressed the wish to stay and work in the USSR to that of civilian employees, after prior agreement on such cases with the MVD of the USSR.

BEGINNING OF REPATRIATION OF INTERNEES, AND NEW "LABOR REPARATIONS"

Regardless of its fragmentary character, the repatriation of internees was launched as early as 1945. Remarkably, at least in 1945 (and even in 1946, according to some sources) Romania refused to receive its former citizens of German ethnic background. The following is a description of the events by E. Klein, who was among the first repatriates from the USSR in late November 1945, and who eventually was transported to Germany instead of Romania:

The train set off on 28 November; and we were full of hope that we would cele-
brate this year's Christmas at home. And what a great disappointment it was to
notice that the train was not heading to the west, to Romania, but instead to the
north: via Kiev to Brest–Litovsk, and further towards Warsaw, Posen (Poznan)
and Frankfurt an der Oder. After we were subjected to disinfection procedures, we
were put aboard passenger carriages with paneless windows and taken to
Neustadt– Orlau in Thuringia. There we were held in quarantine for three weeks.

Then we were placed in an empty factory shop. It was there—and not at
home, with our loved ones—that we marked Christmas. Nonetheless, we were
issued certificates that we were free, and yet—in the middle of a severe winter—
we were quite helpless. Nobody knew when we were going to see our relatives. They
said that the Romanian state did not want us to return.

Only within the period of January through December 1945, a
total of 36,039 people were delivered home, including 10,615 Poles.[23]
Apart from through repatriation, there were other reasons for the sustained "losses" among the internees. According to V. Konasov and
A. Tereshchuk, for example, 75,543 internees in 1945 and 35,485 in
1946 died or became disabled.[24]

The repatriation of internees continued in 1946.[25] NKVD-MVD
directive No. 110 of 30 April 1946 stipulated that all foreign citizens of Jewish ethnic background held in camps, special hospitals
and work battalions of the MVD and Ministry of Armed Forces, be
identified and repatriated (apparently, mainly Polish citizens were
implied).[26]

Under decree No. 1653-726cc "On the transporting of incapacitated German internees to Germany" issued by the Council of Ministers of the USSR on 27 July 1946, the MVD of the USSR was
authorized to send up to 21 thousand people home.[27] The procedure
of handing the internees over was the following: Germans, irrespective of their citizenship (!)[28] were to be repatriated via camp No. 69
in Frankfurt an der Oder; Hungarians and Austrians holding Hungarian and Austrian citizenship—via camp No. 36 (Sziget); Romanians of Romanian citizenship—via camp No. 176 (Focsani);[29] and Polish citizens were received by a camp in Brest.

In autumn of the famine year of 1946, the daily ration of the
POWs and internees was cut down, which further aggravated their
health condition, lamentable as it was. The proportion of those able
to work was melting away.

The unwillingness to feed "spongers" was perhaps an impetus behind the repatriation that was launched. However, the Soviet authorities in Germany itself were facing the same problem.[30]

However, by the end of 1946 the situation changed yet again, and the traffic of labor force between the USSR and Germany started flowing both ways. In particular, USSR Council of Ministers decree No. 2728-1124cc "On the transporting of Germans confined in camps and prisons from Germany" of 23 December 1946 obligated the Soviet Military Administration in Germany and the MVD of the USSR to select 27,500 able-bodied men among the 60,580 inmates of the USSR MVD special camps and prisons in East Germany, and to send them to the enterprises of the USSR Ministry for Coal Industry for work in the eastern regions of the country (15,500 persons to Kuzbass, Karaganda, and Kizel in the Urals), and to the enterprises of the USSR Ministry for Fuel Plant Construction (12 thousand persons to the above-mentioned destinations, and also to the Chelyabinsk Obl., Uzbek SSR, and Guryev Obl. in Kazakhstan). The inflow of the new labor force was compensated by the repatriation of the same number of POWs and internees, unfit for work. This two-way traffic was supposed to be carried on in the period of January–February 1947.[31] However, it was only possible to gather 4,579 able-bodied prisoners from among the German camps; they were sent to the USSR.[32]

At the same time, a few hundred more German civilians were transported from Germany to the USSR in October 1946 under Serov's sanction: this target group comprised highly qualified aviation industry experts that were collected in Dessau, Halle and other cities of East Germany and intended to be engaged in further joint research and development projects with Soviet specialists. Their destinations included the restricted plants and laboratories of the Aviation Industry Ministry, located in the towns of Upravlenchesky near Kuybyshev, Podberezye[33] and Savelovo in the Kalinin Obl., Tushino and Khimki near Moscow, where the German experts were offered decent living and working conditions. The work on the projects in question was commenced in November–December 1946 and lasted until 1948, after which they began gradually to be reduced.

A similar recruitment took place in the case of 150 German missile specialists led by Professor Hertrupp; the team's premises were stationed on the island of Gorodomlya, the largest island in the Seliger lake. These German specialists had to wait for the opportunity of repatriation much longer than "ordinary" internees: in the case of the missile specialists returning home did not take place until 1951–1953, while the aircraft designers had to remain in the USSR even longer, until 1953–1954.[34]

By its resolution of 6 November 1947 the USSR Council of Ministers ruled that German submarine design specialists that had worked in the Antipin Bureau, located in the city of Blankenburg in the eastern zone of Germany, be transferred to the USSR. Soon, however, it was found out that 13 out of 17 specialists intended for the transfer were residing in West Berlin, which made their forced deportation a complicated task.[35]

It is worth noting that there were other outstandingly well qualified specialists and scientists among "ordinary" German internees too, not to mention the POWs. During their confinement in camps, they generated a large number of innovations. For example, engineer Albert Druk developed a device measuring torpedo acceleration, and Aloiz Weber contributed to the evolution of the field of "Transformation of electric power into irradiation."[36]

It took a while for the idea of "labor reparations" to die out. It was not until 28 September 1949 that the Communist Party Central Committee responded to a request, formulated in a letter by Wilhelm Pieck, Otto Grotewohl and Walter Ulbricht to Stalin on 19 September 1949, by admitting the inexpedience of the practice of sending Germans, convicted by the Soviet military tribunals, to the USSR to serve their punishments.

At the same time, Soviet Control Commission head Chuykov was given a ten-day deadline for submitting a proposition concerning the feasibility of releasing a part of prisoners from the camps, and handing over the remaining prisoners to the German authorities.[37]

In conformity with the Communist Party Central Committee resolution of 31 October 1949, a commission was formed comprising representatives of the MGB, MVD and the Prosecutor's Office of the USSR (Comrades Yedunov, Sokolov and Shaver), which was to consider the cases of convicted and non-convicted Germans confined in the USSR MVD special camps with a view to handing these persons over to the German authorities and closing down the MVD special camps in Germany.[38] The results of the commission operation were presented to Stalin, Molotov, Beria and Malenkov on 27 December 1949; and without delay, on 30 December 1949, a corresponding resolution was adopted by the Communist Party Central Committee Politburo. In particular, it envisaged the winding up of the USSR MVD special camps in Buchenwald and Saksenhausen and the handing over of the prisons in the town of Bautzen to the German authorities by 15 March 1950. With regard to the prisoners, the resolution decreed the following: 15,038 Germans, including 9,634 non-convicted and 5,404 convicted for minor offences, were to be released (the same applied to 126 foreign citizens); 13,945 Germans were to be handed over to the GDR Ministry of Internal Affairs, including 10,513 people to continue serving their confinement terms and 3,432 to undergo further investigation and trial. A total of 649 Germans remained under the supervision of the USSR MVD, with 58 of them, convicted for committing felonies, subject to deportation to the MVD camps in the USSR.[39]

On 17 November 1952, Semichastnov, chairman of the Allied Control Commission in Germany, and political counselor Semenov responded to a request of the GDR leadership by agreeing to reconsider 5,063 cases of convicted German citizens by way of prosecutorial supervision.[40]

Only a month before Stalin's death, on 5 February 1953, the Presidium Bureau of the KPSU Central Committee discussed the question regarding the establishment of special camps for Germans, Austrians and other foreign nationals that were convicted by military tribunals of the Soviet occupational forces groups in Germany and Austria.[41] The target group in question comprised a total of 5,337 persons, in particular 4,523 Germans, 649 Austrians and 160 other nationals. In their letter addressed to G. M. Malenkov dated of 17 February 1953, M. Suslov, S. Ignatyev and I. Serov suggested the establishing of four special camps of the USSR MVD for foreigners falling under the mentioned category (two in the Komi ASSR; one in Kazakhstan and one in the Irkutsk Obl.).[42] From that point on, only those foreign citizens convicted for espionage, terrorism, subversions and other felonies committed against the USSR were transported to the territory of the USSR.

FURTHER REPATRIATION PROCESS AND ITS COMPLETION

Under decree No. 1731-426cc by the USSR Council of Ministers of 26 May 1947, the commissary for repatriation affairs of the USSR Council of Ministers took over the control of the POW and internee repatriation process. By way of reinforcing the check-up of repatriates on the USSR frontiers, special departments for POW and internee repatriation affairs were founded within the BSSR MVD, UkSSR MVD and Moldavian SSR MVD in the cities of Brest, Kolomyya and Ungeny in September 1947.[43]

It was planned to repatriate 26,900 internees in 1947. However, later the figure was raised.[44] The total number of POWs and internees repatriated in 1947 made up as many as 550,524 persons.[45]

In his directive of 8 December 1947 (conveying instructions given by USSR minister of internal affairs Kruglov), the new GUPVI chief, Lieutenant General Filippova underlined that the "work with the target groups" had entered its final and crucial stage. With the repatriation process deadline determined, the repatriation acquired a sensitive political character, which entailed stricter requirements with regard to the "target group" custodial conditions and health care, along with the activities aimed at raising their political consciousness. The situation demanded imperative "vigilance" and "intense circumspection" with a view to the prevention of the escape of criminals and "overt enemies." On many occasions the minister condemned the local authorities and administrations, whose involvement in the matter had apparently gone too far over the course of time: on a number of instances they were reminded of the GUPVI camps and camp departments being beyond their remit and even inaccessible to the local authorities.[46]

USSR Council of Ministers directive No. 19064, issued on 23 December 1947, decreed the repatriation of sick and partly incapacitated German internees.[47] A total of 17,514 persons, including 14,116 ethnic Germans holding Romanian citizenship, were intended for the repatriation that was due to be launched in March 1948. However, the Ministry of Foreign Affairs insisted (6 March) that the repatriation be postponed until a special order was given, which was not forthcoming over the course of the next three months. After the matter was agreed upon with the Romanian government, the ministry withdrew its reservations; and Molotov addressed Stalin (4 June

1948) with a request to approve the decision on the repatriation of German internees of Romanian citizenship to Romania.

The mentioned delay in the repatriation could have had a causal connection to a cable message by V. Sokolovsky and A. Kobulov, in which they asked for 50 thousand German POWs of Czechoslovak and Romanian nationalities to be placed at the disposal of the joint-stock company Wismut in Germany (for mining uranium in the Yakhimov mines on Czech territory). On 20 March 1948, S. N. Kruglov (the then USSR internal affairs minister) and B. L. Vannikov (the chief of the 1st department of the USSR Council of Ministers, in charge of the nuclear weapons development project) briefed Beria on the number of able-bodied Germans of non-German nationalities held in the MVD camps (14,759 POWs and 24,481 internees, including 14,948 women[48]), and on their agreement for the transfer of the camp population to the Wismut company provided, the recruitment term at the Yakhimov mines lasted at least three years.

Another USSR Council of Ministers decree was issued as soon as 7 May 1948. It concerned the improvement of custody and working conditions of German internees.[49] As a matter of fact, the numerous ministries, listed in the preamble, were recommended to adhere to the rules and regulations established long before (and apparently rarely observed). There was nothing new, except the instruction to pay the internees a compensation for the leave unused during the first year of work, and the permission to ascribe "civilian employee" status to those highly qualified specialists among the internees who wished to stay and work in the USSR.

In March 1947, the GUPVI administered the supervision of 107,468 internees, 60,498 men and 46,970 women among them. The number of arrested persons (i.e., group "B" internees) constituted 14,327 persons.[50]

As of 15 May 1948, the internees numbered a total of 55,287 persons that were arranged into 98 work battalions distributed among ministries. The internees' health condition was worse, as compared to that of the POWs (see table 16).

While there is no large difference between the data for the POWs and the "D" group internees, the "B" group internees' health condition appears to have been particularly poor.

The health condition of the German POWs considerably deteriorated in 1948, which—to an extent—resulted from the fact that the

Table 16. **Health condition of POWs and internees**
(grouped by degree of work capacity; by percentage; data as of 15 May 1948)

Work capacity group	POWs	"D" group internees	"B" group internees
Group 1	35.9	39.7	14.4
Group 2	37.5	30.9	26.7
Group 3	12.6	14.8	14.2
Disabled	0.7	1.8	4.3
Incapacitated	5.2	no data	7.0
Hospitalized	6.9	3.4	9.3
Group not determined	1.1	9.4	24.1
Total	100.0	100.0	100.0

Source: RGVA, h. 1p, r. 23a, d. 4, l. 7–8

Soviet press announced the 1948 repatriation deadline. Consequently, the enterprises at which the Germans were employed started an advance recruitment campaign in order to fill the work places that were to be vacated by the POWs. Besides, in the course of 1948 the POWs were often transferred to harder, manual and low-paid jobs, which tended to bring them to a state of exhaustion in a short period of time. There were a number of other factors that contributed to the trend. In particular, the reserves of unused looted clothes were coming to an end. And—most importantly—in autumn 1947, 150 thousand POWs were transferred to new enterprises of the Ministries of the Coal Industry and Heavy Engineering Industry, and of the Main Oil and Natural Gas Department,[51] lacking appropriate social facilities (thus, the POWs were placed under disadvantageous circumstances, similar to those initially experienced by German internees). The total number of persons repatriated during 1948 included 646,281 POWs and 29,177 civilian internees.[52]

Under the USSR Council of Ministers resolution No. 1492-572cc "On the repatriation of interned Germans and persons of other nationalities in 1949" of 6 August 1949,[53] it was planned to repatriate some 38 thousand internees in the period of October–December, with more than half of them transported via Sziget.[54]

The ultimate completion of the repatriation of all POWs and internees was supposed to take place in December 1949, which was the reason why MVD deputy minister, Colonel General I. Serov, issued order No. 744 of 28 November 1949 charging all regional departments of the ministry with the task of locating available unregistered members of the target group: the order did not apply to those convicted or on trial; escapees remained on the wanted list and were under investigation; and those residing in special settlements on specific permissions were not subject to detainment.[55]

The most complete and apparently summarized data on the internees are presented in a corresponding certificate signed by GUPVI chief, Lieutenant General I. Petrov, and reflecting the situation as of 20 December 1949.[56] These data are brought together in table 17 below.

So, among the 285 thousand persons in the internee status that were held in the USSR, the "Westarbeiter" were not the only group, although they dominated in terms of numbers. Their total amounted to some 272 thousand persons.[57] The death rate was more than significant: from 19.2% among the "mobilized" people to 38.9% among those "arrested" (compared with the 6.8% among the Poles from the "Armia Krajowa," and 2.1% among the Japanese). The entire number of German internees that died in the USSR reached some 66.5 thousand persons.[58]

By 1950, the internee labor potential was virtually exhausted, which is confirmed by the fact that their repatriation had been large-

Table 17. **Internees as of 20 December 1949** (by categories)

		The "D" group (mobilized)	The "B" group (arrested)	The Japanese	Poles of the "Armia Krajowa"	Total
1. The total number registered	Thousand persons %	205,520 72.2	66,152 23.2	5,554 2.0	7,448 2.6	284,674 100.0
2. Repatriated in 1945–1949	Thousand persons %	164,521 77.5	36,943 17.4	3,968 1.8	6,942 3.3	212,374 100
3. Died or otherwise "withdrawn"*	Thousand persons %	40,737 60.7	25,719 38.3	119 0.2	506 0.8	67,081 100
4. Held in custody as of January 1950	Thousand persons %	271 5.2	3,481 66.7	1,467 28.1	— —	5,219 100

Remark * —Here "otherwise withdrawn" comprises the following categories: shot while attempting to escape; drowned, or suicides (nine persons, all from the "D" group).
Source: RGVA, h. 1p, r. 01e, d. 81, l. 20–21.

ly completed by that time. The "arrested" internees evidently made the most numerous group, whose repatriation was still a matter under consideration; expectably, it was among them that the proportion of those convicted, criminals in particular, was higher.[59]

One more note dealing with internees and dated 17 January 1951 was signed by Petrov. The document shows the year-by-year progress of the repatriation of 213,418 persons interned in the period of 1945–1949, viewed in the context of their citizenship (see table 18).

The mass repatriation of the Reichsdeutsche in 1945 (in fact, these were the returned target groups), of Hungarian Germans in 1947 and of Romanian Germans in 1949 were remarkable events.

Somewhat different statistical values are presented in the documents of the section for repatriation and search for Soviet citizens of the department for SKK affairs in Germany. Camp No. 69 in Grünefeld near Frankfurt an der Oder—the key destination of German repatriates from the Soviet Union, where they were handed over to the German authorities—was one of the most long-lived camps, its dissolution started only as late as 1 June 1950. During the period of 1 June 1946 through 3 May 1950, the camp processed as many as 1,222,819 persons, including 1,195,987 POWs and 32,832 internees. Only 20 persons died directly at the camp or on their way to it. Over one-half of the former internees stayed in the Soviet occupation zone, while the rest moved over to the US and British zones.[60]

Table 18. **The repatriation of internees in 1945–1949**
(persons; by country of citizenship)

Country	Released and repatriated (persons)					
	1945	1946	1947	1948	1949	Total
Germany	32,867	10,526	11,051	11,802	11,446	77,692
Romania	9,064	10,639	9,126	11,439	20,804	61,072
Hungary	3,991	4,860	12,082	3,999	4,169	29,101
Poland	15,490	6,032	4,974	767	740	28,003
Yugoslavia	1,001	1,857	2,506	1,062	2,608	9,034
Japan	—	740	2,210	347	1,715	5,012
Czechoslovakia	876	666	372	248	216	2,378
Austria	13	42	69	27	48	199
Bulgaria and other countries	161	472	182	112	—	927
Total	63,463	35,834	42,572	29,803	41,746	213,418

Source: RGVA, h. 1p, r. 01e, d. 81, l. 24.

On 25 January 1950, there were 3,692 internees on the territory of the USSR, including 2,985 persons held in camps and hospitals and the rest of them apparently imprisoned.[61] The data of 15 July 1950, pertaining exclusively to the persons that had been interned, present their total number as 271,672 persons. The number included 111,831 "mobilized internees" that belonged to the "D" group and were brought to the USSR under the State Defense Committee Decree of 29 December 1944, and 159,841 "arrested internees" of the "B" group, with 155,262 of them transported to the USSR under the State Defense Committee Decree of 3 February 1944 and 4,579 under the USSR Council of Ministers Decree of 23 December 1946. The total of 202,720 persons were subsequently repatriated; 66,468 persons died; and another 1,385 were still held by the USSR.[62]

At this point a certain clarification is required with regard to statistical data. An actual release from the GUPVI establishments is not necessarily coincident with the fact of repatriation, even in terms of statistics. A corresponding comparative examination carried out by the GUPVI showed that the discrepancy between the data of the GUPVI register and that of the repatriate hand-over documents constituted only 2,759 persons in the case of POWs (which made 0.1% of the total of the registered 2,643,263 released persons); 8,260 persons in the case of Japanese POWs (or 1.4% of the registered 574,718 discharged persons); and as many as 34,867 persons in the case of interned western nationals (which makes 16.7% of the registered 208,406 released persons).[63] A similar comparison of the data available as of 1 July 1950 brought about virtually the same results.[64]

As of 1 January 1951, 2,656 convicted internees (both German and Japanese) were still held in the USSR, primarily at the camps of the Sverdlovsk and Minsk Obls., and Khabarovsk Kray.[65] The convicted war criminals (1,605 persons, including 44 women) among the internees probably constituted a part of the group in question, however those that were not convicted (707 persons) were not included. Among the convicted war criminals prevailed citizens of Germany (922 persons), Japan (377 persons), Poland (102 persons) and China (89 persons); while among those not convicted German (529 persons) and Polish (110 persons) nationals predominated.[66]

The number of the convicted internees did not change considerably during the year 1951, constituting 2,237 persons at the end of the year. Germans (1,459 persons) made up the majority of such internees. Their largest numbers were concentrated in camp No. 476 in the Sverdlovsk Obl. (765 persons), camp No. 16 in the Khabarovsk Obl. (524 persons), camp division No. 2 of the Kiev Obl. (362 persons), and in the Brest camp division (201 persons). Besides, there were 1,872 POWs and internees "deferred from repatriation" on various grounds, 684 of them due to their familiarity with the locations and assignment of "special establishments."[67]

On 2 April 1952, the USSR Council of Ministers adopted decree No. 1616-576cc "On the repatriation of German citizens, former POWs and internees, from the USSR" which applied to more than 1,200 persons, including 109 convicted POWs and internees.[68] The number of internees dropped to 1,745 persons by 1 October 1952, convicted persons making a majority of 1,627. The 118 persons that were not convicted were apparently among those "deferred from repatriation."[69]

Chief of the USSR MVD prison department colonel M. Kuznetsov issued a note dated 21 August 1953, which stated that the total number of convicted Germans confined in Soviet detention facilities was 19,848 persons. POWs constituted only a part of them (14,128 persons), the rest being internees (754 persons) and civilians (4,966 persons). Besides, there were 625 Germans that were not convicted, whose repatriation was deferred for undefined terms due to their possession of information concerning state matters.[70]

On 30 November 1953, the CPSU Central Committee Presidium eventually approved the draft resolution of the CPSU Central Committee prepared by Comrades Gorshenin, Kruglov, Rudenko and Pushkin and stipulating the early release of German POWs, internees and civilians convicted by the Soviet courts. Altogether 4,823 Germans held in custody on the territory of the USSR were to be released and repatriated to Germany within one month's period (in addition, 6,150 persons were to be discharged from confinement in Germany itself).[71]

Apparently, Council of Ministers decree No. 2284-rs of 19 April 1956 "On the repatriation of German citizens from the USSR" was the last related official document.[72] So far, we have not located the text of the decree, which probably would shed light on the fate of the remaining 625 Germans, including around a hundred internees: even those that were not convicted but had been unfortunate enough to have been in some way involved with the notorious "special establishments."

Interestingly, at present—owing to a peculiar legal knot—the Germans that were mobilized cannot be officially rehabilitated, for no rehabilitation is envisaged for individuals subjected to administrative repressive measures beyond the borders of the USSR (and on all occasions it is the departure point, from which these people were deported, that is judicially regarded as the place where the actual administrative repressive measure was applied to them).[73]

NOTES

1 APRF, h. 3, r. 58, f. 500, sh. 111–119; particularly sh. 115–119: supplement No. 1: Table of distribution of the 140 thousand arriving German internees among oblasts, and supplement 2: "Directive on the placement, management and employment of mobilized and interned Germans." Other copies: RGANI, h. 89, op. 75, f. 2. sh. 1–9. RTsKhIDNI, h. 644, r. 1, f. 348, sh. 6–8 (Knyshevsky, 1994, 60, 65).

2 Lomako, Petr Fadeyevich (1904—?): in 1939–1957 deputy people's commissar, people's commissar, minister of non-ferrous metallurgy of the USSR.

3 Such commissions were not founded in other regions. However, the first secretaries of the *obkoms* were supposed to provide support in resolving related issues. Among those obliged to assist were also the Sovnarkom [Council of People's Commissars] of the Ukrainian SSR (Comrade Khrushchev), the People's Commissariat of Trade of the USSR (Comrade Lyubimov) and the People's Commissariat of Communications (Comrade Kovalev). Among other assignments, the latter was responsible for providing empty railway carriages, equipped for wintertime, to be used for carrying internees.

4 APRF, h. 3, r. 58, f. 500, sh. 130–133. See other copies in: RGANI, h. 89, op. 75, f. 4. sh. 1, 2. RTsKhIDNI, h. 644, r. 1, f. 372, sh. 177; Knyshevsky, 1994, 59, 65.

5 RGVA, h. 1p, r. 37a, f. 3, sh. 25–30. The document was preceded by "Provisional regulations on the work battalion for delivering services to German internees" of 10 January 1945. See also: "Instruction on the supervision and registration of interned and mobilized Germans" of 28 February 1945 (RGVA, h. 1p, r. 37a, f. 3, sh. 31–38), "Provisional instruction on guard and routine regulations pertinent to interned and mobilized Germans in work battalions" of 5 March 1945 (RGVA, h. 1p, r. 37a, f. 1, sh. 63–66), "Instruction on the procedure for convoying POWs and internees by the USSR NKVD troops" of 4 April 1945 (RGVA, h. 1p, r. 37a, f. 1, sh. 76–81).

6 Konasov, Tereshchuk, 1994, 320.

7 The NKVD agreed upon the particular selection of battalion personnel with the pertinent people's commissariats.

8 Permission for correspondence (once a month) was another incentive measure, envisaged by MVD order No. 00574 of 21 June 1946 (POWs were granted this right starting from July 1945). See: GARF, h. p-9401, r. 205, f. 14, sh. 340.

9 The effective production output standards were to be adhered to starting from the third month of work, while only 60–80% of the standard output was required during the first and second months.

10 See, e.g.: Chukhin, 1995, 12–15.

11 Chukhin, 1995, 7.

12 Not infrequently they even moved into the camp barracks left empty after the camp zones were closed (Chukhin, 1995,10).

13 See a letter of 26 June 1945, sent by the head of the BSSR NKVD finance department, Yaroshenko, and head of the BSSR NKVD 3rd department, Entin, to the USSR NKVD central finance department, commissary service, Major General Berenzon (RGVA, h. 1p, r. 23a, f. 2, sh. 154; f. 3, sh. 141). The inspectors came up with the following suggestions: the use of the labor of POWs of the 1st and 2nd categories for performing tasks within the camps be prohibited; a premium scale for fulfilling and over-fulfilling assigned tasks be introduced as an "incentive" for health department staff; the production departments be granted the right to administer human resources at their discretion and bear the consequent responsibilities; the enterprises be instructed to remunerate the labor resources based on the number of person-days, and—certainly—to improve finance inspection (RGVA, h. 1p, r. 3i, f. 1, sh. 73–73back).

14 RGVA, h. 1p, r. 4i, f. 17, sh. 1–9back.

15 RGVA, h. 1p, r. 4i, f. 15, sh. 17. However, the same proportion in June 1946 was nearly one and half times higher and constituted 88.7% (RGVA, h. 1p, r. 4i, f. 16, sh. 21–21back).

16 And yet, according to the GUPVI data, full sustainability (102.9% and 109.3%) was achieved in the 2nd and 3rd quarters of the year 1946 (i.e., during the warm period of the year). See the operational GUPVI notes of 15 January 1947 and 1 April 1947, prepared by GUPVI deputy head, Major General Ratushnyi (RGVA, h. 1p, r. 23a, f. 2, sh. 154; f. 3, sh. 141).

17 See Chukhin, 1995, 22, 23. Starting from 1948, it was allowed to send the salary home.

18 See "Memo on the distribution of the interned, mobilized and arrested Germans among republics and oblasts" of 1 May 1945 (RGVA, h. 1p, r. 3i, f. 70, sh. 1, 1a). Interestingly, this document differentiates between the people interned (109,940), mobilized (77,741) and arrested (101, 778). The differentiation was not in place any longer in similar memos of 1 June 1945 and 1 August 1945: it was replaced by the division into two more customary target groups, namely "interned persons" (which absorbed "mobilized persons") and "arrested persons" (RGVA, h. 1p, r. 3i, f. 71, sh. 1a, 1b, 1c; f. 72, sh. 1a, 1b, 1c).

19 The State Defense Committee decree No. 9959cc "On the improvement of the life and labor conditions of the German internees employed in industry" of 30 August 1945 (APRF, h. 3, r. 58, f. 501, sh. 169–171; RGANI, h. 89, op. 75, f. 7. sh. 1–3).

20 i.e., persons aged over 50 years, suffering incurable illnesses, the disabled, pregnant women, and women with infants.

21 Nearly one year later (18 June 1946), the sphere of application of virtually the same measures—selection of the disabled, elderly and other protractedly inca-

pacitated individuals in camps and hospitals—was expanded to embrace the POWs of German and other Western ethnic backgrounds (holding the rank of captain or lower), held on the territory of the USSR. It was suggested that by 15 October 1946 they (altogether 150,000 thousand people) be delivered to the Soviet occupation zone in Germany, and—based on agreements with corresponding governments—to Austria, Romania and Hungary. (See decree No. 1263-519cc by the USSR Council of Ministers "On delivery of the sick and incapacitated POWs of German and other Western nationalities to homelands" of 18 June 1946, signed by Stalin and Chadayev. APRF, h. 3, r. 58, f. 502, sh. 51, 52.)

22 Decree No. 1492-572cc "On the improvement of the life and labor conditions of German internees" of 7 May 1948 (APRF, h. 3, r. 58, f. 503, sh. 75–78).

23 RGVA, h. 1p, r. 3i, f. 3, sh. 1, 2. The issue of the Poles was addressed by NKVD-MVD Directive No. 1925 "On the discharge of Poles" of 26 June 1945 and order No. 001301 "On the discharge of interned Poles holding Polish citizenship" of 19 October 1945 (RGVA, h. 1p, r. 15a, f. 3, sh. 275, 275 back).

24 Konasov, Tereshchuk, 1994, 320, with references to RGVA, h. 1p, r. 34f, f. 8, sh. 13, 14. The memo of 15 January 1947 by Major General Ratushnyi indicates 66,659 deceased and 75,843 released internees; on another instance the memo mentions 26,576 released persons (RGVA, h. 1p, r. 23a, f. 2, sh. 163, 164).

25 Decree No. 1253-726cc of 18 June 1946 of the USSR Council of Ministers also envisaged the repatriation of up to 150 POWs (APRF, h. 3, r. 58, f. 502, sh. 51, 52; RGANI, h. 89, op. 75, f. 8. sh. 1, 2).

26 RGVA, h. 1p, r. 15a, f. 3, sh. 275.

27 APRF, h. 3, r. 58, f. 502, sh. 55 (another copy: RGANI, h. 89, op. 75, f. 9. sh. 1). The decree in question partially reduplicates the State Defense Committee decree No. 9959cc of 30 August 1945, which envisaged the repatriation of up to 25 thousand internees to Germany. Under decree No. 1263-519cc by the USSR Council of Ministers "On the delivery of sick and incapacitated POWs of German and other Western nationalities to homelands" of 18 June 1946, the MVD suggested by 12 July 1946 that 20,800 incapacitated German internees employed in the coal industry be repatriated (GARF, h. 9401, r. 16, f. 148, sh. 311–316). At the end of July the following related documents were issued: the Council of Ministers of USSR decree No.1653-726cc of 27 July 1946; MVD order No. 00601 of 27 July 1946; MVD order No. 00731 of 31 July 1946 "On the transporting of incapacitated German internees, assigned to work battalions [of the Defense Ministry], to Germany."

28 Phrase "irrespective of citizenship" meant an actual violation of the Romanian Germans' right to repatriation, or—in other words—it envisaged their expulsion from their homeland.

29 See the USSR MVD order No. 00731 of 31 July 1946 "On the transporting of incapacitated German internees, assigned to work battalions, to Germany" (GARF, h. R– 9401, r. 1c, f. 205, sh. 318, 319).

30 So, on 12 October 1946, the Control Council (with the participation of the Soviet Military Administration in Germany's deputy supreme chief, Colonel

General Kurochkin) adopted directive No. 38 "On the arrest and punishment of German criminals," better known as the directive on de-Nazification. The document confirmed the punishment in the form of imprisonment with regard to principal Nazi criminals, and envisaged the release (with a trial period of up to three years) for minor criminals. As of 1 October 1946, over 80 thousand people were confined in the MVD-MGB prisons and camps on German territory; up to 35 thousand of them qualified under the category of "minor criminals." This was the reason why the Soviet Military Administration in Germany's supreme chief, Marshal Sokolovsky, and Colonel General Serov addressed the Council of Ministers, namely Stalin and Beria, requesting their approval for the subjection of the prisoners to a qualification procedure by a special MVD-KGB commission with subsequent release from the camps (APRF, h. 3, r. 64, f. 805, sh. 1–3; RGANI, h. 89, op. 75, f. 11. sh. 1–3). However, the same issue was brought up again on more than one occasion. For example, in his letter No. 3421 of 29 November 1947 submitted to Stalin (the Council of Ministers) A. A. Kuznetsov (Communist Party Central Committee), state security minister of the USSR, raised the question of the release of some 20 thousand amongst the 60,580 thousand persons, once arrested as a part of the Red Army rear area cleansing operation and held prisoner in the MVD special camps on German territory. Other high-ranking MGB officers—S. Kruglov and S. Ogoltsov—addressed Molotov, as the deputy chairman of the Council of Ministers, on 4 December 1947, putting forward similar suggestions. The USSR Prosecutor's Office (K. Gorshenin) sent a letter to Molotov on 29 December 1947, which dealt with the same question and in addition referred to numerous appeals from the relatives of the MVD camp prisoners (GARF, h. 8131, r. 27, f. 3414, sh. 167, 167 back). Nonetheless, it was not until several months later that an ultimate decision was made regarding the issue. USSR Council of Ministers decree No. 702-223cc "On the reconsideration of the cases of German citizens held in custody in the Soviet occupation zone of Germany" (APRF, h. 3, r. 58, f. 502, sh. 71, 72) of 8 March 1948 envisaged the founding of a corresponding commission comprising Comrades Kovalchuk (chairman), Malkov and Shaver. The commission ruled the release of 27,749 persons, provided for by resolution No. 2386-991cc "On the release of German citizens held in custody in the Soviet occupation zone of Germany" of 30 June 1948 (APRF, h. 3, r. 64, f. 805, sh. 4).

31 See MVD order No. 001196 of 26 December 1945 (GARF, h. 9401, r. 16d, f. 148, sh. 311–316). See also: APRF, h. 3, r. 58, f. 502, sh. 77–79. Interestingly, repatriation on the "compensation basis" was carried out in the Far East too. For example, NKVD-MVD order No. 00385 of 4 May 1946 stipulated the transfer of 20 thousand sick Japanese POWs from MVD camps to Korea with the simultaneous delivery of 20 thousand able-bodied Japanese POWs from Korea to the MVD camps (RGVA, h. 1p, r. 15a, f. 3, sh. 275).

32 See in the letter of 4 September 1947 by Kruglov to Ogoltsov (RGANI, h. 89, op. 18, f. 13. sh. 1, 2). See also Mironenko, S., L. Niethhammer, A. von Plato, (eds.), *Sowjetische Speziallager in Deutschland 1945 bis 1950* (Berlin: Akademie Verlag, 1998), 228, 229. (Studien und Beriche, vol.1).

33 In 1958 the worker settlement of Podberezye was transferred from the Kalinin to Moscow Obl. and transformed into the town of Ivankovo; in 1960 Ivankovo was integrated into the town of Dubna.

34 Voronkov, Yu., V. Zrelov, S. Kuvshinov, Yu. Mikhels, *Germnaskye aviatsionnyye spetsialisty v SSSR. Sudba i rabota. 1945–1954* [German aircraft specialists in the USSR. Fate and work. 1945–1954], Moscow, 1996, 46–49. See also Konovalov, B., "U sovetskikh raketnykh triumfov bylo nemetskoye nachalo" [Soviet rocket triumph had a German origin], *Izvestiya*, 1992, March, nos. 54–59. It is noteworthy that there were many highly qualified specialists and scientists among "ordinary" German internees too (as well as among German POWs). A special note dated 6 January 1949 and signed by GUPVI first deputy chief, Lieutenant General A. Kobulov, mentions an internee among numerous POWs too: engineer A. Druk (RGVA, h. 1p, r. 37a, f. 3, sh. 123–127).

35 GARF, h. 9401, r. 2, f. 171, sh. 406, 407.

36 GARF, h. 9401, r. 2, f. 201, sh. 255–259.

37 APRF, h. 3, r. 64, f. 805, sh. 9.

38 APRF, h. 3, r. 64, f. 805, sh. 10–14.

39 See a letter to Stalin by Abakumov, Kruglov and Safonov, and excerpt No. P72/100 of the Politburo sitting held on 30 December 1949 (APRF, h. 3, r. 64, f. 805, sh. 20–23).

40 A letter to G. Malenkov by Ya. Malik, dated 30 November 1952 (APRF, h. 3, r. 52, f. 92, sh. 131–133).

41 APRF, h. 3, r. 64, f. 805, sh. 223, 224, 228–230.

42 It was recommended to transfer them to camps and prisons on the territory of the GDR one year before the end of their confinement terms.

43 Order No. 00944 of 5 September 1947 (RGVA, h. 1p, r. 37a, f. 3, sh. 123–127).

44 USSR Council of Ministers decrees: No. 413-137cc of 4 March 1947 ("On transportation to Germany of incapacitated Germans employed at ferrous metallurgy enterprises"; the document applied to 6,680 interned and mobilized persons); No. 1022-305cc of 14 March 1947 ("On the transportation to native countries of incapacitated POWs and internees employed at coal industry enterprises in the western regions"; the ruling applied to 18 thousand persons, including 5 thousand internees); No. 1521-402c of 13 May 1947 and No. 1571-414cc of 16 May 1947 ("On the transportation to Germany of incapacitated POWs of the former German army and German internees"); No. 1731-462c of 26 May 1947 and No. 3545-1167cc of 11.10.1947 ("On the repatriation of 100 thousand German POWs").

45 RGVA, h. 1p, r. 23a, f. 3, sh. 186, 187.

46 RGVA, h. 1p, r. 23a, f. 3, sh. 178–185.

47 See Molotov's letter to Stalin dated 4 June 1948 (APRF, h. 3, r. 58, f. 503, sh. 79). The text of the directive itself is not available to us.

48 The distribution of the internees by their native countries looked as follows: 21,042 persons from Romania; 2,991 persons from Yugoslavia; 343 persons from Poland; and 105 persons from Czechoslovakia (Konasov, Tereshchuk, 1994, 331, 332, with a reference to RGVA, h. 1p, r. 24e, f. 6, sh. 87).

49 Council of Ministers decree No. 1492-572 (RGANI, h. 89, op. 75, f. 22. sh. 1, 2).
50 See in: the "taking-over" certificate of 2 April 1947 on the transfer of the GUPVI chief post from Lieutenant General M. S. Krivenko to Lieutenant General T. F. Fillipov on 12 March 1947 (RGVA, h. 1p, r. 23a, f. 3, sh. 115).
51 See: "Report on the operation of the 1st Department of the USSR MVD GUPVI in 1948, and central tasks for 1949" of 26 February 1949, signed by Colonel I. Denisov (RGVA, h. 1p, r. 23a, f. 4, sh. 149–170).
52 See in: report of 26 February 1949 by I. Denisov, deputy chief of the GUPVI 1st department (RGVA, h. 1p, r. 23a, f. 4, sh. 161). See also the letter of 29 December 1948 by Golikov to Molotov (GARF, h. 9526, r. 5, f. 49, sh. 155). Cf. the information concerning more than 211.4 thousand persons transferred only via the camp in Frankfurt am der Oder during the first seven months of 1948, with the internees among them making merely 3.8 thousand persons (GARF, h. 9526, r. 5, f. 48, sh. 191–217).
53 See also MVD order No. 00770 of 13 August 1949 (GARF, h. R-9401, r. 1c, f. 205, v. 17, sh. 178–181).
54 See in a letter of 20 September 1949 by USSR MVD GUPVI chief Lieutenant General Fillipov to the acting USSR Council of Ministers commissary for repatriation affairs Colonel N. A. Filatov (GARF, h. R-9526, r. 6, f. 57, v. 17, sh. 186).
55 GARF, h. R-9401, r. 1c, f. 205, v. 17, sh. 215–218.
56 RGVA, h. 1a, r. 01e, f. 81, sh. 20. Cf. report of 24 May 1950 by Kruglov to Stalin, Molotov and other Politburo members regarding the results of work with POWs and internees in 1941–1949. In particular, he referred to a number of repatriated internees—214,924 persons—that is somewhat higher, as compared to the data of 20 December 1949 (GARF, h. 9401, r. 2, f. 269, sh. 319). At the same time, according to the memo "On comparative data concerning the number of released POWs and internees, as indicated in statistical accounts and available documents confirming the handing over (acts, lists, receipt certificates) as of 1 July 1950," there is an apparent considerable—by 34,833 persons—discrepancy between the former (209,508 persons) and the latter (174,675 persons) in the case of so-called "western nationalities" (RGVA, h. 1p, r. 01e, f. 81, sh. 153).
57 Which, as a matter of fact, makes a little over 3.4% of the total number of Germans (7.95 million) banished or resettled during and after the war. (*Die deutschen Vertreibungsverluste. Bevölkerungsbilanzen für die deutschen Vertreibungsgebiete 1939/50*. Wiesbaden, 1958, 44).
58 According to German data (as of September 1950), the number of the "Volksdeutsche" internees that went missing in the USSR reached at least 39 thousand persons (*Die deutschen Vertreibungsverluste. Bevölkerungsbilanzen für die deutschen Vertreibungsgebiete 1939/50*. Wiesbaden, 1958, 44), which appears to be rather likely.
59 Among the 3,692 internees still remaining in the USSR on 25 January 1950, 2,953 persons (a majority) were held in the MVD camps and special hospitals; 580 persons had been convicted by military tribunals on the territory of the Eastern Germany, and 141 persons had been convicted in the USSR; and

another 18 persons, whose cases were still under investigation, were held in custody in the MVD prisons (RGVA, h. 1p, r. 01e, f. 81, sh. 80).

60 GARF, h. 7317, r. 20, f. 5, sh. 70–72.

61 Of them, 580 persons were convicted by military tribunals on the occupied German territory; 141 persons were convicted in the USSR; and 18 persons' cases were still under investigation. See "Note on the number of internees held in the MVD camps and prisons" of 25 January 1950 (RGVA, h. 1a, r. 01e, f. 81, sh. 80–86).

62 Out of the mentioned 1,385 persons, 516 persons were not convicted, with 15 of them on trial. Out of the 869 convicted persons, 570 were convicted by military tribunals on the occupied German territory; and 299 persons were convicted in the USSR. See "Note on the mobilized internees of the "D" group and arrested internees of the "B" group" of 15 July 1950 (RGVA, h. 1a, r. 01e, f. 81, sh. 123–124).

63 According to the documents, 171,654 persons were handed over, while the operational data refer to another 1,885 persons. Interestingly, in the case of the internees of Eastern nationalities the number of the registered repatriates (6,159 persons) was significantly higher than that of the registered ones (5,012 persons) (RGVA, h. 1a, r. 01e, f. 81, sh. 146–149).

64 RGVA, h. 1a, r. 01e, f. 81, sh. 152–154.

65 RGVA, h. 1a, r. 01e, f. 97, sh. 2–3. Another document: "Note on the number of internees held in the MVD camps and prisons" of 25 January 1950.

66 RGVA, h. 1a, r. 01e, f. 97, sh. 63–65.

67 RGVA, h. 1p, r. 01e, f. 98, sh. 26.

68 See order No. 00337 of 7 April 1952 by MVD Colonel General Kruglov (GARF, h. R-9401, r. 1c, f. 205, v. 17, sh. 51–55).

69 RGVA, h. 1p, r. 01e, f. 98, sh. 76–83.

70 Konasov, Tereshchuk, 1994, 332, 333, with reference to: AVP, h. 082, r. 41, p. 272, f. 28, sh. 93.

71 From excerpt No. P43/66 of the Politburo sitting of 30 November 1953 (APRF, h. 3, r. 64, f. 805).

72 See: RGVA, h. 1p, r. 37a, f. 4, sh. 16.

73 The information was provided by K. S. Nikishkin. A draft legislative act meant to repair this legal oversight has been submitted for the Duma consideration, but has not yet been discussed. Despite this, some cases of rehabilitation applied to former internees are known: for example, Mr. J. Keller from Leipzig was rehabilitated in 1988, after he submitted an individual appeal to the Supreme Council of the USSR ("Bis zu 30 000 Deutsche nach Workuta gezwungen. Überlebende der Lager fordern Wiedergutmachung," *Berliner Zeitung*, 1990, 12 July, 2).

In Lieu of a Conclusion: Geo-demographic Scale and Repercussions of Forced Migrations in the USSR

Forced migrations were practiced in the USSR starting from 1919–1920 until 1952–1953, i.e., during one-third of a century and nearly half of the period of the existence of the Soviet Union, which thus won it the dubious position of becoming the world's leader in the sphere of deportation technology and with regard to the results gained through deportations.

The mass—and ostensibly disorderly—forced resettlement of millions of people produced a most serious demographic and economic impact in the regions of departure and destination, and in the entire country. Apart from a certain historical and geographic logic behind the forced migrations, there were organizational logistics and infrastructure (largely located under OGPU-NKVD-KGB control) that determined their implementation. It was not until the 1920s and the years of collectivization that the activists forming the deportation policy grew increasingly concentrated at the Communist Party Central Committee (the "Andreyev Commission," etc.). As a rule, it was the central supreme authorities that took decisions concerning deportations, even those negligible in terms of numeric strength. However, in particular instances, for example in war-time, the decision-taking level would go down to regional or even military territorial administrations (particularly military districts, and even on the front line).

Deportation operations represented key elements—or shall we say "units"—of the USSR deportation policy. We define the notion as follows: banishment of precisely specified groups of people, implemented on a particular territory within a particular period of time using violence (in case of direct exertion of force) or coercive methods (a threat of direct use of force) and in compliance with a previously drafted plan or scenario. As a rule, the scenario in question was stipulated by official legislative acts issued by the state or party authorities (laws and decrees, directives and resolutions, orders and instructions, etc.).

The deportation operation might include various less apparent stages (for example, so-called first trains [*pervyye eshelony*], i.e., the banishment of the main body of the target group, and the follow-up actions aimed at locating persons that were not affected by the first wave of deportation or those that avoided the resettlement), and particular related actions that did not require immediate contact with the deported population but—as political instruments—constitute components of the operation (for example, administrative and territorial, and toponymic repressions, or measures for rehabilitation and repatriation).

Typically, a number of particular individual operations can be grouped based on a variety of their essential attributes, the most significant of such attributes being the population affected, for example, all kulak banishment operations or all instances of the expulsion of Germans. Essentially, such groups represented parts of a larger operation implemented at a higher level. However, since these larger operations normally comprised several individual deportation operations, in a sense they represented a distinct concept and required a specific term. We suggest that the term "deportation campaign" be employed to indicate them. The notion can be defined as a meaningful totality of individual deportation operations that can be brought together based on the same target population affected by them, but often separated in temporal and spatial terms. One can cite such classical examples of deportation campaigns as the "kulak exile" and "preventive deportation of Soviet Germans," which were carried out in 1930–1934 and 1941–1942 respectively, and included an entire series of individual deportations operations each.

Such an approach allows us to discern a deeper inherent association between the deportation policy and general internal policy pursued by the Soviet state. As a rule, particular deportation campaigns comprising individual deportation operations manifest their correlation with specific "political operations" or "political campaigns" conducted in the corresponding period of time (for example, dekulakization and repatriation).

Leaping a little ahead, we shall remark that the data at our disposal led us to the conclusion that a total of at least 53 deportation campaigns and some 130 deportation operations were carried out. It also transpired that a number of consequential circumstances and issues that had been paid no heed to previously were in place. For example, some legislative acts were of a general character and related to an entire period or stage, and therefore cannot be ascribed to a particular campaign or operation. Our research also revealed some operations that had not been provided for by any legislative basis. In some instances, there are discrepancies relating to various parameters of the operations (dates of the operations, regions of departure and destination, etc.), which in most cases indicates apparent gaps as far as locating and publishing adequate sources is concerned rather than questions the very fact that the operation was carried out. Besides, particular legislative acts refer to operations not registered in supplement 1. And yet, in some cases, the authenticity of both the legislative basis and related operations are questionable.

The following is a tentative list of the operations, compiled as a result of the work we carried out[1]:

I. Deportation of Cossacks from the Terek region (1920);

II. Deportation of the kulak Cossacks from Semirechye (1921);

III. Deportation of scholars ("Philosophers' ships," 1922);

IV. Deportation of former land owners and estate proprietors (1924–1925);

V. Cleansing of the western frontiers: banishment of Finns and Poles (1929–1930);

VI. Cleansing of the eastern frontiers: banishment of Koreans (1930–1931);

VII. "Kulak exile" (1930–1931);

VIII. Resettlement to Communism "construction sites" (*stroyki kommunizma*, 1932);

IX. Resettlement of Kazakhs, caused by imminent starvation (1933);

X. Cleansing of the western frontiers: banishment of Poles and Germans (1935–1936);

XI. Cleansing of the southern frontiers: banishment of Kurds along the entire perimeter (1937);

XII. Cleansing of the eastern frontiers: total deportation of Koreans and other nationalities (1937);

XIII. Cleansing of the southern frontiers: banishment of foreign Jews and Iranis (1938);

XIV. Sovietization and cleansing of the newly established western frontiers: banishment of former Polish and other foreign subjects (1940);

XV. Cleansing of the northern frontiers: banishment from the Murmansk Obl. (1940);

XVI. Sovietization and cleansing of the northwestern and southwestern frontiers: banishment from the Baltic republics, West Ukraine, West Belorussia, and Moldavia (1941);

XVII. Preventive deportations from the RSFSR oblasts, in which martial law was declared (1941);

XVIII. Preventive deportations of the Soviet Germans and Finns (1941–1942);

XIX. Deportations of "labor army" members (1942–1943);

XX. Retreat deportations: from the Crimea and North Caucasus (spring–summer 1942);

XXI. Total deportation of Karachais (August–November 1943);

XXII. Total deportation of Kalmyks (December 1943–June 1944);

XXIII. Total deportation of Chechens and Ingushetians (February–March 1944);

XXIV. Total deportation of Balkars (March–May 1944);

XXV. Cleansing of Tbilisi: deportation of Kurdish and Azerbaijani "spongers" within Georgia (25 March 1944);

XXVI. Deportation of OUN members with families (1944–1948);

XXVII. Total deportation of the Crimean Tatars and other Crimean nationalities (May–July 1944);

XXVIII. Return deportations of Poles to the USSR European part (May–September 1944);

XXIX. Deportation of population from the front-line regions (June 1944);

XXX. Deportation of collaborationists and their family members (June 1944–February 1945);

XXXI. Deportation of "punished confessions": "True Orthodox Christians" (July 1944);

XXXII. Total deportations of Meskhetian Turks, Kurds, Khemshins, Lazs and other nationalities from South Georgia (November 1944);

XXXIII. Forced repatriation of various target groups (1944–1946);

XXXIV. Internment and deportation of German civilians from the occupied European countries (1944–1945; 1947);

XXXV. Deportation of repatriated Finns from Leningrad and the Leningrad Obl. (February–March 1948);

XXXVI. Second deportation of the target groups previously banished from the USSR European part to Siberia and Kazakhstan (March 1948);

XXXVII. Deportation of "bandits and bandit abbetors" from Lithuania (22 May 1948);

XXXVIII. Deportation of Greeks and Armenian Dashnaks from the Black Sea coast region (June 1948);

XXXIX. Deportation of "decree spongers" [*tuneyadtsy-ukazniki*] (June 1948);

XL. Deportation of Kurds, members of the detachment commanded by M. Barzani, from Azerbaijan (August 1948);

XLI. Deportation of kulak "bandits and bandit abbetors" from the Ismail Obl. (October 1948);

XLII. Deportation of kulak "bandits and bandit abbetors" from the Baltic republics (29 January 1948);

XLIII. Deportation of Armenian Dashnaks, Turks and Greeks, holding Turkish, Greek or Soviet citizenship or stateless, from the Black Sea coast region and from Transcaucasia (May–June 1949);

XLIV. Deportation of kulak "bandits and bandit abbetors" from Moldavia (June–July 1949);

XLV. Deportation of kulaks and alleged bandits from the Pskov Obl. (February 1950);

XLVI. Deportation of Iranis without Soviet citizenship from Georgia (March 1950);

XLVII. Deportation of former Basmaches from Tajikistan (August 1950);

XLVIII. Deportation of Anders army members and their family members (after January 1951);

XLIX. Deportation of the "punished confessions": banishment of "Jehovah's Witnesses" from Moldavia (April 1951);

L. Deportation of kulaks from the territories annexed in 1939–1940 (10 December 1951);

LI. Deportation of "anti-Soviet elements" (Greeks) from Georgia (December 1951);

LII. Banishment of kulaks from West Belorussia (March–May 1952);

LIII. Deportation of the "punished confessions": banishment of "*Inokentyevtsy*" and Reformer Adventists[2] (March 1952).

While it is possible to systematize deportation operations chronologically (notwithstanding the vagueness of some important dates), analogous temporal distribution is hardly feasible in the case of deportation campaigns, since particular political campaigns were carried out simultaneously, with some of them (for example, collectivization and repatriation) expanded over years.

All said above manifests a pressing necessity of additional attention to archive sources. Our attempt to systematize available data will hopefully facilitate work with relevant materials in the future.

After forced migrations were turned into a routine instrument of internal policy in Russia during the First World War, the new authority was unlikely to dismiss these convenient means of suppression and coercion. The first attempts undertaken by the Soviet authorities in the "genre" of deportations—namely, the decossackization in the Terskaya Obl. and Semirechye, repression of landowners in Stavropol Kray and the Volga region—appear to have been relatively "innocent" as compared to what was to follow. Cruelty was something the new authorities were remarkably adept at (the executions of the tsar's family, hostages, the introduction of special camps and prisons [*osobogo naznacheniya*] are telling enough). However, when the authorities wanted to get rid of their political opponents, they seemed to prefer them to emigrate voluntarily; banishment represented an additional method of removing adversaries, as in the case of the "Philosophers' ships."

During the second half of the 1920s, forced migrations were scarcely practiced; it was rather time of a planned resettlement.

This "standstill" was made up for and more in the very first two years of the next decade, i.e., the time of collectivization and "kulak exile." Some 35% of the population, deported internally during Soviet times, were deported within the two years in question (the first experiments in cleansing frontier zones were also carried out at the time, but these were negligible in scale as compared to the "kulak exile"). Taking into account the regional collectivization waves, which

continued in the following years, the contribution of the collectivization process to the internal deportation in the USSR exceeded the
estimated 40%. The first internal catastrophe in the USSR—the
famine of 1932–1933, led to the expansion of forced migrations
beyond the country's borders (the famine-driven resettlement of
Kazakhs).

Starting from 1935, the cleansing of most of the Soviet frontier
regions through the use of deportations came into the focus. After the
annexations of 1939–1940 the borders shifted, and new cleansing
operations were needed in the western frontier regions. Deportations
of this type were prevalent until 22 June 1941 and produced at least
10% of the total number of the internal forced migrants.

Of course the war shifted the emphasis. The problem of preventive deportation of unreliable persons—with the registration and
surveillance of them organized well as it was in the USSR—was
brought to the forefront, as it had been during the First World War.
After the first two months of war, the political aspect of "unreliability" was replaced by the ethnic one. Consequently, by virtue of their
belonging to the titular nationality of the country-aggressor, all Soviet Germans became the key target of the deportation operations of
1941–1942; the Finns were affected on the same grounds in 1942.
Germans and Finns of working age were deported again, and constituted the backbone of the labor army that was organized in winter
1942. Soviet Romanians and Hungarians resided in the western outskirts of the country, and were already beyond the Kremlin's reach at
that time. As far as Italians were concerned, their number was negligibly small in the USSR. Nevertheless, the deportation affected all
those that were within reach, as in the case of Germans and Finns
but, as a rule, immediately before the army's retreat rather than earlier (in particular, from the Crimea).

The campaign of total deportation of so-called punished peoples
started in November 1943. Related operations in the North Caucasus (Karachais, Kalmyks, Chechens, Ingushetians, and Balkars) were
completed by spring 1944. They were followed by a series of total
deportations in the Crimea and the North Caucasus again (affecting
the Crimean Tatars and Greeks most notably). At the same time the
first deportation operations against families of OUN (Organization
of Ukrainian Nationalists) members were launched, and against various categories of collaborationists in the North Caucasus. Besides, it

was then that a confessional group (the sect of the True Orthodox Christians) became a target of the deportations for the first time. At the end of 1944, a number of operations were carried out in Transcaucasia, in particular the total deportation of the Meskhetian Turks (which had initially been scheduled for an earlier period).

Internal deportation prevailed until a turn took place in 1944, when organized mass repatriation of Soviet citizens started. The inflow of repatriates originated from both the territories liberated by the Red Army and from those under the control of the Allies or defeated adversaries, as in the case of Ingermanland Finns that had been evacuated to Finland by Germans and Finns. Within less than 15 months starting from mid-October 1944, the Soviet authorities repatriated almost 5.3 million persons, which represented an outstanding "achievement" in terms of intensity, especially taking into account the fact that other deportations were carried out at that time too. These other deportations included international ones, in particular deportations of German civilians holding foreign citizenship from the countries of Eastern and Southeastern Europe (these persons may be termed the "Westarbeiter" by analogy with the Ostarbeiter).

The repatriation continued in 1946–1947 but gradually declining, while no internal deportation campaigns were conducted up until the end of 1947 or the beginning of 1948 at all. Once these campaigns were resumed, they comprised two streams: the territorial redistribution of those deported earlier, and the continuation of cleansing operations in the frontier areas, first of all the western territories where sovietization encountered certain hindrances. The main target groups of the time included OUN members, "kulaks," "bandits and bandit abettors," "anti-Soviet elements," "Dashnaks," and "basmaches." There emerged some new groups, such as "spongers" [tuneyadtsy] and a number of repressed confessions ("Jehovah's Witnesses," [Innokentyevtsy], "Reformer Adventists").

According to our estimation, during the years of Soviet rule at least 5.9 million people were subjected to internal deportations alone, i.e., those who did not spread beyond the steadily expanding borders of the Soviet state. Approximately the same number (around 6 million persons) of the deportees were affected by the international migrations. Therefore, the total number of forced migrants produced by the Soviet state amounted to some 12 million persons, or around 14.5 million, when taking into account compensatory migrants.

Along with the Stalin deportations, Soviet citizens became victims to the forced migration policy pursued by Hitler's Germany as well. The herding to Germany ("recruitment to the Reich") of 4.2 million Ostarbeiter, refugees and evacuees was the most large-scale deportation campaign carried out by Hitler's Germany[3]; by its magnitude it surpassed even the OGPU-NKVD-conducted operations of the 1930s and 1940s. And yet, in terms of size and intensity it was eventually left behind by the mass repatriation of Soviet citizens, with its forced nature predetermined by the Yalta agreements.

When talking about the deportations of "interned and mobilized" German civilians from a number of European countries, one can remark that the NKVD bodies felt at ease in their alien surroundings and acted as confidently as they did at home, in the USSR: the campaign was carried out within short time scales and in the same manner as the deportations of the "punished peoples" from the Caucasus and Crimea. Even almost all those marshals and generals that directed the operations were the same.

The summary data showing the numbers of deportees in particular periods are presented in table 19:

Table 19. **The scale of forced migrations in the USSR in 1920–1952**

Distinctive periods	The number of deportees					
	Internal (thousands persons)	%	International* (thousands persons)	%	Total (thousands persons)	%
1920–1925	100**	1.7	0	0.0	100**	0.9
1930–1931	2050	35.0	-	-	2,050	17.2
1932–1934	335	5.7	200	3.3	535	4.5
1935–1938	260	4.4	-	-	260	2.2
1940–1941	395	6.7	-	-	395	3.3
1941–1942	1,200	20.5	-	-	1,200	10.1
1943–1944	870	14.8	-	-	870	7.3
May 1944-1945	260	4.4	5,565	93.0	5,825	49.0
May 1945–1952	400	6.8	255	3.7	655	5.5
TOTAL	5,870	100.0	6,020	100.0	11,890	100.0

Sources: Polian, 2001; Polian, 2002.
  * Without taking into account the deportations of Soviet citizens (the Ostarbeiter and others) carried out by Germany in 1941–1944.
  ** Including the estimated numbers covered by deportation campaigns II and III.

Forced migrations on such a scale were bound to produce—and did produce—a considerable impact on the entire population system of the former Soviet Union. Having abruptly subverted or obstructed the natural flow of the demographic progress of entire ethnic groups, the deportations affected the macro-patterns of the population distribution over the country, and contributed to a successive shift of the USSR population "gravitation" center: first to the north, and then to the east and southeast.

At the same time, nearly all deported groups manifested outstanding acclimatization capacity and managed to adjust themselves to the new living conditions, to find or create particular economic niches for themselves, and provide their children with a good-quality education, notwithstanding the status discrimination they were generally subjected to.

The deportation of peoples, or a forced change of their residence location, may also be described in terms of their absence in their homelands, and presence in alien parts. As such, these phenomena certainly predetermined a particular impact on other population groups residing in both the places of departure and destination of the deportees. In the former case, they shaped preconditions for compensatory migrations, and in the latter one they predetermined the emergence of mixed marriages and inter-ethnic economic communication. Both developments encompassed certain potential for inducing conflicts in the distant future.

Some peoples, not affected by the deportations immediately, still proved to be indirectly involved in the events, especially in the compensatory processes. For example, Russians, Georgians, Ossetians, Kabardians, Avars, Laks and others would be resettled—often against their own will—to the lands left abandoned as a result of the deportations. In a way this was unavoidable, since an economic vacuum would inescapably emerge in the areas where the deported ethnic groups had lived.

In a number of cases we estimated the ratio of the deported population to the number of compensatory migrants as five to two. Assuming that the ratio is valid in the case of all deported target groups, the number of the deportees can be supplemented by approximately 2.4 million forced migrants! It is noteworthy that it is not a mere coincidence that it was precisely in the areas previously populated by the deported peoples (for example, the Saratov and Crimea

Obls.) where the maximum mechanical outflow of the population was registered in the early 1950s.

Forced migrations led to the formation of "internal diasporas" of almost all repressed peoples (following the pattern "homeland"— "exile destination"). After the USSR collapse and the emergence of 15 independent states on the same territory, the "internal diasporas" in question unexpectedly attained official international status, which implied both positive and negative consequences for these peoples.

Today, it is generally recognized that any departure from the practices, both balanced and justifiable in historical terms, may give rise to a most serious economic and political aftermath. Apropos, a remark should be made with regard to two radical shifts in the ethnic structure of the Soviet and post-Soviet population itself. First, as a result of the Holocaust launched by Hitler's Germany, Stalin deportations and the mass emigration of Jewish and German population, there has been a dramatic and universal reduction of both populations on the former USSR territory, especially in the 1990s.

The decrease of Jewish population in the USSR was foremost brought about by the Nazi Germany's genocide inflicted on Jews on the occupied Soviet territories, which included deportation policy as its inseparable constituent. Apart from the Holocaust practiced directly in the regions of Jewish residence, forced transportation of Jews to other areas was also widely exercised: most often they were delivered to concentration camps and so-called extermination camps (where the technology of killing was advanced to the utmost degree of rationalization), and sometimes to larger ghettos that often proved nothing else but transit stations on the way to the mentioned camps. The first to be exterminated were women, children, the elderly, and sick men; the chances of able-bodied men to survive were somewhat higher.

Should the foundation of the state of Israel in 1948 be regarded as the reaction of the world community to the Holocaust, the process of Jewish emigration from the USSR (and from Russia in the recent decade) can be perceived as an indirect consequence of the same historic catastrophe in the first place, while the state anti-Semitic policy administered by the Soviet regime (which allegedly was developing actual deportation plans in 1953[4]) can be seen as a secondary—albeit direct—determining factor in this case.

Germans are another ethnic group that suffered a sharp population decline in the years of the USSR existence. The failure of the state to administer a timely and satisfactory restoration of the German autonomy brought about mass emigration of Soviet ethnic Germans, humiliated by both deportation and deficient rehabilitation, from Russia and the states of Central Asia. The mass departure of German population from the countries in question implies substantial negative consequences for them, but they have hardly been able to restrain the process once it had started.

Forced migrations of the 1920s, which affected only some tens of thousands of persons, brought about generally negligible geo-demographic and economic consequences. The essential significance of these actions belongs to a different domain: in a sense, they constituted the first experimental attempts at repressive deportations and helped the system to develop the necessary practical methodology (and "technology" in particular), which was subsequently widely applied in the course of far more consequential mass operations.

The first experience—dekulakization and collectivization—brought about the sought-after social and political outcomes (namely, the social exclusion of kulaks and middle-income peasants, as a politically unwelcome element). However, there were other consequences too, and these were not directly linked to the political needs of the state and possibly were even undesirable from the latter's perspective. Provided we put aside attempts to "demonize" the Stalin regime (if this were the case then the events in question were also preplanned and designed!), it raises no doubts that—most importantly—it was the famine of 1932–1933, an immediate product of collectivization, that constituted such a "side effect." The "kulak exile" certainly brought about a radical decrease of the number of mouths in the rural areas of Ukraine, the North Caucasus, the Volga region and other areas. However, this was but a slight "benefit" brought about through the far greater blow that was inflicted on the countryside, stripping it of millions of fertile women.

For many former peasants, cities and large construction project sites (i.e., would-be cities) became resorts to turn to, places where they hoped to survive, which would replace the hard and almost unpaid labor in the countryside. The proportion of urban population was growing nearly every month, which gives one a clear idea of the origin of the "seven-mile steps" taken in the first Soviet five-year periods, the unprecedented pace of the "Soviet-version" urbanization and industrialization: urbanization in bast shoes, and industrialization with handbarrows and spades.

To an extent, the mechanism in question was also stimulated by the mass "outpouring" (or rather "flight") from the countryside to cities of those peasants that did not want to subject themselves and their families to the risk of expropriation and exile of, so-called, remaining kulaks [*nedoraskulachennyye*]. This campaign within the Soviet deportation policy, therefore, made another specific contribution to the building of the new socialist society. In 1932, the large-scale and initial lack of control over this "building" process urged the authorities to introduce a passport system, at least in the case of urban population.

However, even considered separately from other developments, the "kulak exile" itself represented a mass migration and, as such, had a momentous impact on settlement patterns and involved an evident geographic component. From a qualitative perspective it is obvious that the rural population center shifted in the USSR to the north in 1930, and the northwest in 1931. It poses a greater difficulty to determine the geographic vector of the additional dekulakization [*doraskulachivaniye*] campaign of 1933–1935.

The second half of the 1930s was remarkable for the deliberate and purposeful cutback of the population (and in some cases even total depopulation) of territories adjacent to the frontier, in particular in the southern part of the Far East (Koreans) and along the southern and western borders of the USSR. The width of the zone to be cleansed of socially dangerous (and prevalently rural) population ranged from 800 meters to 100 kilometers. Remarkably though, at the time the western frontiers themselves had a tendency to shift further to the west and deeper into Eastern Europe and, therefore, the campaign needed regular "updates." Those banished from the frontier zones were transported in an opposite direction, to the Asian part of the country: Kazakhstan and West Siberia (the notorious Narym) commanded particular "popularity" in this respect at the time.

"Attachment" to Kazakhstan was retained in 1941, as the authorities carried out mass preventive deportations of the German and Finn populations from the Volga region, Crimea, the North Caucasus, Transcaucasia, and Kola Peninsula. However, in the case of the million-strong target group of Soviet Germans the destination areas were not limited to the mentioned ones. They also included Kyr-

gyzstan, West and partially East Siberia. Siberia became the destination for some peoples deported in 1943–1944, Kalmyks in particular, while the four North Caucasian peoples were distributed
between Kyrgyzstan and Kazakhstan. At the same time, Crimean
Tatars and then Meskhetian Turks were placed predominantly in
Uzbekistan.

Consequently, there can be no doubt with regard to the shift of
the USSR population to the east in the war years, but its quantitative
intensity is difficult to determine. Even more so, as—in their turn—
other factors and processes contributed to the migration in that direction, particularly mass evacuation of civilian population to the east
and southeast. On the whole it was precisely in these directions that
a considerable population distribution shift took place in the war-time
USSR.

As far as the abandoned territories were concerned, the forced
migrations in question preconditioned the population decline—and
sometimes partial (or, rather, temporary) depopulation—of a magnitude that had had no precedents in the history of forced migrations
in the USSR. In many cases the process proved irreversible, or hardly reversible, since the "volunteers" settled on the vacated territories
were, as a rule, considerably—on average two and a half times—less
numerous than the resettled native population. This induced repeated waves of "volunteers" that were recruited for compensatory settlement by all possible means (and many of those that did resettle
developed a firm intention to leave once the first opportunity presented itself).

In the destination regions, the special settlers often made up a
rather significant proportion of the population. In many oblasts of
Central Asia and Kazakhstan, Germans and sometimes representatives of other "punished peoples" ranked the second or third largest
ethnic group in the local ethnic structure. Intensive ethnic merging
of the new settlers and native population was in progress, with mixed
marriages as one of its typical forms. Gradually, the proportion of
urban residents among the resettlers grew, and the process of forming a local ethnic intelligentsia and elite started.

While the list of the largest repressed peoples of the USSR (as of
1989) included, in descending order, Germans, Chechens, Koreans,
the Crimean Tatars and Ingushetians, within the Russian Federation
those included on the list and their sequence were different:

Chechens, Germans, Ingushetians, Kalmyks, and Karachais (at this point it should be remembered that the German population is rapidly declining).

One aspect of forced migrations should be touched upon by way of summarizing.

The significance of forced resettlements for the deportees themselves is obvious. At best, it meant a catastrophe, exclusion from the environment which their ancestors and they themselves had been used to, crushed hopes, grief and longing for their dearly loved homeland.

However, let us see whether this whole game the state played with human lives was "worth the candle." Was it not the hands of convicts and special resettlers that built "Magnitka," Kuzbass, Komsomolsk-on-Amur, the Moscow metro, and thousands of kilometers of railways? Was it not the convicts and special resettlers that produced millions of cubic meters of wood, excavated tons of gold, etc.? Was it not their "planned" labor that formed the foundation of the industrial power of the world's first state of proletarian dictatorship? What was the economic effect of the whole sequence of operations of uprooting, transporting and settling in new regions of millions of families? What were the economic costs of all those industrial projects that were fulfilled by means of the forced labor of millions of forced migrants deprived of political rights?

No single bibliographical or archival source that we had at our disposal has confirmed the few optimistic statements that were put forward by some Cheka economic experts regarding the supposed higher efficiency of forced labor as compared to that of free employees. This is—to use their habitual vocabulary—pure rubbish. If anyone gained any economic profit through the use of deportee labor, it was not the state but the NKVD itself, which indeed made serious attempts in the 1930s to become one of the largest economic powers of the country.

On the macroeconomic scale of the state, however, the deportations were disadvantageous, since they scratched millions of well-settled, economically productive families off the production cycle; rendered vast lands and numerous settlements deserted and neglected; caused the loss of population labor skills and traditions, and a dramatic decline in agricultural and industrial production; required additional expenses for the transportation of deportees and settling them down at new locations; and so on and so forth. Besides, due to the loss of millions of lives as a result of famine and to other negative demographic effects brought about by the deportations, the state had to face immense difficulties during the Great Patriotic War, in particular as far as mobilization to the armed forces was concerned. The practical inadequacy of the economic rationale behind the deportee forced labor use was further enhanced by the sheer size of the Soviet Union's vast territory.

NOTES

1 We left out dubious or arguable cases.
2 Reformer Adventists: A reform movement within the Church of the Seventh Day Adventists, which emerged in the years of the First World War in Germany. The followers of the movement reject using arms and giving oaths of allegiance. There are numerous followers on the territory of the former USSR, also known as members of the Church of True and Free Seventh Day Adventists [Tserkov vernykh i svobodnykh adventistov 7-go dnya] and Seventh Day Adventists of True Remainder [Adventisty 7-go dnya vernogo ostatka].
3 See Polian, 2002.
4 Since no documents directly validating such allegations are available today, we are not in a position to make judgements on how well grounded such suspicions are.

Afterword

AT THE CROSSROADS OF GEOGRAPHY AND HISTORY

The book by Pavel Polian, *Against Their Will,* is the first systematic research of mass forced migrations in the USSR.

The multi-million-strong movement of human mass over the entire territory of the USSR constituted an inseparable part of the 70-year-long economic, social and political history of the country. Undoubtedly, not all migrations were literally "forced," but the question is whether they were absolutely voluntary. Any self-initiated movement of people within the country—putting aside going abroad—was complicated in the Soviet times, to say it mildly. Mass movement of peasants to cities took place as early as the 1930s (the USSR urban population grew from 26 up to 56 million persons in the period of 1926 through 1939). However, who can tell to what extent this movement was voluntary, and to what extent it represented a flight dictated by the desertion of the countryside through famine, forced collectivization, the infringement of rights practiced in collective farms, and threat of political repression?

At the end of the 1930s, Stalin made a public statement: "...there have been no unemployed and homeless peasants that strayed from their villages and live in fear of hunger [...] for a long time now [...] Today we can only talk about asking the *kolkhozy* to meet our request and let at least a million and a half young collective farmers annually leave in order to develop our growing industry." [Report on the Communist Party Central Committee activities at the 8th Party Congress, 10 March 1939. *Voprosy leninizma* no.11 (Moscow, 1952): 625–626.]

By no means can one discern even an allusion to one's "free will" in these words, uttered by Stalin in his favorite hypocritical manner. One could leave if they "let" one leave. To either drag or prohibit is the Prishibeyev[1] wisdom of the "migration policy" practiced during many Soviet decades with its planned voluntary resettlements, with passports issued to some citizens and not to others, with the "passport regime," with *propiska* regulations, with restricted towns, with exit visas and so on.

Even against this medieval—and not quite yet extinct today—background, two historical tragedies, which affected millions of USSR citizens in the first half of the 20th century, still stand out as the most large-scale repressive operations carried out on social and ethnic grounds. These are dekulakization and the deportation of entire peoples. It is these events that P. Polian examines in his book, without omitting "combined" instances, i.e., repression administered based on both social and ethnic grounds (for example, directed against the Lithuanian, Latvian and Estonian "bourgeois") or less known to the Russian-speaking audience the internment of German civilians and citizens of other countries at the end of the Second World War, along with other precedents of forced migrations on a smaller or larger scale.

Although these tragic events are known to virtually everybody today, there are still only a few thorough research works written about them. One may get an impression that the topic had been exhausted and closed once and for all by A. Solzhenitsyn. In reality, this is far from the actual state of things. And whereas the heights of *Gulag Archipelago* can hardly be expected to be achieved again, the archives that have become accessible nowadays open new opportunities for serious research and deeper knowledge and understanding of the events that were taking place in the Soviet Union in the 1920–1950s.

Pavel Polian is among the few authors that—through their creative work—keep asserting that it is not time yet for the pages of so recent a history to be turned. It must be noted, however, that P. Polian is not a professional historian, but an expert on economy and geography in the classical sense, dealing with a wide range of geographic issues reflected in a score of books and nearly three hundred articles. However, in recent years the researcher has manifested clear adherence to historical—or, rather, historico–geographic—analysis of large-scale and, as a rule, barely researched events and phenomena of the 20th century. The reading audience is already familiar with his monograph published in 1996 under the title "Victims of Two Dictatorships," a historico–geographic depiction of the experience of the POWs and the Ostarbeiter. The book represents a detailed account of the tragedy of forced stay and labor of Soviet POWs and civilian workers in the Third Reich and their similarly forced repatriation to the USSR (there is a short German-language version under the title "Deported Home," issued by the Vienna-Munich publishing house, Oldenburg).

Pavel Polian's long-lasting commitment to the problem of forced migrations, his scrupulous work with a variety of sources (remarkably, his book *Against Their Will* is based primarily on documents, already published but insufficiently systematized and analyzed) and evident determination to avoid hasty conclusions, allowed the researcher to produce a monograph that demonstrates two essential achievements.

First, it represents a sizable well-systematized collection of factual data, which renders the book an especially valuable reference guide on the issues pertaining to forced migrations in the USSR under the rule of Stalin (the summarizing chronological tables given as supplements are particularly noteworthy in this respect). Having critically processed an immense amount of sources and archival materials, Polian presents the reader with essential information and data, indispensable for any student of Soviet history.

Second, the book is remarkable for its interpretation of the facts in the context of the objective social reality of the years in question. The author's inherent human feeling of horror and citizenly resentment still remain in the background: in the first place he is focused on analyzing the logic behind the actions taken by the authorities, which were affiliated with the repressive apparatus and launched a war against their own people on a scale rarely encountered in history.

The book by Polian represents an interesting and quite original synthesis of historical and geographic approaches, of chronological and spatial perspectives. Polian shows the "geographic" image of the repressive operations with an unprecedented thoroughness. It is not only the "geographic" design developed by the authorities that is analyzed in the book, but also the "geographic" outcomes and practical implementation of that design, the outcomes that can still be observed in all their poignancy today. The author remarks that "the origins of some of today's hot spots, for example the Ossetian–Ingush conflict, can be traced down to the deportation policy of the Soviet state."

The work is saturated with the understanding of the undeniable (although, regrettably, often overlooked by many researchers) fact that no major event of Russian or Soviet history can be adequately described, comprehended and examined without analyzing its geographical aspect, without demonstration of its regional structure and regional features.

Mass repression against innocent people, often indiscriminate of either their age or gender, was carried out in the world's largest country, which has been making hard, yet vain, efforts to cultivate its vast territory for centuries. Whatever original motives had been behind the mass repression it was only a question of time before the process acquired a form that accurately fitted into the centuries-long tradition of territorial expansion. And that repression was so precisely and conventionally pursued that the physical outcome of opening up the wilderness was assured, at least as effectively as can be through the use of slave labor in the 20th century.

The author makes a reasonable observation pointing to the fact that—having inherited the essential age-old "experience" of the Russian Empire—the deportation policy of the USSR was closely linked with the practice of forced labor usage and can be comprehended only in conjunction with the planned voluntary resettlement operations and the GULAG activities.

The very topic itself, dealt with by P. Polian in his book, is far from becoming a frozen stagnant historical issue, and has not even today lost its topicality. Regrettably, bloody conflicts between the peoples that developed mutual hostility as a result of the deportations are still all too frequent. Every day newspaper reports may contribute new "colors" to the theme, and the author carefully monitors all such developments.

It seems to me that, all in all, the author managed to produce a book designed for a broad audience, and not merely an academic "monograph"—although valuable—intended for a relatively narrow circle of experts. In his work, the author successfully combined a strict academic style and methodology with a lively language and

high-quality journalistic technique. Ultimately, the material presented cannot fail but to grip any potential reader who holds an interest
in history.

Anatoly Vishnevsky

NOTES

1 Prishibeyev—the main character of the satiric story "Unter Prishibeyev" by
A. Chekhov.

Supplement 1

REPRESSIVE FORCED MIGRATIONS IN THE USSR
(THE DATA ARE ROUNDED OFF)*

Date Y	M	D	Target group	Total (thousands persons)	Regions of departure	Destinations
1920	04	17	The Terek Cossacks	45	8 *stanitsa* settlements along the Terek river	Ukraine, the north of the European part of the USSR
1922	09		Philosophers and other humanity scholars	0.1	Petrograd, Moscow, Kazan	Stettin (Germany)
1924– 1925			Former estate- and land-owners	No data	North Caucasus and other regions	
1930			Socially dangerous elements from frontier zones of the UkSSR and BSSR	18	22 km zone along the western border of the USSR	West Siberia, and the Far East
1930	02–04		1st and 2nd-category kulaks	472	The blanket collectivization regions	The North Kray, the Urals, West Siberia
	03–04; 08–10		3rd-category kulaks	250	Nizhny Novgorod Kray, Low Volga Kray, Central Volga Kray, North Caucasus Kray, Far East Kray, the Central-Chernozem Oblast, the West Obl. and other regions	Within the regions of previous residence
	05–12		1st and 2nd-category kulaks	30	The blanket collectivization regions	Siberia, Kazakhstan The Stavropol and
1931	01–02		1st and 2nd-category kulaks	45	Kuban maritime, and forest and mountain regions	Salsk districts of North Caucasus Kray

* The supplement presents recently found data on some deportation operations which were not included in the main text.

Y	Date M	D	Target group	Total (thousands persons)	Regions of departure	Destinations
	03–04; 05–09		1st and 2nd-category kulaks	1,230	Ukraine, the North Caucasus and other blanket collectivization regions	The Urals, the North Kray, Siberia, Kazakhstan
1932	11–12		Peasants (for "subversions")	45	*Stanitsa* settlements: Poltavskaya (Krasnoarmeyskaya), Medvedovskaya, Urupskaya	The North Kray
1933			Nomadic Kazakhs	Around 200	Kazakhstan	Moved to China, Mongolia, Iran, Afghanistan, Turkey
			Kulaks	268	Various regions	West Siberia, the Urals, Kazakhstan and other regions
1935	02–05		Ingermanland Finns	30(?)	The Leningrad Obl., frontier zone	The Vologda Obl., Tajik SSR, Kazakh SSR, West Siberia
	02–03		Poles and Germans (predominantly) from the Kiev and Vinnitsa Obl.	412	The Kiev and Vinnitsa Obl. Ukrainian SSR, frontier zone	Eastern regions of the Ukrainian SSR
	No data		Kulaks	23	The North Caucasus	Various regions
1936	05		Poles and Germans	45	Frontier zones of the Ukrainian SSR	The Karaganda and other Obl. of the Kazakh SSR
	Circa 10		Kulaks	5	The Daghestan and Chechen–Ingush ASSR	The Kyrgyz and Kazakh SSR
1937	07		Kurds and others	2	Frontier zones of Georgia, Armenia, Azerbaijan, Turkmenistan, Uzbekistan and Tajikistan	The Kyrgyz and Kazakh SSR
	09–10		Koreans	172	Spassk, Posyet, Grodekovo, Birobidzhan, Vladivostok, the Buryat–Mongol ASSR, Chita Obl.	The Kazakh SSR (towns and settlements of the northern part), Uzbek SSR
	09–10		Chinese, repatriates from Harbin and others	9	Southern part of the Far East	The Kazakh SSR, Uzbek SSR

Date Y	M	D	Target group	Total (thousands persons)	Regions of departure	Destinations
1938	No data		Iranian Jews	6	The Mary Obl. (the Turkmen SSR)	Northern (desert) regions of the Turkmen SSR
1940	01		Iranians	No data	Frontier zones of the Azerbaijan SSR	The Kazakh SSR
	02	10	Poles	Around 140	Western parts of the UkSSR and BSSR	North of the European part of the USSR, the Urals, Siberia
	04	09, 13	Poles	61	Western parts of the UkSSR and BSSR	The Kazakh SSR, part of the Uzbek SSR
	06	29	Refugees from Poland	75	Western parts of the UkSSR and BSSR	North of the European part of the USSR, the Urals, Siberia
	07	05–10	Foreign nationals		The Murmansk Obl.	The Karel–Finn ASSR, Altay Kray
1941	05	22	Counter-revolutionaries and nationalists	11	Western Ukraine	The South-Kazakhstan Obl., Krasnoyarsk Kray, the Omsk and Novosibirsk Obl.
	06	12–13	Counter-revolutionaries and nationalists	30	The Moldavian SSR, Ismail and Chernovtsy Obl.	The Kazakh SSR, Komi ASSR, Krasnoyarsk Kray, the Omsk and Novosibirsk Obls.
		14	Counter-revolutionaries and nationalists	18	Lithuania	Altay Kray and the Novosibirsk Obl., Kazakh SSR, Komi ASSR
		14	Counter-revolutionaries and nationalists	17	Latvia	Krasnoyarsk Kray, the Novosibirsk Obl., Kazakh SSR (the Karaganda Obl.)
		14	Counter-revolutionaries and nationalists	10	Estonia	Kirov and Novosibirsk Obl.
		19/20	Counter-revolutionaries and nationalists	21	Western Belorussia	
	06	07	Administratively exiled on the basis of their unreliability (for a 10-year term)		RSFSR oblasts, in which martial law was declared under the Supreme Soviet Presidium decree of 22 June 1941	No data

	Date		Target group	Total (thousands persons)	Regions of departure	Destinations
Y	M	D				
	08	end	Germans	53	Crimean ASSR	Ordzhonikidze Kray and the Rostov Obl.
	09	03–20	Germans	439	The Volga German ASSR, Saratov and Stalingrad Obl.	The Kazakh SSR, Krasnoyarsk Kray, Altay Kray, Novosibirsk and Omsk Obls.
			Finns and Germans	91	The Leningrad Obl.	Krasnoyarsk Kray, the Novosibirsk and Omsk Obls., Kazakh SSR, Altay Kray
		15–20	Germans	36	Moscow, the Moscow and Rostov Obls.	The Kazakh SSR
	09–10	25.09–10.10	Germans	Around 138	Krasnodar Kray, Ordzhonikidze Kray, the Tula Obl., Kabardian–Balkar ASSR and North-Ossetian ASSR (in fact also the Crimean residents that had been evacuated to Krasnodar Kray earlier)	Krasnoyarsk Kray, the Irkutsk Obl., Kazakh SSR
		25.09–10.10	Germans	110	The Zaporozhye, Stalino, Voroshilovgrad Obls.	The Kazakh SSR, Astrakhan Obl.
	10	15–22	Germans	5	The Voronezh Obl.	The Novosibirsk, Omsk Obls.
		15–30	Germans	46	The Georgian, Azerbaijani, and Armenian SSR	The Kazakh SSR, Novosibirsk Obl.
		25–30	Germans	6	The Daghestan and Chechen–Ingush ASSR	The Kazakh SSR
	11		Germans	No data	The Kalmyk ASSR	
1942	01	28–29	Italians	No data	The Kerch Peninsula, Crimea, Mariupol (presumably)	The Kazakh SSR Akmolinsk Obl.

Y	Date M	D	Target group	Total (thousands persons)	Regions of departure	Destinations
	03		Germans	No data	The Kharkov, Crimea, Dnepropetrovsk, Odessa, Kalinin Obls.	No data
			Ingermanland Finns	around 9	The Leningrad Obl.	The Irkutsk Obl., Krasnoyarsk Kray, Yakut ASSR
	04		Greeks, Romanians and others		The Crimea, North Caucasus	
	06		Germans, Romanians, Crimean Tatars, foreign nationals (Greeks)	No data	Krasnodar Kray	No data
1943	08	09	Karachais ("gang leaders" and "active bandits")	0.5	The Karachai–Circassian AO	Beyond the Obl. boundaries
	11	02	Karachais	around 70	The Karachai–Circassian AO	The Kazakh SSR (the South-Kazakhstan and Dzhambul Obls.), Kyrgyz SSR
	12	28–31	Kalmyks	around 93	The Kalmyk ASSR	Altay and Krasnoyarsk Kr., Novosibirsk, Omsk Obls.
1944	02	23–29	Chechens (first trains)	393	The Chechen–Ingush ASSR and Daghestan ASSR	The Kazakh SSR, Kyrgyz SSR
		23–29	Ingushetians (first trains)	91	The Chechen–Ingush ASSR, Vladikavkaz	The Kazakh SSR, Kyrgyz SSR
	03	08	Balkars (first trains)	38	The Kabardian–Balkar ASSR	The Kazakh SSR, Kyrgyz SSR
		25	Kalmyks	3	The Rostov Obl.	The Novosibirsk, Omsk Obl.
	04 (?)	25	Kurds, Azerbaijanis	3	Tbilisi	The Tsalka, Borchalo and Karayaz districts of the Georgian USSR
	05	05–10	Balkars	0.1	The Klukhori district of the Georgian USSR	The Kazakh SSR, Kyrgyz SSR
		18	The Crimean Tatars	182	The Crimean ASSR	The Uzbek SSR

Y	Date M	D	Target group	Total (thousands persons)	Regions of departure	Destinations
	05–06		Crimea's peoples (Greeks, Bulgarians, Armenians, Turks and others)	42	The Crimean ASSR	The Uzbek SSR (?)
	05–07		Kalmyks	26	Northern and eastern regions	The European part of the RSFSR (the Saratov, Voronezh Obls., Krasnodar Kray), the Ukrainian SSR
	06	04	Kalmyks	1	The Stalingrad Obl.	The Sverdlovsk Obl.
		20	Kabardians – family members of collaborators that left with Germans	2	The Kabardian ASSR	The Dzhambul and South-Kazakhstan Obl.
	07	27	Bulgarians, Armenians, Greeks	around 4	The Crimea	The Uzbek SSR
			"Truely Orthodox Christians"	1	The Ryazan, Voronezh and Orel Obls.	The Tomsk and Tyumen Obls., Krasnoyarsk Kray
	08–09		Poles	Around 30	Urals, Siberia, the Kazakh SSR	The Ukrainian SSR, the European part of the RSFSR
	11	15–18	Meskhetian Turks, Kurds and Khemshins	Around 92	The Georgian SSR	The Uzbek, Kazakh and Kyrgyz SSR
		25–26	The Laz and frontier zone residents	1	Adjaria	The Uzbek, Kazakh and Kyrgyz SSR
	12		Family members of the Volksdeutsche that voluntarily left with Germans	1	Cities of the Caucasus Minvody region	The Novosibirsk Obl. (according to other sources, the Tajik SSR)
1945	01	25	Traitors and enemy's abettors from the Caucasus Minvody region	2	The Caucasus Minvody region	The Tajik SSR
1947	08		Families of convicted and killed OUN members	No data	Western Ukraine	
	09		OUN members		Western Ukraine	
1948	05	22	Kulak bandits and bandit abettors	49	The Lithuanian SSR	Krasnoyarsk Kray, Irkutsk Obl., Buryat–Mongol ASSR

Y	Date M	D	Target group	Total (thousands persons)	Regions of departure	Destinations
	06		Greek, "Dashnak" Armenians	58	The Black Sea coast region	The Kazakh SSR (the South-Kazakhstan and Dzhambul Obls.)
	06		"Decree spongers"	16	No data	No data
	10		OUN members	175 (including those deported in September 1947)	Western Ukraine	
	10		Kulaks	1	The Ismail Obl.	The Tomsk Obl.
1949	01	29	Kulak bandits and bandit abettors	42	The Latvian SSR	The Omsk and Amur Obls.
		29	Kulak bandits and bandit abettors	20	The Estonian SSR	Krasnoyarsk Kray, Irkutsk Obl.
		29	Kulak bandits and bandit abettors	32	The Lithuanian SSR	Krasnoyarsk Kray, Irkutsk Obl.
	05–06		Dashnaks, Turks and Greeks holding Turkish, Greek or Soviet citizenship, or stateless	No data	The Black Sea coast region, Georgia, Armenia, Azerbaijan	The Kazakh SSR (the South-Kazakhstan and Dzhambul Obls.)
	07	06–07	Kulak bandits and bandit abettors	36	The Moldavian SSR	The Kurgan, Tyumen, Irkutsk, Kemerovo Obls., Altay Kray, Khabarovsk Kray, Buryat–Mongol ASSR
1950	No data		Kulaks charged with banditry (with families)	1.4	The Pskov Obl.	Khabarovsk Kray, Kemerovo Obl.
1951	03		The Basmaches	3	The Tajik SSR	The Kazakh SSR (Kokchetav Obl.)
	04	01–02	Jehovah's Witnesses	3	The Moldavian SSR	The Tomsk Obl.
	10		Kulaks	35	The Baltic republics, Moldavia, Western Ukraine, Western Belarus	Krasnoyarsk Kray, the Yakut ASSR, Tyumen Obl., Kazakh SSR
1952	03–05		Kulaks	6	Western Belarus	The Irkutsk Obl., Kazakh SSR

Supplement 2

CHRONOLOGY OF OFFICIAL LEGISLATIVE ACTS ISSUED BY THE STATE AND PARTY BODIES OF THE USSR AND ITS SUCCESSOR STATES, CONCERNING FORCED MIGRATIONS OR THEIR CONSEQUENCES

Date Y	M	D	Legislative acts and other documents	Archival sources (first publications or references to the sources are indicated in brackets)
1919	1	24	Russian Communist Party Central Committee directive on decossakization	
1922	8	10	All-Union Central Executive Committee decree "On administrative banishment"	(Zaytsev, 1993, 12)
	10	16	All-Union Central Executive Committee decree "On instituting amendments to the Resolutions 'On the GPU' and 'On administrative banishment'"	(Zaytsev, 1993, 104)
1923	1	03	NKVD Resolution "Instruction on the application of the All-Union Central Executive Committee decree 'On administrative banishment'"	(Zaytsev, 1993, 105–106)
1924	5	31	Circular No. 370/166 by People's Commissar of Agriculture Smirnov concerning the banishment of former estate owners and land proprietors from their estates	Mentioned in GASK, h. 217, r. 1, f. 1, sh. 1, 51
	11	28	Circular No. 2887 by People's Commissar of Agriculture Smirnov concerning the banishment of former estate owners and land proprietors from their estates	Mentioned in GASK, h. 217, r. 1, f. 1, sh. 1, 51
1925	3	25	USSR Central Executive Committee resolution concerning banishment of former estate owners and land proprietors from their estates	Mentioned in GASK, h. 217, r. 1, f. 1, sh. 1, 51
1929	9	20	RSFSR Smaller Council of People's Commissars decree "Concerning the banishment of superfluous and—foremost—socially dangerous elements from frontier regions of the RSFSR"	TsGA SPb, h. 100, r. 87, f. 1, sh. 168. (Ken, Rupasov, 2000, 487)
	11	13	UkSSR Council of People's Commissars decree No.20369 "Concerning the banishment of socially dangerous elements from frontier *okrug*s of the UkSSR"	RGAE, h. 5675, r. 1, f. 43, sh. 42–43 (Protocol of the UkSSR Council of People's Commissars No. 46/950)

Date			Legislative acts and other documents	Archival sources
Y	M	D		
		21	USSR Central Executive Committee Presidium resolution "On the declaration of the outlaw status of the officials, USSR citizens abroad, who defected to the camp of the enemies of the working class and peasantry and refused to return to the USSR"	(Zaytsev, 1993, 32–33)
1930	1	11	Instruction concerning the application of the regulations on exile and banishment, employed under the OGPU Special Council resolution	UFSB Current Archive of Altay Kray, Russian Federation, f. 1, sh. 16–17.
		18	OGPU directives No.775 and 776 on intended mass banishment of kulak families	GARF, h. 9414, r. 1, f. 1944, sh. 13 (Ivnitsky, 1996, 108)
		30	Communist Party Central Committee resolution "On measures for liquidation of kulak households in the regions subject to blanket collectivization"	RGASPI, h. 17, r. 162, f. 8, sh. 60, 64–69 (Adibekov, 1994, 147–152)
	2	1	USSR Central Executive Committee and Council of People's Commissars resolutions "On measures for the reinforcement of socialist restructuring of agricultural production in the regions subject to blanket collectivization, and for fighting kulaks"	(Ivnitsky, 1996, 72)
		2	OGPU order No. 44/21 on the organized liquidation of kulaks	GARF, h. 9414, r. 1, f. 1944, sh. 17–25 (Zaytsev, 1993, 107–110; Ivnitsky, 1996, 111)
		4	USSR Central Executive Committee and Council of People's Commissars instruction on measures for dekulakization, the eviction of kulaks and the confiscation of their property	(Ivnitsky, 1996, 72)
	3	4	Leningrad Oblast Communist Party Committee resolution on the resettlement of the local population from the Leningrad Oblast frontier zone	(Kiuru, 1992)
		5	Communist Party Central Committee resolution "Concerning Polish settlements in frontier oblasts"	RGA SPI, h. 17, r. 162, f. 8, sh. 103, 109–110 (Ken, Rupasov, 2000, 508–510)
	4	1	Council of People's Commissars decree on the establishment of a special commission chaired by V. V. Schmidt	(Ivnitsky, 1996, 231)
		1	North Kray Communist Party Committee resolution "On the placement and employment of banished kulaks in the North Kray"	(Ivnitsky, 1996, 232)

Date Y M D	Legislative acts and other documents	Archival sources
1	Narkomzem resolution "On locations for settling kulak households banished from the blanket collectivization regions"	(Ivnitsky, 1996, 237)
10	RSFSR Council of People's Commissars decree "On measures for regulating the temporary and permanent settlement of banished kulaks and their families"	GARF, h. 393, r. 2, f. 1796, sh. 230 (Ivnitsky, 1996, 233, 268)
23	Resolution of Prigorodnyi district executive committee, Leningrad Obl., concerning the banishment of local population	(Gildi, 1996, 26)
8 13	RSFSR Council of People's Commissars decree "On measures for conducting special colonization in the North Kray, Siberia Kray and Urals Oblast"	(Ivnitsky, 1996, 243)
10 3	RSFSR Council of People's Commissars decree on approval of the regulations for special settlements and special resettlers	(Ivnitsky, 1996, 243)
1931 2 1	USSR Central Executive Committee and Council of People's Commissars decree "On authorizing kray (oblast) executive committees of the union republics to banish kulaks from the areas subject to the blanket collectivization of agricultural industry"	
20	Communist Party Central Committee Politburo decree concerning the banishment of 200–300 thousand kulak families	(Ivnitsky, 1996, 181–182)
3 20	Communist Party Central Committee Politburo decree "On kulaks"	RGASPI, h. 17, r. 162, f. 9, sh. 174, 176–178 (Adibekov, 1994, 152–155)
20	Council of People's Commissars decree "On the resettlement of kulak households"	GARF, h. R-5446, r. 57, f. 14, sh. 148 (Krasilnikov et al., 1993, 13)
6 5	Communist Party Central Committee Politburo decree "On the banishment of kulak families from the Leningrad Oblast and Tatarstan"	RGASPI, h. 17, r. 162, f. 10, sh. 66, 74 (Adibekov, 1994, 159)
7 1	Council of People's Commissars decree "On settlement of 'special resettlers'"	GARF, h. R-5446, r. 57, f. 15, sh. 81–83 (Krasilnikov et al., 1993, 14–15)
3	USSR Central Executive Committee resolution on the procedure for the restoration of the rights of banished kulaks	(Krasilnikov et al., 1993, 15–16)

Date Y M D	Legislative acts and other documents	Archival sources
20	Communist Party Central Committee Politburo decree "On kulaks"	RGASPI, h. 17, r. 162, f. 10, sh. 123, 126 (Adibekov, 1994, 159–160)
8 2	Communist Party Central Committee Politburo decree "On special resettlers"	RGASPI, h. 17, r. 162, f. 10, sh. 141, 144–148 (Adibekov, 1994, 161–164)
10	Communist Party Central Committee Politburo decree "On special resettlers"	RGASPI, h. 17, r. 162, f. 10, sh. 151, 154–159 (Adibekov, 1994, 164–169)
16	Council of People's Commissars decree "On special resettlers"	GARF, h. R-5446, r. 57, f. 15, sh. 165–174 (Krasilnikov et al., 1993, 16–23)
30	Communist Party Central Committee Politburo decree "On special resettlers"	RGASPI, h. 17, r. 162, f. 10, sh. 176, 180–181 (Adibekov, 1994, 170–172)
10 25	Temporary regulations on the rights and duties of special resettlers, and on administrative functions of local administrations in the areas of settlement of special resettlers	(Ivnitsky, 1996, 244, with reference to: *Iz istorii raskulachivanya v Karelii v 1930–1931 gg.* [From the history of dekulakization in Karelia in 1930–1931], Petrozavodsk, 1991, 227–232
12 23	Communist Party Central Committee Politburo decree "On the economic employment of special resettlers in Narym Kray"	RGASPI, h. 17, r. 162, f. 11, sh. 102–106 (Adibekov, 1994, 172–175)
28	Council of People's Commissars decree "On the economic employment of special resettlers in Narym Kray"	GARF, h. R-5446, r. 57, f. 16, sh. 193–199 (Krasilnikov et al., 1993, 23–28); TsDNI TO, h. 206, r. 1, f. 1, sh. 8 (Maksheyev, 1997, 17–18)
1932 1 28	Communist Party Central Committee Politburo decree "On special resettlers"	RGASPI, h. 17, r. 162, f. 11, sh. 162, 167–169 (Adibekov, 1994, 175–178)

Date Y M D	Legislative acts and other documents	Archival sources
2 3	Communist Party Central Committee Politburo decree "On special resettlers"	RGASPI, h. 17, r. 162, f. 11, sh. 174, 176–177 (Adibekov, 1994, 178–180)
21	Council of People's Commissars decree "On the hygienic services and social amenities for special resettlers"	GARF, h. R-5446, r. 57, f. 18, sh. 77–79 (Krasilnikov et al., 1993, 29–31)
4 04	Council of People's Commissars decree "On special resettlers"	GARF, h. R-5446, r. 57, f. 19, sh. 7–9 (Krasilnikov et al., 1993, 33–34)
11 16	Tajik SSR Central Executive Committee and Council of People's Commissars decree "On resettlement to Vakhsh"	(Kurbanova, 1993, 67)
12 27	Council of People's Commissars decree "On the introduction of the passport system"	
1933 4 17	Communist Party Central Committee Politburo decree "On organizing OGPU labor settlements"	(Ivnitsky, 1996, 220)
5 8	Communist Party Central Committee instruction No. P-6028 on termination of mass banishment and other forms of repression in the countryside	(Zaytsev, 1993, 110–111)
1934 5 27	All-Union Central Executive Committee decree "On the restoration of the rights of labor settlers"	
1935 3 25	NKVD directive "On the cleansing of the frontier zone of the Leningrad Oblast and Karelia from kulaks and anti-Soviet elements, as a repressive measure"	(Bugay, 1991e; Kiuru, 1992)
1936 1 23	* Council of People's Commissars decree No. 111-21cc "On resettlement from the UkSSR to the Kazakh ASSR"	
2 16	Kazakh SSR CP Central Committee and Council of People's Commissars resolution "On resettlers from Ukraine"	(Eisfeld, Herdt, 1996, s. 26–27)
4 28	* Council of People's Commissars decree No. 776–120cc "On the resettlement of 15,000 Polish and German households from Ukraine and their economic employment in the Kazakh SSR"	GARF, h. R-9479, r. 1, f. 641, sh. 363 (Bugay, 1995, 9–11; Eisfeld, Herdt, 1996, 27–29)
5 20	Communist Party Politburo protocol No. 39, item 242 "Concerning the resettlement of Kulak households from Daghestan and Chechen–Ingushetia"	(Politburo-II, 2001, 767).

Date Y M D	Legislative acts and other documents	Archival sources
21	Council of People's Commissars decree No. 911–150cc on the banishment of 500 kulak households from the Daghestan ASSR and 500 kulak households from the Chechen–Ingush ASSR	GARF, h. R-9479, r. 1, f. 36, sh. 33
1937 7 17	USSR Council of People's Commissars and Central Executive Committee decree No. 103/1127-267cc on establishing special restriction zones along the southern border of the USSR, and on the deportation of foreign citizens and stateless persons (in cases of the presence of compromising evidence)	GARF, h. R-9479, r. 1, f. 597, sh. 292 (Bugay, 1995, 17); APRF, h. 3, r. 58, f. 182, sh. 17–24 (referred to in Artizov, A. et al., *Rehabilitation: The Way It Was*, vol. 2, 99)
8 21	* USSR Council of People's Commissars and Central Executive Committee decree No. 1428-326cc "On the banishment of the Korean population from the Far East Kray frontier districts"	(Bugay, 1992, 142–143)
9 5	* Council of People's Commissars decree No. 1527-349cc "On the procedure for the settlement of financial issues with the Koreans to be resettled to the Kazakh and Uzbek SSR"	GARF, h. 5446, r. 57, f. 52, sh. 29 (Bugay, 1992, 143)
08	Council of People's Commissars decree No. 1539-354cc "On the resettlement of Koreans"	GARF, h. 5446, r. 57, f. 52, sh. 30 (Bugay, 1992, 144)
11	* Council of People's Commissars decree No. 1571-356cc "On estimating expenditures for the resettlement of Koreans from the Far East Kray"	GARF, h. 5446, r. 57, f. 52, sh. 31 (Bugay, 1992, 144)
25	* Council of People's Commissars decree No. 1672-371cc "On deliveries of and compensation for the grain produced by Koreans to be resettled"	
28	* Council of People's Commissars decree No. 1697-77 "On the resettlement of Koreans from the territory of Far East Kray"	
10 7	* Council of People's Commissars decree No. 1722-388cc "On estimating expenditures for the resettlement of the second target group of Koreans from the Far East Kray"	GARF, h. 5446, r. 57, f. 52, sh. 40 (Bugay, 1992, 147)
1938 10 8	Council of People's Commissars decree No. 1084-269cc "On the resettlement of Iranians from the Azerbaijani SSR frontier districts to the Kazakh SSR"	GARF, h. 5446, r. 30, f. 29, sh. 27–28 (Bugay, 1994c) (Zemskov, 1992, 5, 19)
22	Council of People's Commissars decree No. 1143-280c "On the discharge of children aged over 16 years from labor settlements"	

Date Y M D	Legislative acts and other documents	Archival sources
11 06	Kazakh SSR Council of People's Commissars and CP Central Committee resolution "On the reception and placement of 2,000 resettled Iranian households"	GARF, h. 5446, r. 30, f. 29, sh. 6–10 (Bugay, 1994c)
1939 7 3	NKVD directive "On the discharge of the disabled from labor settlements"	(Zemskov, 1992, 5, 19)
10 11	NKVD order No. 001223 "On the banishment of anti-Soviet elements from the Lithuania, Latvia and Estonia"	(*These Names Accuse*, 1982, XXXVI–XXXXI)
12 2	NKVD memo No. 5332 "On the resettlement of all *osadniki* families from Western Ukraine and Belorussia from 15 January 1940"	APRF, h. 3, r. 30, f. 199, sh. 3–5 (Guryanov, 1997a, 117)
4	Communist Party Central Committee Politburo resolution No. P9/158 "On the resettlement of *osadniki* and their employment for timber harvesting under the supervision of the USSR Narkomles"	APRF, h. 3, r. 30, f. 199, sh. 1–2 (Guryanov, 1997a, 117)
5	Council of People's Commissars decree No. 2010-558cc "On the resettlement of *osadniki* and their employment for timber harvesting under the supervision of the USSR Narkomles"	APRF, h. 93, Council of People's Commissars Decree Collection (Guryanov, 1997a, 117)
29	Politburo resolution No. P1/68 "On special resettlers— *osadniki*"	APRF, h. 3, r. 30, f. 199, sh. 30–38 (Guryanov, 1997a, 118)
29	Council of People's Commissars decree No. 2122-617cc approving the "Resolution on special settlement and labor employment of *osadniki* banished from western oblasts of UkSSR and BSSR," "Instruction on the procedure for the resettlement of *osadniki* from the western oblasts of UkSSR and BSSR," "Staff for district and settlement *komendatura*s of the NKVD special settlements"	GARF, h. 9479, r. 1, f. 52, sh. 8–10; h. R-9401, r. 1, f. 4475, sh. 13 (Bugay, 1995, 12) GARF, h. 5446, r. 57, f. 65, sh. 163–165 (Guryanov, 1997a, 118)
1940 1 14	Communist Party Central Committee and Council of People's Commissars decree No. P1/175 "On the additional settlement of special settlers *osadniki* and their labor employment in the mining and timber-harvesting industries under the supervision of the Narkomtsvetmet"	APRF, h. 3, r. 30, f. 199, sh. 47 (Guryanov, 1997a, 118)
19	Ukrainian Communist Party Central Committee Politburo resolution "Issues concerning the banishment of *osadniki*"	(Filippov, 1997, 52)
2 27	Central Red Army Department directive No. 22/181387 "On the procedure for assigning labor-settlement youth to the military registration and enlistment offices"	GARF, h. 9479, r. 1, f. 89, sh. 20 (Zemskov, 1992, 3)

Date Y M D	Legislative acts and other documents	Archival sources
3 2	Communist Party Central Committee Politburo resolution No. P13/114 "On the resettlement of Polish POWs that were imprisoned from the western regions of the UkSSR and BSSR"	APRF, h. 93, Council of People's Commissars Decree Collection (Guryanov, 1997a, 118)
2	Council of People's Commissars decree No. 289-127cc "On the resettlement from western regions of the UkSSR and BSSR of family members of Polish POWs and prisoners" (in practice this was applied to all western regions of the USSR, including the Moldavian SSR)	GARF, h. R-9479, r. 1, f. 52, sh. 12–13 (Passat, 1994, 24; Bugay, 1995, 12); APRF, h. 3, r. 61, f. 861, sh. 93–94 (Guryanov, 1997a, 118)
5	Communist Party Central Committee Politburo resolution concerning the execution of Polish POW officers and imprisoned Polish nationals	APRF, h. 3, r. 67 (Katyn, 2001, 43–44)
4 10	Council of People's Commissars resolution No. 497-177cc approving the instruction for the banishment of persons under the Council of People's Commissars decree of 2 March 1940	GARF, h. R-9479, r. 1, f. 52, sh. 13 (Bugay, 1995, 13); GARF, h. 5446, r. 57, f. 68, sh. 123–124
24	NKVD order without number "On the procedure for the banishment to remote northern areas of the USSR of family members of activists of counter-revolutionary organizations of Ukrainian, Belorussian, Polish nationalists and persons in hiding"	GARF, h. 9401, r. 2, f. 1, sh. 284–288
6 23	NKVD order No. 00761 "On the banishment of citizens of foreign nationalities from the city of Murmansk and Murmansk Oblast"	GARF, h. 9401, r. 2, f. 1, sh. 207–210 (*Neues Leben*, 28 August 1991; facsimile – Kotsonis, 1997, 83, 89).
1941 5 14	Council of People's Commissars and Communist Party Central Committee decree No. 1299-526cc (?) "Concerning the arrests and 20-year exile and settlement in USSR remote areas of family members of activists of Ukrainian and Polish counter-revolutionary nationalist organizations" (with the instruction to conduct discussion of similar operations in Western Belorussia)	GARF, h. 9479, r. 1, f. 57, sh. 40–41 (Guryanov, 1997a, 120)
14	Council of People's Commissars and Communist Party Central Committee decree No. 1299-526 "Concerning seizure of counter-revolutionary organizations in western regions of the Ukrainian SSR"	(Guryanov, 1997, 143).

Date			Legislative acts and other documents	Archival sources
Y	M	D		

	6	14	Plan on the measures for the transportation, placement and labor employment of special target groups banished from the Lithuanian, Latvian, Estonian and Moldavian SSR (approved by Beria)	(Passat, 1994, 23–24)
		22	USSR Supreme Soviet Presidium decree No. 277 "On martial law"	(Ved. VS, 1941, No. 29)
		22	USSR Supreme Soviet Presidium decree No. 278 "On declaring martial law" in some parts of the USSR	(Sovetskaya Yustitsiya. 1941, No. 24–25)
		27	Communist Party Central Committee decree "On the procedure for the transportation and placement of human target groups and valuable property"	(Izvestiya TsK KPSS 1990, No. 6, 208–213)
	7	4	NKVD and NKGB directive No. 238-131 "On measures for the banishment of socially dangerous persons from the districts declared under martial law"	(Zaytsev, 1993, 112)
	8	12	Council of People's Commissars and Communist Party Central Committee decree No. 2060-935cc "On the placement of Volga Germans in Kazakhstan"	RGASPI, h. 17, r. 3, f. 1042, sh. 20 (Milova, 1995, 15)
		12	USSR Supreme Soviet Presidium decree No. 19-160 "On the amnesty for Polish citizens held in custody on the territory of the USSR"	GARF, h. 7523, r. 4, f. 49, sh. 128
		15	Evacuation Council resolution concerning the evacuation of Germans from the Crimean ASSR	GARF, h. 9479, r. 1, f. 86, sh. 122–123 (German, A., Kurochkin, 2000, 29)
		17	USSR Supreme Soviet Presidium decree on the discharge of Poles from special settler status	(Bugay, 1995, 192–193)
		19	NKVD directive on allowing the Poles discharged from special settler status to reside on the territory of the USSR	(Bugay, 1995, 192–193)
		26	Council of People's Commissars and Communist Party Central Committee decree "On the resettlement of all Germans of the Volga German ASSR, Saratov and Stalingrad Obl. to other krays and oblasts"	(German, A., 1996, 139)
		26	Leningrad Front Military Council resolution No. 196cc on the evacuation of the Finnish population	GARF, h. R-9479, r. 1, f. 896, sh. 119 (Bugay, 1995, 191)
		27	NKVD order No. 001158 "On measures for conducting the resettlement of Germans of the Volga German ASSR, Saratov and Stalingrad Obl." with a corresponding instruction delivered	GARF, h. R-9401, r. 2, f. 1, sh. 415–125 (German, A., 1996, 138)
		28	USSR Supreme Soviet Presidium decree No. 21-160 "On the resettlement of Germans residing in the Volga region"	GARF, h. 7523, r. 4, f. 49, sh. 151–154; also r. 82, f. 146, sh.

Date			Legislative acts and other documents	Archival sources
Y	M	D		

				184, 185 (*Bolshevik* 30 August 1941; *Nachrichten*, 30 August 1941; Ved. VS, 1941, No.38)
		30	* Council of People's Commissars decree No. 2016-95 "On approving the instruction with regard to the procedure for the reception of the property of resettled collective farms and collective farmers"	
		30	NKVD order No. 001175 "On measures for conducting the operation for the resettlement of Germans and Finns from the Leningrad suburbs to the Kazakh SSR"	GARF, h. R-9401, r. 2, f. 1, sh. 426–427
		31	Communist Party Central Committee Politburo decree concerning Germans residing on the territory of Ukraine	(*Izvestiya* TsK KPSS. 1990, No.9, 195)
	9	3	Council of People's Commissars decree No. 2030/920 concerning resettlement to the Saratov and Stalingrad oblasts	(Bugay, 1999, 88)
		6	Council of People's Commissars and Communist Party Central Committee decree "On the administrative structure of the territory of the former Volga German ASSR"	(German, A., 1996, 141)
		6	* State Defense Committee resolution No. 363cc "On the banishment of Germans from the city of Moscow and the Moscow and Rostov Oblasts"	RGASPI, h. 644, r. 1, f. 8, sh. 171–172 (Auman, Chebotareva, 1993, 161–162)
		7	USSR Supreme Soviet Presidium decree No. 21/160 "On the administrative structure of the territory of the former Volga German ASSR"	GARF, h. 7523, r. 4, f. 49, sh. 163 (Ved. VS, 1941, No.40)
		8	NKVD order No. 001237 "Concerning measures for conducting the operation for the resettlement of Germans from Moscow and the Moscow Oblast" with a corresponding instruction delivered	GARF, h. R-9401, r. 2, f. 1, sh. 430–431 (*Neues Leben*, 28 August 1991)
		12	* Council of People's Commissars and Communist Party Central Committee decree No. 2060-935cc "On the placement of Volga Germans in Kazakhstan"	
		21	* State Defense Committee resolution No. 698cc "On the resettlement of Germans from Krasnodar, Ordzhonikidze Krays, the Tula Oblast, Kabardian–Balkar and North Ossetian ASSR"	RGASPI, h. 644, r. 1, f. 10, sh. 42–43 (Auman, Chebotareva, 1993, 164–165)
		22	* State Defense Committee resolution No. 702cc "On the resettlement of Germans from the Zaporozhye, Stalino and Voroshilovgrad Oblasts"	RGASPI, h. 644, r. 1, f. 10, sh. 62–63 (Milova, 1995, 15)

Date Y M D	Legislative acts and other documents	Archival sources
22	NKVD order No. 001347 "On measures for conducting the operation for the resettlement of Germans from Krasnodar, Ordzhonikidze Krays, the Tula Oblast, Kabardian–Balkar and North Ossetian ASSR"	(Bugay, 1992, 55–57)
23	NKVD order No. 001354 "On measures for conducting the operation for the resettlement of Germans from the Zaporozhye, Stalino and Voroshilovgrad Oblasts of the Ukrainian SSR"	GARF, h. R-9401, r. 2, f. 1, sh. 461–464; RGASPI, h. 644, r. 1, f. 10, sh. 63 (Auman, Chebotareva, 1993, 165)
26	NKVD order No. 001398 "On the reorganization of NKVD construction battalions into labor columns"	
10 07	* Council of People's Commissars decree No. 2130-972cc "On forming labor columns from persons subject to the army draft"	
8	* State Defense Committee resolution No. 743cc "On the resettlement of Germans from the Voronezh Oblast"	RGASPI, h. 644, r. 1, f. 10, sh. 195 (Auman, Chebotareva, 1993, 166)
8	* State Defense Committee resolution No. 744cc "On the resettlement of Germans from the Georgian, Azerbaijani and Armenian SSR"	RGASPI, h. 644, r. 1, f. 10, sh. 195 (Auman, Chebotareva, 1993, 167)
22	* State Defense Committee resolution No. 827cc "On the resettlement of Germans from the Daghestan and Chechen–Ingush ASSR"	RGASPI, h. 644, r. 1, f. 12, sh. 176 (Auman, Chebotareva, 1993, 168)
25	State Defense Committee resolution "On the establishment of the committee for evacuation"	(*Izvestiya* TsK KPSS 1991, No.2, 219)
30	* Council of People's Commissars directive No. 57k "On the resettlement of ethnic Germans from industrial to agricultural areas"	
11 3	* Council of People's Commissars directive No. 84c "On the resettlement of Germans from the Kalmyk ASSR"	GARF, h. 5446, r. 56c, f. 42, sh. 59–60 (Milova, 1995, 16)
14	* Council of People's Commissars directive No. 180c "On the resettlement of ethnic Germans from frontier regions to the front rear areas within the Chita Oblast"	GARF, h. 5446, r. 56c, f. 43, sh. 45 (Milova, 1995, 16)
21	* Council of People's Commissars directive No. 280c concerning the deportation of repatriated Germans	APRF, h. 3, r. 58, f. 182, sh. 17–24 (referred to *Rehabilitation: The Way It Was*, vol. 2, 100)

Date Y M D	Legislative acts and other documents	Archival sources
24	State Defense Committee resolution on the resettlement of Poles from the northern areas of the USSR to the Kazakh SSR	
26	Council of People's Commissars decree "Concerning measures for agriculture in the former Volga German ASSR"	GARF, h. A-327, r. 2, f. 393. sh. 1–6. (Bugay, 1999, 88)
1942 1 6	Council of People's Commissars and Communist Party Central Committee resolution No. 19cc concerning the resettlement of 50 thousand ethnic Germans from other regions of the country to fishing and fish-processing enterprises	GARF, h. 9479, r. 1, f. 108 (German, A., Kurochkin, 2000, 40)
10	* State Defense Committee resolution No. 1123cc "On the employment of German resettlers aged from 17 to 50 years"	RGASPI, h. 644, r. 1, f. 19, sh. 49 (Auman, Chebotareva, 1993, 169)
12	NKVD order declaring the "Regulations concerning the order of the supervision of, discipline and labor employment of German resettlers mobilized into work columns"	GARF. h. 9414, r. 1, f. 1146, sh. 34–38 back. (GULAG 1918–1960, 129–132)
28, 29	Unknown legislative act concerning the deportation of Italians from the Kerch Peninsula, Crimea and (presumably) Mariupol to the Akmolinsk Obl., Kazakh SSR	Presentation by M. Le Conte-Libedinskaya and V. Malyshev at the conference "Repression against Foreigners in the USSR: the Case of Italians," Milan, 10 April 2002 (see also www.gulag-italia.it)
2 14	* State Defense Committee resolution No. 1281cc "On the mobilization of male Germans of the call-up age of 17 to 50 years, permanently residing in oblasts, krays, autonomous and union republics"	RGASPI, h. 644, r. 1, f. 21, sh. 51 (Auman, Chebotareva, 1993, 170)
3 9	Leningrad Front Military Council resolution No. 00713 "On the evacuation of the Finnish population from the city of Leningrad and surrounding areas	(Bugay, 1995, 191)
20	Leningrad Front Military Council resolution No. 00714 "On the evacuation of the Finnish population from the city of Leningrad and surrounding areas"	(Bugay, 1995, 45)
4 2	Approval by Chernyshev of not resettling the Karaims from the Crimea	(Bugay, 1995, 201)

Date			Legislative acts and other documents	Archival sources
Y	M	D		

		3	Leningrad Front Military Council resolution "On the requisitioning of ethnic Finnish military service members from the front-line army forces and their transfer to the NKVD labor battalions and columns"	(Kiuru, 1992)
		11	State Defense Committee resolution No. 1575cc allowing the call-up of former kulaks for military service	
5	5		USSR Supreme Soviet Presidium decree "Concerning the renaming of some districts and towns of the Saratov Obl."	(Bugay, 1999, 86, with reference to: the Current Archive of the Ministry for Nationalities Affairs of the Russian Federation)
		29	* State Defense Committee resolution No. 1828cc "On the additional banishment of socially dangerous Germans, Romanians, Crimean Tatars and foreign citizens (Greeks) from Krasnodar Kray and the Rostov Oblast"	RGASPI, h. 644, r. 1, f. 36, sh. 170 (Auman, Chebotareva, 1993, 171; facsimile – Kotsonis, 1997, 88)
		30	State Defense Committee resolution No. 1828-cc "On the banishment of the German population from different regions of the country"	
6	5		USSR Supreme Soviet Presidium decree "Concerning the renaming of some settlements and village soviets of the Saratov Obl."	(Bugay, 1999, 86, with reference to: the Current Archive of the Ministry for Nationalities Affairs of the Russian Federation)
		20	USSR Council of People's Commissars directive "On the banishment of the German population from some regions of the country"	
7	9		State Defense Committee resolution "On the banishment of socially dangerous elements from Leningrad and its suburban districts"	(Kiuru, 1992)
8	20		NKVD order "On the order of convoying by the USSR NKVD convoy detachments of the trains carrying special resettlers" with a corresponding distributed instruction	GARF, h. 9401, r. la, f. 118, sh. 145–149
		26	State Defense Committee resolution "On the mandatory evacuation of the German and Finnish population from Leningrad frontier districts"	(Kiuru, 1992)

Date Y M D	Legislative acts and other documents	Archival sources
10 7	* State Defense Committee resolution No. 2383cc "On the additional mobilization of Germans for the people's economic needs"	RGASPI, h. 644, r. 1, f. 61, sh. 138–140 (Auman, Chebotareva, 1993, 172–173)
14	* State Defense Committee resolution No. 2409 "On the application of State Defense Committee Resolutions No. 1123 and No. 1281 to other citizens of the ethnic backgrounds of the nations fighting against the USSR"	
24	Council of People's Commissars and CPSU Central Committee decree No. 1702 "On the mobilization of the banished German population to the labor army"	
24	USSR Council of People's Commissars and Party Central Committee decree No. 1732 "On the resettlement of workers and special resettlers to the northern part of the country for employment as labor force"	RGASPI, h. 17, r. 3, f. 1042, sh. 259–286 (German, A., Kurochkin, 2000, 40)
1943 1 15	Council of People's Commissars decree "On the issuing of passports to former Polish citizens"	(Bugay, 1995, 194)
3 2	State Defense Committee resolution No. 3857cc "On the mobilization of the resettled German population to the labor army"	
4 15	NKVD and Prosecutor's Office of the USSR Joint directive No. 52-6927 "On the forceful banishment of the families of 'gang leaders' and 'active bandits' beyond the boundaries of the Karachai–Circassian Autonomous Oblast"	(Bugay, 1995, 61)
7 30	Agreement with the Polish government in exile on the formation of a Polish army on the territory of the USSR, and amnesty for all Polish citizens	(Bugay, 1995, 194)
8 9	The banishment of 110 families (472 persons) from the Karachai–Circassian AO under the Directive of 15 April 1943	(Bugay, 1995, 61)
19	* State Defense Committee resolution No. 3960cc "On the mobilization of the resettled German population to the labor army"	RGASPI, h. 644, r. 1, f. 146, sh. 108–109 (Auman, Chebotareva, 1993, 173–175)
10 12	USSR Supreme Soviet Presidium decree No. 115/136 "On the liquidation of the Karachai–Circassian AO and the new administrative structure of its territory"	GARF, h. 7523, r. 4, f. 198, sh. 79–80 (DNS-1, No.6)
14	* Council of People's Commissars decree No. 1118-342cc "USSR NKVD issues concerning the banishment of persons of Karachai nationality from the Karachai AO"	(Bugay, 1995, 61–62)

Date			Legislative acts and other documents	Archival sources
Y	M	D		

		15	Council of People's Commissars decree No. 1118-346cc "On the preparation for the reception of Kalmyk special resettlers in Altay and Krasnoyarsk Krays, and the Omsk and Novosibirsk Oblasts"	(Bugay, 1995, 69)
	11	6	* Council of People's Commissars decree No. 1221-368 "On the order of populating districts of the former Karachai AO, Stavropol Kray"	
	12	27	USSR Supreme Soviet Presidium decree No. 115/144 "On the liquidation of the Kalmyk ASSR and establishment of the Astrakhan Obl. under the RSFSR jurisdiction, and on administrative structure of its territory"	GARF, h. 7523, r. 4, f. 200, sh. 151–152
		28	Council of People's Commissars decree No. 1432-425 (525c) "On the banishment of Kalmyks residing in the Kalmyk ASSR to Altay and Krasnoyarsk Krays, and the Omsk and Novosibirsk Oblasts"	
1944	1	7	NKVD order No. 0013 "On the establishment of a special Chernogorsky camp in Krasnoyarsk Kray" (for the Volksdeutsche). According to another version: NKVD directive No. 20/b (with the Volksdeutsche designating former Soviet citizens—along with their family members—that became German citizens and were active accomplices of the occupiers)	GARF, h. 9401, r. la, f. 157, sh. 7–8; See also: APRF, h. 3, r. 58, f. 182, sh. 17–24 (referred to *Rehabilitation: The Way It Was*, vol. 2, 101)
		29	NKVD instruction "On the order of conducting the banishment of Chechens and Ingushetians"	(Bugay, Gonov, 1998, 142)
		31	* State Defense Committee resolution No. 5073cc "On measures for the placement of special resettlers within the Kazakh and Kyrgyz SSR"	GARF, h. 7523, r. 4, f. 49, sh. 163 (Bugay, Gonov, 1998, 143)
		31	* State Defense Committee resolution No. 5074cc "On measures for the purchases of cattle and agricultural goods in the North Caucasus"	
	2	26	NKVD order No. 00186cc "On measures for the banishment of the Balkar population from the Kabardian–Balkar ASSR"	GARF, h. 9401, r. l, f. 3, sh. 315–319 (Bugay, 1995, 128–131)
		28	NKVD order No. 00193 "On measures with respect to the completion of the operation for the banishment of Chechens and Ingushetians"	GARF, h. 9401, r. l, f. 3, sh. 315–319
	3	3	State Defense Committee directive No. 0741 "On the assignment of Karachai military service members to special settlements"	(Bugay, 1995, 63)
		5	* State Defense Committee resolution No. 5309cc "The NKVD questions" (on the banishment of Balkars from the Kabardian–Balkar ASSR)	

Date	Legislative acts and other documents	Archival sources
Y M D		

7	USSR Supreme Soviet Presidium decree No. 116/102 concerning the liquidation of the Chechen–Ingush ASSR and on the administrative structure of its territory	GARF, h. 9479, r. l, f. 925, sh. 129; GARF, h. 7523, r. 4, f. 208, sh. 51–54
9	Council of People's Commissars decree No. 255-74cc "On the populating and development of districts of the former Chechen–Ingush ASSR"	(Bugay, Gonov, 1998, 203)
9	USSR Supreme Soviet Presidium decree on the liquidation of the Kalmyk district, Rostov Oblast	
11	*Council of People's Commissars decree No. 5473cc "On the resettlement from highland districts of Daghestan to the lands of the Aukhov district, Daghestan ASSR"	(Bugay, Gonov, 1998, 204)
11	* Council of People's Commissars directive No. 5475cc "On the resettlement of Kalmyks from the Rostov Oblast to Omsk Oblast"	(Bugay, 1995, 74–75)
13	Daghestani Council of People's Commissars and Daghestani Communist Party Oblast Committee decree No. 186/241 "Concerning top-priority measures for developing the Aukhov District, Daghestani ASSR, and Kurchaloy, Nozhay-Yurt, Vedeno, Sayasan districts and a part of Gudermes district, Chechen–Ingush ASSR, which were incorporated into the Daghestani ASSR"	TsGA RD, h. P-186, r. 35P, f. 22, sh. 55.
31	NKVD Order (NKVD directive No. 122) "On the banishment of OUN members' families to Krasnoyarsk Kray, the Omsk, Novosibirsk and Irkutsk Oblasts"	(Bugay, 1995, 205–206)
4 2	State Defense Committee resolution No. 5943cc "On the banishment of the Crimean Tatar population from the territory of the Crimean ASSR to the Uzbek SSR"	(Bugay, 1995, 150–151)
5	Council of People's Commissars decree No. 359-105cc "On the resettlement of Poles residing in the northern and eastern regions to regions with more suitable climatic conditions"	(Bugay, 1995, 195)
7	NKVD directive No. 130 concerning OUN members	APRF, h. 3, r. 58, f. 182, sh. 17–24 (referred to *Rehabilitation: The Way It Was*, vol. 2, 101)
7	USSR Supreme Soviet Presidium decree No. 116/102 "Concerning liquidation of the Chechen–Ingush ASSR and administrative structure of its territory"	GARF, h. 7523, r. 4, f. 208, sh. 51–54

Date Y M D	Legislative acts and other documents	Archival sources
8	USSR Supreme Soviet Presidium decree No. 117/6 "On the banishment of Balkars from the Kabardian–Balkar ASSR, and on renaming the Kabardian–Balkar ASSR the Kabardian ASSR"	GARF, h. 7523, r. 4, f. 220, sh. 62–65
13	NKVD and NKGB joint resolution "On measures for the cleansing of the territory of the Crimean ASSR from anti-Soviet elements"	(Bugay, 1995, 149)
15	NKVD order on the location and transportation to special settlements of Kalmyks residing beyond the former Kalmyk ASSR boundaries	(Bugay, 1995, 76)
25	State Defense Committee resolution No. 5729c "On assigning of 1,000 families of Kalmyk special resettlers for work at the mica mines of the Irkutsk Obl. and Yakut ASSR" (According to other sources, the act is dated 25 July 1944)	(Pavlova, 1992)
29	RSFSR Supreme Soviet Presidium decree "On renaming the districts transferred from the Chechen–Ingush ASSR to the North Ossetian SSR"	
5 4	Stavka Commander-in-Chief directive "On the resettlement of residents of the 23 km zone adjacent to the front line"	(Bugay, 1995, 215)
11	* State Defense Committee resolution No. 5859cc "On the Crimean Tatars"	(Bugay, 1995, 150–151)
15	RSFSR Supreme Soviet Presidium decree concerning the liquidation of the Priyutninsky district of Stavropol Kray, transferred to the latter after the liquidation of the Kalmyk ASSR	
18	USSR Council of People's Commissars decree No. 546 "On the resettlement of 700 Avar households from the Georgian SSR to the Chechen–Ingush ASSR"	
21	* State Defense Committee resolution No. 5937 "On the banishment of additional groups of the Crimean Tatar population from the territory of the Crimean ASSR to the Mari ASSR, Gorky, Ivanovo, Kostroma, Molotov and Sverdlovsk Obl."	(Bugay, 1995, 150–151)
25	NKVD–NKGB order No. 00620/001/190 "On the banishment from the Kabardian ASSR of the families of German accessories, traitors and betrayers of the Motherland, who voluntarily left with the Germans"	GARF, h. 9401, r. 2, f. 3, sh. 627–629 (Bugay, Gonov, 1998, 185–186)
25	RSFSR Supreme Soviet Presidium decree "On the liquidation in the Astrakhan Obl. and the incorporation into the oblast of four districts that formerly constituted part of the Kalmyk ASSR"	

Date			Legislative acts and other documents	Archival sources
Y	M	D		

		29	RSFSR Supreme Soviet Presidium decree "On the renaming of former Balkar districts"	
		29	Council of People's Commissars decree No. 627-176cc "On allotting cattle and consumer grain for Karachai, Chechen, Ingushetian, Balkar and Kalmyk special resettlers in exchange for the cattle and grain received from them at the places of departure"	(Bugay, Gonov, 1998, 254)
		29	* State Defense Committee resolution No. 1828cc "On the banishment of the Crimean Tatars and Greeks from Krasnodar Kray and the Rostov Obl."	(Bugay, 1995, 150–151)
	6	7	RSFSR Supreme Soviet Presidium decree concerning the renaming of the Aukhov District, Daghestani ASSR, the Novolaksky district	A. Nurbagandov, Memorandum of 13 March 1989 concerning the former Aukhov district of the Daghestani ASSR; TsGA RD (reported by Sh. Muduyev)
		24	* State Defense Committee resolution No. 6100cc "On the banishment from the Crimea of local residents of Turkish, Greek and Iranian citizenship holding expired passports"	(Bugay, 1995, 198)
	7	2	State Defense Committee resolution No. 5984cc "On the banishment from the Crimea of Greeks, Armenians and Bulgarians"	RGASPI, h. 644, r. 1, f. 26, sh. 64–68 (Bugay, 1995, 197)
		11	Council of People's Commissars decree No. 854-224cc "On the partial resettlement of former Polish citizens" (from USSR eastern regions)	GARF, h. R-9401, r. 1, f. 178, sh. 287 (Bugay, 1995, 196)
		14	NKVD order No. 2863-1/12933 "On the resettlement of family members of 'True Orthodox Christians'"	(Bugay, 1995, 217)
		26	Council of People's Commissars directive No. 15372 "On the resettlement of 213 Czechs from the Dzhambul Obl. to the UkSSR"	(Bugay, 1995, 217)
		31	* State Defense Committee resolution No.6279cc "On the banishment of Turks, Kurds and Khemshins from the frontier areas of the Georgian SSR: the Akhaltsikhe, Adigen, Aspindzi, Akhalkalaki and Bogdan districts"	(Bugay, 1995, 169, 172)
	8	2	NKVD order No. 001036 "Concerning the banishment from the cities of Caucasian Minvody of the families of collaborationists and those, who voluntarily left with the Germans" (according to other sources, the order is dated 24 August 1944)	GARF, h. 8131, r. 32, f. 4288, sh. 74–77 (referred to *Rehabilitation: The Way It Was*, vol. 2, 210–212)

Date Y M D	Legislative acts and other documents	Archival sources
9	Georgian SSR Council of People's Commissars and CP Central Committee decree "On the resettlement of 113 households from the Adjar ASSR"	(Bugay, 1995, 169)
9 20	NKVD order "On the banishment of Turks, Kurds and Khemshins from the frontier areas of the Georgian SSR"	(Bugay, 1995, 171–174)
11 19	State Defense Committee resolution No. 6973 "Concerning the resettlement from Finland of the former residents of the Leningrad Obl. of Ingermanland descent" (those resettled were banned from residing in Leningrad and the Leningrad Oblast and placed in the Velikiye Luki, Novgorod, Yaroslavl, Kalinin and Pskov Obls.)	
No data	Georgian SSR Supreme Soviet Presidium decree "On renaming five settlements of the Zemo-Svaneti district established on the lands transferred from the Kabardian–Balkar ASSR"	
12 14	RSFSR Supreme Soviet Presidium decree "On renaming districts and district centers of the Crimean Obl."	(Bugay, 2002, 121)
29	NKVD order No. 274 "On the registering of citizens of Finnish origin as special resettlers (removed from the register in 1946 with their status changed to 'administratively exiled')"	(Bugay, 1995, 192; Gildi, 1996, 28)
No data	Georgian SSR Supreme Soviet Presidium decree "On changing Balkar toponyms"	
1945 1 6	NKVD order No. 008 "On the banishment of families of collaborators and those that voluntarily left with the Germans from the city of Stavropol, Circassian AO, and districts of Stavropol Kray"	GARF, h. 9401, r. 2, f. 5, sh. 51–91
8	Council of People's Commissars decree No. 34-14c "Enactment on the NKVD Special *Komendatura*s"	(Zaytsev, 1993, 114)
8	Council of People's Commissars decree No. 35 "On the legal status of special resettlers"	GARF, h. 9479, r. 1, f. 213, sh. 1 (*Neues Leben.* 14 August 1991; Zemskov, 1992; Bugay, 1992a, 123–124; Zaytsev, 1993, 113)
16	NKVD directive No. 323 concerning the residents of the Baltic republics	APRF, h. 3, r. 58, f. 182, sh. 17–24 (referred to *Rehabilitation: The Way It Was*, vol. 2, 102)

Date			Legislative acts and other documents	Archival sources
Y	M	D		
	3	5	Council of People's Commissars decree No. 399-cccc "On the procedure of financial compensation for property received from resettlers from Georgia"	(Bugay, Gonov, 1998, 220)
	6	30	USSR Supreme Soviet Presidium decree "On the transformation of the Crimean ASSR into the Crimean Obl. under the jurisdiction of the RSFSR"	GARF, h. 7523, r. 4, f. 349, sh. 206
	7	28	Council of People's Commissars decree No. 1927 "On benefits for special resettlers"	RGANI, h. 3, r. 58, f. 179, sh. 17(Bugay, Gonov, 1998, 233)
	8	18	State Defense Committee resolution No. 9871 "On the banishment of Vlasov army members"	(Bugay, 1995, 221)
		18	State Defense Committee resolution "Concerning the labor employment in industries of Red Army servicemen delivered from German captivity and repatriates of call-up age"	RGASPI, h. 644, r. 1, f. 457. sh. 194–198 (Zemskov, 1993., 16).
		21	USSR Supreme Soviet Presidium decree No. 619/3 "On the renaming of 327 Tatar settlements in the Crimea"	(Chervonnaya, 1997, 164)
		22	NKVD directive No. 140 "On assigning the resettled peoples' representatives that were demobilized from the army to move to the places of main group residence"	(Bugay, Gonov, 1998, 171)
	9	19	USSR Council of Ministers decree No. 13925cc concerning the ban on Ingermanland Finns residing in the Leningrad Obl., with exemption for Great Patriotic War veterans decorated with government awards and their family members	(Bugay, 1992c).
	11	28	Council of People's Commissars directive No. 17074cc "On the banishment of the Vlasov army members to the Sverdlovsk Obl."	(Bugay, 1995, 221)
	12	21	Council of People's Commissars decree No. 3141-950cc "On the banishment of the Vlasov army members to the Kemerovo Obl."	APRF, h. 3, r. 58, f. 182, sh. 17–24 (referred to *Rehabilitation: The Way It Was* vol. 2, 98); Cf. (Bugay, 1995, 221, with 21 December 1948 indicated as th date of the document issuance)
1946	1	5	NKVD order No. 3/0-39 "On the liquidation of residence zones for those mobilized for employment in the oil industry"	GARF, h. 9479, r. 1, f. 148, sh. 162 (Bugay, 1995, 55)

Date Y M D	Legislative acts and other documents	Archival sources
7	USSR Council of Ministers directive "On the banish- ment of Vlasov army members to the Kemerovo Obl."	(Bugay, 1995, 222)
28	NKVD order concerning the removal of Ingermanlan- dians and Finns from the special settlement register	(Zemskov, 1994, 159)
3 29	USSR Council of Ministers decree No. 691-271cc "On the assigning of special target groups subject to reset- tlement to USSR northern parts to the enterprises of the Ministry of Ferrous Metallurgy"	APRF, h. 3, r. 58, f. 182, sh. 17–24 (referred to *Rehabili- tation: The Way It Was*, vol. 2, 98);
4 13	USSR Council of Ministers resolution concerning exempting repatriated natives of the Baltic republics from mobilization to labor battalions and delivery to special settlements in the inland of the USSR	GARF, h. 5446, r. 49, f. 2513, sh. 9–10 (Zemskov, 1993, 18).
16	USSR Council of Ministers directive "On the banish- ment of Vlasov army members to the Karel–Finn ASSR"	(Bugay, 1995, 222)
20	MVD directive No. 97 "On a six-year term banishment of 'legionaries,' Vlasov army members and police mem- bers to special settlements"	(Zaytsev, 1993, 114–116)
6 13	NKVD directive No. 155 concerning the discharge of Ingermanlandians from work columns	(Gildi, 1996, 29).
16	NKVD telegraphic directive (concerning the deporta- tions from the Baltic republics)	(Zemskov, 1993, 4–5)
25	RSFSR Supreme Council decree "On the abolition of the Chechen–Ingush ASSR and the transformation of the Crimean ASSR into the Crimean Obl."	
29	USSR Council of Ministers directive "On the banish- ment of Vlasov army members to the Bashkir ASSR, Kazakh and Turkmen SSR, Molotov, Kirov and Sakhalin Obls."	(Bugay, 1995, 222)
8 5	USSR Council of Ministers directive No. 10297cc "On the banishment of the Vlasov army members to the Gorky Obl."	(Bugay, 1995, 222)
13	USSR Council of Ministers decree No. 1767-796cc "On the cancellation of special regulations in special settlements of Stavropol Kray"	(Bugay, Gonov, 1998, 273)
28	USSR Council of Ministers directive No. 10382cc "On the banishment of the Vlasov army members to the Tajik SSR"	GARF, h. 9479, r. 1, f. 248, sh. 17 (Bugay, 1995, 222)
12 10	MVD directive (concerning the deportations from the Baltic republics)	(Zemskov, 1993, 4–5)
18	MVD order No. 01164 concerning the banishment from the Lithuanian SSR of family members of "gang leaders" and "active members"	(Zemskov, 1993, 4–5) APRF, h. 3, r. 58, f. 182, sh. 17–24

Date			Legislative acts and other documents	Archival sources
Y	M	D		

				(referred to *Rehabilitation: The Way It Was,* vol. 2, 101)
1947	5	7	USSR Council of Ministers directive No. 5211cc "On banning Finns from settling in their former places of residence in the city and oblast of Leningrad"	(Bugay, 1992c; Kiuru, 1992)
		21	MVD order concerning the banishment from Leningrad and the Leningrad Obl. of Finns that returned there in 1946–1947	(Gildi, 1996, 30)
	8	13	USSR Council of Ministers decree "On banishment of families of active nationalists and bandits, those convicted, killed and in hiding, from western regions of Ukraine"	
	9	10	USSR Council of Ministers decree concerning the banishment of OUN members	APRF, h. 3, r. 58, f. 182, sh. 17–24 (referred to *Rehabilitation: The Way It Was,* Vol. 2, 97)
		29	USSR Council of Ministers decree No. 3387-1107cc "On the banishment of the families of bandits, bandit abettors and kulaks from the Lithuanian SSR"	
	11	26	USSR Supreme Soviet Presidium decree "On the criminal liability for escaping from places of compulsory and permanent settlement of persons banished to remote areas of the Soviet Union during the Great Patriotic War"	
1948	2	21	USSR Council of Ministers decree No. 417-160cc "On the banishment of the families of bandits and nationalists in hiding, along with their abettors and kulak families from the territory of the Lithuanian SSR"	(Bugay, 1995, 226)
		21	USSR Council of Ministers decree No. 418-161cc "On the banishment, expulsion and special settlements"	(Ivanova, 1997, 66–67; see also Bugay, 1995, 223)
		21	USSR Supreme Soviet Presidium decree "On the assignment of special dangerous state criminals to special settlements in remote areas of the USSR after serving punishment"	(Zaytsev, 1993, 46)
		21	NKVD order No. 00544 "On measures for the expulsion from the city of Leningrad and Leningrad Obl. of persons of Finnish nationality and Ingermanland Finns repatriated from Finland"	

Date			Legislative acts and other documents	Archival sources
Y	M	D		

		21	USSR Council of Ministers decree No. 417-160cc "Concerning OUN members"	(Bugay, 1995, 221) APRF, h. 3, r. 58, f. 182, sh. 17–24 (referred to *Rehabilitation: The Way It Was*, vol. 2, 101)
		22	USSR Council of Ministers decree No. 413-162 "On the resettlement of deportees from the European part of the USSR to Siberia and Kazakhstan"	GARF, h. 9479, r. 1, f. 371, sh. 4 (Bugay, 1995, 224)
	3	16	MGB Instruction to the USSR Council of Ministers decree No. 417-160cc	GARF, h. R-8131, r. 32, f. 7351, sh. 56–64 (Bugay, 1995, 226)
	5	19	USSR Supreme Soviet Presidium decree No. 745/3 "On the renaming of 1,062 Tatar settlements in the Crimea"	(Chervonnaya, 1997, 164)
	6	2	USSR Council of Ministers decree No. 1841-730cc "On the banishment to remote areas of individuals persistently avoiding their labor duties in the agricultural industry and leading an antisocial parasitic life"	TsAODM, h. 203, r. 1, f. 116, sh. 10 (Zaytsev, 1993, 123–124; Ivanova, 1997, 63, with reference to the TsAODM)
	8	9	USSR Council of Ministers decree No. 2943-210cc "On the resettlement of Kurds from the M. Barzani detachment from the Azerbaijani SSR to Uzbek SSR"	(Bugay, 1995, 233)
	10	4	USSR Council of Ministers decree No. 3728-1524cc "On authorizing the USSR MGB to banish bandits and pogromists, and their families residing on the UkSSR western oblasts' territories to special settlements under Special Council rulings"	APRF, h. 3, r. 58, f. 182, sh. 17–24 (referred to *Rehabilitation: The Way It Was*, vol. 2, 98)
		6	USSR Council of Ministers decree No. 3785.1538 "On the banishment of kulaks from the Ismail Obl."	
	11	24	* USSR Council of Ministers decree No. 4367-1726cc "On resettlers"	(Bugay, Gonov, 1998, 234)
		26	USSR Supreme Soviet Presidium decree "On the criminal liability for escaping from the places of compulsory and permanent settlement of persons banished to remote areas of the Soviet Union during the Great Patriotic War"	GARF, h. 7523, r. 36, f. 450, sh. 87 (*Neues Leben*. 14 August 1991; Kiuru, 1992; Zaytsev, 1993, 124)
	12	29	USSR Council of Ministers decree No. 4722 "On the banishment of kulaks and those accused of banditry, with their families, from the territories of the districts of Pytalovo, Pechora and Kachanovsky, the Pskov Obl."	(Bugay, 1992, 46)

Date			Legislative acts and other documents	Archival sources
Y	M	D		

1949	1	29	USSR Council of Ministers decree No.the 390-138cc "On the banishment of kulaks with families, and families of bandits and nationalists from the territories of the Lithuanian, Latvian, and Estonian SSR"	(Passat, 1994, 41)
	2	28	MGB order No. 0068 "On operation 'Priboy' on the territory of the Baltic republics"	RGVA, h. 38650, r. 1, f. 408 (Strods, 1999, 130)
	4	6	USSR Council of Ministers decree No. 1230-467cc "On the banishment of kulaks, White Army's abettors, members of underground organizations, with their families, from the territory of the Moldavian SSR"	(Bugay, 1995, 238–239, another number of the document—1290-467—is cited); Also APRF, h. 3, r. 58, f. 182, sh. 17–24 (referred to *Rehabilitation: The Way It Was*, vol. 2, 98)
	5	16	Joint MVD and USSR Prosecutor directive concerning the application of the USSR Supreme Soviet Presidium decree of 26 November 1948 to special settlers' children	APRF, h. 3, r. 58, f. 182, sh. 17–24 (referred to *Rehabilitation: The Way It Was*, vol. 2, 98)
		17	Communist Party Central Committee resolution "On the banishment of Greek citizens, currently stateless former Greek citizens, and former Greek citizens holding Soviet citizenship"	(Kotsonis, 1997, 87, facsimile)
		29	* USSR Council of Ministers decree No. 2214-856cc "On the provision of transportation, placement and labor employment for persons banished from the territories of the Georgian, Armenian and Azerbaijani SSR, and from the Black Sea coast zone"	(Bugay, 1995, 239)
	6	11	MVD order on the proceedings pertinent to the transportation, placement and labor employment of those banished from Moldavia	
	12	1	Karel–Finn SSR Communist Party Central Committee and Council of Ministers decree "Concerning the recruiting of 8,000 Ingermanland families in 1950 in addition to those earlier recruited for working in the republic's timber industry"	(Bugay, 1992c).
		29	USSR Council of Ministers decree No. 5881-2201cc "On the banishment of the families of kulaks, bandits and those convicted for anti-Soviet activities, from the territories of the districts of Pytalovo, Pechora and Kachanovsky, the Pskov Obl."	GARF, h. 9479, r. 1, f. 641, sh. 368 back; and f. 607, sh. 201 (Bugay, 1995, 243–244)

Date Y M D	Legislative acts and other documents	Archival sources
1950 1 11	USSR Council of Ministers decree No. 135-26cc "On the banishment of former members of the Basmach gangs and their family members residing on the territory of the Tajik SSR"	GARF, h. 9479, r. 1, f. 641, sh. 382 (Bugay, 1995, 244–145)
2 21	USSR Council of Ministers decree No. 727-269cc "On the banishment of Iranians"	(Bugay, 1995, 244)
4 6	USSR Council of Ministers decree No. 1398-508 concerning OUN members	APRF, h. 3, r. 58, f. 182, sh. 17–24 (referred to *Rehabilitation: The Way It Was*, vol. 2, 102)
20	Karel–Finn SSR Communist Party Central Committee and Council of Ministers decree "Concerning the partial alteration of the Karel–Finn SSR Communist Party Central Committee and Council of Ministers Decree of 1 December 1949" (signed by Yu. Andropov; on the discontinuance of the organized resettlement of Ingermanland Finns from frontier districts)	(Bugay, 1992c).
1951 1 23	USSR Council of Ministers decree No. 189-88cc "On the banishment of the families of kulaks from western oblasts of the UkSSR and BSSR"	(Bugay, 1995, 245)
2 13	USSR Council of Ministers decree No. 377-190cc "On the resettlement of former military servicemen of the Anders army"	(Bugay, 1995, 245)
19	USSR MGB Memorandum "Concerning the need for the banishment of members of the anti-Soviet 'Iyegovisty' sect and their family members from western regions of the Ukrainian, Belorussian, Moldavian, Latvian, Lithuanian and Estonian SSRs"	APRF, h. 3, r. 58, f. 180, sh. 52–53 (Passat, 1994, 612–613)
3 3	USSR Council of Ministers decree No. 667-339cc "On the banishment of active participants of the anti-Soviet 'Iyegovisty' sect, with families, from the UkSSR, BSSR, Moldavian, Latvian, Lithuanian, and Estonian SSRs"	(Bugay, 1995, 245)
24	Moldavian SSR Council of Ministers decree "On the confiscation and selling of the property of individuals banished from the territory of the Moldavian SSR"	(Passat, 1994, 53)
4 2	Report of Moldavian SSR state security minister Mordovets and MGB commissioner Misyurov concerning the operation "Sever"	(Passat, 1994, 632)
9 5	USSR Council of Ministers decree No. 3309-1568cc "On the banishment of kulaks and their family members manifesting hostile attitudes *kolkhozy*" (The Baltic republics are implied by the decree!)	GARF, h. R-9479, r. 1, f. 641, sh. 103 (Bugay, 1995, 234, 245)

Date			Legislative acts and other documents	Archival sources
Y	M	D		

				Also: APRF, h. 3, r. 58, f. 182, sh. 17–24 (referred to *Rehabilitation: The Way It Was*, vol. 2, 101)
		18	USSR Council of Ministers resolution No. 3358-1643 "On the banishment of kulaks and their family members from the territory of western oblasts of the BSSR"	APRF, h. 3, r. 58, f. 182, sh. 17–24 (referred to *Rehabilitation: The Way It Was*, vol. 2, 101)
	10	9	USSR Supreme Soviet Presidium decree stipulating eternal banishment for seven punished peoples and the Greeks	
		24	MGB order No. 00776 "On announcing the content of the USSR Supreme Soviet Presidium decree of 9 October 1951 against written acknowledgement, and on cancellation of the MVD directive No. 97 of 20 April 1946"	(Zaytsev, 1993, 125)
	11	29	USSR Council of Ministers decree No. 4893-2113cc "Concerning the banishment of hostile elements from the territory of the Georgian SSR"	APRF, h. 3, r. 58, f. 182, sh. 17–24 (referred to *Rehabilitation: The Way It Was*, vol. 2, 100); GARF, h. 8131, r. 32, f. 4288, sh. 74–77 (referred to *Rehabilitation: The Way It Was*, vol. 2, 212)
	12	12	USSR Communist Party Central Committee and Council of Ministers resolution on the banishment from the Lithuanian SSR of kulaks and their families that avoided the banishment in October 1951	
1952	7	7	USSR Council of Ministers decree "On keeping the special settlement restrictions with regard to individuals banished in the period of the Great Patriotic War"	GARF, h. 9179, r. 2, f. 611, sh. 287–288
	1	14	USSR Supreme Soviet Presidium decree "On renaming railway stations on the territory of the Crimean Obl."	
	3	11	USSR Supreme Soviet Presidium decree "On the assigning of convicted individuals that have served their punishment terms to special settlements, in which their families reside"	GARF, h. 7523, r. 56, f. 588, sh. 1 (*Neues Leben*. 14 August 1991); GARF, h. 9401, r. 12, f. 207 (Zemskov, 1993б, 9)

Date Y M D	Legislative acts and other documents	Archival sources
25	USSR Council of Ministers directive No. 6435cc "On the eternal banishment of kulaks and their families from the BSSR"	
4 7	USSR Council of Ministers No. 436 "On the banishment of kulaks and their families from the oblasts of Grodno, Molodecheno, Brest, Pinsk and Polotsk"	(Bugay, 1995, 249)
1954 2 19	USSR Supreme Soviet Presidium decree "On the transfer of the Crimean Obl. from the RSFSR to the UkSSR"	(Ved. VS—1954 / no.4—147).
3 15	Letter of the Crimean CPSU Oblast Committee to Ukrainian SSR CPSU Central Committee secretary O. I. Kirichenko requesting him to submit a petition to the CPSU Central Committee for banning citizens deported in 1944 from returning to the Crimea	(*Natsionalni vidnosyny v Ukrayini u XX st.* [National Relations in Ukraine in the 20th century], Kiev, 1994, 326–327).
7 5	USSR Council of Ministers decree No. 1439-649C "On lifting some restrictions relative to the legal status of special settlers"	Vesnovskaya, 1999, 2b, 263–264
16	USSR Prosecutor General, MVD and KGB order No. 127c/0391/078 "On the discharge from exile to special settlement"	
20	USSR Prosecutor General directive No. 12/132c concerning the USSR Council of Ministers decree of 5 July 1954	(Zaytsev, 1993, 126–127)
8 13	USSR Council of Ministers decree No. 1738-789cc "On lifting special settlements restrictions relative to former kulaks, Germans registered at the place of residence, and Germans that were mobilized for industrial work and exempted from banishment"	(Zaytsev, 1993, 127–128; Bugay, 1995, 260)
13	CPSU Central Committee Presidium decree No. 7 "On lifting special settlement restrictions pertaining to kulaks and other persons"	RGANI, h. 3, r. 8, f. 136, sh. 1 (referred to *Rehabilitation: The Way It Was*, vol. 2, 158–159)
1955 3 10	USSR Council of Ministers decree "On issuing passports to special settlers"	(Pavlova, 1992)
23	CPSU Central Committee Presidium decree No. 113 "Concerning the conscription of some categories of special settlers for military service"	APRF, h. 3, r. 58, f. 181, sh. 54 (referred to *Rehabilitation: The Way It Was*, vol. 2, 206–207)

Date			Legislative acts and other documents	Archival sources
Y	M	D		
	5	9	CPSU Central Committee resolution "On lifting special settlements restrictions relative to German CPSU members and candidate members, and their family members"	(Bugay, 1995, 260)
	6	29	CPSU Central Committee Presidium decree No. 128 "Concerning measures for the intensification of mass political agitation among special settlers"	RGANI, h. 3, r. 10, f. 151, sh. 66; f. 152, sh. 109–114 (referred to *Rehabilitation: The Way It Was*, vol. 2, 224–227)
	8	23	USSR Council of Ministers directive No. 2708cc providing for the conscription of children of German special settlers for military service	(Bugay, 1995, 260)
	9	17	USSR Supreme Soviet Presidium decree "On the amnesty for Soviet citizens that collaborated with the occupiers in the time of the Great Patriotic War of 1941–1945"	(Polian, 1996, 328–329)
	11	24	USSR Council of Ministers decree No. 1963-1052 "Concerning the removal of some categories of special settlers from the special settlement register"	(Pavlova, 1992); The text of the document is available at RGANI, h. 3, r. 10, f. 199, sh. 21; r. 8, f. 334, sh. 78–80 (referred to *Rehabilitation: The Way It Was*, vol. 2, 286–287)
		24	CPSU Central Committee Presidium decree "On lifting special settlement restrictions pertaining to Soviet citizens of Greek nationality banished from the Georgian SSR in 1949"	RGANI, h. 3, r. 10, f. 199, sh. 14–15 (Protocol No. 170, item 46) (referred to *Rehabilitation: The Way It Was*, vol. 2, 286–287)
		24	CPSU Central Committee Presidium decree No. 170 concerning the ratification of the USSR Council of Ministers Draft Resolution "Concerning the removal of some categories of special settlers from the special settlement register"	RGANI, h. 3, r. 10, f. 199, sh. 14–15 (Protocol No. 170, item 41) (referred to *Rehabilitation: The Way It Was*, vol. 2, 286)
	12	13	USSR Supreme Soviet Presidium decree No. 129/23 "On lifting restrictions relative to the legal status of Germans and their family members assigned to special settlements"	GARF, h. 7523, r. 72, f. 576, sh. 79 (Auman, Chebotareva, 1993, 177)

Date			Legislative acts and other documents	Archival sources
Y	M	D		

1956	1	17	USSR Council of Ministers decree No. 62-41cc "On lifting restrictions relative to individuals of Polish nationality, banished from the UkSSR regions adjacent to the Polish border in 1936"	
	3	10	USSR Supreme Soviet Presidium decree "On the cancellation of USSR Supreme Soviet Presidium Decree 'On assignment of special dangerous state criminals to special settlements in remote areas of the USSR after serving punishment' of 21 February 1948"	
		17	USSR Supreme Soviet Presidium decree No. 134/33 "On lifting restrictions relative to the legal status of Kalmyks and their family members assigned to special settlements"	GARF, h. 7523, r. 72, f. 606, sh. 66
		27	USSR Supreme Soviet Presidium decree No. 139/47 "On lifting restrictions relative to the legal status of Greeks, Bulgarians, Armenians, and their family members, assigned to special settlements"	
	4	28	USSR Supreme Soviet Presidium decree No. 0-134/42 "On lifting special settlement restrictions relative to the Crimean Tatars, Turks holding Soviet citizenship [Meskhetian Turks], Kurds, Khemshins, and their family members, banished in the period of the Great Patriotic War"	
	7	16	USSR Supreme Soviet Presidium decree No. 139/19/20 "On lifting special settlement restrictions relative to Chechens, Ingushetians, Karachais, and their family members, banished in the period of the Great Patriotic War"	GARF, h. 7523, r. 4, f. 629, sh. 201 (Naimark, 1998, p. 52)
	9	22	USSR Supreme Soviet Presidium decree No. 144/29 "On lifting special settlement restrictions relative to some categories of foreign nationals, stateless persons, and former foreign nationals granted Soviet citizenship"	
	11	9	Ukrainian SSR Supreme Soviet Presidium decree banishing former leaders of the Ukrainian underground organizations, who were convicted and served their punishment, from returning to western oblasts of the UkSSR	
	12	25	CPSU Central Committee decree "On the territory of the Chechen–Ingush ASSR"	RGANI, h. 5, r. 32, f. 56, sh. 103–104 (Naimark, 1998, p. 52)

Date Y M D	Legislative acts and other documents	Archival sources
1957 1 9	USSR Supreme Soviet Presidium decree No. 149/11 "On the establishment of the Kalmyk AO within the RSFSR"	GARF, h. 7523, r. 72, f. 701, sh. 64–67
9	USSR Supreme Soviet Presidium decree No. 149/12 "On the transformation of the Circassian AO into Karachai–Circassian AO"	GARF, h. 7523, r. 72, f. 701, sh. 68–69
9	USSR Supreme Soviet Presidium decree No. 149/13 "On the transformation of the Kabardian ASSR into Kabardian–Balkar ASSR"	GARF, h. 7523, r. 72, f. 701, sh. 70
9	USSR Supreme Soviet Presidium decree No. 149/14 "On the restoration of the Chechen–Ingush ASSR within the RSFSR, and on abolishing the Grozny Obl."	GARF, h. 7523, r. 72, f. 701, sh. 72–73
11	USSR Supreme Soviet Presidium decree No. 149/22 "On the transfer of a part of the territory of the Dusheti and Kazbegi districts from the Georgian SSR to the RSFSR"	GARF, h. 7523, r. 72, f. 701, sh. 119
21	Lithuanian SSR Supreme Soviet Presidium decree "On banning former leaders of Lithuanian bourgeois governments and bourgeois political parties, active members of the Lithuanian nationalist underground organizations, leaders of anti-Soviet organizations, convicts and discharged convicts, from returning to the Lithuanian SSR"	GARF, h. 9401, r. 12, f. 207 (Zemskov, 1993b., 12).
25	MVD order No. 055 "On the sanctioning of residence and registration of the Kalmyks, Balkars, Karachais, Chechens, Ingushetians, and their family members, banished in the period of the Great Patriotic War"	GARF, h. 207, v. 14, section 15, sh. 1–3 (Bugay, Gonov, 1998, 283)
2 11	The Law "On the enactment of USSR Supreme Soviet Presidium decrees on the restoration of the national autonomy of the Balkar, Chechen, Ingushetian, Kalmyk, and Karachai peoples"	GARF, h. 7523, r. 71, f. 154, sh. 27
22	BSSR Supreme Soviet Presidium decree banishing former leaders and active participants of Belorussian underground organizations, who were convicted and served their punishment, from returning to the obls. of Brest, Grodno, and Molodecheno	
4 12	RSFSR Council of Ministers resolution No. 205 "Concerning granting privileges and providing assistance to collective farmers, workers and office employees returning to the Chechen–Ingush SSR, the Kabardinian–Balkar ASSR, Stavropol Kray's Kalmyk Autonomous Obl. and Karachai–Circassian Autonomous Obl., the Daghestani ASSR and some districts of the North Ossetian ASSR, Astrakhan and Rostov Obls."	GARF, h. A-259, r. 42, f. 4830, sh. 33–34 (Kozlov, 1999, 130)

Date			Legislative acts and other documents	Archival sources
Y	M	D		

	6	10	CPSU Central Committee Presidium decree "Concerning the unauthorized resettlement of Chechen and Ingushetian families to the district of the city of Grozny"	GARF, h. P-9401, r. 2, f. 491, sh. 122 (Kozlov, 1999, 131)
	10	31	USSR Supreme Soviet Presidium decree No. 161/29 "On lifting restrictions relative to USSR citizens of Azerbaijani nationality, banished from the Georgian SSR in 1944"	
		31	Latvian SSR and Estonian SSR Supreme Soviet Presidium decree "On banning former leaders of bourgeois governments and bourgeois political parties, active members of nationalist underground organizations, leaders of anti-Soviet organizations, convicts and discharged convicts from returning to the homeland"	GARF, h. 9401, r. 12, f. 207 (Zemskov, 1993b., 13).
1958	3	8	RSFSR Council of Ministers decree No. 245 "Concerning providing assistance to the population that returned to their former places of residence and to the residents that resettled from highland districts to the plain within the Chechen–Ingush ASSR"	(Reported by Sh. Muduyev)
	4	21	RSFSR Council of Ministers directive No. 2027-p "Allowing the Daghestani ASSR to spend 300,000 rubles from the 1958 budget on providing assistance to impoverished Chechen returnees to the Daghestani ASSR"	(Reported by Sh. Muduyev)
	5	19	USSR Supreme Soviet Presidium decree No. 161/29 "On lifting restrictions relating to some categories of special settlers"	GARF, h. 9401, r. 12, f. 207 (Zemskov, 1993b., 14).
	7	16	Daghestani SSR Council of Ministers decree "Concerning the resettlement from the Kyrgyz SSR and the economic employment of the Chechen population in the republic"	A. Nurbagandov, Memorandum of 13 March 1989 concerning the former Aukhov district of the Daghestani ASSR; TsGA RD, h. 168, r. 34, f. 923, sh. 171–173 (reported by Sh. Muduyev)
		29	USSR Supreme Soviet Presidium decree No.the 108/1 "On the transformation of the Kalmyk AO into the Kalmyk ASSR"	GARF, h. 7523, r. 77, f. 20, sh. 8
	10	16	Daghestani SSR CPSU Oblast Committee Bureau and Council of Ministers decree "Concerning the economic situation and employment of Chechen families that returned to the republic"	TsGA RD (reported by Sh. Muduyev)

Date			Legislative acts and other documents	Archival sources
Y	M	D		

Date			Legislative acts and other documents	Archival sources
1959	3	27	MVD order No. 097 "On the liquidation of the Special Settlement Department"	(Pavlova, 1992)
	5	29	Daghestani SSR CPSU Oblast Committee Bureau and Council of Ministers decree "Concerning the reception and employment of Chechen families in the city of Khasavyurt"	A. Nurbagandov, Memorandum of 13 March 1989 concerning the former Aukhov district of the Daghestani ASSR; TsGA RD (reported by Sh. Muduyev)
1960	1	7	USSR Supreme Soviet Presidium decree "On lifting special settlement restrictions relative to some categories of special settlers"	GARF, h. 9401, r. 12, f. 207 (Zemskov, 1993б., 15).
1963	1	7	USSR Supreme Soviet Presidium decree "On lifting special settlement restrictions relative to former members of underground nationalist organizations, traders, land proprietors, and industrialists, banished from Western Ukraine, the Moldavian SSR, Lithuanian SSR, Latvian SSR, and Estonian SSR"	
	5	10	Daghestani SSR CPSU Oblast Committee Bureau and Council of Ministers decree No. 236/91 "On additional measures for assistance relative to the employment and cultural life of the Chechen population of the republic"	TsGA RD (reported by Sh. Muduyev)
1964	12	6	USSR Supreme Soviet Presidium decree "On lifting special settlement restrictions relative to some categories of special settlers"	
	8	29	USSR Supreme Soviet Presidium decree "On instituting amendments to the Supreme Soviet Presidium decree 'On the resettlement of Germans residing in the Volga region' of 28 August 1941"	GARF, h. 7523, r. 82, f. 146, sh. 184–185 (Ved. VS, 1964, No.52, 592)
1965	9	30	USSR Supreme Soviet Presidium decree No. 4020-VI "On lifting special settlement restrictions relative to members of the 'Iyegovisty' sect, True Orthodox Christians, members of the 'Innokentyevtsy' sect and Reformer Adventists and their family members"	GARF, h. 6991, r. 4, f. 119, sh. 15
1967	9	5	USSR Supreme Soviet Presidium decree No. 1361 "On citizens of the Tatar nationality residing in the Crimea"	GARF, h. 7523, r. 92, f. 134, sh. 65–66 (Ved. VS, 1967, No.36, 493)
		5	USSR Supreme Soviet Presidium resolution "On the procedure for the application of Article 2 of the Supreme Soviet Presidium Decree of 28 April 1956"	(Ved. VS, 1967, No.36, 494)

Date Y M D	Legislative acts and other documents	Archival sources
1968 5 30	USSR Supreme Soviet Presidium resolution "On the procedure for the application of Article 2 of the USSR Supreme Soviet Presidium decree of 28 April 1956 and Article 2 of the USSR Supreme Soviet Presidium decree of 31 December 1957 to Turks, Kurds, Khemshins, and Azerbaijanis that hold USSR citizenship and previously resided in the Georgian SSR"	(Ved. VS, 1968, No.23, 188)
1972 11 3	USSR Supreme Soviet Presidium resolution No. 3521-VIII "On lifting the restrictions concerning the choice of place of residence, hitherto stipulated, relating to particular categories of citizens" [Germans, Greeks, Bulgarians, and former Greek, Turkish, and Iranian citizens]	(Dumay, Chebotare-va, 1993, 179)
12 27	USSR Supreme Soviet Presidium decree "On lifting the restrictions concerning the choice of place of residence, hitherto stipulated, relating to particular categories of citizens"	
1974 1 9	USSR Supreme Soviet Presidium decree "On declaring the invalidity of certain USSR legislative acts, under the USSR Supreme Soviet Presidium decree 'On lifting the restrictions concerning the choice of place of residence, hitherto stipulated relating to particular categories of citizens'"	
4 16	Kazakhstan Communist Party Central Committee Bureau decree "On intensification of ideological and educational work among citizens of German nationality"	(Auman, Chebotare-va, 1993, 180–183)
1977 6 28	Kazakhstan Communist Party Central Committee Bureau decree No. B32-2 "On the further intensification of ideological and educational work among citizens of German nationality"	(Auman, Chebotare-va, 1993, 185–190)
1978 4 25	Uzbek SSR MVD directive prohibiting the Uzbek SSR militia passport departments from cancelling the Uzbek *propiska* of those Crimean Tatars that failed to produce certificates from their future place of residence confirming the availability of employment and housing there	(Alekseyeva, 1992, 107)
10 15	USSR Council of Ministers decree No. 700 "On additional measures for controlling the observation of passport regulations in the Crimean Oblast" (according to other sources, the date was 15 August 1978)	(Alekseyeva, 1992, 107; see also: Bugay, 1995, 289)
1979 5 31	USSR Communist Party Central Committee Politburo decree No. 153/XI "On the formation of the German Autonomous Oblast"	(Dumay, Chebotare-va, 1993, 195)

Date Y M D	Legislative acts and other documents	Archival sources
1986 3 18	Kazakhstan Communist Party Central Committee Bureau decree "On the further intensification of ideological and educational work among citizens of German nationality, residing in Kazakhstan"	(Auman, Chebotareva, 1993, 216–219)
1987 12 8	Georgian SSR Council of Ministers decree No. 600 "On problems of Meskhetian Turks"	
24	USSR Council of Ministers decree "On restrictions relating to citizens' residence registration in some settlements of the Crimean Oblast and Krasnodar Kray"	(Bugay, 1995, 289)
1988 6 24	Georgian SSR Council of Ministers decree No. 600 "On problems of Meskhetian Turks"	
1989 1 16	USSR Supreme Soviet Presidium decree "On additional measures for restoring justice with regard to victims of repressions that took place in the period of 1930–1940s and early 1950s"	(Ved. VS. 1989, No.3, 19)
11 14	USSR Supreme Soviet declaration "On the recognition as unlawful and criminal of the repressive acts against peoples who were subjected to forced resettlement, and on guaranteeing their rights"	(Vedomosti Syezda narodnykh deputatov i VS SSSR. 1989, No.23, 449)
28	USSR Supreme Soviet Presidium "On conclusions and suggestions of the commissions for problems of Soviet Germans and the Crimean Tatar people"	(Ved. VS. 1989, No.25, 495)
12 21	USSR Council of Ministers decree No. 1117 "On instituting a commission for implementing the USSR Supreme Soviet Presidium decree 'On the conclusions and suggestions of the commissions for the problems of Soviet Germans and the Crimean Tatar people'"	(Auman, Chebotareva, 1993, 279–280)
1990 1 29	USSR Council of Ministers decree No. 90 "On Instituting a commission for the problems of Soviet Germans"	(Auman, Chebotareva, 1993, 287–292)
4 6	Resolution of the Executive Committee of the Ulyanovsk Oblast Soviet of People's Deputies No. 135 "On the organization of the placement of Soviet Germans in the Ulyanovsk Oblast"	(Auman, Chebotareva, 1993, 299–300)
8 13	Decree of the President of the USSR "On the restoration of the rights of all victims of the political repressions of the 1920–1950s"	(*Sovetskaya Rossiya.* 14 August 1990)
11 24	USSR Council of Ministers decree No. 1184 "On the preparation and holding of a Congress of Soviet Germans"	(Auman, Chebotareva, 1993, 349–350)
1991 3 7	USSR Supreme Soviet Presidium decree 2031-1 "On cancellation of corresponding legislative documents, in conformity with the USSR Supreme Soviet Declaration 'On the recognition as unlawful and criminal of the repressive acts against peoples who were subjected to forced resettlement, and on guaranteeing their rights' of 14 November 1989"	(Vedomosti syezda narodnykh deputatov SSSR i VS , 1991, No.11, 302)

Date			Legislative acts and other documents	Archival sources
Y	M	D		

		11	Ukraine Supreme Soviet Presidium decree on the transformation of the Crimean Oblast to the Crimean ASSR	
		26	USSR Cabinet of Ministers directive No. 225p "On the implementation of the USSR Supreme Soviet Presidium Decree of 7 March 1991"	(Auman, Chebotareva, 1993, 359)
	4	22	USSR Supreme Soviet Presidium decree "On high-priority measures for resolving the problems of the Germans residing in the oblast"	(Auman, Chebotareva, 1993, 361–362)
		26	RSFSR Law "On the rehabilitation of the repressed peoples"	(Auman, Chebotareva, 1993, 362–363)
	6	6	USSR Cabinet of Ministers decree No. 336 "On the reversal of the resolutions by the former State Defense Committee of the USSR and Decrees by the USSR government, relative to the Soviet peoples subjected to repression and forced resettlement"	(Auman, Chebotareva, 1993, 382–385)
		18	Resolution of the Executive Committee of the Altay Kray Soviet of People's Deputies No. 258 "On restoration of the German National Okrug on the territory of Altay Kray"	(Auman, Chebotareva, 1993, 386)
		21	Decree of the President of the USSR "On awarding medal 'For valorous labor during the Great Patriotic War of 1941–1945' to the USSR citizens that were mobilized into labor columns"	(Auman, Chebotareva, 1993, 386–387)
	7	12	Azerbaijani SSR Cabinet of Ministers decree No. 214 "On the reversal of the resolutions by the former State Defense Committee of the USSR and decrees by the USSR government, relating to the Soviet peoples subjected to forced resettlement"	(Bugay, Gonov, 1988, 18)
	8	2	USSR Cabinet of Ministers decree No. 565 "On the committee for the problems of Soviet Germans"	(Auman, Chebotareva, 1993, 389–391)
	10	11	Law of the Russian Federation "On rehabilitation of victims of political repression"	
		15	RSFSR Cabinet of Ministers decree No. 546 "On instituting within the RSFSR State Committee for Nationalities of Department for the Affairs of Peoples not Possessing National or State Administrative Units"	(Auman, Chebotareva, 1993, 394)
		18	RSFSR Law No. 1761-1 "On the rehabilitation of victims of political repression"	(Vedomosti syezda narodnykh deputatov RSFSR i VS RSFSR. 1991. No.44, 1428)
		18	RSFSR Supreme Soviet Presidium decree "On the procedure for the implementation of the RSFSR Law 'On the rehabilitation of victims of political repression'"	(Vedomosti syezda narodnykh deputatov RSFSR i VS RSFSR. 1991. No.44, 1429)

Date			Legislative acts and other documents	Archival sources
Y	M	D		

	11	1	Chechen–Ingush ASSR Supreme Soviet Proclamation of the Sovereign Chechen Republic	
	12	6	Georgian SSR Supreme Soviet Presidium decree No. 321 "On instituting a Commission for Cooperation with the Council of the Society for the Salvation of (Meskhi) Georgians"	(Bugay, Gonov, 1998, 18)
1992	1	23	Decree of the President of Ukraine No. 51 "On instituting a Ukrainian–German Foundation"	(Auman, Chebotareva, 1993, 402–403)
		29	Decree of the President of the Republic of Kyrgyzstan "On instituting German national cultural okrugs, and national production and commercial structures in the Republic of Kyrgyzstan"	(*Gazeta nemtsev Kyrgyzstana*, 1992, No.1—2)
	2	11	Republic of Kyrgyzstan Cabinet of Ministers decree "On the establishment of a Kyrgyz–German Trade Center in the city of Beshkek"	(*Gazeta nemtsev Kyrgyzstana*, 1992, No.1—2)
		21	Decree of the President of the Russian Federation No. 231 "On high-priority measures for the rehabilitation of Russian Germans"	(*Rossiyskaya gazeta*, 5 March 1992)
	4	9	Russian Federation Government directive No. 681 "On the formation of a Commission for Affairs of the Russian Germans"	(Auman, Chebotareva, 1993, 412–413)
		14	Law of the Supreme Soviet of the Republic of Kazakhstan "On the rehabilitation of victims of political repression"	(Bugay, 1995, 302)
	5	21	Decree of the President of the Russian Federation No. 514 "On the establishment of agricultural industrial facilities, satellite settlements for Russian Germans in the Volga region, and on guarantees of the settlements' social and economic development"	(Auman, Chebotareva, 1993, 414)
		18	Resolution of a Session of Saratov Oblast's Engels district council decreeing opposition to the institution of a German national territorial unit on the districts' territory	(Auman, Chebotareva, 1993, 415)
		26	Russian Federation Supreme Soviet decree No. 3131-1 "On procedure for providing benefits to rehabilitated persons residing on the territory of the Russian Federation"	(Auman, Chebotareva, 1993, 415–416)
	6	1	Russian Federation Supreme Soviet decree "On the rehabilitation of the Cossacks"	(Bugay, Gonov, 1988, 17)
		15	Decree of the President of the Russian Federation "On the rehabilitation of the Cossacks"	(Bugay, Gonov, 1988, 17)
		23	Decree of the President of the Russian Federation "On the declassification of legislative and other acts envisaging mass repressions and infringements on human rights"	(Zaytsev, 1993, 5–6)

Date Y M D	Legislative acts and other documents	Archival sources
26	Russian Federation Supreme Soviet decree "On procedure for providing benefits to rehabilitated persons residing on the territory of the Russian Federation"	(*Rossiyskaya gazeta*, 4 July 1992)
7 4	Russian Federation Law "On instituting the transitional period for state-territorial division within the Russian Federation"	(Auman, Chebotareva, 1993, 416–417)
9	Russian Federation Government resolution No. 475 "On signing the 'Protocol on cooperation between the Government of the Russian Federation and the Government of the FRG for gradual restoration of Soviet German statehood'"	(Auman, Chebotareva, 1993, 417–423)
10 9	Bishkek agreement of the CIS countries concerning the restoration of the rights of deported persons, national minorities and peoples	
11 2	Decree of the President of the Russian Federation on the introduction of a state of emergency in the zone of Ossetian–Ingushetian conflict	
12 15	Decree of the President of the Russian Federation No.1562 "On instituting the Foundation 'Russian Germans'"	(Auman, Chebotareva, 1993, 427)
22	Russian Federation Law No. 4185.1 "On instituting changes and additions to the RSFSR Law 'On the rehabilitation of victims of political repression'"	(*Rossiyskaya gazeta*, 6 January 1993)
1993 4 1	Russian Federation Supreme Soviet decree No. 4721-1 "Concerning the rehabilitation of Russian Koreans"	(Vesnovskaya, 1999, part 1, 247–249
5 18	Directive of the Head of the Republic of Georgia No. 106 "On resolving some social problems of the deported Meskhetian Turks"	(Bugay, 1995, 302)
6 29	USSR Supreme Soviet Presidium Russian Federation "On the recognition of Russian Finns as a repressed people"	
7 23	Russian Federation Supreme Soviet decree No. 5503-1 "On instituting changes and additions to the RSFSR Law 'On the rehabilitation of victims of political repression'"	(Vedomosti syezda narodnykh deputatov RSFSR i VS RSFSR, 1993. No.1, 21)
1994 4 14	Decree of the President of Ukraine "On measures for marking the memory of the victims of the deportation from the Crimea"	(Chervonnaya, 1997, 164)
5 3	Russian Federation Government resolution No. 419 "On approval of the Enactment of the procedure for providing benefits to rehabilitated persons and persons recognized as victims of political repressions"	(Bugay, 2000, 47)

Date			Legislative acts and other documents	Archival sources
Y	M	D		
		25	Republic of Armenia Supreme Soviet decree No. 1062-1 "On passing the draft legislation 'On repressed persons'"	
	6	1	Russian Federation Government resolution No. 616 "On the burying of rehabilitated persons at the expense of state in the event of their deaths"	
	8	12	Russian Federation Government decree "Concerning the procedure for the restoration to citizens of their property that was illegally confiscated, expropriated or otherwise alienated due to political repression, reimbersement of its cost or paying out monetary compensation"	(Bugay, 2000, 47)
		23	Republic of Georgia Cabinet of Ministers decree No. 589 "On the repatriation of persons deported from Samtskhe-Dzhavakheti in 1944"	(Bugay, Gonov, 1988, 19)
1996	3	14	Decree of the President of the Russian Federation No. 378 "On measures for the rehabilitation of clergy and believers that were subjected to ungrounded repression"	
	6	6	Decree of the President of the Russian Federation "On additional measures for the rehabilitation of Russian Germans"	

* Legislative acts issued by the State Defense Committee, Council of People's Commissars and Council of Ministers, invalidated by the USSR Supreme Soviet Presidium decree No. 2031-1 of 7 March 1991 and the USSR Cabinet of Ministers decree No. 336 of 6 June 1991.

Supplement 3

REPORT NO. 800 "ON PLANNED RESETTLEMENT FROM THE KURSK OBLAST," 20 MARCH 1938

Head of the Kursk Oblast NKVD Department, State Security Captain Boyechin, to the People's Commissar of Internal Affairs of the USSR State Security Senior Major Zhukovsky:

The substantial experience of these matters, acquired in 1936–1937 in the course of resettlement from the Kursk Oblast, demonstrated that—due to poorly organized control on the part of the USSR NKVD Resettlement Department, and the local executives' negligent approach to the practical implementation of the directions—there were occasions when the resettlement measures fell short of requirements, which caused resentment among those to be resettled.

The USSR NKVD Resettlement Department conveyed directives concerning the resettlement prior to the approval of the plans by the Sovnarkom [Council of People's Commissars]. Based on the directives in question, the local executives launched preparatory work, thus engendering unrest among the district population, and—in point of fact—disorienting *kolkhoz* members.

A couple of particular facts are described below:

The central Resettlement Department conveyed information that 14 thousand households would be resettled from the Kursk Oblast in 1937 and 1930, and suggested that the practicability of the possible resettlement of 9 thousand households in spring 1937 be discussed.

The matter was considered by the local authorities, and the possibility of the resettlement of the indicated number of households was confirmed by the delivery of the Oblast Executive Committee's resolution of 5 October 1936. Subsequently, a large-scale instructive campaign was launched among *kolkhoz* members, and registration of potential volunteer resettlers was commenced.

As of 7 January 1937, the registered number of households that handed in applications stating their willingness to resettle reached 1,455. However, no resettlement was carried out, as the due dates passed. Those persons that submitted applications grew increasingly concerned and started besieging the resettlement section in scores, since a part of the applicants considered themselves already recruited and had sold their houses, quit their work in *kolkhoz* and were eating away the resources at their disposal, while waiting for the planned resettlement.

Due to this situation, and left with no specific instructions from the Resettlement Department, the oblast authorities had to terminate all activities for the recruitment of resettlers and to issue a categorical ban on property sale and dismissals from *kolkhozy*.

With regard to those who had already sold their property, measures were taken to include them into the industrial resettlement campaign conducted by the oblast Planning Committee.

A similar situation took place in the case of the resettlement of 500 households to Azov-Black Sea Kray. The Resettlement Department conveyed the dates for transporting resettlers by trains; and recruitment was carried out accordingly. Some 200 families sold their houses. Corresponding contracts were concluded with relevant oblast organizations concerning the provision of health care, hygiene and veterinary services for the resettlers and their cattle; railway carriages were ordered too. On the eve of the departure date, however, a directive was received, which stipulated the reversal of the resettlement and withdrawal of the executives from the destination regions, who had arrived in the Kursk Oblast in order to take over and escort the trains carrying the resettlers.

It was only by means of categorical instant demands that 232 out of all recruited families that had sold their houses were delivered to their destinations (according to the letter of the Resettlement Department No. P-0/1016243 of 20 April 1937 and cable notification No. 0206228).

I inform you of the above facts in order to avoid such incidents in the future.

Source: RGAE, h. 5675, op. 1, d. 196, l. 23–25 (registered by the USSR NKVD Resettlement Department on 28 March 1938 under number No. 1814).

Supplement 4

USSR SUPREME SOVIET DECLARATION "ON
THE RECOGNITION AS UNLAWFUL AND CRIMINAL OF
THE REPRESSIVE ACTS AGAINST PEOPLES WHO WERE
SUBJECTED TO FORCED RESETTLEMENT, AND ON
GUARANTEEING THEIR RIGHTS"

Today, in the period of the revolutionary renewal of Soviet society, the process of democratization—the process of cleansing all aspects of life from the deformities and distortions of the universal humanist principles—has commenced, and the aspiration to learn the whole truth about the past in order to grow from the experience for the sake of the future has been gaining momentum in the country.

The memory has been returning to us with a remarkable bitterness towards the years of the Stalin repressions. No single republic or people were able to avoid their unlawfulness and arbitrariness. The sanctioned mass arrests, camp martyrdom, the wretched fates of women, elderly people and children in the resettlement zones keep prodding our conscience and injuring our moral dignity. These must not be forgotten.

The barbaric actions of the Stalin regime included the banishment of Balkars, Ingushetians, Kalmyks, Karachais, Crimean Tatars, Germans, Meskhetian Turks, and Chechens from their native lands during the Second World War. The forced resettlement policy also affected the fates of Koreans, Greeks, Kurds and other peoples.

The Supreme Soviet of the USSR unconditionally denounces the practice of the forced resettlement of entire peoples as a gravest crime contravening the foundations of international law, and the humanist nature of the socialist order.

The Supreme Soviet of the USSR guarantees that no infringement of human rights or humanity norms will ever occur in our country at state level.

The Supreme Soviet of the USSR considers it necessary to take corresponding legislative measures for the unconditional restoration of the rights of the Soviet peoples who were subjected to repression.

The Supreme Soviet of the USSR Moscow, Kremlin, 14 November 1989

Bibliography

The bibliography includes only main sources used in the research. References to publications cited only once are given in the immediate notes and are not included in the general list.

BOOKS AND COLLECTIONS OF DOCUMENTS

Aizenstadt, Ya. O. "O podgotovke Stalinym genotsida yevreyev" [Concerning Stalin's plan of Jewish genocide]. *Judicial research of the stages of the Jewish genocide as planned by Stalin*. Jerusalem, 1994.

Alekseyeva, L. M. *Istoriya inakomysliya v SSSR. Noveyshy period*. [The History of nonconformist thinking in the USSR. The contemporary period]. Moscow: Vest, 1992.

Aliyeva, S. U. (comp.). "Tak eto bylo: Natsionalnyye repressii v SSSR. 1919–1952 gody." [This is how it was: Ethnic repressions in the USSR. 1919–1952]. Moscow: Insan, 1993.

Andreyev, Ye. M. and L. Ye. Darsky, and T. L. Kharkova. *Istoriya naseleniya SSSR. 1920–1959* [The history of population of the USSR. 1920–1959]. Issue 3–5 (Part 1). (Series: Express-informatsiya. "The History of Statistics"). Moscow: Goskomstat SSSR, 1990.

Anikeyev, A. A. *Agrarnaya politika natsistkoy Germanii v gody Vtoroy mirovoy voyny* [Agrarian policy of Nazi Germany in the years of the Second World War]. Rostov-on-Don: Rostov University Publishing House, 1990.

Artizov, A., Yu. Sigachev, I. Shevchuk and V. Khlopov (comps.). *Reabilitatsiya: Kak eto bylo. Dokumenty Prezidiuma TsK KPSS i drugiye dokumenty. Mart 1953–fevral 1956.* [Rehabilitation: The way it was. Documents of the USSR Communist Party Central Committee Presidium, and other materials. March 1953–February 1956.]. Moscow, 2000.

Auman, V. A. and V. G. Chebotareva (comps.). *Istoriya rossiyskikh nemtsev v dokumentakh* [The history of Russian Germans in documents] V. 1: (1763–1992). Moscow: International Humanitarian Program Institute, 1993.

———. "Obshchestvenno-politicheskiye dvizheniya za vosstanovleniye natsionalnoy gosudarstvennosti (1965–1992)" [The public and political movements for the restoration of ethnic sovereignty (1965–1992)]. Vol. 2. In *Istoriya rossiyskikh nemtsev v dokumentakh* [The history of Russian Germans in documents]. Moscow: Rossiysky ekonomichesky zhurnal, 1994.

Avtorkhanov, A. *Memuary* [Memoirs]. Frankfurt-am-Main: Posev, 1983.

Azamatov, K. G., M. O. Temirzhanov, B. B. Temukuyev, A. I. Tetuyev and I. M. Chechenov. *Cherekskaya tragediya* [The tragedy of Cherek]. Nalchik: Elbrus, 1994.

Belaya kniga. O deportatsii koreyskogo naseleniya Rossii v 30-40-e gody. [The White Book. On the deportations of the Korean population of Russia in 1930–1940s]. Book 1. Moscow: Publisher?, 1992.

"Berlinskaya (Potsdamskaya) konferentsiya rukovoditeley trekh soyuznykh derzhav—SSSR, SShA i Velikobritanii (17 iyulya–2 avgusta 1945 g.)" [The Berlin (Potsdam) Conference of the leaders of the three Allied nations: The USSR, USA and Great Britain. 17 July–2 August 1945]. Collection of documents, MID SSSR. Vol. 6. In Gromyko, A. A. (Editor-in-Chief) and I. N. Zemskov et al. (eds.*).* *Sovetsky Soyuz na Mezhdunarodnykh konferentsiyakh perioda Velikoy Otechestvennoy voyny 1941–1945 gg.* [The Soviet Union at the international conferences in the period of the Great Patriotic War of 1941–1945]. Moscow: Politizdat, 1984.

"Bitva za Berlin (Krasnaya armiya v poverzhennoy Germanii)" [The Battle for Berlin (The Red Army in the conquered Germany)]. Documents and materials. Vol. 15. In *Russian Archive: The Great Patriotic War*. Moscow: Terra, 1995.

Bugay, N. F. *Operatsiya "Ulusy"* [Operation "Ulusy"]. Elista: Kalmyk Book Publisher, 1991.

———. *"Po svedeniyam NKVD, byli pereseleny…"* ["According to the NKVD data, those resettled included…"]. Kiev, 1992.

——— (comp.). *Jozef Stalin—Lavrentiyu Beria: "Ikh nado deportirovat"* [Jozef Stalin to Lavrenty Beria: "They must be deported…"]. Documents, Facts, Comments. Moscow: Druzhba narodov, 1992.

———. *Turki iz Meskhetii: dolgy put k reabilitatsii (1944–1994)* [Turks from Meskhetia: A long way to rehabilitation (1944–1994)]. Moscow: ROSS Publisher, 1994.

———. *L. Beria—J. Stalin: "Soglasno vashemu ukazaniyu…"* [L. Beria to J. Stalin: "Following your order…"]. Moscow: AIRO–KHKH?, 1995.

———. *Mobilizovat nemtsev v rabochiye kolonny… J. Stalin* ["Germans are to be mobilized to labor columns… J. Stalin"]. Collection of documents (1940s). Moscow: Gotika, 1998.

———. *Sotsialnaya naturalizatsiya i etnicheskaya mobilizatsiya (opyt koreytsev v Rossii)* [Social rehabilitation and ethnic mobilization (Experience of Koreans in Russia)]. Moscow: Centre for Inter-ethnic Relations Studies of the Russian Academy of Sciences, N. N. Miklukho-Maklay Institute of Ethnology and Anthropology, 1998.

———. *Deportatsiya narodov Kryma. Dokumenty, fakty, kommentarii.* [Deportation of the peoples of the Crimea. Documents, facts, comments]. Moscow: Insan, 2002.

————, T. M. Broyev and R. M. Broyev. *Sovetskiye kurdy: vremya peremen* [The Soviet Kurds: The time of change]. Moscow: Kap, 1993.

———— and A. M. Gonov. *Kavkaz: narody v eshelonakh (20-60-ye gody)* [The Caucasus: Peoples on trains (1920–1960s)]. Moscow: Insan, 1998.

Chervonnaya, S. M. *Krymskotatarskoe natsionalnoye dvizhenie (1991–1993 gg.)* [The Crimean Tatar National Movement (1991–1993)]. Moscow: The Russian Academy of Sciences N. N. Miklukho-Maklay Institute of Ethnology and Anthropology, 1994.

Dugas, I. A. and Cheron, F. Ya. *Vycherknutyye iz pamyati. Sovetskie voyennoplennye mezhdu Gitlerom i Stalinym* [Crossed out of memory. The Soviet POWs between Hitler and Stalin]. Research into contemporary Russian history.— Paris: YMCA–Press, 1994.

Dugin, A. N. *Neizvestny GULAG. Dokumenty i fakty.* [The unknown GULAG. Documents and facts]. Moscow: Nauka, 1999.

Gakaev, D. *Ocherki politicheskoy istorii Chechni (XX vek)* [Sketches of the political history of Chechnya (the XXth century)]. Moscow: Chechen Cultural Center, 1997.

German, A. A. *Istoriya respubliki nemtsev Povolzhya v sobytiyakh, faktakh, dokumentakh* [The history of the Volga German Republic in events, facts and documents]. Moscow: Gotika, 1996.

Gildi, L. A. *Rasstrely, ssylki, muchenya* [Executions, exile, torments]. Saint Petersburg, 1996.

Gonov, A. M. *Severny Kavkaz: reabilitatsiya repressirovannykh narodov (20–90-ye gody XX veka)* [The North Caucasus: Rehabilitation of the repressed peoples (1920–1990s of the 20th Century). Moscow: Nalchik, 1998.

Grossman, V. and I. Erenburg (comps.). *Chernaya kniga o zlodeyskom povsemestnom ubiystve evreev nemetsko–fashistskimi zakhvatchikami vo vremenno–okkupirovannykh rayonakh Sovetskogo Soyuza i v lageryakh Polshi vo vremya voyny 1941–1945 gg.* [The Black Book on the malicious total murdering of Jews by the German Fascist invaders in the temporarily occupied regions of the Soviet Union and in camps of Poland during the war of 1941–1945]. Vilnus: Yad, 1993.

Istoriya rossiyskikh nemtsev v dokumentakh (1763–1992) [The history of Russian Germans in documents (1763–1992)]. Moscow, 1993 (abbreviated: IRND–1).

Ivanova, G. M. *Gulag v sisteme totalitarnogo gosudarstva* [The Gulag in the totalitarian state system]. Moscow: The Moscow Public Scientific Foundation, 1997.

Ivnitsky, N. A. *Kollektivizatsiya i raskulachivanie: nachalo 30–kh gg.* [Collectivization and dekulakization: The early 1930s]. Moscow: Magist, 1997.

Iz istorii raskulachivaniya v Karelii. 1930–1931. [From the History of Dekulakization in Karelia. 1930–1931]. Petrozavodsk: Publisher?, 1991.

K 50–letiyu Pobedy v Velikoy Otechestvennoy voyne 1941–1945 gg. [To the 50th anniversary of the victory in the Great Patriotic War]. Moscow: The CIS Interstate Statistics Committee, 1995.

Kabuzan, V. M. *Russkie v mire: Dinamika chislennosti i rasseleniya (1719–1989). Formirovanie etnicheskikh i politicheskikh granits russkogo naroda.* [Russians in the world: The dynamics of the size and territorial distribution of population. The formation of ethnic and political boundaries of the Russian people]. Saint Petersburg: Blits, 1996.

Ken, O. N. and A. I. Rupasov. *Politburo TsK VKP(b) i otnosheniya SSSR s zapadnymi sosednimi gosudarstvami (konets 1920kh–1930ye gg). Problemy. Documenty.* [Communist Party Central Committee Politburo and relations between the USSR and neigboring Western countries (Late 1920s–1930s). Problems. Documents]. Saint Petersburg: Yevropeysky dom, 2000.

Khrebtovich–Buteneva, O. A. *Perelom (1939–1942)* [The rupture (1939–1942)]. The All-Russian Library of Memoirs. Vol. 3. Paris: YMCA–Press, 1984.

Kim, G. N. *Sotsialno–kulturnoe razvitiye koreytsev Kazakhstana* [The social and cultural development of the Koreans of Kazakhstan]. Alma–Ata: Publishing House Nauka of the Kazakh SSR, 1989.

Knyshevsky, P. *Dobycha tayny germanskikh reparatsy* [Discovering the secrets of German reparations]. Moscow: Soratnik, 1994.

Kokurin, A. I. and N. V. Petrov (comps.). *Lubyanka: VChK—OGPU—NKVD—MGB—MVD—KGB. 1917–1960.* [The Lubyanka: VChK—OGPU—NKVD—MGB—MVD—KGB. 1917–1960]. (Series: Russia. The XXth Century.) Moscow: International Foundation Democracy, 1997.

———. *GULAG: Glavnoye upravleniye lagerey. 1918–1960.* [GULAG: The Chief Camp Administration. 1918–1960.]. Moscow: MF "Demokratiya," 2000.

Kolerov, M. A. (ed.), Ye. D. Grinko, Ye. A. Danilina, O. K. Lokteva and K. G. Lyashchenko (comps.). *"Osobaya papka" Berii* [The "Special File" of Beria]. From the materials of the secretarial office of the USSR NKVD–MVD of 1946–1949. Vol. 4. (Series: The archive of the contemporary history of Russia.) Moscow, 1996.

Kozlov, V. A. *Massovyye besporyadki v SSSR pri Khrushcheva i Brezhneve (1953–nachalo 1980kh).* [Mass disturbances in the USSR during the Khrushchev and Brezhnev rule (1953–the early 1980s)]. Issue 1. (Series: "Issledovaniya") Novosibirsk: Sibirskiy Khronograf, 1999.

Knyshevsky, P. N., O. Yu. Vasilyeva, V. V. Vysotsky and S. A. Solomatin (comps.). *Skrytaya pravda voyny: 1941 god. Neizvestnyye dokumenty* [The hidden truth of the War: 1941. Unknown documents]. (Series: Rossiya v litsakh, dokumentakh, dnevnikakh.) Moscow: Russkaya kniga. 1992 (in the text referred to as "hidden truth").

Krasilnikov, S. A., V. L. Kuznetsova, T. N. Ostashko, T. F. Pavlova, L. S. Pashchenko and R. K. Sukhanova (comps.). *Spetspereselentsy v Zapadnoy Sibiri: 1930–vesna 1931 goda* [Resettlers in West Siberia: 1930–Spring 1931]. Novosibirsk: Ekor, 1992.

———. *Spetspereselentsy v Zapadnoy Sibiri: vesna 1931–nachalo 1933 goda* [Resettlers in the West Siberia: Spring 1931–Early 1933]. Novosibirsk: Ekor, 1993.

———. *Spetspereselentsy v Zapadnoy Sibiri: 1933–1938* [Resettlers in West Siberia: 1933–1938]. Novosibirsk: Ekor, 1994.

————. *Spetspereselentsy v Zapadnoy Sibiri: 1939–1945* [Resettlers in West Siberia: 1939–1945]. Novosibirsk: Ekor, 1996.

Kritchlou, D. *Repressirovannye narody Sovetskogo Soyuza. Nasledie stalinskikh deportatsy* [The repressed peoples of the Soviet Union. The legacy of the Stalin deportations]. A report by the Helsinki Human Rights Group. N.p.: Helsinki Watch, Committee of Human Rights Watch, 1991.

Krivosheina, N. A. *Chetyre treti nashey zhizni* [Four-thirds of our life]. The All-Russian Library of Memoirs. Vol. 2. Paris: YMCA–Press, 1984.

Krym mnogonatsionalnyy: voprosy i otvety [The Crimea multiethnic: Questions and answers]. Issue 1. Simferopol: Tavria, 1988.

"Krymskaya konferentsiya rukovoditeley trekh soyuznykh derzhav—SSSR, SShA i Velikobritanii (4–11 fevralya 1945 g.)" [The Crimea conference of the leaders of the Three Allied Nations: the USSR, USA and Great Britain. 4–11 February 1945]. Collection of documents MID SSSR. Vol. 4. In Gromyko, A. A. (Editor-in-Chief), I. N. Zemskov et al. (eds.). *Sovetsky Soyuz na mezhdunarodnykh konferentsiyakh perioda Velikoy Otechestvennoy voyny 1941–1945 gg.* [The Soviet Union at the international conferences of the period of the Great Patriotic War of 1941–1945]. Moscow: Politizdat, 1984.

Kurbanova, Sh. I. *Pereselenie: kak eto bylo* [Resettlement: The way it was]. Dushanbe: Irfon, 1993.

Kynin, G. P. and J. Laufer (comps.). *SSSR i germansky vopros. 1941–1949: Dokumenty iz Arkhiva vneshney politiki Rossiyskoy Federatsii.* [The USSR and the German Question. 1941–1949: Documents from the Russian Federation Foreign Policy Archive]. Vol. 1: 22 June 1941–8 May 1945. Moscow: Mezhdunarodnyye otnosheniya, 1996.

Lebedeva, N. S. (comp.). *Katyn. Mart 1940 g.–sentyabr 2000 g.: Rasstrel. Sudby zhivykh. Ekho Katyni. Dokumenty.* [Katyn. March 1940–September 2000: Execution. Fates of survivors. The echo of Katyn. Documents]. Moscow: Ves mir, 2001.

Lugin, I. A. *Polglotka svobody* [Half a Swallow of Freedom]. The All-Russian Library of Memoirs. Vol. 6. (Series: Nashe nedavneye.) Paris: YMCA–Press, 1984.

Maksheyev, V. N. (comp.) *Narymskaya khronika* [The Narym Chronicles]. Vol. 3. (Series: Research into contemporary Russian history) Moscow: Russky put, 1997.

Milova, O. L. (comp.) *Deportatsii narodov SSSR (1930–1950-e gody)* [Deportations of the Peoples of the USSR (1930–1950)]. Part 1. Dokumentalnye istochniki Tsentralnogo Gosudarstvennogo Arkhiva Oktyabrskoy Revolyutsii, vysshikh organov gosudarstvennoy vlasti i organov gosudarstvennogr upravleniya (TSGAOR) SSSR [The document sources of the October Revolution Central State Archive and of the Higher State Authorities of the USSR]. Issue XII. (Series: Peoples and cultures.) Introduction by O. L. Milova. Moscow, 1992.

————. *Deportatsii narodov SSSR (1930–1950-e gody)* [Deportations of the peoples of the USSR (1930–1950)]. Part 2. Deportatsiya nemtsev (sentyabr

1941–fevral 1942 gg.) [The Deportation of Germans (September 1941–
February 1942)]. (Series: Peoples and cultures.) Moscow, 1995.

Mukomel, V. I. *Deportirovannye narody v Sredney Azii: problemy i perspektivy sotsialno–demograficheskogo razvitiya* [The deported peoples in Central Asia:
problems and prospects of the social and demographic development].
Ashkhabad, 1991.

Narodonaseleniye [The Population]. Encyclopedic dictionary. Moscow: Bolshaya
Rossiyskaya entsiklopediya, 1994.

Narody Rossii: problemy deportatsii i reabilitatsii [The peoples of Russia: The problems of deportations and rehabilitation]. Maykop: Meoty, 1997.

Nekrich, A. *Nakazannye narody* [The punished peoples]. New York: Khronika,
1978.

Okorokov, A. V. (ed.). *Materialy po istorii russkogo osvoboditelnogo dvizheniya: Statyi,
dokumenty, vospominaniya* [Materials on the history of the Russian liberation
movement: Articles, documents, memoirs]. Moscow: Archive ROA, 1999.

Ollkott, M. B., V. Tishkov and A. Malashenko (eds.). *Identichnost i konflikt
v postsovetskikh gosudarstvakh* [Identity and conflict in the post-Soviet states].
Moscow: The Carnegie Moscow Center, 1997.

Organy gosudarstvennoy bezopasnosti v Velikoy Otechestvennoy voyne [State security
bodies during the Great Patriotic War]. Collection of documents. Vol. 1.
Book 1: Nakanune. Noyabr 1938–dekabr 1940 g. [On the eve. November
1938–December 1940]. Moscow: Kniga i biznes, 1995.

Organy gosudarstvennoy bezopasnosti v Velikoy Otechestvennoy voyne [State security
bodies during the Great Patriotic War]. Collection of documents. Vol. 1.
Book 2: Nakanune. 1 yanvarya–21 iyunya 1941 g. [On the eve. 1 January–
21 June 1941]. Moscow: Kniga i biznes, 1995.

Organy gosudarstvennoy bezopasnosti v Velikoy Otechestvennoy voyne [State security
bodies during the Great Patriotic War]. Collection of documents. Vol. 2.
Book 1: Nachalo. 22 iyunya–31 avgusta 1941 goda. [The beginning. 22 June–
31 August 1941]. Moscow: Rus, 2000.

Organy gosudarstvennoy bezopasnosti v Velikoy Otechestvennoy voyne [State security
bodies during the Great Patriotic War]. Collection of documents. Vol. 2.
Book 2: Nachalo. 1 sentyabrya–31 dekabrya 1941 goda. [The beginning.
1 September–31 December 1941]. Moscow: Rus, 2000.

Osipov, A. G. and O. I. Cherepova. *Narushenie prav vynuzhdennykh migrantov i
etnicheskaya diskriminatsiya v Krasnodarskom kraye (Polozhenie meskhetinskikh
turok)* [Infringements on the rights of forced migrants and ethnic discrimination in Krasnodar Kray (The situation of Meskhetian Turks)]. Moscow:
Memorial, 1996.

Osipov, A. G. *Rossiysky opyt etnicheskoy diskriminatsii: meskhetintsy v Krasnodarskom kraye* [The Russian experience of ethnic discrimination: The Meskhetians in Krasnodar Kray]. Moscow: Zvenya, 1999.

Palibin, N. V. *Zapiski sovetskogo advokata. 20–30-e gody.* [Notes of a Soviet
Lawyer. 1920–1930s]. Vol. 9. (Series: Nashe nedavneye.) Paris: YMCA–Press,
1988.

Parsadanova, V. S. *Sovetsko–polskie otnosheniya v gody Velikoy Otechestvennoy voyny 1941–1945* [Soviet-Polish relations in the years of the Great Patriotic War of 1941–1945]. Moscow: Nauka, 1982.

Passat, V. I. *Trudnye stranitsy istorii Moldovy: 1940–1950* [The bitter pages of the history of Moldova: 1940–1950s]. Moscow: Terra, 1994.

Polian, P. M. *Zhertvy dvukh diktatur. Voennoplennye i ostarbaytery v Tretyem Reykhe i ikh repatriatsiya.* [Victims of two dictatorships. The Ostarbeiter and POWs in the Third Reich and their repatriation]. Moscow: TSIRZ "Vash vybor," 1996.

———. *Geografiya prinuditelnykh migratsy v SSSR* [Geography of forced migrations in the USSR]. Abstract of dissertation for the doctoral degree in geographic sciences. Moscow: Geography Institute of the Russian Academy of Sciences, 1998.

———. *"Vestarbaytery": internirovannye nemtsy v SSSR (predystoriya, istoriya, geografiya)* [The "Westarbeiter": German internees in the USSR (Prehistory, history, geography)]. Special course handbook. Stavropol–Moskow: Stavropol State University, 1999.

Politburo TsK RKP(b). Povestki dnya zasedaniy. 1919–1952 [USSR Communist Party Central Committee Politburo. Agenda of sittings. 1919–1952]. Catalogue. Vol. 1. 1919–1929. Moscow: Rosspen, 2000 (in the text referred to as: Politburo-I).

Politburo TsK RKP(b). Povestki dnya zasedaniy. 1919–1952 [USSR Communist Party Central Committee Politburo. Agenda of sittings. 1919–1952]. Catalogue. Vol. 2. 1930–1939. Moscow: Rosspen, 2001 (in the text referred to as: Politburo-II).

Politburo TsK RKP(b). Povestki dnya zasedaniy. 1919–1952 [USSR Communist Party Central Committee Politburo. Agenda of sittings. 1919–1952]. Catalogue. Vol. 3. 1940–1952. Moscow: Rosspen, 2001 (in the text referred to as: Politburo-III).

Repressii protiv polyakov i polskikh grazhdan. [Repressions against Poles and Polish citizens]. History collections of the Memorial Society. Issue 1. Moscow: Zvenya, 1997.

Shabayev, D. V. *Pravda o vyselenii balkartsev* [The truth about the banishment of Balkars]. Second edition, revised. Nalchik: Elbrus, 1994.

Shcherbakova, I. L. (ed. and comp.). *Repressii protiv sovetskikh nemtsev. Nakazanny narod.* [Repressions against Soviet Germans. The Punished People.]. Moscow: Zvenya, 1999. (From the materials of conference "Repressions against Soviet Germans in the Soviet Union in the context of the Soviet national policy" held on 18–20 November 1998 by the Goethe German Cultural Center, Moscow, and the Memorial Society.)

Shirer, U. *Vzlet i padenie Tretyego Reykha* [The Rise and Fall of the Third Reich]. Translated from English, introduced and edited by O. A. Rzheshevsky. Moscow: Voyenizdat, 1991.

Slavko, T. I. *Kulatskaya ssylka na Urale 1930–1936* [The Kulak Banishment in the Urals]. Moscow: Mosgorarkhiv, 1995.

Smirnov, M. B. (comp.). *Sistema ispravitelno–trudovykh lagerey v SSSR. 1923–1960* [The system of correction labor camps in the USSR. 1923–1960]. Reference book. Moscow: Zvenya, 1998.

Sokolov, B. V. *Narkomy strakha. Yagoda, Ezhov, Beria, Abakumov* [People's commissars of fear. Yagoda, Ezhov, Beria, Abakumov]. Moscow: Ast-Press, 2001.

Solzhenitsyn, A. I. *Arkhipelag GULAG. 1918–1956: opyt khudozhestvennogo issledovaniya.* [The GULAG Archipelago. 1918–1956: The experience of artistic research]. Paris: YMCA–Press, 1973–1975.

Sovetskie nemtsy: istoriya i sovremennost [Soviet Germans: History and contemporaneity]. Materials of the All-Russian academic and practical conference. Moscow, 1990.

Ssylka kalmykov: kak eto bylo [The banishment of Kalmyks: The way it was]. Collection of documents and materials. Vol. 1. Book 1. Elista: Kalmyk Publishing House, 1993.

Tishkov, V. A. (ed.). *Narody Rossii* [The peoples of Russia]. Encyclopedia. Moscow: Bolshaya Rossiyskaya Entsiklopediya, 1994.

———. *Migratsiya i novye diaspory v postsovetskikh gosudarstvakh* [Migration and new diasporas in the post-Soviet states]. Moscow: The Russian Academy of Sciences N. N. Miklukho-Maklay Institute of Ethnology and Anthropology, 1996.

Tolstoy, N. *Zhertvy Yalty* [The Victims of Yalta]. Transl. from English by Ye. S. Gessen. Paris: YMCA–Press, 1988.

Tsutsiyev, A. A. *Osetino–ingushsky konflikt (1992–…): ego predystoriya i faktory razvitiya* [The Ossetian-Ingushetian conflict (1992–…): Its prehistory and development factors]. Moscow: Rosspen, 1998.

Ubushayev, V. *Kalmyki. Vyselenie i vozvrashcheniye* [The Kalmyks banishment and return]. Elista: Sanan, 1991.

Verbitsky, G. G. *Pochta ostarbaiterov Vtoroy mirovoy voyny. Dokumenty i perepiska.* [The correspondence of the Ostarbeiter of the Second World War. Documents and letters]. Tenafly: Hermitage, 1996. (Published in Russian and English.)

Vermel, S. S. *Moskovskoe izgnaniye (1891–1892 gg.): Vpechatleniya, vospominaniya* [The Moscow exile (1891–1892): Impressions, memories]. Moscow, 1924.

Vesnovskaya, G. F. (ed.) *Sbornik zakonodatelnykh i normativnykh aktov o repressiyakh i reabilitatsii zhertv politicheskikh repressiy* [Collection of legislative and normative acts concerning the repression and rehabilitation of political repression victims]. Kursk: GUIPP "Kursk," 1999.

Vishnevsky, A. G. *Serp i rubl. Konservativnaya modernizatsiya v SSSR.* [The sickle and ruble. Conservative modernization in the USSR]. Moscow: O.G. I., 1998.

Volkov, Ye. Z. *Dinamika naseleniya SSSR za vosemdesyat let* [The USSR population dynamics over eighty years]. Moscow: Gosizdat, 1930.

Zaytsev, Ye. A. (comp.). *Sbornik zakonodatelnykh i normativnykh aktov o repressiyakh i reabilitatsii zhertv politicheskikh repressy* [Collection of legislative and regulatory acts relative to the persecution and rehabilitation of the victims of political repressions]. Moscow: Respublika, 1993.

Zdravomyslov, A. G. *Mezhnatsionalnye konflikty v postsovetskom prostranstve* [The intra-national conflicts in the post-Soviet space]. Moscow: Aspekt–Press, 1997.

————. *Osetino–ingushsky konflikt: perspektivy vykhoda iz tupikovoy situatsii* [The Ossetian-Ingushetian conflict: The prospects of breaking the deadlock]. Moscow: Rosspen, 1998.

Zhurnaly zasedaniy vremennogo pravitelstva. Vol. 1: March–October 1917. Arkhiv noveyshey istorii Rossii. Moscow: Rosspen, 2001.

Aly, G. *"Endlösung"*. *Völkerverschiebung und der Mord der europäischen Juden*. Frankfurt–am–Main: Fisher Taschebuch Verlag, 1995.

Beer, S. *Judenburg 1945–im Spiegel britischer Besatzungsakten*. Judenburger Museumschriften. Judenburg: Publisher?, 1990.

Conquest, R. *Soviet Deportations of Nationalities*. London: McMillan and Co Ltd–New York: St Martin's Press, 1960.

Dahlman, D. and G. Hirschfeld (ed.). *Lager, Zwangsarbeit, Vertreibung und Deportation. Dimensionen der Massenverbrechen in der Sowjetunion und in Deutschland 1933 bis 1945*. Schriften der Bibliothek für Zeitgeschichte. Vol. 10. Essen: Klartextverlag, 1999.

Dallin, A. J. *Deutsche Herrschaft in Russland 1941–1945. Eine Studie über Besatzungspolitik*. Düsseldorf: Droste Verlag, 1958.

Der Prozess gegen die Hauptverbrecher vor dem Internationalen Militärgerichtshof. Nurnberg. 14. November 1945—1. Oktober 1946. Nürnberg: Publisher?, 1948.

Didier, F. *Europa arbeitet in Deutschland. Sauckel mobilisiert die Leistungsreserven*. Berlin: Zentralverlag der NSDAP Franz Eher Nachf. G.M.B.H., 1943.

Die deutschen Vertreibungsverluste. Bevölkerungsbilanzen für die deutschen Vertreibungsgebiete 1939–50. Wiesbaden: Publisher?, 1958.

Dörf, F., W. Kerl and Osmipreß GmbH (comps.). *Ostdeutschland und die deutschen Siedlungsgebiete in Ost– und Südosteuropa in Karte, Bild und Wort*. Munich: Südwestverlag, 1991.

Eisfeld, A. and V. Herdt (eds.) *Deportation, Sondersiedlung, Arbeitsarmee: Deutsche in der Sowjetunion 1941 bis 1956*. Der Göttinger Arbeitskreis: Veröffentlichung Nr. 453. Cologne: Verlag Wissenschaft und Politik, 1996.

Gatrell, P. *A Whole Empire Walking. Refugees in Russia during World War I*. Bloomington and Indianapolis: Indiana University Press, 1999.

Gatterbauer, R. H. *Arbeitseinsatz und Behandlung der Kriegsgefangenen in der Ostmark während des Zweiten Weltkrieges* (Dissertation). Salzburg, 1975.

Gilbert, M. *Atlas of Russian History*. Place?: Doprset Press, 1985.

Gross, J. *Revolution from Abroad: The Soviet Conquest of Poland's Western Ukraine and Western Belorussia*. Princeton: Princeton University Press, 1988.

Herbert, U. *Fremdarbeiter. Politik und Praxis des "Ausländer–Einsatzes" in der Kriegswirtschaft des Dritten Reiches*. Berlin–Bonn: Verlag J.H.W. Dietz Nachf., 1986.

The Holdings of the Berlin Document Center. A Guide to the Collection. Berlin: The Berlin Documentation Center, 1994.

Homze, Ed. L. *Foreign Labor in Nazi Germany*. Princeton: Princeton University Press, 1967.

Jacobmeyer, W. *Vom Zwangsarbeiter zum Heimatlosen Auslaender*. Kritische Studi-
en zur Geschichtswissenschaft. Vol. 65. Göttingen: Vandenhoeck u. Ruprecht
in Göttingen, 1985.

Jakobson, M. *Origin of Gulag: The Soviet Prison Camp System 1917–1934*.
Louisville: University Press of Kentucky, 1993.

Karner, S. *Im Archipel GUPVI. Kriegsgefangenschaft und Internirung in der Sowjetunion 1941–1956*. Kriegsfolgen–Forschung. Vol. 1. Vienna–Munich: R. Oldenbourg Verlag, 1995.

Lewin, M. *Russia, USSR, Russia: The Drive and Drift of a Superstate*. New York:
New Press, 1995.

Lohr, E. *Enemy Allien Policies Within the Russian Empire During World War I*. (Dissertation.) Cambridge, Mass.: Harvard University Press, 1999.

Magocsi, P. R. *Historical Atlas of East Central Europe*. Seattle—London: University of Washington Press, 1993.

Mitzka, H. *Zur Geschichte der Massendeportationen von Ostdeutschen in die Sowjetunion im Jahre 1945: ein historisch–politischer Beitrag*. Einhausen: Atelier
Huber, 1987.

Naimark, N. *Die Russen in Deutschland. Die sowjetische Besatzungszone 1945 bis
1949*. Berlin: Propyläen, 1997.

———. *Ethnic Cleansing in Twentieth Century Europe*. The Donald W. Treagold
Papers in Russian East European and Central Asian Studies. No. 19. Seattle: The Henry M. Jackson School of International Studies. The University
of Washington, 1998.

———. *Fires of Hatred. Ethnic Cleansing in Twentieth-Century Europe*. Cambridge,
Mass.: Harvard University Press, 2002.

Nekrich, A. *The Punished Peoples. The Deportation and Fate of Soviet Minorities at
the End of the Second World War*. New York: W. W. Norton, 1979.

Pfahlmann, H. *Fremdarbeiter und Kriegsgefangen in der Deutschen Kriegswirtschaft
1939–1945*. Beiträge zur Wehrforschung. Vols. 16–17. Darmstadt: Wehr und
Wissen Verlaggesellschaft GMBH [1968].

Pohl, J. O. *The Stalinist Penal System. A Statistical History of Soviet Repression and
Terror, 1930–1953*. Jefferson, North Carolina and London: McFarland &
Company, Inc., Publishers, 1997.

Proudfoot, M. J. *European Refugees: 1939–1952. A Study in Forced Population
Movement*. London, 1957.

Rhode, G. *Phasen und Formen der Massenzwangswanderungen in Europa. Die Vertriebenen in Westdeutschland*. Vol. 1. Kiel, 1959.

Schieder, T. (comp.). *Dokumentation der Vertreibung der deutschen aus Ost–Mit-
teleuropa*. Vols. 1–5. Wolfenbüttel, 1953–1961.

Sobczak, J. *Hitlerowskie przesiedlenia ludnisci niemeckej w dobie II woyny Swjatowej*.
Poznan, 1966.

Speer, A. *Errinerungen*. Augsburg: Weltbild Verlag GmbH, 1993.

Streibel, R. (ed.). *Flucht und Vertreibung: zwischen Aufrechnung und Verdrängung*.
Vienna: Picus–Verlag, 1994.

Streit, C. *Keine Kameraden. Die Wehrmacht und die sowjetischen Kriegsgefangenen
1941–1945*. 2nd edition. Bonn: Verlag J. H. W. Dietz Nachf, 1991.

Stühlpfarrer, K. *Umsiedlung Südtirol 1939–1940*. Vienna, 1985.

These Names Accuse: Nominal List of Latvians Deported to Soviet Russia in 1940–41.
2nd edition with supplementary list. Stockholm, 1982.

Ther, P. *Deutsche und polnische Vertriebene: Gesellschaft und Vertriebenenpolitik in
der SBZ//DDR und in Polen 1945–1956.* Vol. 127.(Series: Kritische Studien zur Geschichtswissenschaft.) Göttingen: Vandenhoeck und Ruprecht,
1998.

UNRRA in Europe 1945–1947. UNRRA European Office. Operational Analysis
Paper. No. 49. London, 1947.

Vertreibung und Vertreibungsverbrechen 1945–1978. Bericht des Bundesarchivs vom
28.05.1974. Archivalien und ausgewählte Erlebnisberichte Red., Spieler S.
Bonn: Kulturstiftung der deutschen Vertriebenen, 1989.

Weber, G., R. Weber–Schlenther, O. Sill and G. Kneer. *Die Deportation von
Siebenbürger Sachsen in die Sowjetunion 1945–1949.* Vols. 1–3. Cologne—
Weimar: Böhlau Verlag, 1996.

Weischer, H. *Russenlager. Russische Kriegsgefangene in Heessen (Hamm) 1942–1945.*
Vorwort von L. Kopelew. Essen: Klartextverlag, 1992.

Williams, B. G. *The Crimean Tatars. The Diaspora Experience and the Forging of
a Nation.* Vol. 2. (Series: Brill's Inner Asian Library.) Leiden—Boston—
Cologne: Brill, 2001.

Wysocki, G. *Arbeit für den Krieg. Herrschaftsmechanismen in der Rüstungsindustrie
des "Dritten Reiches". Arbeitseinsatz, Sozialpolitik und staatspolizeiliche Repression bei den Reichswerken "Hermann Göring" im Salzgitter-Gebiet 1937–38 bis
1945.* Braunschweig: Steinweg Verlag, 1992.

ARTICLES AND PUBLICATIONS

Abylkhozhaev, Zh. B., M. K. Kozybaev and M. B. Tatimov. "Kazakhstanskaya
tragediya" [The tragedy of Kazakhstan]. *Voprosy istorii,* no. 7 (Moscow,
1989): 53–71.

Adibekov, G. M. "Spetspereselentsy—zhertvy 'sploshnoy kollektivizatsii'" [The
special resettlers—victims of the 'blanket collectivization']. *Istorichesky arkhiv,*
no. 4 (Moscow, 1994): 145–180.

Auman, V. A. and V. G. Chebotareva. "Gordiev uzel nemetskikh natsionalnykh
problem" [The Gordian knot of the German ethnic problem]. In Auman,
Chebotareva, 1993, 3–10.

Baratashvili, A. and K. Baratashvili. "My—meskhi" [We are Meskhetian]. *Literaturnaya Gruziya,* no. 9 (1988).

Belitser, N. and O. Bodruk. "Krym kak region potentsialnogo konflikta" [The
Crimea as a region of potential conflict]. In *Etnicheskie i regionalnyye konflikty v Evrazii* [Ethnic and Regional Conflicts in Eurasia]. Book 2: Rossiya,
Ukraina, Belorussiya [Russia, Ukraine, Belorussia]. Moscow: Publisher?,
1997, 83–113.

Belkovets, L. "Spetsposelenie nemtsev v Zapadnoy Sibiri (1941–1955 gg.)" [German special settlements in the West Siberia (1941–1955)]. In *Repressii protiv
sovetskikh nemtsev.* Moscow: Nakazannyy narod, 1999, 158–179.

Bokov, Kh. *Ekho nevozvratnogo proshlogo* [The echo of the irrevocable past].
Moscow, 1989, no.1, 160–167.

Broydo, Ya. B. and V. Yu. Prokhorov. "Turki–meskhetintsy" [The Meskhetian
Turks]. In *Narody Rossii* [The Peoples of Russia]. Moscow: Encyclopedia,
1994, 342–343.

Brul, V. "Deportirovannye narody v Sibiri (1935–1965)" [The punished peoples
in Siberia (1935–1965)]. In *Repressii protiv sovetskikh nemtsev.* Moscow:
Nakazannyy narod, 1999, 95–118.

Bugay, N. F. "K voprosu o deportatsiyakh narodov SSSR v 30–40–kh godakh"
[On the question of the deportations of peoples of the USSR in 1930–1940s].
Voprosy istorii, no. 6 (Moscow, 1989): 135–143.

———. "O deportatsii kalmytskogo naroda" [On the deportation of the Kalmyk
people]. *Teachin Gerl,* no. 3 (Elista, 1990): 20–30.

———. "Deportatsiya" [Deportation]. *Politichesky sobesednik,* no. 6 (Minsk, 1990a):
39–41.

———. "Pravda o deportatsii chechenskogo i ingushskogo narodov" [The truth
about the deportation of the Chechen and Ingushetian peoples]. *Voprosy
istorii,* no. 7 (Moscow, 1990b): 32–44.

———. "Deportatsiya narodov s Ukrainy (30–50–e gody)" [The deportation of
peoples from Ukraine (1930–1950s)]. *Ukrainsky istorichesky zhurnal,* no.10
(Kiev, 1990c): 32–45.

———. "Deportatsiya narodov s Ukrainy (30–50–e gody)" [The deportation of
peoples from Ukraine (1930–1950s)]. *Ukrainsky istorichesky zhurnal,* no. 11
(Kiev, 1990d): 20–25.

———. "Pogruzheny v eshelony i otpravleny k mestam poseleniy" [They have been
put on trains and dispatched to the settlement destinations]. *Istoriya SSSR,*
no. 1 (1991a): 143–160.

———. "Vyselenie proizvesti po prikazu tov. Berii..." [The banishment shall be
carried out in accordance with the order by Comrade Beria]. *Istoricheskie
nauki v Moldove,* no. 1 (1991b): 64–68.

———. 40–e gody: "Avtonomiyu nemtsev Povolzhya likvidirovat..." [The 1940s:
The Volga Germans' autonomy shall be liquidated...]. *Istoriya SSSR,* no. 2
(1991c): 172–180.

———. "Deportatsiya. Beriya dokladyvaet Stalinu" [The deportation. Beria reports
to Stalin]. *Kommunist,* no. 3 (1991d): 123–128.

———. "Sever v politike pereseleniya narodov" [The North in the policy of peoples resettlement]. *Sever,* no. 4 (Petrozavodsk, 1991e): 92–98.

———. "Shli poezda na vostok" [The trains were moving eastwards]. *Politichesky
sobesednik,* no. 5 (Minsk, 1991f): 33, 61–63.

———. "Deportatsionnye i migratsionnye protsessy v Tsentralnom Chernozemye:
40–e gody" [The deportation and migration processes in the Central Chernozem zone: the 1940s]. In *Istoriya zaseleniya i sotsialno-ekonomicheskogo
razvitiya Tsentralnogo Chernozemya* [The history of the population, and social
and economic development of the Central Chernozem Zone]. Voronezh,
1991, 17–20.

————. "Konets 30-kh—40-e gody. Evropeysky Sever: deportatsiya narodov." [Late 1930s–1940s. The European North: deportation of peoples]. *Works of the Institute for language, literature and history of the Academy of Sciences Komi Center*, Issue 52 (Syktyvkar, 1991h): 84–97.

————. "Nastoyashchim dokladyvaem, na osnove ukazany deportiruyutsya..." (O pereselenii narodov v Bashkiriyu v 40–50–e gody [It is hereby reported that, under the directives, the deportation is being carried out... (On the resettlement of the peoples of Bashkiria in 1940–1950s)]. In *Stranitsy istorii bashkirskoy istorii: novye fakty, vzglyady, otsenki* [Pages of History of the Bashkir History: New Facts, Views and Evaluations]. Ufa: Publisher?, 1991i, 69–77.

————. "40–50–e gody: posledstviya deportatsii narodov" (svidetelstvuyut arkhivy NKVD–MVD SSSR) [1940–1950s: consequences of the deportation of peoples (USSR NKVD–MVD archive evidence)]. *Istoriya SSSR*, no. 1 (1992a): 122–143.

————. "Deportatsiya krymskikh tatar v 1944 g" [The deportation of the Crimean Tatars in 1944]. *Ukrainsky istorichesky zhurnal*, no. 1b (Kiev, 1992b): 29–44.

————. "Ingermanlandtsy pod grifom 'sekretno'" [The Ingermanlands, "classified"]. *Sever*, no. 3 (Petrozavodsk, 1992c): 123–128.

————. " 'Koreysky vopros' na Dalnem Vostoke i deportatsii 1937 g." [The "Korean question" in the Far East, and the deportations of 1937]. *Problemy Dalnego Vostoka*, no. 4 (1992d): 152–161.

————. "20–40–e gody: deportatsiya naseleniya s territorii Evropeyskoy Rossii" [The 1920–1940s: Deportations from the territory of European Russia]. *Otechestvennaya istoriya*, no. 4 (Moscow, 1992e): 37–49.

————. "Kharuki Vada. Iz istorii deportatsii 'russkikh koreytsev'" [Kharuki Vada. From the history of the deportation of the "Russian Koreans"]. *Druzhba narodov*, no. 7 (1992f): 218–224.

————. "O vyselenii koreytsev iz Dalnevostochnogo kraya" [On the banishment of Koreans from the Far East Okrug]. *Otechestvennaya istoriya*, no. 6 (Moscow, 1992g): 141–168.

————. "Iz istorii deportatsy i trudoustroystva koreytsev v Kazakhstane i Uzbekistane" [From the history of the deportations and labor use of Koreans in Kazakhstan and Uzbekistan]. *Information bulletin of the Korean Eurasian Association "Koren."* Issue 2 (Moscow, 1992h.): 54–94.

————. "40–e gody: deportirovannye i mobilizovannye nemtsy na Dalnem Vostoke" [1940s: The deported and mobilized Germans in the Far East]. *Problemy Dalnego Vostoka*, no. 2 (1993a): 172–177.

————. "O pereselenii i deportatsiyakh evreyskogo naseleniya v SSSR" [On the resettlement and deportations of the Jewish population in the USSR]. *Otechestvennaya istoriya*, no. 2 (Moscow, 1993b): 175–185.

————. "Vlast satany. O deportatsiyakh narodov iz Pribaltiki v 40–50–e gody" [The power of Satan. On the banishment of peoples from the Baltic republics in the 1940–1950s]. *Molodaya Gvardiya*, no. 4 (1993c): 40–48.

————. "20–50–e gody: prinuditelnye pereseleniya narodov" [The 1920–1950s: Forced resettlement of peoples]. *Obozrevatel*, no. 11 (1993d): 122–127.

————. "Repressirovannye narody: kazaki" [The repressed peoples: The Cossacks]. *Shpion*, no. 1 (1994a): 38–68.

————. "Vyselenie sovetskikh koreytsev s Dalnego Vostoka" [The banishment of the Soviet Koreans from the Far East]. *Voprosy istorii*, no. 5 (Moscow, 1994b): 141–148.

————. "O deportatsiyakh irantsev iz Azerbaydzhana i Kazakhstana" [On the deportation of Iranians from Azerbaijan and Kazakhstan]. *Vostok*, no. 6 (1994c): 146–154.

————. "Avtonomiya nemtsev Povolzhya: problemy destruktuirovaniya i sotsial-noy naturalizatsii" [Volga German autonomy: the problems of restructuring and social naturalization]. In *Repressii protiv sovetskikh nemtsev*. Moscow: Nakazannyy narod, 1999, 84–94.

Bukalov, D. "Ostarbaytery Donbassa" [The Ostarbeiter from the Donbass]. In *Korni travy* [Grass Roots]. Collection of articles by young historians. Moscow: Memorial, 1996, 155–159.

Burgart, L. "Sudba cheloveka—sudba naroda. Lichnye dela nemtsev–spetspere-selentsev kak istochnik po probleme deportatsii i rezhima spetsposeleniya" [Fate of an individual as the fate of the people. Personal files of German spe-cial resettlers as a source relating to the problem of deportation and special settlement regulations]. In *Repressii protiv sovetskikh nemtsev*. Moscow: Nakazannyy narod, 1999, 180–187.

Chebrikov, V. "O vyselenii v 40–50 godakh nekotorykh kategory grazhdan iz zapadnykh rayonov SSSR" [On the banishment of some categories of citi-zens from the USSR western regions in the 1940–1950s]. *Istochnik*, no. 1 (1996).

Chebykina, T. "Deportatsiya nemetskogo naseleniya iz evropeyskoy chasti SSSR v Zapadnuyu Sibir (1941–1945 gg.)" [The deportation of German popula-tion from the European part of the USSR to West Siberia (1941–1945)]. In *Repressii protiv sovetskikh nemtsev*. Moscow: Nakazannyy narod, 1999, 118–127.

Chernova, T. "Problema politicheskikh repressy v otnoshenii nemetskogo nase-leniya v SSSR (obzor otechestvennoy literatury)" [The problem of political repression against the German population in the USSR (a review of domestic publications)]. In *Repressii protiv sovetskikh nemtsev*. Moscow: Nakazannyy narod, 1999, 261–278.

Chervonnaya, S. M. "Vozvrashchenie i integratsiya krymskikh tatar v Krymu: 1990–e gody" [The return and integration of the Crimean Tatars in the Crimea: the 1990s]. In *Vynuzhdennyye migranty: integratsiya i vozvrashcheniye*. Moscow: Publisher?, 1997, 145–182.

Danilov, V. P. and N. A. Ivnitsky. "O derevne nakanune i v khode sploshnoy kollektivizatsii" [On the countryside before and during the blanket collec-tivization]. *Dokumenty svidetelstvuyut. Iz istorii derevni nakanune i v khode kollektivizatsii 1927–1932 gg.* [Documents testify. On the history of the coun-tryside before and during the blanket collectivization of 1927–1932]. Moscow, 1989, 9–50.

Krasilnikov, S. A. and V. L. Kuznetsova et al. "Introduction." In Danilov, V. P. and S. A. Krasilnikov. *Spetspereselentsy v Zapadnoy Sibiri: vesna 1931–nachalo 1933 goda* [Special resettlers in West Siberia: spring 1931–early 1933]. Novosibirsk: Ekor, 1993, 3–9.

Dugin, A. N. "Govoryat arkhivy: neizvestnye stranitsy GULAGa" [Archives testify: Unknown pages of the GULAG]. *Sotsialno–politicheskie nauki*, no. 7 (1990): 90–101.

———. "Stalinizm (Legendy i fakty)" [Stalinism (Legends and Facts)]. *Slovo*, no. 7 (1990): 23–26.

———. and A. Ya. Malygin. "Solzhenitsyn, Rybakov: tekhnologiya lzhi" [Solzhenitsyn, Rybakov: The technology of lying]. *Voyenno-istorichesky zhurnal*, no. 7 (Moscow, 1991): 68–73.

Erkenov, Ye. "Chechentsy i ingushi: Paket dokumentov No.1" [Chechens and Ingushetians. Collection of documents No.1]. *Shpion*, no. 1 (1993): 16–33.

———. "Chechentsy i ingushi: Paket dokumentov No.2" [Chechens and Ingushetians. Collection of documents No.2]. *Shpion*, no. 2 (1993): 53–72.

Filippov, S. G. "Deyatelnost organov VKP(b) v zapadnykh oblastyakh Ukrainy i Belorussii v 1939–1941 gg" [Activities of the Communist Party bodies in the western oblasts of Ukraine and Belorussia in 1939–1941]. In *Repressii protiv polyakov i polskikh grazhdan*. Issue 1. Moscow: Zvenya, 1997, 44–76.

Genis, V. L. "Raskazachivanie v Sovetskoy Rossii" [Decossackization in Soviet Russia]. *Voprosy Istorii*, no. 1 (Moscow, 1994): 42–56.

———. "Deportatsiya russkikh iz Turkestana v 1921 godu ("Delo Safarova")" [The deportation of Russians from Turkestan in 1921 ("The case of Safarov")]. *Voprosy istorii*, no. 1 (Moscow, 1998): 44–58.

Glezer, O. B. and P. M. Polian. "Karta deportatsy narodov v SSSR 30–50–kh godov" [The map of the deportations of peoples in the USSR in 1930–1950s]. *Moskovskie novosti*, no. 26 (30 June 1991): 6.

Guryanov, A. E. "Masshtaby deportatsii naseleniya vglub SSSR v mae–iyune 1941 g". [The scale of the deportation of population inland of the USSR in May–June 1941]. In *Repressii protiv polyakov i polskikh grazhdan*. Issue. 1. Moscow: Zvenya, 1997, 137–175.

———. "Polskie spetspereselentsy v SSSR v 1940–1941 gg". [Polish special resettlers in the USSR in 1940–1941]. *Repressii protiv polyakov i polskikh grazhdan*. Issue 1. Moscow: Zvenya, 1997, 114–136.

Holquist, P. "Rossiyskaya katastrofa (1914–1921) v evropeyskom kontekste. Totalnaya mobilizatsiya i 'politika naseleniya'" [The Russian catastrophe (1914–1921) in the European context. The total mobilization and "resettlement policy"]. *Rossia*, no. 11–12 (1998): 26–54.

Ibragimbeili, Kh. M. "Skazat pravdu o tragedii narodov" [To say the truth about the tragedy of peoples]. *Politicheskoe obrazovanie*, no. 4 (1989): 58–63.

Illarionova, T. "Reabilitatsiya: trudnyy put iz tupika. Problemy rossiyskikh nemtsev v sovetsko–zapadnogermanskikh peregovorakh 1957–1958 gg". [Rehabilitation: Hard way out of deadlock. Problems of Russian Germans in the Soviet–West German negotiations of 1957–1958.]. In *Repressii protiv sovetskikh nemtsev*. Moscow: Nakazannyy narod, 1999: 237–252.

Iontsev, V. A. "Deportatsiya narodov" [The deportation of peoples]. In *Narodonaselenie. Encyclopedic Dictionary*. Moscow, 1994, 124–125.

Isupov, V. A. "Demograficheskaya sfera v epokhu stalinizma" [The demographic sphere in the epoch of Stalinism]. In *Aktualnye problemy istorii sovetskoy Sibiri* [Topical Problems of the History of Soviet Siberia]. Novosibirsk, 1990, 180–201.

Ivanov, V. A. "Operatsiya 'Byvshie lyudi' v Leningrade (fevral–mart 1935 g.)" [The operation "The Déclassé" in Leningrad (February–March 1935)]. *Novyy chasovoy* (Russian military and political journal), no. 6–7 (Saint Petersburg, 1998): 118–130.

Kichikhin, A. N. "Sovetskie nemtsy: otkuda, kuda i pochemu?" [Soviet Germans: where from, where to, and why?]. *Voyenno-istorichesky zhurnal*, no. 9 (Moscow, 1990): 26–28.

Kim, S. "Ispoved soren–saram–sovetskogo cheloveka" [A confession by a Soren-Saram-Soviet person]. *Druzhba narodov*, no. 4 (1989): 168–195.

Kirillov, V. "Sovetskie nemtsy v Tagillage" [Soviet Germans in the camps of Tagil]. In *Repressii protiv sovetskikh nemtsev*. Moscow: Nakazannyy narod, 1999, 146–148.

Kiuru, Ye. "Rossiyskie finny do sikh por ne reabilitirovany" [Russian Finns have not been rehabilitated so far]. *Izvestiya*, 25 February 1992.

Knyshevsky, P. N. "Gosudarstvennyy komitet oborony: metody mobilizatsii trudovykh resursov" [The State Defense Committee: the methods of labor force mobilization]. *Voprosy istorii*, no. 2 (Moscow, 1994): 53–65.

Kokurin, A. I. "Spetspereselentsy v SSSR v 1944 godu, ili god bolshogo pereseleniya" [Special resettlers in the USSR in 1944, or a year of great resettlement]. *Otechestvennye arkhivy*, no. 5 (1993): 98–111.

———. "GULAG v gody voyny. Doklad nachalnika GULAGa NKVD SSSR V. G. Nasedkina. Avgust 1944 g". [The GULAG in the war years. A report by USSR NKVD GULAG Chief V. G. Nasedkin. August 1944]. *Istorichesky Archiv*, no. 3 (Moscow, 1995): 60–86.

Konasov, V. B. and A. V. Tereshchuk. "Budut nemedlenno predany sudu voennogo tribunala..." [They shall be immediately handed over to the military tribunal...]. *Russkoe proshloe*, no. 5 (1994): 318–337.

Kondakov, G. I. "Ostrov Olderni (Velikobritaniya) i Frantsiya" [The island of Aldernie (UK) and France]. In Komolova N. P. (ed.). *Sovetskie lyudi v Evropeyskom soprotivlenii* [Soviet People in the European Resistance]. (Memoirs and documents). Part II. Moscow: Chernakova, 1991, 256–361.

Kotsonis, A. N. "Deportatsiya grekov Severnogo Kavkaza v 30–50–e gody" [The deportation of Greeks from the North Caucasus in the 1930–1950s]. In *Pontiyskie greki* [The Greeks of Pontissi]. Krasnodar, 1997, 80–89.

Kozlov, V., S. Somonova and N. Teptsov. "Occupation: I. A review of the measures by the German authorities on temporarily occupied territories, prepared based on trophy documents, foreign press and intelligence data received in the period of June 1941 through March 1943." Vol. 2. In Ponomarev, A. *Neizvestnaya Rossiya. XX vek.* Moscow: Mosgorarkhiv, 1993, 231–365.

Krasilnikov, S. A. "...Svobodnyy trud svobodno sobravshikhsya lyudey" ["...Free labor by a free assembly of people"]. *EKO*, no. 8 (Novosibirsk, 1991): 183–196.

Kriger, V. "V nachale puti. Chast 3: Demograficheskie i migratsionnye protsessy sredi nemetskogo naseleniya SSSR (SNG)" [At the beginning of the path. Part 3: Demographic and migration processes among the German population of the USSR (CIS)]. *Vostochnyy ekspress*, no. 8 (Alen, 1997): 5.

Krupnik, I. I. and M. S. Kupovetsky. "'Lakhlukhi': kurdistanskie evrei v SSSR" [The 'Lakhlush': The Jews of Kurdistan in the USSR]. *Sovetskaya etnografiya*, no. 2 (1988): 102–111.

Kupovetsky, M. S. "Evrei iz Meshkheda i Gerata v Sredney Azii" [The Jews from Meshkhed and Herat in Central Asia]. *Etnograficheskoe obozrenie*, no. 5 (1992): 54–63.

Kurkchi, A. "Krymskie tatary" [The Crimean Tatars]. Otechestvo. *Regional studies almanac*, no. 1 (Moscow, 1991): 184–196.

Kurtsev, A. N. "Bezhentsy pervoy mirovoy voyny v Rossii v 1914–1917 gg." [Refugees in the First World War in Russia in 1914–1917]. *Voprosy istorii*, no. 8 (Moscow, 1998).

Malamud, G. "Mobilizovannye sovetskie nemtsy na Urale v 1942–1948 gg." [Mobilized Soviet Germans in the Urals in 1942–1948]. In *Repressii protiv sovetskikh nemtsev*. Moscow: Nakazannyy narod, 1999, 128–145.

Muduyev, Sh. S. "Vliyanie prinuditelnoy migratsii na rasselenie laktsev (na primere Lakskogo, Kulinskogo i Novolakskogo rayonov)" [The impact of migration on the territorial distribution of Laks (by the examples of the Laksky, Kuli and Novolaksky districts)]. *Novoluniye*, no. 2 (Makhachkala, 1993): 36–59.

Mukomel, V. "Vooruzhennye mezhnatsionalnye i regionalnye konflikty: lyudskie poteri, ekonomichesky ushcherb i sotsialnye posledstviya" [Armed inter-ethnic conflicts: human casualties, economic damage and social repercussions]. In *Identichnost i konflikt v postsovetskikh gosudarstvakh*. Moscow: Publisher?, 1997, 298–324.

Nelipovich, S. G. "Rpressii protiv poddannykh 'tsentralnykh derzhav'" [Repressions against subjects of "central states"]. *Voyenno-istorichesky zhurnal*, no. 6 (Moscow, 1996): 32–42.

Okhotin, N. and A. Roginsky. "Iz istorii 'nemetskoy operatsii' NKVD 1937–1938 gg." [From the history of the NKVD "German operation"]. In *Repressii protiv sovetskikh nemtsev*. Moscow: Nakazannyy narod, 1999, 35–74.

Osipov, A. "Ofitsialnye ideologemy regulirovaniya mezhnatsionalnykh otnosheny kak faktor razvitiya etnicheskoy konfliktnosti (regionalny aspekt)" [Official ideological assumptions of the inter-ethnic relations regulation, as a factor in ethnic conflict development (the regional aspect)]. In *Identichnost i konflikt v postsovetskikh gosudarstvakh*. Moscow, 1997, 250–297.

Osokina, Ye. A. "Zhertvy goloda 1933 goda: skolko ikh?" [Victims of the famine of 1933: how many are there?]. (Analysis of the demographic statistics of the USSR TsGANKh.) *Istoriya SSSR*, no. 5 (1991): 18–26.

Panesh, Ye. Kh. and L. B. Yermolov. "Meskhetinskie turki" [Meskhetian Turks]. *Voprosy istorii*, no. 9–10 (Moscow, 1991): 212–217.

Parsadanova, V. S. "Deportatsiya naseleniya iz Zapadnoy Ukrainy i Zapadnoy Belorussii v 1939–1941 gg." [Deportation of population from Western Ukraine and Western Belorussia in 1939–1941]. *Novaya i noveyshaya istoriya*, no. 2 (Moscow, 1989): 26–44.

Pashkov, A. and G. Dudarets. "Deportatsii na Sakhaline" [Deportations on Sakhalin]. *Karta*, no. 5 (Ryazan, 1994): 14–17.

Pavlova, T. F. "Dokumenty TSGAOR SSSR po istorii deportatsii narodov v 40–50–e gody" [Documents of the USSR October Revolution Central State Archive on the history of the deportation of peoples in the 1940–1950s]. In *DNS-1.*, 7–28.

Polian, P. M. "K voprosu o planovom pereselenii s gor na ravninu" [On the issue of the planned resettlement from the highlands to the plain]. In *Problemy sotsialno–ekonomicheskogo razvitiya gornykh territory Severnogo Kavkaza*. Rostov–on–Don: Publisher?, 1989, 58–60.

———. "Chelovek i bolshoy terror" [The person and the Great Terror]. *Znamya*, no. 1 (1990a): 230–234.

———. (Introduction) "Pobeda nad derevney: tsel i rezultat" [The conquest of the countryside: the goal and result] (S. Maksudov. "Nachalo 37 goda: perepis" [The beginning of 1937: Census]). *Selskaya molodezh*, no. 9 (1990b): 46–51.

———. *Ne po svoey vole* [Against their will]. *Grazhdanskoe dostoinstvo*, no. 16 (1990c, April): 5.

———. "Prinuditelnye migratsii v SSSR" [Forced migrations in the USSR]. *Russkaya mysl*, Paris, 1990d, 18 May.

———. "Spetskontingent" [The special target group]. In *Migratsiya naseleniya*. Moscow: Social and Economic Population Problems Institute, 1992, 48–60.

———. "Velikoe pereselenie nemtsev" [The great resettlement of Germans]. *Evropa–Tsentr*, no. 14 (Berlin, 1997a,): 6.

———. "'Reparatsii trudom': motivy i predystoriya poslevoennogo trudoispolzovaniya 'internirovannykh i mobilizovannykh' nemetskikh grazhdanskikh lits v SSSR" ["Labor reparations": Motivation and prehistory of the post-war labor use of the "interned and mobilized" German civilians in the USSR]. In *Problemy voyennogo plena: Istoriya i sovremennost* [POW Problems: History and Contemporaneity]. (Materials of international practical and academic conference, 23–25 October 1997, Vologda.) Part 2. Vologda, 1997b, 59-67.

———. "Nasilstvennye migratsii v byvshem SSSR" [Forced migration in the former USSR] "Migratsionnaya situatsiya v stranakh SNG" [The migratory situation in the CIS states]. Moscow: The Center for Research of the Problems of Forced Migration in the USSR, 1999a., 265–276.

———. "Ostarbaytery i vestarbaytery" [The Ostarbeiter and Westarbeiter]. *Russkaya mysl*, no. 4285 (Paris, 1999b): 18.

———. "Deportatsii evreev v Rossii" [Deportations of Jews in Russia]. *Forward*, no. 206 (New York, 1999c): 9.

———. "Geografiya prinuditelnykh migratsy v SSSR" [Geography of forced migrations in the USSR]. *Academy of Sciences Bulletin*, no. 6 (Geography Series, 1999d): 55–62.

———. "Geografiya nasilstvennykh migratsy v SSSR" [Geography of forced migrations in the USSR]. *Naseleniye i obshchestvo* (Information bulletin of the Center for Human Demography and Ecology of the Russian Academy of Sciences Economic Forecast Institute), no. 37 (1999e, June): 4.

————. "Vestarbaytery. Internirovannye nemtsy na sovetskikh stroykakh." [The Westarbeiter. German internees at the Soviet construction sites]. *Rodina*, no. 9 (1999): 21–25.

————. "Ne po svoey vole" [Against their will]. *Priroda*, no. 2 (2000): 3–12.

————. "Internirovannye nemtsy v SSSR" [German internees in the USSR]. *Voprosy istorii*, no. 8 (2001): 113–23.

Prozumenshchikov, M. "'Natsionalisticheskie elementy postoyanno provotsirovali vystupleniya.' Kak nakalyalas obstanovka v Checheno–Ingushetii." ["The nationalistic element kept provoking public unrest." The way the situation was growing tense in the Chechen-Ingush Republic]. *Istochnik*, no. 4 (1997): 48–64.

Semiryaga, M. "Prikazy, o kotorykh my ne znali. Stalin khotel vyvezti iz Germanii v SSSR vsekh trudosposobnykh nemtsev" [The orders that we did not know about. Stalin wanted to bring all able-bodied Germans from Germany to the USSR]. *Novoe vremya*, no. 15 (1994): 56–57.

Shevyakov, A. A. "Gitlerovsky genotsid na territoriyakh SSSR" [The Hitler genocide on the territories of the USSR]. *Sotsiologicheskiyye issledovaniya*, no. 12 (Moscow, 1991): 3–11.

————. "Repatriatsiya sovetskogo mirnogo naseleniya i voennoplennykh, okazavshikhsya v okkupatsionnykh zonakh gosudarstv antigitlerovskoy koalitsii" [Repatriation of the Soviet civilian population and POWs from the occupation zones of the anti-Hitler coalition countries]. *Naselenie Rossii v 1920–1950-e gody: chislennost, poteri, migratsii* [The Population of Russia in the 1920–1950s: size, losses, migrations]. Collection of academic publications. Moscow, 1994, 195–222.

Shulga, I. I. "Sudby krasnoarmeytsev—nemtsev Povolzhya v germanskom plenu v 1941–1945 gg." [Fates of German Red Army servicemen in German captivity in 1941–1945]. In *Migration Processes among Russian Germans: Historical Aspect* (Materials of International Academic Conference. Anapa, 26–30 September 1997). Moscow, 1998, 323–337.

Sidorenko, V.P. "'Dlya vyseleniya chechentsev i ingushey napravit chasti NKVD.' Dokumenty o provedenii spetsoperatsii po deportatsii narodov ChI ASSR. 1943–1944" ["NKVD units shall be dispatched for resettling Chechens and Ingushetians." Documents about the implementation of the special operation for the deportation of the peoples of the Chechen-Ingush ASSR. 1943–1944]. *Istorichesky arkhiv*, no. 3 (2000): 66–89.

Silayeva, O. "Iz istorii bez viny vinovatykh" [From the history of those guilty without fault]. *Argumenty i fakty*, 7 February 1991, 2.

Streletsky, V. "Etnoterritorialnye konflikty: sushchnost, genezis, tipy" [Ethnic-territorial conflicts: essence, genesis, types]. In *Identichnost i konflikt v postsovetskikh gosudarstvakh*. Moscow: Publisher?, 1997, 225–249.

Strods, Kh. P. "Deportatsiya naseleniya Pribaltiyskikh stran" [Deportation of the population of the Baltic states]. *Voprosy istorii*, no. 9 (Moscow, 1999): 130–136.

Tsaplin, V. V. "Statistika zhertv stalinizma v 30-e gody" [The statistics of Stalinism victims in the 1930s]. *Voprosy istorii*, no. 4 (Moscow, 1989): 175–181.

Verigin, S. G. and L. V. Suni. "Pereselenie ingermanlandtsev v Kareliyu v kontse 1940–kh godov" [The banishment of the Ingermanlands to Karelia in the late 1940s]. (Materials of the series "Narody i kultura.") Issue X. *Voprosy istorii* (Moscow, 1992): 200–216.

Viola, L. "OGPU. Raskulachivanie i spetspereselentsy." [The OGPU. Dekulakization and Special Resettlers]. *Krestyanovedenie: teoriya, istoriya, sovremennost.* Moscow: Intertsentr, 1999, 115–161.

Vormsbekher, G. "Nemtsy v SSSR" [Germans in the USSR]. *Znamya*, no. 11 (1988): 193–203.

Vyltsan, M. A. "Deportatsiya narodov v gody Velikoy Otechestvennoy voyny" [The deportations of peoples in the years of the Great Patriotic War]. *Etnograficheskoe obozrenie*, no. 3 (1995): 26–44.

Zayonchkovskaya, Zh. A. and Polian, P. M. "Ostarbaytery: v Germanii i doma (Po materialam anketnogo obsledovaniya)" [The Ostarbeiter in Germany and at home (based on the data of questionnaire research)]. In *In Memoriam. The F. F. Perchenko historical collection.* Saint Petersburg: Publisher?, 1995, 396–413.

Zelenin, I. Ye. "O nekotorykh 'belykh pyatnakh' zavershayushchego etapa sploshnoy kollektivizatsii" [On some "blank spots" in the concluding stage of blanket collectivization]. *Istoriya SSSR*, no. 2 (1989): 3–19.

Zemskov, V. N. "K voprosu o repatriatsii sovetskikh grazhdan 1944–1951 gg." [On the question of repatriation of Soviet citizens in 1944–1951]. *Istoriya SSSR*, no. 4 (1990a): 26–41.

———. "'Chernye dyry' istorii" ["Black voids" of history]. *Raduga*, no. 9 (1990b): 56–62.

———. "'Kulatskaya ssylka' v 30–e gody" [The "kulak exile" in the 1930s]. *Sotsiologicheskiye issledovaniya*, no. 10 (Moscow, 1990c): 3–21.

———. "Spetsposelentsy (po dokumentam NKVD–MVD SSSR)" [Special settlers (based on the USSR NKVD-MVD documents)]. *Sotsiologicheskiye issledovaniya*, no. 11 (Moscow, 1990d): 3–17.

———. "Massovoe osvobozhdenie spetsposelentsev i ssylnykh (1954–1960)" [The mass discharge of special settlers and exiles (1954–1960)]. *Sotsiologicheskiye issledovaniya*, no. 1 (Moscow, 1991a): 5–26.

———. "Ob uchete spetskontingenta NKVD vo Vsesoyuznykh perepisyakh naseleniya 1937 i 1939 gg." [On the registration of special target groups in the All-Union Censuses of 1937 and 1939]. *Sotsiologicheskiye issledovaniya*, no. 2 (Moscow, 1991b): 74–75.

———. "Zaklyuchennyye, spetsposelentsy, ssylnoposelentsy, ssylnyye i vyslannyye (statistiko–geografichesky aspekt)" [Convicts, special settlers, exiles and deportees (statistical and geographical pattern)]. *Sotsiologicheskiye issledovaniya*, no. 5 (Moscow, 1991c): 151–165.

———. "'Kulatskaya ssylka' nakanune i v gody Velikoy Otechestvennoy voyny" [The "kulak exile" before and during the Great Patriotic War]. *Sotsiologicheskiye issledovaniya*, no. 2 (Moscow, 1992): 3–26.

———. "Repatriatsiya sovetskikh grazhdan v 1945–1946 godakh. Opirayas na dokumenty." [The repatriation of Soviet citizens in 1945–1946. Based on documents]. *Rossiya*, no. 5 (1993): 74–81.

————. "Prinuditelnye migratsii iz Pribaltiki v 1940–1950-kh godakh" [Forced Migrations from the Baltic republics in the 1940–1950s]. *Otechestvennye arkhivy*, no. 1 (1993b): 4–19.

————. "Spetsposelentsy (1930–1959 gg.)" [Special settlers (1930–1959)] *Naselenie Rossii v 1920–1950–e gody: chislennost, poteri, migratsii* [The Population of Russia in the 1920–1950s: Size, Losses, Migrations] (Collection of academic publications). Moscow, 1994a: 145–194.

————. "Sudba 'kulatskoy ssylki' (1930—1954 gg.)" [The fate of the "kulak exile" (1930–1954)]. *Otechestvennaya istoriya*, no. 1 (Moscow, 1994b): 118–147.

————. "Repatriatsiya sovetskikh grazhdan i ikh dalneyshaya sudba (1944–1956 gg.)" [The repatriation of Soviet citizens and their subsequent fate (1944–1956)]. *Sotsiologicheskiye issledovaniya*, no. 5 (Moscow, 1995a): 3–13.

————. "Nekotorye problemy repatriatsii sovetskikh peremeshchennykh lits" [Some problems of repatriation of Soviet DPs]. *Rossiya*, no 5–6 (1995b): 183–192.

————. "Zaklyuchennye v 30–e gody (demografichesky aspekt)" [Convicts in the 1930s (the demographic aspect)]. *Sotsiologicheskiye issledovaniya*, no. 7 (Moscow, 1996): 3–14.

Bierschenk, Th. "Zahlen über die während des Zweiten Weltkrieges umgesiedelten deutschen Volksgruppenzugehörigen." *Zeitschrift für Ostforschung*, no. 1 (1954): 80–83.

Browning, C. R. "Deportations." In *Encyclopedia of the Holocaust*. New York: Publisher?, 1995, 365–369.

Djordzevic, D. "Migrations during the 1912–1913 Balkan Wars and World War One." In *Migrations in Balkan History*. Belgrade, 1989, 115–130.

Gelb, M. "An Early Soviet Ethnic Deportation: The Far Eastern Koreans." *The Russian Review*, (1885, July): 389–412.

————. "The Western Finnic Minorities and the Origins of the Stalinist Nationalities." *Deportations Nationalities Papers*, no. 2 (1896): 237–267.

Gerlach, C. "The Wannssee Conference, the fate of German Jews, and Hitler's decision in principle to exterminate all European Jews." *The Journal of Modern History*, no. 4 (1998 December): 759–812.

Gestwa, K. "'Es lebe Stalin' Sowjetischer Zwangsarbeiter nach Ende des Zweiten Weltkrieges. Das Beispiel der Stadt Hamm in Westfalen." *Geschichte in Wissenschaft und Unterricht*, no. 2 (1993): 71–86.

Gleser, O., and P. M. Polian. "Ethnische Deportationen im Raum der ehemaligen UdSSR." *Geographica Slovenica* (Geografija in narodnosti. [Geography and Ethnicity.]) (Ljubljana, 1993): 139–152.

Dahlmann, D. "'Operation erfolgreich durchgeführt'. Die Deportationen der Wolgadeutschen 1941." In *Flucht und Vertreibung: zwischen Aufrechnung und Verdraengung*. Vienna: Picus Verlag, 1994, 201–226.

Heidemeyer, H. "Flucht und Zuwanderung aus der SBZ." In *DDR: Flüchtlingspolitik der Bundesrepublik Deutschland bis zum Bau der Mauer*. Düsseldorf, 1993.

Holquist, P. "Conduct merciless mass terror: decossackization on the Don, 1919." *Cahiers du monde russe*, no. 1–2 (1997): 127–162.

Lemberg, H. "Ethnische Säuberung: ein Mittel zur Lösung von Nationalitäten-problemen?" *Aus Politik und Zeitgeschichte*, no. 46 (1992): 27–38.

Martin, T. "The Origin of Soviet Ethnic Cleansing." *The Journal of Modern History*, no. 4 (1998, December): 812–861.

Merl, S. "Das System der Zwangsarbeit und die Opferzahl im Stalinismus." *Geschichte im Wissenschaft und Unterricht*, no. 46 (1995): 277–301.

Müller, R. D. "Die Rekrutierung sowjetisher Zwangsrarbeiter fuer die deutsche Kriegswirtschaft." In Herbert, U. (ed.). *Europa und der "Reicheinsatz". Auslaendische Zivilarbeiter, Kriegsgefangene und KZ–Häftlinge in Deutschland 1938–1945*. Essen: Publisher?, 1991, 234–250.

Münz, R. and R. Ohliger. "Deutsche Minderheiten in Ostmittel– und Osteuropa, Aussiedler in Deutschland. Eine Analyse ethnish privilegierter Migration." In *Demographie aktuell. Vorträge Aufsätze Forschungsberichte*. Berlin: Humboldt Universität zu Berlin, 1998, 43.

———. "Vergessene Deutsche Erinnerte Deutsche. Flüchtlinge, Vertrienebe, Aussiedler." *Transit*, no. 15 (1998): 141–157.

Overmans, R. "Personelle Verluste der deutschen Bevölkerung durch Flucht und Vertreibung." *Dzieje Najnowesye*, no. 2 (1994): 51–66.

Polian, P. "Westarbeiter: Reparationen durch Arbeitskraft. Deutsche Häftlinge in der UdSSR." In Dahlmann, D. and G. Hirschfeld (eds.). *Lager, Zwangsarbeiter, Vertreibung und Deportation: Dimensionen der Massenverbrechen in der Sowjetunion und in Deutschland 1933 bis 1945*. Essen: Klartextverlag, 1999, 337–367.

———. "Ethnische Deportation im Raum der ehemaligen Sowjetunion." In Streibel, Robert (ed.). *Flucht und Vertreibung: zwischen Aufrechnung und Verdrängung*. Vienna: Picus–Verlag, 1994, 227–236.

———. "Die Deportation der Ostarbeiter im Zweiten Weltkrieg." In Gestrich, A., G. Hirschfeld and H. Sonnabend (eds.). *Ausweisung und Deportation. Formen der Zwangsmigration in der Geschichte*. (Stuttgarter Beiträge zur historische Migrationforschung). Vol 2. Stuttgart: Franz Steiner Verlag, 1995, 115–140.

Sundhaussen, H. "Bevölkerungsverschiebungen in Südosteuropa seit der Nationalstaatswerdung (19/20 Jahrhundert)." *Zwabgsmigrationen in Mittel– und Südosteuropa, Comparativ: Leipziger Beiträge zur Universalgeschichte und vergleichende Gesellschaftsgeschichte*, no. 1 (1996): 25–40.

Ther, P. "The Integration of Expellers in Germany and Poland after World War II: A Historical Reassessment." *Slavic Review*, no. 4 (1996): 779–805.

———. "Die Vertriebenenproblematic in Brandenburg und im Oppelner Schlesien 1945 1952. Ausgewalte Aspekte einer vergleichenden Landesgesvhichte." *Zeitschrift für Ostmitteleuropa–Forschung*, no. 4 (1997): 513–534.

Wheatcoft, S. "German and Soviet repressions and mass death." *Europa–Asia Studies*, no. 8 (1996).

Glossary of Russian Terms

Aul: A highland village settlement in the Caucasus (the association with a highland location has weakened lately)

Bai (Turkish): A rich land and cattle owner.

Basmaches (Turkish): Literally "bandits," an armed anti-Soviet movement in Central Asia in the 1920–1930s.

Dashnaks: A shortened name of the followers of the Armenian nationalistic political party "Dashnaktsutyun," which was founded in 1890 and supported the autonomy of Western Armenia within Turkey and the consequent establishment of an independent Armenian state.

Dessiatina: obsolete Russian measure of area (= approx. 2.75 acres)

Gubernia, also *Gub.* and *Gubs.* (plural): A territorial administrative unit in the Russian Empire, abolished by the Soviet government in 1923.

Innokentyevtsy: An Orthodox sect founded in 1908 by Innokenty, a hieromonk of the Baltsky Monastery, a self-proclaimed embodiment of the Holy Spirit.

Khutor: A small (initially containing one household) village settlement, a seasonal or permanent residence of a group of relatives who maintain economic relations with a village or a *stanitsa*, of which the *khutor* had once been a part.

Kray: A territorial administrative unit, similar to an oblast, but usually containing an autonomous oblast within its boundaries.

Oblast, also Obl. and Obls. (plural): A territorial administrative unit, corresponding to a province.

Okrug: An administrative territorial unit forming part of an oblast.

Stanitsa: A large Cossack settlement (derived from the name of a Cossack detachment).

Troika: An "arbitrary" court system of three people to accelerate arrests and prosecution on a local level, abolished in fall 1938.

Uyezd: A territorial administrative unit in the Russian Empire, larger than a present district; was abolished by the Soviet authorities in the 1920s, but continued to exist in the Baltic states and Bessarabia until the 1940s.

Abbreviations

AO – Autonomous Oblast
APRF – The Archive of the President of the Russian Federation [Arkhiv Presidenta Rossiyskoy Federatsii]
ASSR – Autonomous Soviet Socialist Republic

BDC – Berlin Document Center (Берлинский Центр документации), Берлин
BSSR – The Belorussian Soviet Socialist Republic

Cheka, also VChK – The All-Russian Extraordinary Commission for the Struggle against Counter-revolution and Sabotage [VChK, Vserossiyskaya Chrezvychaynaya Komissiya]
CP – The Communist Party
CPSU – The Communist Party of the Soviet Union

DDR – German Democratic Republic [Deutsche Demokratische Republik]
Dr. – Doctor

EWZ – Central Bureau for Immigration [Einwanderungszentralstelle], Berlin

f. – file number (in references to archival sources)
FRG – The Federal Republic of Germany
FSB – Federal Security Service of the Russian Federation [Federalnoy sluzhby bezopasnosti]

GANO – The State Archive of the Novosibirsk Oblast [Gosudarstvennyi arkhiv Novosibirskoy oblasti]
GARF – The State Archive of the Russian Federation [Gosudarstvennyi arkhiv Rossiyskoy federatsii] (formerly: TsGAOR – The State Archive of the October Revolution and Socialist Development)
GASK – The State Archive of Stavropol Kray [Gosudarstvennyi arkhiv Stavropolskogo kraya], Stavropol
GDR – The German Democratic Republic
GKO – The State Defense Committee [Gosudarstvenny komitet oborony SSSR]

Gosplan – The State Planning Committee [Komitet gosudarstvennogo planiro-vaniya]

GPU – The Chief Political Directorate [Glavnoye politicheskoye upravleniye]

GULAG – The Chief Administration of Camps of the USSR NKVD [Glanoye upravleniye lagerey NKVD SSSR]

GUPVI – The Main Administration for Affairs of Prisoners of War and Internees of the USSR NKVD/MVD [Glavnoye upravleniye po delam voyennoplen-nykh i internirovannykh] (before 1945—UPVI)

GUPVI Archive – Archive of the Main Administration for Affairs of Prisoners of War and Internees [Arkhiv Glavnogo upravleniya po delam voennoplennykh i internirovannykh MVD SSSR], Moscow

h. – holding (in references to archival sources)

Izv. RAN – journal "Izvestiya Rossiyskoy Akademii Nauk" [Russian Academy of Sciences Bulletin], Moscow

KGB – The Committee of State Security [Komitet gosudarstvennoy bezopas-nosti]

Komsomol, also VLKSM – The All-Union Lenin Communist Youth League [Vsesoyuznyi Leninsky Kommunistichesky Soyuz molodezhi]

M. – Moscow

MGB – The Ministry of State Security of the USSR [Ministerstvo gosudarst-vennoy bezopasnosti SSSR]

MID – The Ministry of Foreign Affairs of the USSR [Ministerstvo inostrannykh del SSSR] (before 1946 – NKID)

MTS – Machine Tractor Stations [Motoro-traktornoye stansii]

MVD – The Ministry of Internal Affairs of the USSR [Ministerstvo vnutrennikh del SSSR]

Narkomchermet – People's Commissariat of Ferrous Metallurgy of the USSR [Narodny komissariat chernoy metallurgii SSSR]

Narkomelektrostantsy – People's Commissariat of Power Plants of the USSR [Narodny komissariat elektrostantsy SSSR]

Narkomgrazhdanzhilstroy – People's Commissariat of the Civilian Construction Industry of the USSR [Narodny komissariat grazhdanskogo zhilishche-stroyeniya SSSR]

Narkomles – People's Commissariat of the Forest Industry of the USSR [Naro-dny komissariat lesnoy promyshlennosti SSSR]

Narkommesttopprom – People's Commissariat of the Local Fuel Industry of the USSR [Narodny komissariat mestnoy toplivnoy promyshlennosti SSSR]

Narkompishcheprom – People's Commissariat of the Food Industry of the USSR [Narodny komissariat pishchevoy promyshlennosti SSSR]

Narkompros – People's Commissariat of Education of the USSR [Narodny komissariat prosveshcheniya SSSR]

Narkomsredmash – People's Commissariat of the Mechanical Industry of the USSR [Narodny komissariat sredego mashinostroyeniya SSSR]

Narkomstroy – People's Commissariat of the Construction Industry of the USSR [Narodny komissariat stroitelnoy promyshlennosti SSSR]

Narkomstroymaterialov – People's Commissariat of the Construction Materials Industry of the USSR [Narodny komissariat stroymaterialov SSSR]

Narkomtankprom – People's Commissariat of the Tank Construction Industry of the USSR [Narodny komissariat tankostroyeniya SSSR]

Narkomtorg – People's Commissariat of Trade of the USSR [Narodny komissariat torgovli SSSR]

Narkomugol – People's Commissariat of the Coal-Mining Industry of the USSR [Narodny komissariat ugolnoy promyshlennosti SSSR]

Narkomvooruzheniya – People's Commissariat of the Armament Industry of the USSR [Narodny komissariat vooruzheniya SSSR]

Narkomzdrav – People's Commissariat of Health Care of the USSR [Narodny komissariat zdravookhraneniya SSSR]

Narkomzem – People's Commissariat of Agriculture of the USSR [Narodny komissariat zemleustroystva SSSR]

NKGB – People's Commissariat of State Security [Narodny komissariat gosudarstvennoy bezopasnosti]

NKID – People's Commissariat of Foreign Affairs of the USSR [Narodny komissariat inostrannykh del SSSR] (from 1946—MID)

NKO – People's Commissariat of Defense of the USSR [Narodny komissariat oborony SSSR]

NKPS – People's Commissariat of Communication of the USSR [Narodny komissariat putey soobshcheniya SSSR]

NKVD – People's Commissariat of Internal Affairs [Narodny komissariat vnutrennikh del]

NTS – National Labor Union [Natsionalno-Trudovoy Soyuz]

Obl. – Oblast

OGPU – The Unified Chief Political Directorate [Obyedinennoye glavnoye politicheskoye upravleniye]

OUN – Organization of Ukrainian Nationalists

Politburo – Political Buro (The USSR Communist Party Central Committee Political Bureau)

r. – register (in references to archival sources)

RGAE – Russian State Archive of the Economy [Rossiysky gosudarstvenny arkhiv ekonomiki] (former TsGANKh – Central State Archive of the National Economy of the USSR [Tsentral'nyi gosudarstvenny arkhiv narodnogo khoziaistva SSSR])

RGAKFD – Russian State Archive of Documentary Films and Photographs [Rossiysky gosudarstvenny arkhiv kinofotodokumentov], Krasnogorsk

RGALI – Russian State Archive of Literature and the Arts [Rossiysky gosu-darstvenny arkhiv literatury i iskusstva], Moscow

RGANI – Russian State Archive of Contemporary History [Rossiysky gosu-darstvenny arkhiv noveishei istorii], Moscow (former TsKhSD – Center for Preservation of Contemporary Documentation [Tsentr khraneniia sovre-mennoi dokumentatsii])

RGASPI – Russian State Archive of Social and Political History [Rossiysky gosu-darstvennyi arkhiv sotsialno-politicheskoy istorii] (formerly: RTsKhIDNI – The Russian Center for the Holding and Examination of Contemporary His-tory Documents; previously: TsPA IMEL – The Central Party Archive of the Marx-Engels-Lenin Institute)

RGVA – Russian State Military Archive [Rossiysky gosudarstvenny voennyi arkhiv], Moscow (former TsKhIDK – Center for the Preservation of His-torico-Documentary Collections [Tsentr khraneniia istoriko-dokumen-tal'nykh kollektsii], now part of the RGVA, Moscow; before: TsGOA SSSR – Central State Special Archive of the USSR [Tsentral'nyi gosudarstvenny Osobyi arkhiv SSSR])

ROA – Russian Liberation Army [Russkaya osvoboditel'naya armiya]

RSFSR – The Russian Soviet Federal Socialist Republic

SBZ – Soviet Occupation Zone in Germany [Sowjetische Besatzungszone]

SD – SS Security Service [Sicherheitsdiens der SS]

SEMRPK – Bulletin "Set etnologicheskogo monitoringa i rannego preduprezh-deniya konfliktov" [Network for ethnologic monitoring and early conflict prevention], Moscow (International Project "Conflict Resolution in the Post-Soviet States")

sh. – sheet (in references to archival sources)

SMERSH (GUKR/SMERSH) – Main Directorate of the Military Counter-Intel-ligence Service [Glavnoye upravleniye voyennoy kontrrazvedki] (during the later part of the Second World War; derived from the Russian words "smert shpionam" or "Death to Spies!")

Sovnarkom – The Council of People's Commissars

SPb. – Saint-Petersburg

SSR – Soviet Socialist Republic

TsAMO – Russian Federation Central Archive of the Ministry of Defense [Tsen-tralnyi arkhiv Ministerstva oborony RF], Podolsk

TsAODM – Central Archive of Social Movements of Moscow [Tsentralnyi arkhiv obshchestvennykh dvizhenii Moskvy]

TsDNI TO – Center of Documentation of Contemporary History of the Tomsk Oblast [Tsentr dokumentatsii noveishei istorii Tomskoi oblasti]

TsGA RD – National Archive of the Republic of Daghestan [Natsionalnyi arkhiv Respubliki Dagestan], Makhachkala

TsGA SPb – Central State Archive of Saint-Petersburg [Tsentralnyi gosu-darstvennyi arkhiv Sankt-Peterburga], Saint-Petersburg

TsKhDMO – Center for the Preservation of Records of Youth Organizations [Tsentr khraneniia dokumentov molodezhnykh organizatsii] (former VLKSM Central Committee Archive, now: part of RGASPI

USSR – The Union of Soviet Socialist Republics
UWZ – Resettlement Center [Umwanderungszentrale]

VChK, also Cheka – The All-Russian Extraordinary Commission for the Struggle against Counter-revolution and Sabotage [VChK, Vserossiyskaya Chrezvychaynaya Komissiya]
Ved. VS – journal "Vedomosti Verkhovnogo Soveta SSSR" [Bulletin of the USSR Supreme Soviet]
VKP(b) – The All-Union Communist Party (Bolsheviks) [Vsesoyuznaya Kommunisticheskaya partiya (bolshevikov)]
VLKSM, also Komsomol – The All-Union Lenin Communist Youth League [Vsesoyuznyi Leninsky Kommunistichesky Soyuz molodezhi]
VPK – USSR Council of People's Commissars Committee for Resettlement [Vsesoyuznyi pereselenchesky komitet]

Index of Personal Names*

* Compiled by N. Pobol

Index of
Geographical Names*

* Compiled by N. Pobol

134, 136, 144–146,
167, 174, 190, 205,
330, 331, 349, 350
Ordzhonikidze Kray
126, 134, 135, 140,
228, 330, 344, 347
Orel Obl.158, 159, 163,
332
Orenburg Obl. 24
Osh Obl. 148

Pacific Ocean 36
Padoozero 242
Palestine 19, 42, 66
Pamir 67, 231
Parabel district 105, 107
Parbigsky 85
Pavlodar Obl.118, 148,
190
Pearl Harbor 37
Pechora district 167,
357, 358
Pest-Pilis 273
Penza Obl. 158, 163
Perm 116
Perm Gub. 24
Perm Railroad 258
Pervomaysk 161
Petrograd (see also
Leningrad, Saint
Petersburg) 61, 327
Petrozavodsk 242, 268,
283, 338
Piaseczna 25
Piedmont 63, 104
Pinsk Obl. 361
Ploieşti 258, 273
Podberezye 287
Podolia Gub. 26
Poland 19, 20, 24, 25,
28, 33–35, 38–42,
51–55, 56 115, 117,
119. 244, 270, 275,
294, 301
Polotsk Obl. 361
Polszta 273

Poltava Obl. 26, 175
Poltavskaya *stanitsa* 109,
328
Pomerania 54, 282
Popov, khutor 233
Portugal 18, 19
Posyet 99, 328
Posyet district 98
Potsdam 38, 39, 248,
249
Poznan (Posen) 51, 286
Pregradnensky district
141, 143
Priangarsky *Okrug* 73
Pribilof islands 37
Prigorodnyi district
(Leningrad Obl.) 107
Prigorodnyi district
(North Ossetian
ASSR) 148, 197, 200,
201, 227–231, 233,
238
Prikumsky district 77
Primorsky Kray 24, 64,
93, 98, 101, 189, 233
Privolzhsky *ulus* 176
Priyutninsky *ulus* 144,
176
Prokopievsky mines 107
Prut 21, 273
Psedakh district 148, 200
Pskov Obl. 163, 167,
170, 309, 333, 353,
357, 358
Psykhod 218
Pulin district 113
Pulin, National *Okrug*
113
Putivl camp 122
Pyatigorsk 177
Pytalovo 167, 170
Pytalovo district 357,
358

Radom Gub. 25
Radoszczicy 25

Ratlub 161
Redant 228, 233
Resita 257
Riga 35
Right-Bank Moldavia
51, 171
Ritlyab 160
Ritlyab district 160–161
Romania 32, 36, 38, 52,
63, 115, 242, 246,
249–251, 253,
255–256, 260, 266,
267, 270–272, 285,
286, 291, 294, 299,
301
Romanovskaya *stanitsa*
60
Rostov Obl. 134, 139,
140, 144, 145, 152,
159, 174, 187, 220,
278, 279, 331, 344,
347, 350, 352, 364
Rostov-on-Don 19, 109
Rote-Fahne 174
Rot-Front 174
Rovno 205
Rovno Obl. 175
Ryazan Gub. 25
Ryazan Obl. 163, 189, 332
Ryki 25

Saalty 217
Saalty district 218, 222
Saar-Pfalz 35
Saint Petersburg (see
Leningrad,
Petrograd) 24, 103
Sakhalin 36, 65, 99, 190,
224, 355
Saksenhausen 289
Salsk steppe 79
Salzburg 385
Samarkand Obl. 60, 152
Samashki 60
Samashkinskaya *stanitsa*
60